THE PHOTOGRAPHER'S BUILD-IT-YOURSELF BOOK

THE PHOTOGRAPHER'S BUILD-IT-YOURSELF BOOK

BY TOM BRANCH

AMPHOTO
American Photographic Book Publishing
An Imprint of Watson-Guptill Publications
New York, New York

All photographs of the author and his hands were taken by Judy Branch.
All other photographs were taken by the author.

Copyright © 1982 by Tom Branch

First published in New York, New York by American Photographic Book Publishing:
an imprint of Watson-Guptill Publications, a division of Billboard Publications,
Inc., 1515 Broadway, New York, NY 10036.

Library of Congress Cataloging in Publication Data

Branch, Tom.
    The photographer's build-it-yourself book.

    1. Photography—Apparatus and supplies—Design and
construction—Amateurs' manuals. I. Title.
TR196.B68   771   82-1684
ISBN 0-8174-5406-3   AACR2
ISBN 0-8174-5407-1 (pbk.)

Manufactured in the United States of America

First Printing, 1982

3 4 5 6 7 8 9/87 86 85

I wish to dedicate this book to my wife Judy.
Without her help, the book wouldn't have been possible.

Contents

Why Do-It-Yourself?

The reason most people make or build something is to save money. Making the photo equipment in this book can save you a lot. The cost of building something is usually only a small fraction of the cost of buying the manufactured item.

I have tried to avoid giving a dollar-and-cents cost to each project because in a short time inflation will make the stated cost sound ridiculous. At times, though, I resorted to saying that something cost a few dollars. Shop around before you begin building and compare the cost of the manufactured item to the cost of the materials you will need to make it. I'm sure that you'll be amazed at the amount of money you can save by making your own equipment.

Saving money isn't the only reason for building your own equipment. Ironically, a do-it-yourself project can also save time. If you have to spend a lot of time shopping to find what you want or have to special order it, making it can save hours, days, or even weeks. I've had small items on order for weeks and even months — some I'll probably never receive. If you're like me and want something right away, sometimes the fastest way to get it is to make it yourself.

Much of the equipment in this book isn't manufactured and sold. Many times you'll know exactly what you want and then find out that no one makes it. Then if you really want or need the equipment, you have to make it for yourself or have someone make it for you. The latter can become extremely expensive.

Quality is another reason for building your own photo equipment. Often the only way to get the high quality you desire is to make it yourself. This is why I use real leather, hardwood, and heavy metal in so many of the projects. I'm tired of the plastic, cardboard, and flimsy metal so often found in commercially manufactured equipment.

Self-satisfaction is another aspect of designing and building things you need. It's very satisfying to design and build quality equipment. This book describes simple ways of making almost anything. Change the design of these projects to meet your specific needs. After you have made the equipment to the best of your ability and with the best materials, you will feel a real sense of accomplishment.

Each photographer has different equipment needs and these needs change as one's photographic interests and skills grow. A manufacturer of photo equipment has to make a product for the average photographer. If you're not average, you may have no choice but to make the special equipment you need.

Most of the equipment made in these projects was designed for my needs and interests. Often I begin a project identifying a problem I was having and then designing the equipment to solve the problem. Many of you will have the same types of problems and can make use of the same equipment. Remember to design and build your photo equipment to solve the problems you're encountering and I'm sure it will cost less, work better, and last longer than any item you could buy.

Metric Confusion

I've used both standard and metric measurements throughout this book. I've worked with the standard measurements and in most cases gave the mathematical metric equivalent. The main exception to this is for wood dimensions. I referred to the wood by its common North American name — for example, calling a two by four 2″ × 4″. The metric equivalent is given as 3.8 × 8.9 cm, the actual metric measurement of the wood.

For the dimensions of pipe, tubing, sheet metal, drill bits, and wire, I used the material with the standard measurement and gave a mathematical metric equivalent. If you're using metric material, this exact size probably won't be available, so choose the nearest metric size you can find.

Bolts and nuts that attach cameras and photo accessories have a standard size and thread. The American standard is ¼″ with twenty threads to the inch. The European standard, which is used on some equipment, is ⅜″ with sixteen threads to the inch. I've used the ¼″ size for these projects. You can substitute the larger size if it fits your equipment. I didn't give the metric equivalent to these nut and bolt sizes because, as far as I know, no metric equivalent exists.

COMMON METRIC CONVERSIONS IN THIS BOOK

1/16″ = 1.6 mm	2″ = 5.1 cm	40″ = 1 m
1/8″ = 3.2 mm	3″ = 7.6 cm	53″ = 1.35 m
3/16″ = 4.8 mm	3½″ = 8.9 cm	107″ = 2.72 m
¼″ = 6.4 mm	4″ = 10.2 cm	140″ = 3.56 m
5/16″ = 7.9 mm	5″ = 12.7 cm	1 ft. = 30.5 cm or .3 m
⅜″ = 9.5 mm	5½″ = 14 cm	2 ft. = 61 cm or .6 m
½″ = 12.7 mm	6″ = 15.2 cm	3 ft. = 91.4 cm or .9 m
⅝″ = 15.9 mm	7″ = 17.8 cm	4 ft. = 1.2 m
¾″ = 19.1 mm	8″ = 20.3 cm	6 ft. = 1.8 m
7/8″ = 22.2 mm	9″ = 22.9 cm	12 ft. = 3.7 m
1″ = 2.5 cm	16″ = 40.6 cm	18 ft. = 5.5 m
1¼″ = 3.2 cm	18″ = 45.7 cm	12 yds. = 11 m

WOOD (Equivalent Metric Sizes)

1″ × 1″ = 1.9 cm × 1.9 cm
2″ × 4″ = 3.8 cm × 8.9 cm
1″ × 2″ = 1.9 cm × 3.8 cm
1″ × 4″ = 1.9 cm × 8.9 cm
4′ × 8′ = 1.2 m × 2.4 m

TEMPERATURE

150 F = 66 C
170 F = 77 C

WEIGHT

3 oz = 85 gm
12 oz = 340 gm

18 teeth/inch = 7 teeth/centimeter

NONCONVERTIBLE NUMBERS

¼″ bolts that are used to attach cameras and accessories do not have a metric equivalent, i.e. a 6 mm bolt won't work.

Tools

I tried to keep the number of tools needed to make these projects to a minimum. Some of the simpler projects can be made using only a sharp knife or a pair of scissors. Even the more complex equipment can be built with simple and basic hand tools that most people have.

The only power tool I frequently used is an electric drill. A variable-speed drill will be most useful — slow speeds are used with large drill bits and higher speeds with the small bits. You can tell the speed is right when drilling metal by watching the drill bit. When it produces large spiral metal shavings, the speed is correct.

The major hazard encountered when using the drill is having the bit *bind*, causing the small object being drilled to spin. The spinning object can cut your hand or perhaps fly dangerously from the bit. This can be prevented by using a clamp or vise to hold what you're drilling. If this isn't possible, use a block to prevent the object from rotating.

An electric saber saw was a late addition to my tools and was purchased after most of the projects were already finished. None of the projects requires the use of an electric saw — hand saws are sufficient. If you do use an electric saw, follow the manufacturer's directions for safe operation. Be sure that the material being sawed is well supported and the path of the saw blade is free from obstructions and foreign objects. Keep hands and fingers well away from the blade. With both electric drills and power saws, it's best to wear eye protection. Safety goggles are available in most hardware stores.

If you have a very limited number of tools, start with the simpler projects. Add more tools, a few at a time as needed, to make additional photo equipment. Buy quality tools and they will give you many years of use. Bargain tools will often break after being used only once or twice, so they aren't really such a bargain after all.

Some of the tools I frequently use are:

soldering iron	screwdrivers
leather punch	"C" clamps
metal shears	pliers (various types)
hacksaw	wire cutters
miter box and finishing saw	set of socket wrenches
files, large and small	multimeter
wood rasps	oilstones for sharpening
ball peen hammer	caulking gun
claw hammer	set of wrenches
chisel and punch	pocketknife
riveting tool	razor knife (regular and plastic-cutting)
vise	
carpenter's saw	small levels
tubing cutter	taps, ¼″ and ⅜″
rulers in several sizes	electric saber saw
carpenter's square	divider and compass
drill and bits, both large and small	

With these tools, I've made all the photo equipment in this book.

Safety

Do-it-yourself safety is a big enough topic for another book, so all I can do here is give some general guidelines. Unfortunately, it's a fact that more accidents occur in the home than anywhere else. Most, if not all, of these accidents could be prevented if proper precautions were taken.

Chemical Safety A photographer, especially one building his or her own equipment, works with a lot of chemicals. To start with, there are the photographic chemicals. Then there are paints, lacquers, solvents, glues, cements, stains, and dyes.

The starting point for chemical safety is reading the label. It will tell you the specific hazards associated with each product. As terrible as the label's warnings may seem, they should be taken as understatements. One classic understatement is the warning "Use in a well-ventilated area." This really means to use it outside with a breeze blowing. Few houses or apartments have an area with adequate ventilation.

I tried to choose the safest possible chemicals for these projects, but there still are hazards. Uncured silicone is a dangerous eye irritant, the super glues bond to skin instantly, and epoxy is possibly carcenogenic so avoid contact with the skin and inhaling the vapors. Almost all the chemicals used in the paints, glues, and so on are poisonous and should be kept away from young children. Always replace the childproof caps and keep the chemicals in a locked cabinet.

Right now there are no safe substitutes for these substances. Reading the directions and warnings on the labels and following them carefully is the best way of preventing accidents.

Oven Drying In several of the projects, I suggested oven drying at a low temperature to speed the drying time for epoxy or silicone. Place the object on a foil-lined cookie sheet to prevent any of the epoxy or silicone from dripping. Don't use the oven, especially a gas oven, to speed the drying of any flammable substance. Use the ventilator over the oven to remove the fumes.

As I said earlier, the fumes from epoxy are possibly hazardous, but the epoxy is going to emit the same amount of fumes whether it is dried in the oven or at room temperature. With the oven, the exhaust fan will remove most of the fumes from the room. I've never noticed any smell from the oven drying. Oven drying of the epoxy is probably safe because of the small amount used for these projects. If you are concerned, the best advice I can give is to mix, use, and dry the epoxy outside.

With silicone cement, the fumes given off are acetic acid (stop bath) and there is a smell similar to vinegar. As far as I know, this isn't dangerous and the exhaust fan easily takes care of the odor.

Electrical Safety Common household current can electrocute you. There is only one safe way to make electrical equipment and that is with the equipment *unplugged*. As simple as this is, it's amazing the number of accidents that happen because someone thought the item was unplugged.

Plug in the electrical projects only when the equipment is finished and all the wires are properly connected and insulated. Be certain and be safe.

A potentially lethal shock can also come from even the smallest battery-operated electronic flash unit. Repairing or modifying an electronic flash unit is something that should be left to professionals. The flash projects in this book only involve additions to the basic flash unit, and never should the insulating case of the flash be opened or removed.

Sharp Tools There is an old saying that you're more likely to cut yourself with a dull knife than a sharp one. This is true for a couple of reasons. A person treats a razor-sharp edge with care and respect. If you wish to see an example of this, hand someone a straight razor to examine. The person will be extremely careful with it.

Another reason that a sharp edge is safer to use is that it will cut with only a little pressure and the blade is easier to control. If it should slip, it will travel only an inch or so before you can stop it. With a dull blade, you have to use a lot of pressure to make it cut. If it slips, there is no stopping the blade before you seriously cut yourself.

Use pocketknives, razor knives, and other edged tools just as carefully as you would that straight razor. Keep the edges almost as sharp as the razor and use the blades with just moderate pressure and you won't cut yourself.

Eye Protection As photographers, we should be especially aware of the importance of vision. Good quality safety glasses, goggles, or a face shield are essential equipment for the do-it-yourselfer. These should be used with all power tools, even a high-speed drill.

Eye protection should also be worn when using some hand tools. I frequently specify using a ball peen hammer for many of the projects. There is a reason for this. The only uses for a claw hammer are driving and pulling nails. Using a claw hammer with a hard metal punch or chisel is dangerous. The hard metal of the hammer or chisel can shatter, sending splinters of metal flying into your face and eyes. Use the appropriate hammer and wear some kind of eye protection for any hard hammering.

As terrible as these warnings are, the dangers are very real. If you understand the dangers and take proper precautions, accidents won't happen. With all the equipment I've made both for this book and other projects, the worst thing that has ever happened to me is that I got a blister. It taught me one thing — the next time I'll wear gloves.

PART ONE

CAMERA ACCESSORIES

Quick and Easy Camera Raincoat

Raindrops glistening on the grass, ocean spray breaking over the bow of a boat — these are photographs begging to be taken. Unfortunately water, especially salt water, can be devastating to cameras. You can protect your camera in these situations by making a raincoat for it out of a Ziploc plastic bag and a rubber band.

The only tools you need are a lens filter and the eyepiece on the camera. For large cameras, the gallon-sized (3.8 liters) bag, which is approximately 11″ (28 cm) square, should be used. For compact cameras, the quart-sized (.9 liters) bag (7″ × 8″ [18 × 20 cm]) would work.

Begin by removing the filter and the eyepiece from the camera. Place your camera in the plastic bag with the zipper at the bottom. Then set the camera on the working surface with the lens facing upward. Screw the filter onto the lens through the plastic and then remove the filter. This action perforates the plastic, making it easy to remove a circle the size of the lens. Use the rubber band to secure the plastic to the barrel of the lens and replace the filter.

Next, turn the camera so that the back is facing you. Use the eyepiece to cut the opening for viewing. Remove the eyepiece and the circle of plastic and then reattach the eyepiece to hold the plastic in place. To attach the camera strap, just hold the camera's split ring in one hand and push the snap swivel on the strap through the plastic, with the other hand, securing the strap to the camera. Attach the other end of the strap in the same manner. Zip the bag and the camera raincoat is finished.

You'll find that all the camera's controls are operable through the plastic bag, but you should be careful when focusing. Use several short turns to focus rather than the continuous turn normally used. If this is too awkward, an alternative is to attach the plastic behind the focusing ring so that you can focus in the usual manner. A winder or motor drive is helpful for advancing film, but the film can still be advanced manually through the plastic.

This "raincoat" will last through a lot of shooting and does a good job of keeping the camera dry, even in the hardest downpour. But don't save it just for rainy days and salt water spray. It is also great for sandy beaches, in blowing sand or dust, and other times when your camera needs some extra protection. These bags work so well that it's a good idea to keep one in your gadget bag.

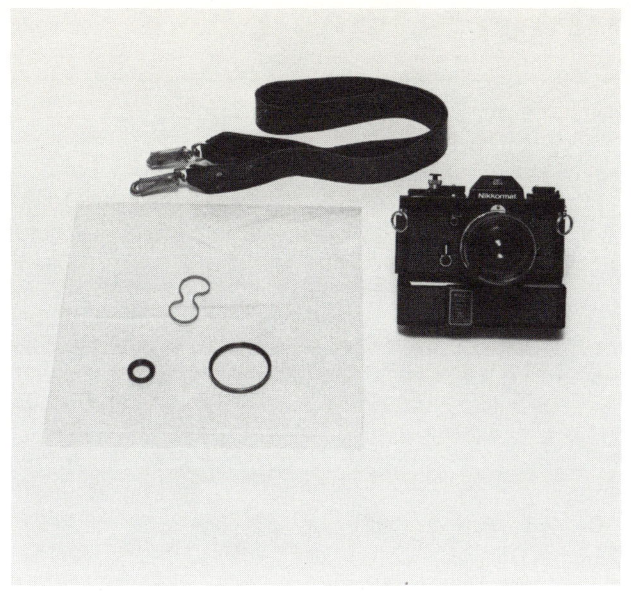

1. All you need to make a "raincoat" for your camera are a lens filter, the camera's eyepiece, the camera strap, a Ziploc plastic bag, and a rubber band.

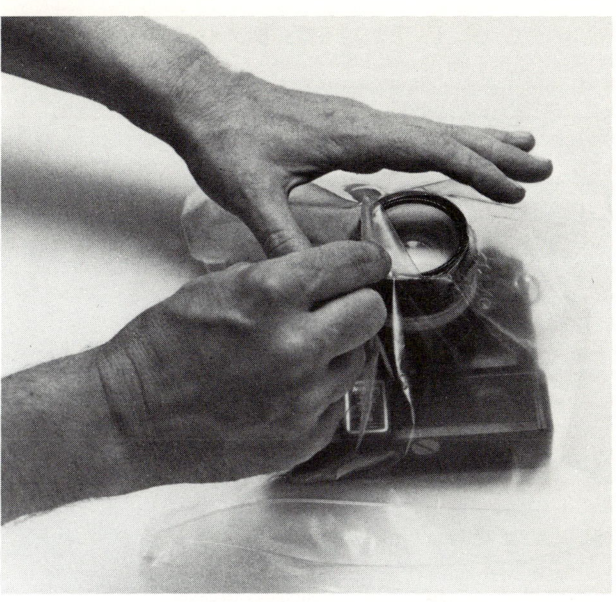

2. Center the camera in the plastic bag and screw the filter onto the lens through the plastic. Screwing on the filter makes it simple to remove a circle the size of the lens.

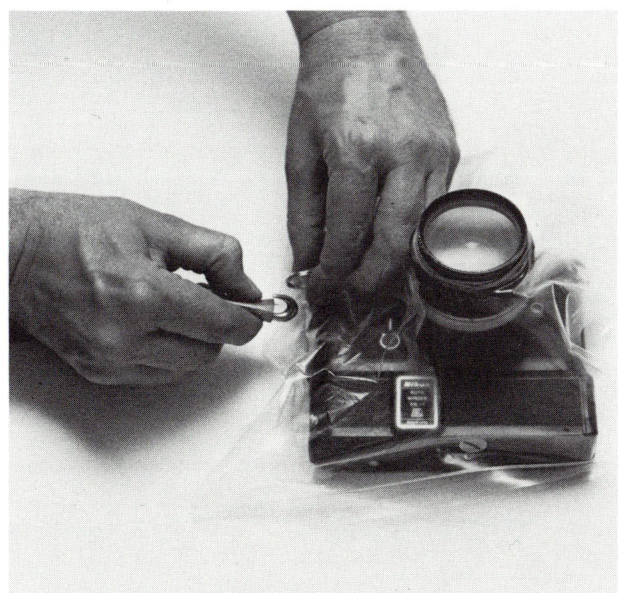

3. To attach the camera strap, grasp the split ring on the camera and force the snap swivel on the camera strap through the plastic.

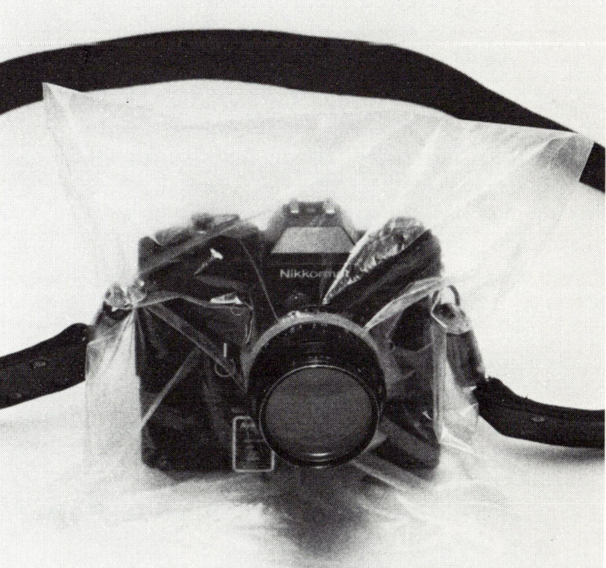

4. All camera controls are operable through the plastic and the camera is well protected from water and dust.

Indestructible Lens Cases

<table>
<tr><td>

MATERIALS

⅜″ (9.5 mm) closed-cell foam sleeping pad
Two 3″ or 4″ (7.6 or 10.2 cm) pipe end caps
3″ or 4″ plastic pipe
Clear silicone cement
Two ¾″ (19.1 mm) "D" rings
Scrap of leather
⅛″ (3.2 mm) diameter long aluminum or steel rivets
   and spacers

TOOLS

Hacksaw
Scissors
Razor knife
Emery paper, 150 or 180 grit
File
Rivet tool
Drill and ⅛″ bit
Ruler
Pencil

</td></tr>
</table>

Many of today's photographers are extremely active and combine photography with boating, hiking, camping, mountain climbing, skiing, and many other activities. This type of photography calls for carrying a minimum of equipment. It is difficult to be active when loaded down with a heavy camera bag and two or three cameras. Photography, in these situations, is best done with one camera and a couple of lenses.

An extra lens requires some kind of protective case. Lens cases found in stores are usually made of fake leather and cardboard with a little foam lining. When you're active, a lens needs more protection than these cases can provide. Ideally, a lens case should be waterproof, crushproof, impact- and abrasion-resistant to stand up to the abuse an active photographer might give it. It would also be nice if the case were brightly colored for easy visibility. If you want a lens case like I have just described, you'll have to make your own. As far as I know, none is being manufactured.

The ⅜″ (9.5 mm) foam can be found in the sporting goods section of most stores in the form of a sleeping pad for backpacking. These pads are made from a tough closed-cell foam that is perfect for protecting the lens. Plumbing supply stores will have the plastic pipe and end caps, and a leather shop will carry the leather and "D" rings.

The material list shows what you'll need for a lens case 3″ (7.6 cm) or 4″ (10.2) in diameter. To find out which you require, measure your lens. If the lens is 2½″ (6.4 cm) or less at the widest part, it will fit inside the 3″ pipe with room for the padding. If the lens is larger (up to 3 ½″ [9 cm]), the 4″ pipe should be used.

The case should be just large enough to hold the lens without allowing it to move about inside. Measure the height of the lens with both front and rear lens caps in place. Then saw a length of pipe ½″ (12.7 mm) shorter than this measurement. The portion of the lens that extends beyond the pipe is housed in the end caps.

The hacksaw with its finer teeth is better for precise sawing than a carpenter's saw. I usually cut partially through the pipe and then rotate it gradually as I complete the cut. Keep the saw perpendicular to the pipe for an even cut. Marking the pipe before sawing is a good idea but not essential. Trim the ragged edge with a razor knife. Then use coarse emery paper, 150 or 180 grit, to remove the saw marks. It is best to lay the paper on a flat surface and rub the pipe over it with a circular motion. If there is yellow or another color of printing on the pipe, it can be removed by wiping with alcohol.

Next, examine the end caps. Inside you'll find a ridge (or ridges) that prevents the pipe from being inserted all the way into the cap. Use the razor knife to remove the ridge from one of the caps. This end cap will become the bottom of the lens case.

Take the other end cap and drill a 1/16″ (1.6 mm) hole about ½″ below what will be the top of the case. This hole is needed so the top of the case will slip on and off easily. Without the hole the case would be airtight. The compression created when putting on the cap and the vacuum created when taking it off would be a problem. The 1/16″ hole is sealed by the pipe when the lid is pushed down fully and the case is still waterproof.

Test the fit of the lid by opening and closing it. If it is too tight, it can be made to fit better by sanding the top of the pipe with emery paper.

Cut the foam lining for the inside of the case with a scissors. Circles of foam are needed for the top and bottom and a rectangular piece for the side. For the 3″ pipe, the rectangular foam should be 9½″ (24.1 cm) long and for the 4″ pipe, it should be 12¾″ (32.4 cm) long. Both should be the height of the pipe. These dimensions are slightly larger than needed, but the foam will compress to make a proper fit.

My lenses have external coupling prongs that would cut into the foam, so I left a gap in the foam for the prong. Most lenses do not have this type of coupling, so the gap would not be needed.

The ⅜″ foam might be too thick or thin for a proper fit for your lens. The lens should be immobilized by the foam but still be easy to insert and remove. Correct the thickness of the foam by slicing it with the razor knife. The cut side may be a bit ragged, but it will be glued to the pipe and hidden from view. If a slightly thicker lining is needed, a double layer of foam can be used: one layer the full thickness and the other sliced to whatever extra thickness is required.

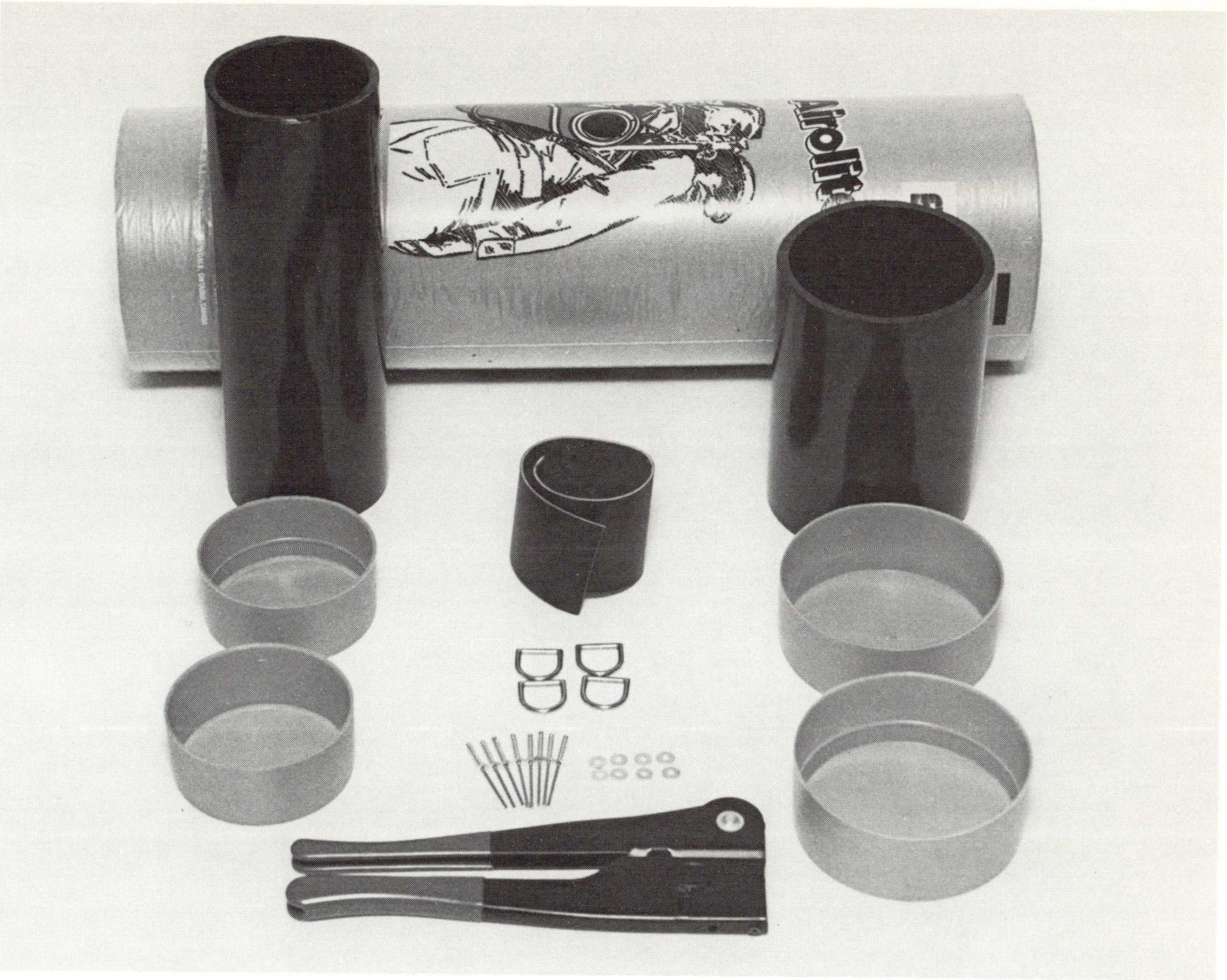

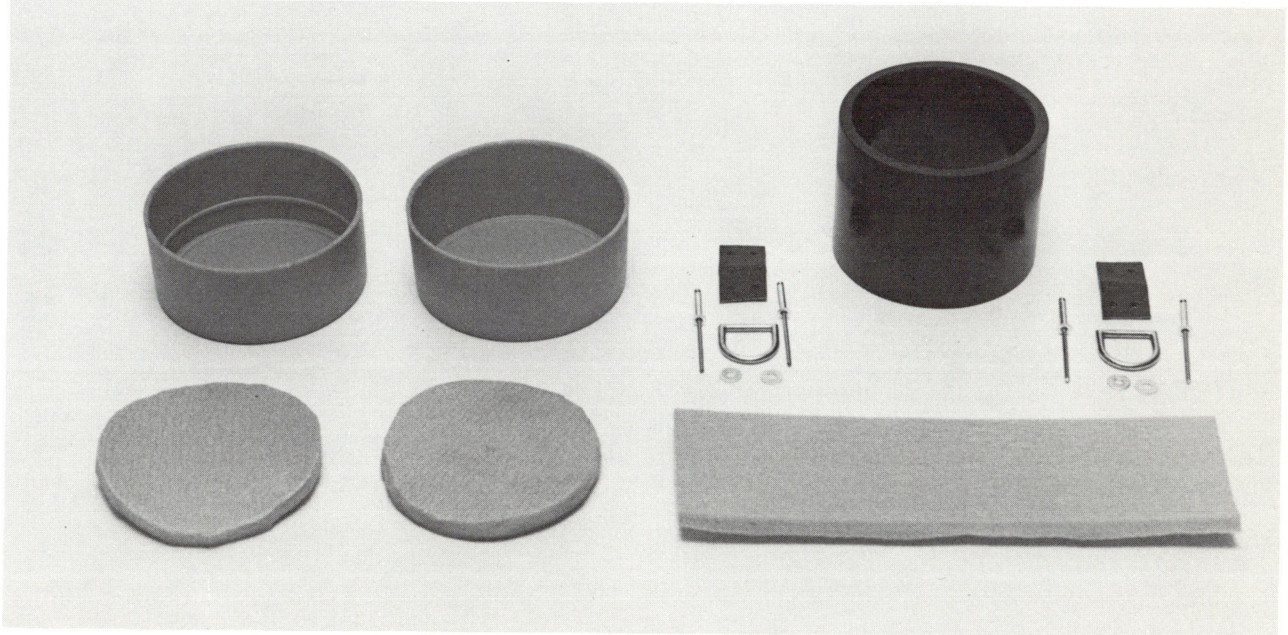

1. Lens cases can be made from plastic plumbing parts and cushioned with foam rubber cut from a sleeping pad. A riveting tool and rivets are used to attach the leather and "D" rings to the case.

2. Here are all the pieces for a case laid out and ready to be assembled. The interior ridge has been cut out of one end cap that will become the bottom of the case.

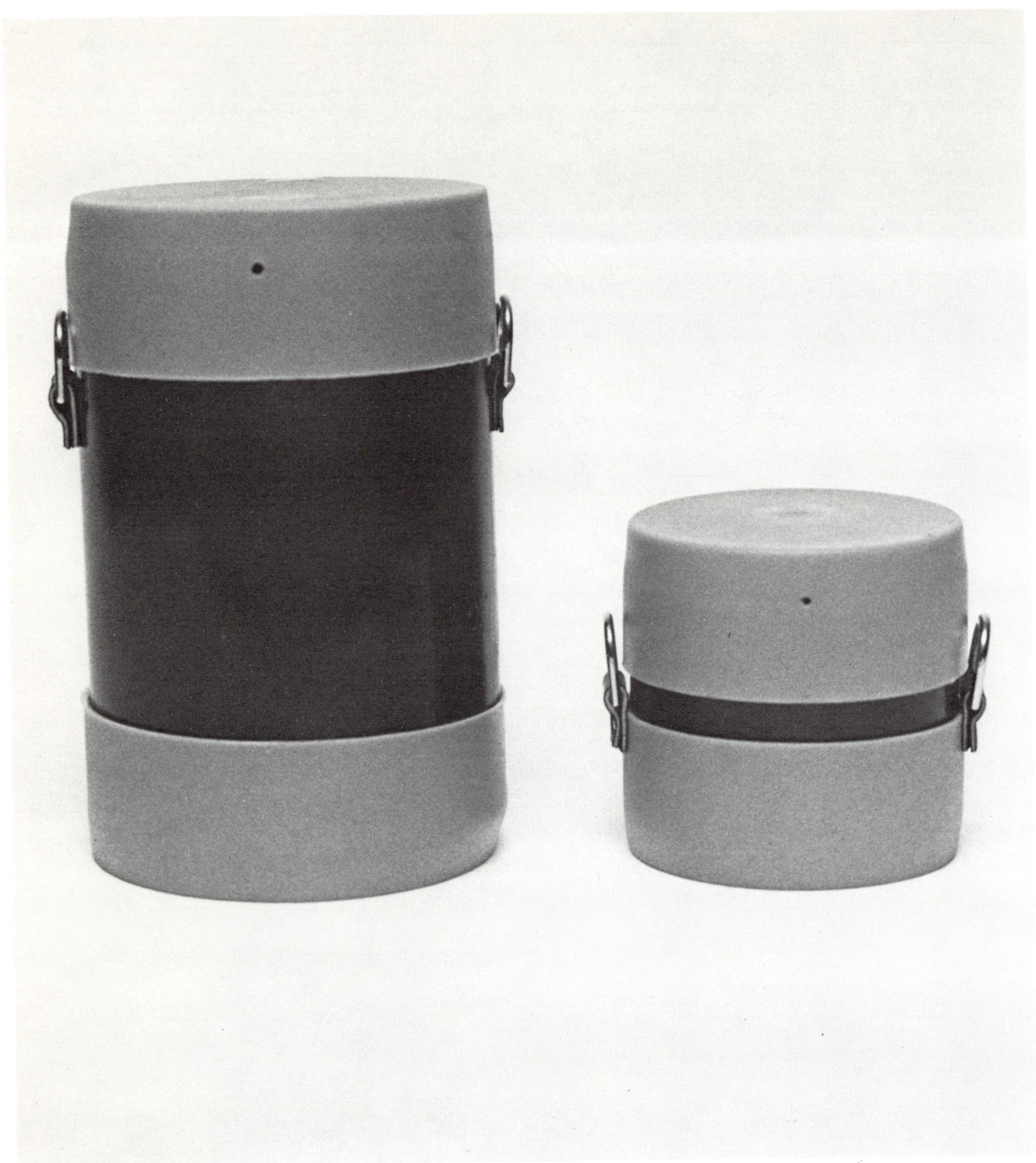

3. Almost any size of lens case can be made with these techniques. Lenses up to 2½″ in diameter will fit inside the 3″ pipe. Lenses up to 3½″ will fit inside the 4″ pipe.

I used blue foam and blue end caps to make these lens cases. End caps are available in blue and black and perhaps other colors as well. Different colors of foam are also available, so there is some choice for the lens cases. The brighter colors make the cases easier to spot if you set them down.

I added "D" rings to the sides of the case so a shoulder strap or a strap that attaches to my belt can be used. To add the rings, start by cutting a scrap of leather to make two strips, each ¾" × 1½" (1.9 × 3.8 cm). Fold the strips in half and punch two holes for the rivets in each. Position the leather on the pipe and mark the location of the holes. Drill ⅛" (3.2 mm) holes in the pipe for the rivets. Use the rivet tool to insert the rivets with spacers (small washers) inside the pipe. Add a little silicone around the rivets before fastening for waterproofing. Also add silicone to the holes in the rivets.

Long solid regular rivets could be used if you don't have a rivet tool. To set the regular rivets, use two hammers — one inside the pipe to serve as an anvil and the other hammer to pound the end of the rivet flat on the outside.

Glue the foam inside the bottom, top, and side of the lens case. Use just a little silicone so that the lining can be removed and replaced at some time in the future if necessary. Let the silicone dry and the lens case is finished and ready to protect your valuable lens.

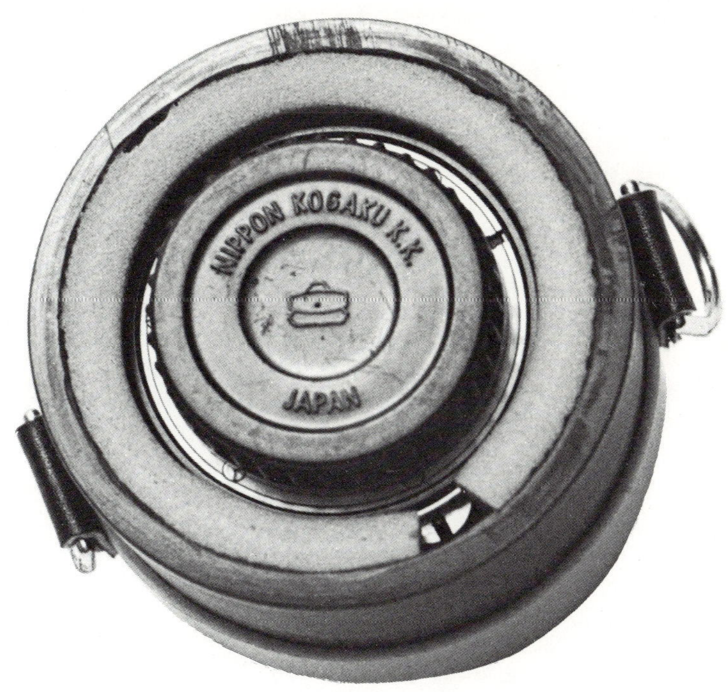

4. My lenses have an external coupling prong, so I left a gap in the foam lining to house the prong. This isn't necessary for most lenses.

Camera and Accessories Suitcase

MATERIALS

Suitcase or briefcase
Upholstery foam, 72″ × 24″ × 2″ (182.9 × 61 × 5.1 cm)
Clear silicone cement
Masking tape
Cardboard
Fiberboard

TOOLS

Saber saw with knife blade
Serrated knife
Ruler
Pencil
Black marker

When traveling, I carry my photo equipment in a suitcase fitted with custom foam padding to hold the cameras and lenses. The suitcase is an old, battered, hard-sided Samsonite model that is no longer being made. This was the sturdiest suitcase I could find and I bought it in a pawn shop for much less than the original price. I've used it constantly for over ten years and hope to use it for many more. The fact that the suitcase is dirty and battered is important, as this makes it less likely to be stolen. Thieves seem to have a marked preference for new luggage and hopefully would not give mine a second look. Besides being less likely to be stolen, the camera suitcase does an excellent job of protecting the equipment.

Making your own camera suitcase is easy. If you don't have enough equipment to fill a large suitcase, or if you want to carry only a small amount, a wide briefcase could be used instead.

Upholstery foam, used to cushion the equipment, presents a problem. The foam is soft and difficult to cut without making a ragged edge. I found that the best way to cut the foam was to use a saber saw (jigsaw) with a sharp, toothless knife blade. The blade must be very sharp to leave a smooth, clean edge on the foam. An electric carving knife can be used if you don't have a saber saw. As a last resort, the foam can be cut with a sharp, serrated knife. Unfortunately the serrated knife will make a ragged edge as it cuts the foam.

The foam comes in different thicknesses and colors. I use white foam, but green, red, and orange are also available. The white foam will yellow with age, so you may prefer a colored foam for this reason. Camera stores sometimes have dark gray foam that is used to line camera cases. This foam is more expensive than the other kinds, but would fit the inside of a briefcase very well.

Begin by measuring the size of the suitcase or briefcase. Cut the foam to the size required. I used 2″ (5.1 cm) foam and split some of it into sheets 1″ (2.5 cm) thick. Use the 1″ sheets to cushion the bottom of the equipment and for the center partition. If you wish, you can buy an additional sheet of 1″ foam instead of cutting the 2″ foam down to size. Other thicknesses of foam are available and can be used if they fit your case better.

Use an electric carving knife or a serrated knife to split the foam. It doesn't matter if the surface is ragged, since it will be glued and will not be seen.

Cut two 2″ sheets and three 1″ sheets of foam the size of the case. These sheets can be cut with a sharp serrated knife, as a long straight cut can be made smoothly. It is only the cutouts that are hard to make with a serrated knife.

Cut two sheets of cardboard the same size as the 2″ foam. Position your equipment on the cardboard and determine the optimum location for each piece. Leave at least an inch between each item. When satisfied with the placement, outline each item with a pencil.

Set the camera equipment aside and retrace the final pattern with a black marker. Make these lines slightly inside the pencil outline so the cutouts will be smaller than the equipment. This ensures that the foam will hold the equipment tightly in place. Simplify the pattern as much as possible.

When the pattern is finished, tape the cardboard to the foam you wish to cut. Rest this foam on a second sheet of thick (2″) foam. This second sheet prevents the blade of the saber saw or electric knife from striking the tabletop or working surface.

To start each cut, press the saw blade through the cardboard and into the foam before turning it on. This makes it easier to start the cut. Turn on the saw and cut out the opening. Another person can assist by moving the foam, but one person can manage almost as well. Follow the pattern as closely as possible and take your time cutting. *Keep hands and fingers well away from the blade.* The saber saw does a super job of cutting the cardboard and foam.

The cardboard gives the saw a smooth surface to move over and isn't needed if you use an electric carving knife or a serrated knife. When using these, the pattern can be drawn on the foam with a fine line marker.

When the cutting is finished, the sheets of foam can be glued inside the case using silicone cement. Use only a little bit of glue so the foam can be easily removed if you wish to change the compartments. I used a sheet of fiberboard and some books to press the foam and center partition together while the silicone was drying.

I use the camera suitcase to protect the camera equipment when I'm traveling. Because of its size, I don't use it as a working camera case. When shooting, I use a canvas camera bag instead.

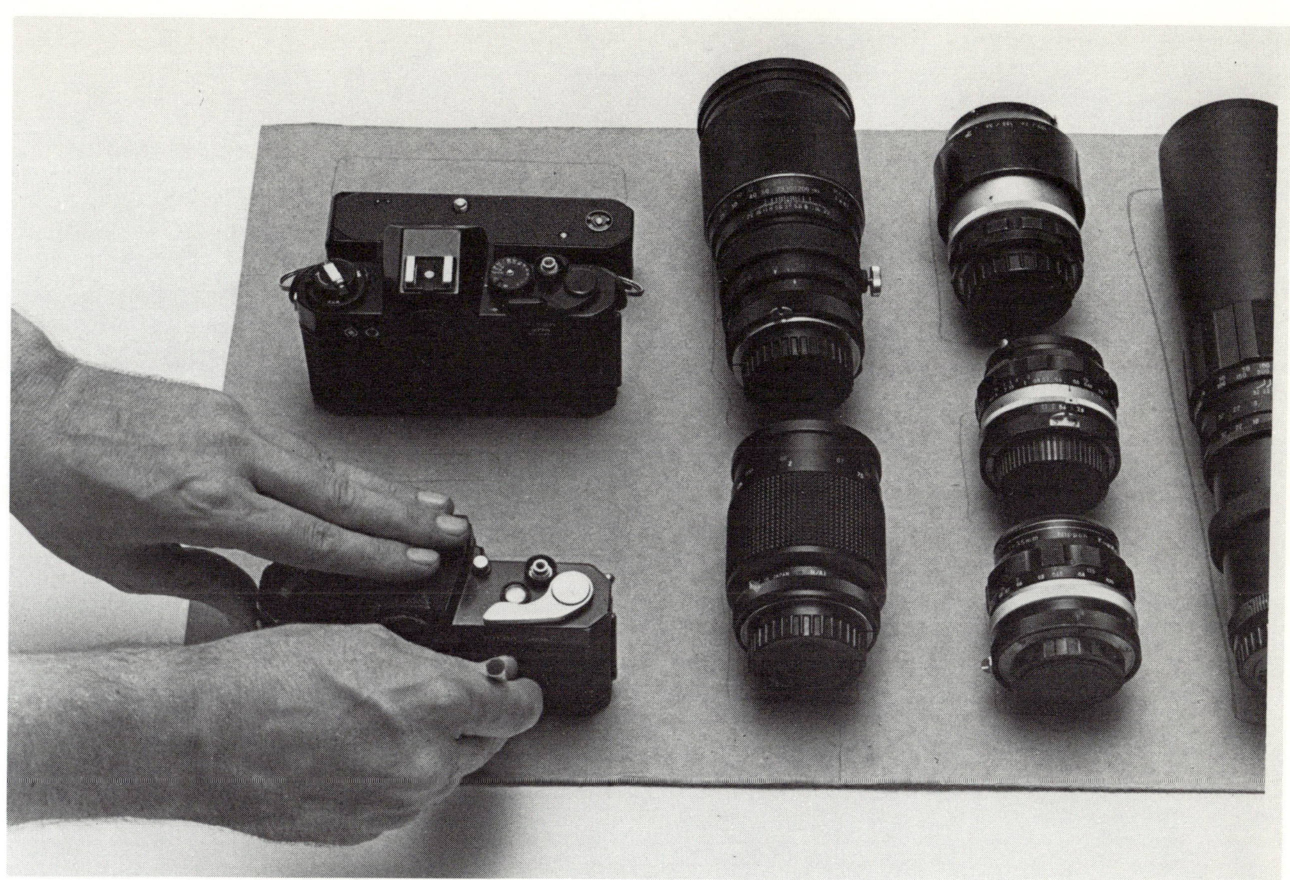

1. Find the best location for your equipment on a piece of cardboard that is the size of the suitcase. Outline each item with a pencil. Leave at least an inch between each item.

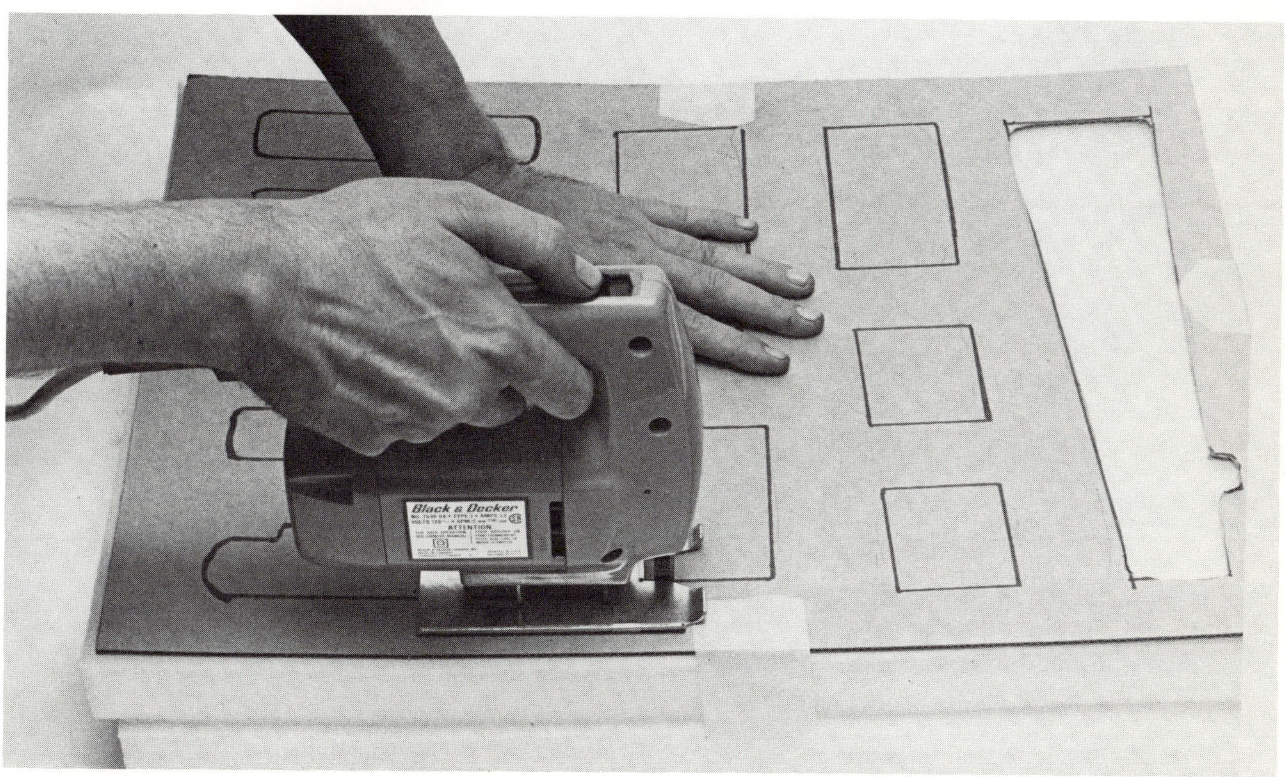

2. A saber saw fitted with a sharp knife blade is used to cut the openings in the cardboard-covered foam. Use an extra sheet of foam underneath to prevent the blade from striking the tabletop.

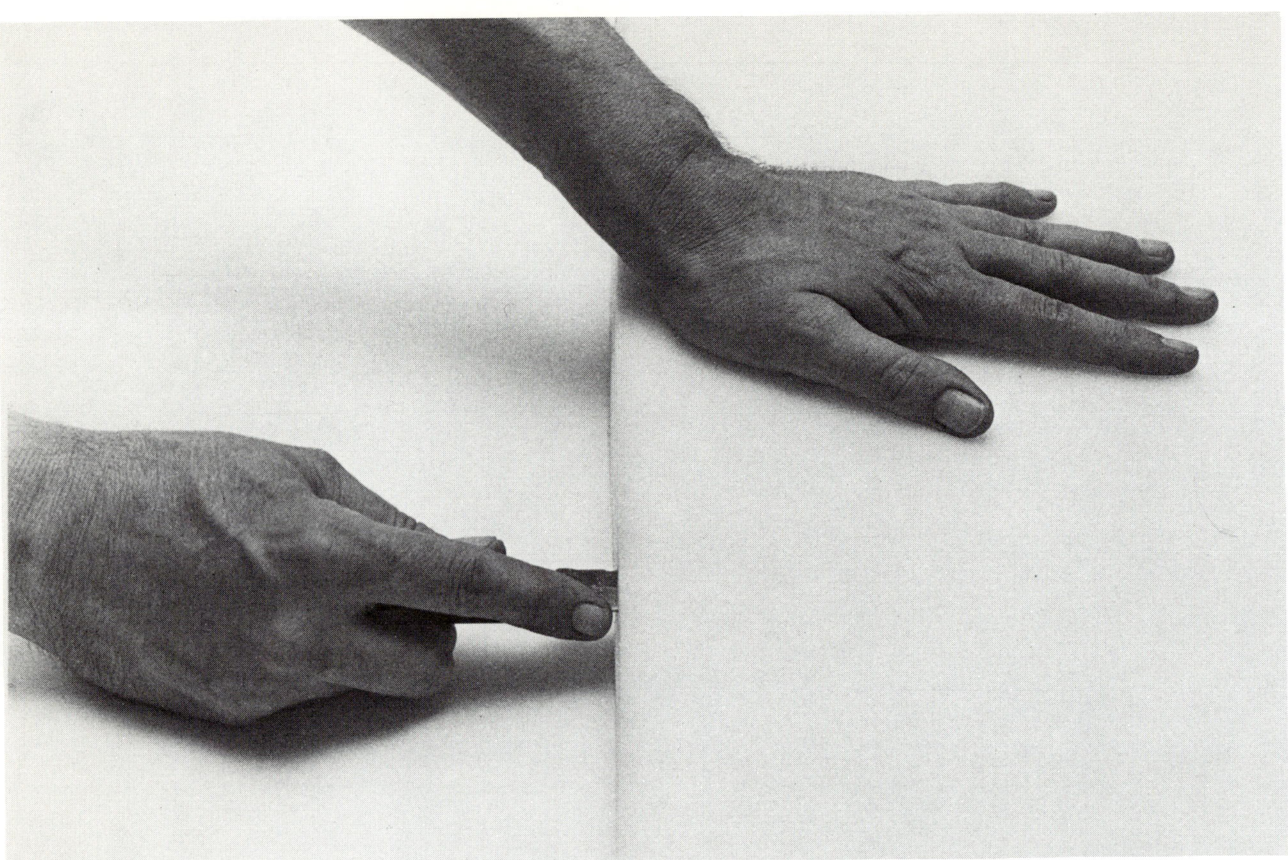

3. Split the 2″ foam with a serrated knife to make the 1″ sheets of foam for the bottom of the compartment and the divider.

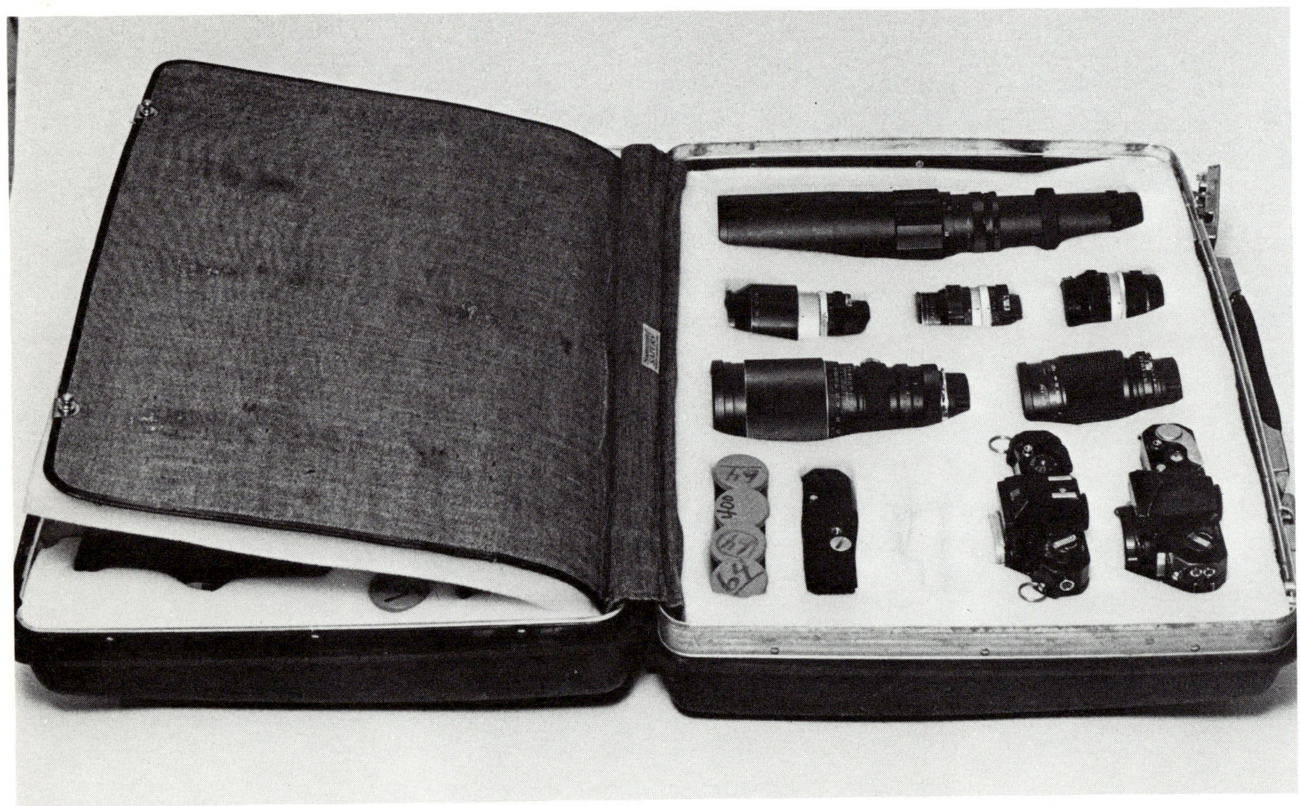

4. A suitcase can hold a lot of camera equipment. For less equipment, a briefcase can be used instead. A 1″ foam pad is glued to the center divider to cushion the top of the equipment.

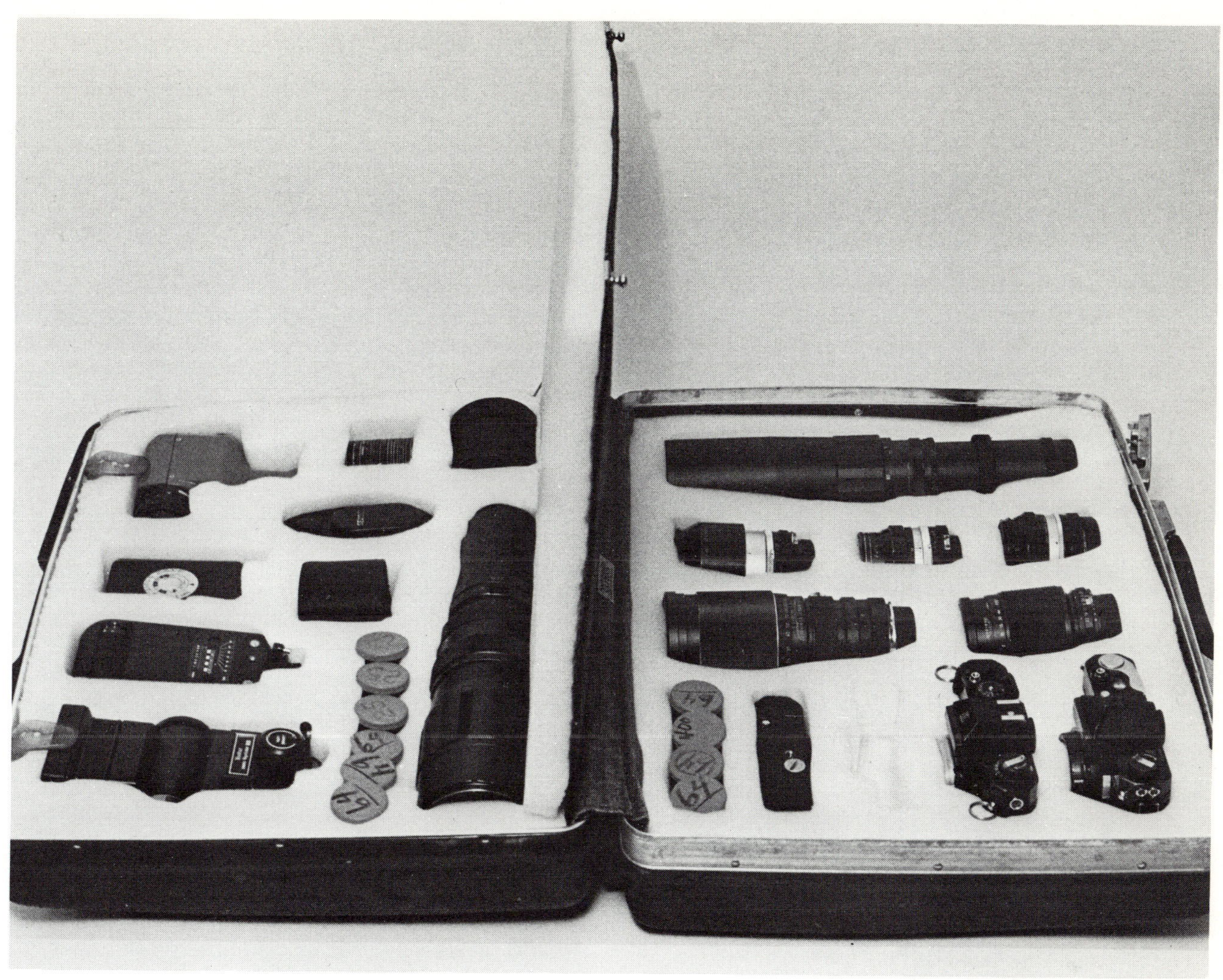

5. This camera suitcase protects the equipment in two ways — the foam lining protects it from physical harm, and the old and dirty outside of the case protects it from theft.

Camera Hold-Down

MATERIALS

10″ (25.4 cm) of leather, 1″ (2.5 cm) wide
24″ (61 cm) of elastic, ¾″ (19.1 mm) wide
Velcro, 1″ wide
Instant glue for wood and leather
Leather rivets, large size
Small scraps of fiberboard

TOOLS

Razor knife
Leather punch
Ball peen hammer
Scissors
Spring clamp or "C" clamp

There are many types of camera straps for the active photographer. These straps hold the camera in place and prevent it from bouncing and swinging around as the photographer moves. All of these are rather complicated with extra straps going around the back or waist. Some are so complicated that you need an instruction manual and a valet to put them on.

If you normally wear a belt there is a simpler way to hold your camera in place. The belt that holds up your pants can also be used to keep the camera from bouncing around. All that is needed is an attachment that connects the camera to the belt and any camera strap can be used.

Begin by folding over 3 ½″ (8.9 cm) of leather. If the leather is thick, dampen it with a little water where you wish it to bend. Use an instant glue for wood and leather to attach the 1″ strip of Velcro to the leather. I tried several other types of glues but couldn't find another type that would hold this combination of materials. Carefully read the directions on the glue as it really does bond to skin instantly.

First, coat both the leather and the Velcro with the glue and allow them to dry. Recoat the two surfaces and use the spring clamp and the small scraps of fiberboard to hold the leather and Velcro together. The fiberboard prevents the clamp from marring the leather. Allow about a half hour for the glue to reach maximum strength.

Next, add the two loops of elastic. These loops will be used to hold the camera in place on your chest. Their length will depend on your height and the position you carry your camera. Hook the leather over your belt with the long portion of the leather toward the front and fasten it in place. Put on your camera and make a loop in the elastic. Hook the loop under your camera lens and run it over the top of the camera and down to the leather. Allow for the inch of leather that will be folded over and an inch of the elastic that will overlap. The elastic should be stretched a little but not enough to tilt the camera. When you find the correct length for this loop, cut the elastic.

Make another loop in the elastic, hook it over the lens on the camera, and run it below the camera and up to the leather in back. Again, stretch the elastic a little to find the correct length. This will be a shorter loop. Once the length is determined, cut the elastic.

Remove the leather strip from your belt and fold over 1″ of the end. Form the loops with elastic, overlapping the ends about an inch. Place the four thicknesses of elastic between the folded portions of the end of the leather and use the leather punch to make two holes for rivets through the double thickness of leather and the four thicknesses of elastic. Punching all the holes at the same time will ensure proper alignment. Insert the two-part leather rivets. If the leather is thick, large rivets should be used. For thinner leather, medium rivets will work.

Insert the rivets, but before setting them, test the lengths of the elastic loops by attaching the hold-down to your camera and belt. The larger loop goes up behind the camera and then over the top to hook onto the lens while the shorter loop goes under the camera and hooks over the top of the lens. If the length is correct, there should be a comfortable amount of tension. Remove the attachment and set the rivets by pounding on them with a ball peen hammer.

With the hold-down, your camera won't bounce and swing around when you are active and will stay securely pressed to your body. With a little practice, the hold-down can be quickly attached and removed, and it will take up very little space in your gadget bag.

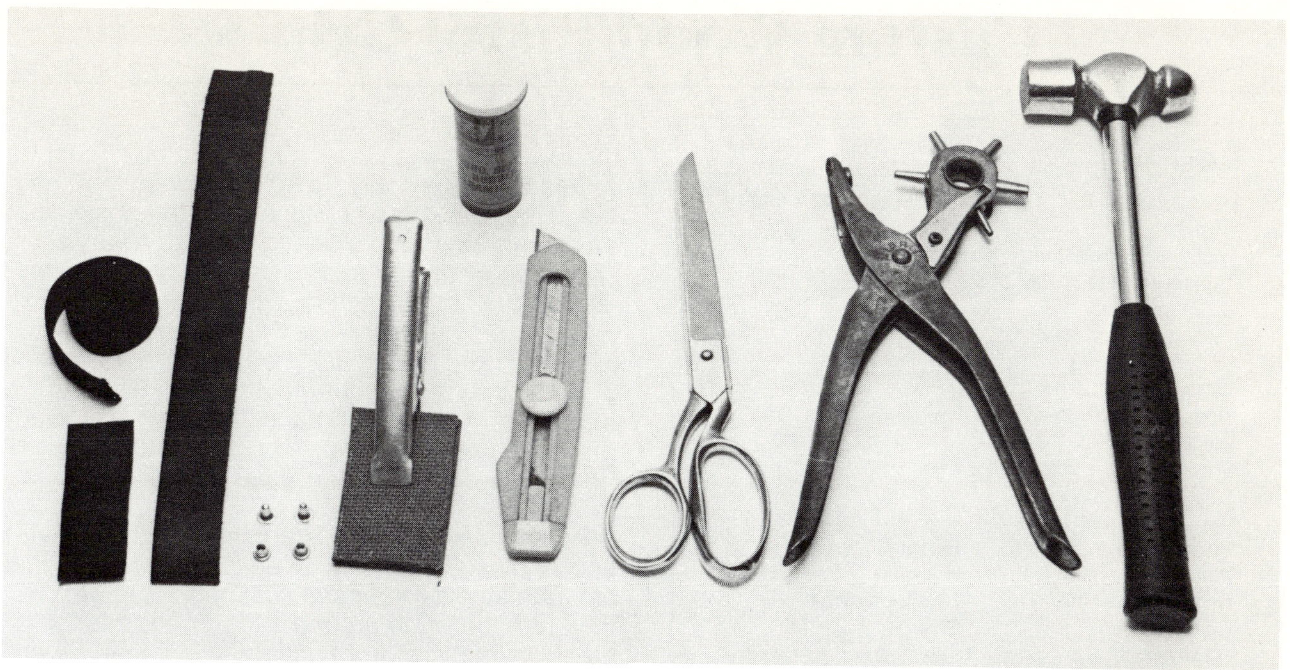

1. These are the materials needed to make the hold-down. Leather and elastic are used to secure the camera to your belt.

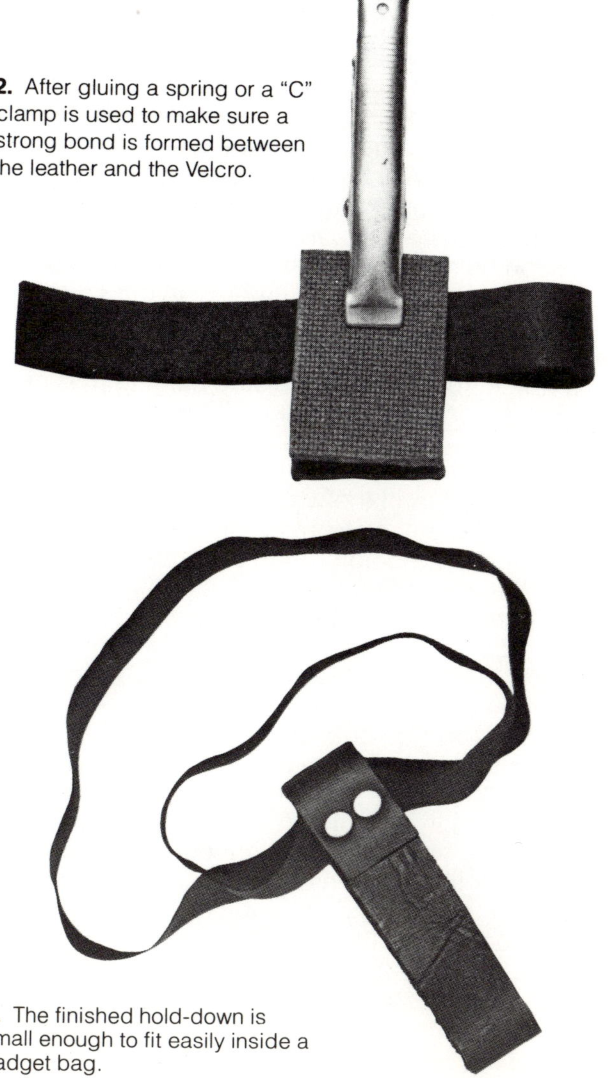

2. After gluing a spring or a "C" clamp is used to make sure a strong bond is formed between the leather and the Velcro.

3. The finished hold-down is small enough to fit easily inside a gadget bag.

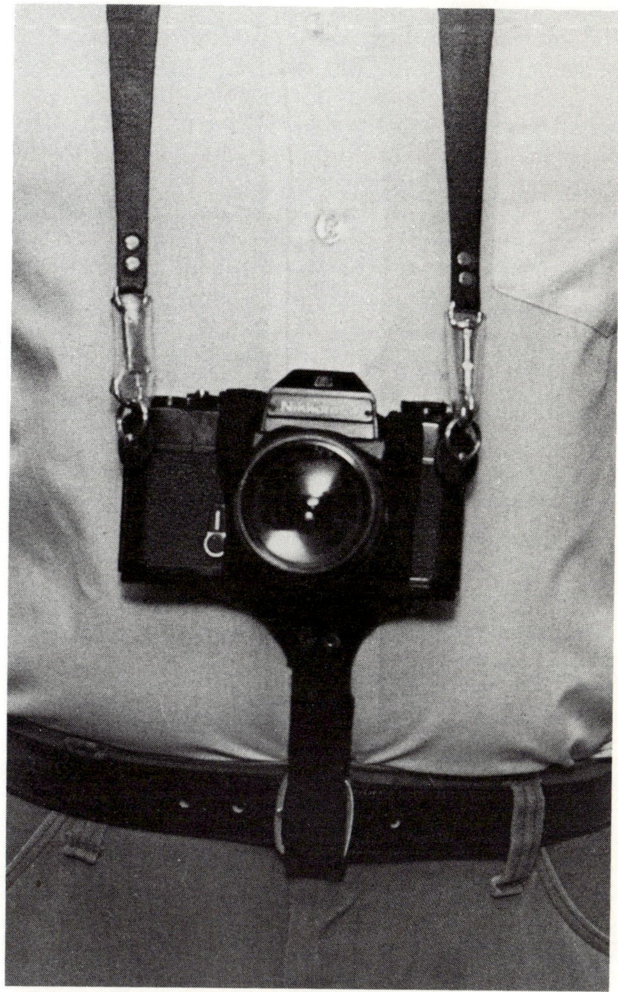

4. The hold-down with its two elastic loops can prevent your camera from swinging and bouncing around when you are active.

Custom Wood Pistol Grip

MATERIALS

Hardwood block 1″ × 2″ × 5″ (2.5 × 5.1 × 12.7 cm) or larger
Tripod screw (photographic thumb screw)
Aluminum, 1/16″ or 3/32″ (1.6 or 2.4 mm)
Scrap of leather
4 wood screws, 5/8″ or 6″ (15.9 × 152.4 mm)
Silicone cement (clear or black)
Sandpaper
Fine steel wool
Poster paint
Shoe polish the color of the wood

TOOLS

Pocket knife	Pencil
Whetstone	Hacksaw
Drill and small bits	Leather punch
Countersink	Saw
Metal punch	File
Hammer	Screwdriver

Plastic pistol grips have indentations for fingers and are contoured to fit a hand. Unfortunately, these grips aren't custom-shaped to fit *your* hand, and everyone's hand and way of gripping are different. The only way to get a custom pistol grip is to make your own — one that fits your hand and way of gripping like a glove.

This pistol grip was my first attempt at making something by whittling. I wasn't sure that I could do it, so I took a block of soft pine and just started cutting with my pocket knife. In about an hour, I had shaped a grip and had confidence that I could really make a pistol grip from hardwood.

A hardwood specialty store has small blocks of wood. These blocks are inexpensive. I chose black walnut, but many beautiful woods would be suitable. Be sure to select wood without knots. I started with a block 1″ × 2″ × 5″ (2.5 × 5.1 × 12.7 cm). Hardwood is usually full cut, so a 1″ × 2″ (2.5 × 5.1 cm) block really measures 1″ × 2″, not the ¾″ × 1¾″ (1.9 × 4.4 cm) measurement of softwood. This grip is small and simple, but if you want a larger grip you can use a block of wood 1½″ × 2″ (3.8 × 5.1 cm), 2″ × 2″ (5.1 × 5.1 cm), or even larger.

A tripod screw (photographic thumb screw) is used to attach the grip to a camera or lens. New screws, sold in camera stores, are made of plastic and aluminum and could be used, but I prefer using an old steel screw. You may be able to find a similar one among the miscellaneous bits and pieces in the "junk box" in camera stores that carry used equipment.

First decide if you want a right- or left-handed grip. Most right-handed photographers will want a left-handed grip so the right hand will be free to advance the film and trip the shutter.

Begin by sawing a notch for the thumb screw in the top of the block of wood. The notch should be wide and deep enough to hold the wheel portion of the screw. With the whetstone hone the pocketknife as sharply as possible before carving. A very sharp knife makes carving easier. Use the pocket knife to smooth the notch and remove the saw marks.

Now paint the palm side of your gripping hand with the poster paint, using a light color for dark wood and a dark color for light wood. Grip the wood with your painted hand. This leaves a hand-print that can be used as a cutting guide. Dry the "painted" wood in a warm (150F [66C]) oven for a few minutes.

When the paint is dry, start shaping the grip at a corner by cutting the grooves for your fingers that are indicated by the paint. Cut half of the groove, then turn the wood around to complete the cut. Make several cuts from one direction, then several from the other. Always start carving on the corners and work your way toward the middle. Take your time and pare a thin shaving with each cut, and you'll soon get the feel of whittling. Respect the sharp edge of the knife and keep your fingers out of the way of the blade. Needless to say, this kind of work is best done sitting under a shade tree, drinking your favorite cold beverage.

When all the paint marks have been whittled away, repaint your hand to make another print. As you proceed, keep testing the feel of the grip. You will soon be able to feel where the wood needs to be removed. (Walnut is fairly easy to cut so I soon had a pile of shavings around my feet.) As the shape of the wood starts to feel comfortable when you grip it, force yourself to stop carving. It is easy to get carried away and take off too much wood. Don't let the complicated appearance of the grip fool you. It is a lot simpler to make than it looks.

Leave the top of the wood squared off to make adding the metal plate easier. Smooth off the edges around the notch with the knife. At this point, begin sanding the wood, starting with a 150 or 180 grit paper and following up with 220 and 320 grits. For an extra smooth surface, finish up with a 400 grit paper. Continue using the coarser paper until all the whittling marks have been removed before you change to a finer paper.

The metal plate for the top of the grip is approximately 1″ × 2″, but you should outline the top of the wood on the aluminum to obtain a precise match. Use the hacksaw to cut out the top plate. Then mark the location of the center hole for the threaded portion of the thumb screw and for the four wood screws that attach the plate. Use the hammer and center punch to make an indentation where the holes will be drilled. This makes accurate drilling a lot easier. File and sand the edges of the metal smooth.

The holes for the wood screws should be countersunk so the tops of the screws will be flush with the metal. Use the countersink in the electric drill to ream out the metal so it will hold the head of the screws.

Holes for the screws must also be drilled in the wood. These holes should be slightly smaller than the diameter of the screw and not as deep as the screw is long. These holes prevent the wood from splitting when the screws are applied. Attach the metal plate. If the heads of the screws protrude slightly, you can file them down. The edge of the metal plate should be filed as well to make it fit precisely with the wood.

Cut a pad the size of the metal plate from the leather strap and make a hole in the center with the leather punch. Attach the pad to the metal plate using silicone. The silicone can be dried in a warm oven in about an hour. When dry, trim the pad to a precise fit. This pad cushions the camera and prevents the base from being marred.

The wood can be protected in many ways using wax, unrefined linseed oil, or varnish. I used a brown shoe polish. Don't knock it until you've tried it — this method of finishing wood works very well. Rub the polish in with fine steel wool. A few coats of wax applied this way give a smooth, almost velvety texture. Give it a final polish with a soft cloth, then spend a few minutes admiring the rich look of the wood. The work involved in making the custom grip is worth the effort once you feel the finished grip in your hand.

The pistol grip is more than just a handle for a camera. It can be used in the tripod socket of telephoto lenses. If you add a tripod flash adapter, it can be used as a handle for off-camera flash. It is also the starting point for making the flash bracket that is the next project.

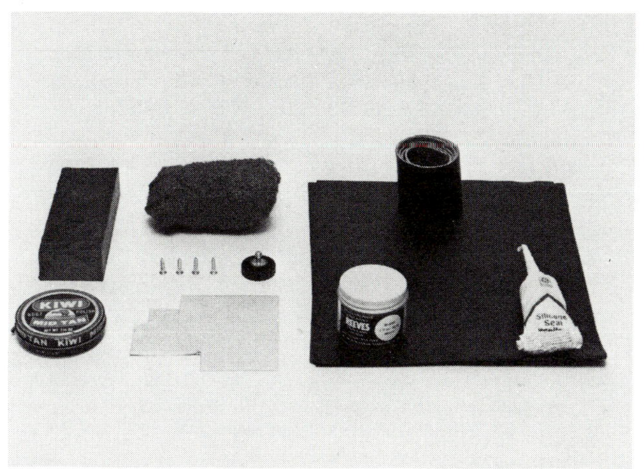

1. The materials used to make the pistol grip: poster paint, silicone, leather, sandpaper, aluminum, wood screws, a tripod screw, steel wool, shoe polish, and a block of hardwood.

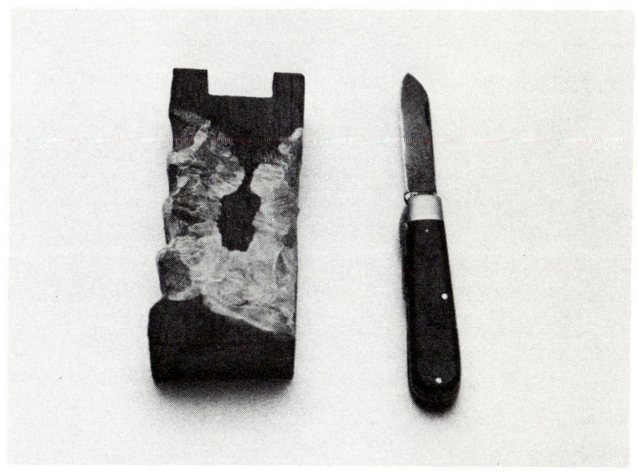

2. A notch for the thumbscrew is sawed in the top of the block of wood. Handprints are made with poster paint to provide a carving guide.

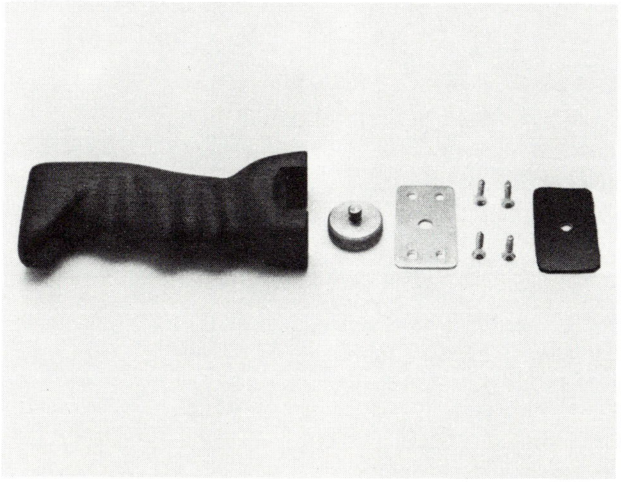

3. Here the parts of the pistol grip are laid out ready to be assembled. I used an old steel tripod screw rather than the plastic and aluminum ones usually sold in camera stores.

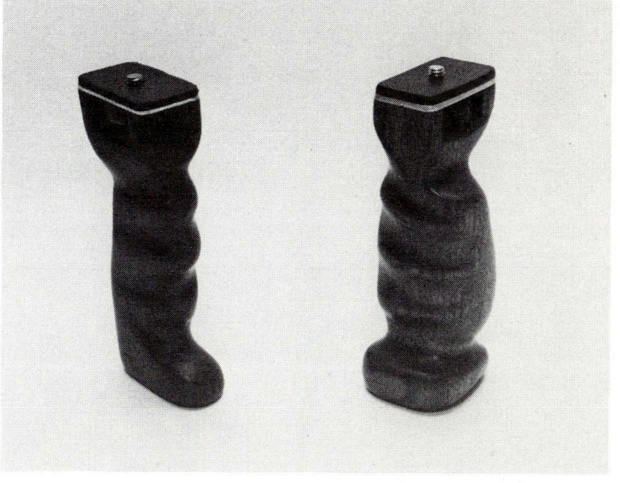

4. I had so much fun making the simple grip on the left that I also made a right-hand grip from a larger block of wood. You can make your pistol grip as simple or as fancy as you wish.

Flash Bracket Made of Wood and Metal

MATERIALS

Aluminum, ⅛″ (3.2 mm) thick
Two "T" nuts, ¼″ (6.4 mm)
Tripod screw
Machine screws, ¼″ and ½″ (12.7 mm) long, standard
 thread
Scrap of leather
Silicone cement, black
Cable release, if desired

TOOLS

Ball peen hammer	File
Metal punch	Emery paper
Hacksaw	Leather punch
Drill and bits	Pocket knife
Ruler	Pliers
Countersink	

Cameras keep getting smaller and smaller while popular electronic flash units are becoming larger and more powerful. A compact SLR with a large electronic flash may look impressive, but the combination is hard to hold and a lot of stress is placed on the camera's flash shoe. A better way of combining the two is to use a flash bracket.

Most flash brackets have a plastic grip. They tend to look cheap, even if they aren't. There is something incongruous about combining an expensive SLR and flash with a bracket that looks like a refugee from a dime store.

Using your own homemade, hardwood-and-metal flash bracket is a much better way of mounting your flash. The pistol grip made in the last project is the starting point for making a flash bracket. Two "T" nuts added to the base of the pistol grip allow machine screws to be attached to the wood. The metal portion of the bracket can be attached to the base of the pistol grip by means of the machine screws.

Begin by cutting the ⅛″ (3.2 mm) aluminum into a strip as wide as the base of your camera and about 9″ (22.9 mm) long. This is longer than necessary, but the excess can be cut off later. Cutting the aluminum with a hacksaw will be easier if you use a new blade with the correct number of teeth. A coarse blade with 18 teeth to the inch (18T) 7T/ cm is best for the thick metal.

Also use the nacksaw to cut a slot in the base of the pistol grip. This saw is better for precise sawing than a regular carpenter's saw because it has finer teeth. Saw two parallel cuts about 3/16″ (4.8 mm) deep and slightly closer together than the width of the aluminum. Next use two diagonal cuts to remove most of the wood from between the original parallel cuts. Do not saw any deeper than 3/16″. With the pocketknife, remove

additional wood and widen the slot to the width of the aluminum.

Use a drill and a 5/16″ (7.9 mm) bit to make two holes to seat the "T" nuts. Avoid drilling too deeply, as a hole only ⅜″ (9.5 mm) deep is all that is needed. Hammer the "T" nuts into the wood. Coat the nuts with epoxy so they will stay firmly in place. If the bracket is for extra-heavy equipment, use three or four "T" nuts and screws to attach the grip.

Measure the position for the screw holes in the aluminum. These holes must match the position of the "T" nuts. Use the ball peen hammer and center punch to locate the position of the holes. Drill ¼″ (6.4 mm) holes in the aluminum and then use the countersink to ream out the metal so that it will hold the heads of the screws. Now the screws will be flush with the metal.

Attach the aluminum to the handle with the machine screws. Position your camera to the left of the grip on the metal. Locate and mark the place for the hole needed for the tripod screw that attaches the camera. Also mark the necessary length of the metal bracket. Remove the handle, saw off the extra metal, and drill the ¼″ mounting hole. If your have two or more different cameras that you plan to use with the flash bracket, additional holes will have to be drilled so that each camera can be correctly positioned on the bracket. Use the file to round off the corners and edges of the aluminum and then smooth the metal further with emery paper.

Squeeze some black silicone around the "T" nuts, attach the metal to the grip, and tighten the machine screws. The silicone acts both as a glue and as a filler, filling the gaps between the wood and the aluminum that were created by the metal base of the "T" nuts.

Next cut a piece of leather slightly larger than the metal and punch a hole for the tripod screw. Glue the leather to the metal with silicone. The flash bracket can now be placed in a warm oven (150F [66C]) so that the silicone will dry in about an hour. When dry, trim the leather to the size of the aluminum.

I built this flash bracket so that it could be used with an auto-winder. Since the film is advanced automatically, I decided to use a right-handed grip and add a cable release to it. With this bracket, my right hand holds the camera and trips the shutter while my left focuses. If you decide to make a left-handed grip and use your right hand to advance the film, there is no need for the cable release unless you wish to trip the shutter with your left hand.

Cable releases have enough plunger travel (the distance the plunger moves) to trip any type of camera. There may be a few cameras that take over an inch of travel to trip the shutter, but most SLRs only require a fraction of the total travel. Attach the cable to your camera and see how much travel you need. Mine takes less than a ¼". The rest of the plunger length gets in the way when used on the grip, so it must be modified.

Remove the trigger button with pliers. This button usually just unscrews. Then cut off the extra cable with the hacksaw. Leave enough plunger to allow for only a little extra travel and about an additional ⅛" to fit inside the button. File the end of the plunger to reduce its diameter so that it will fit. Reattach the button with a little epoxy. Then test the cable release by putting it back on your camera to see how it works. There should be enough travel to trip the shutter with a little bit to spare.

Drill a hole through the grip's upper section that is equal to the diameter of the cable release's metal portion. Start drilling the hole at the point where the button will be under your index finger and angle the hole so that the bit will come out the rear of the grip, slightly above where your hand will grip the back of the handle. Use a little silicone to hold the cable release in place. This allows you to replace the cable release if necessary at some point in the future.

A tripod adapter is used to attach the flash to the grip. Several types of adapters are available. Some have a cable that attaches to the hot shoe of the camera so the adapter will then act as the hot shoe, requiring no PC cord. Manufacturers of cameras with dedicated flash units have special adapters and cables that allow the flash to work automatically when off the camera. Bounce flash adapters are also available. These various attachments will fit the tripod screw on top of the handle. This screw also provides a very secure way of mounting a flash unit, which is important when the flash unit is large and heavy.

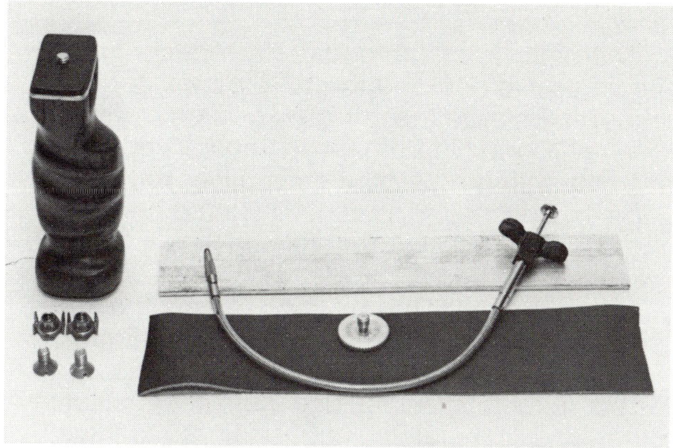

1. Once you've made a pistol grip, adding the parts to make a flash bracket is simple. The aluminum bar, cable release, leather, thumb screw, "T" nuts, and machine screws will be added to the grip to make the flash bracket.

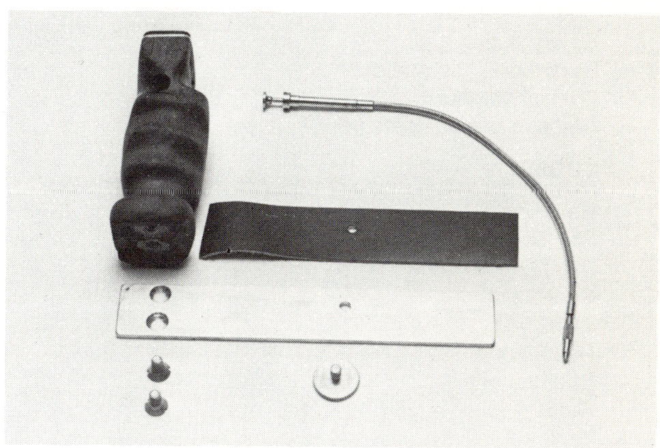

2. Everything here is ready to be assembled. "T" nuts have been glued into the base of the grip, holes drilled in the aluminum and in the grip, and the cable release has been modified by shortening the plunger, and by removing the plastic finger grip and the locking screw.

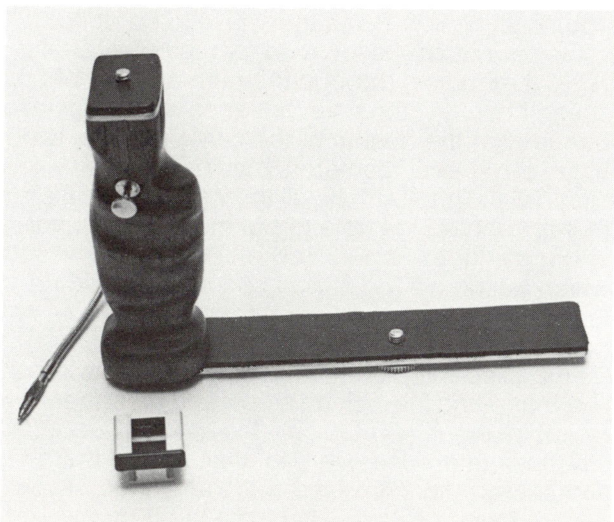

3. The finished flash bracket with the ¼" screw in the grip can be used with a variety of different flash adapters. A non-hot shoe type of adapter is shown in front of the grip.

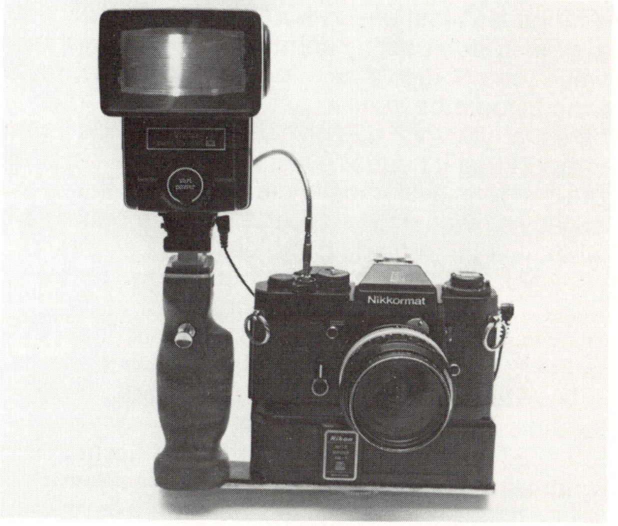

4. Using a flash bracket is a better way of mounting a heavy flash than using the shoe on top of the camera. For maximum stability, use the flash bracket with a camera strap.

Riflestock for Action Shots

MATERIALS

1' (.3 m) of ¾" (19.1 mm) rigid copper pipe
1' of ½" (12.7 mm) rigid copper pipe
1' of ½" flexible copper pipe
¾" close-off caps (2)
½" close-off caps (2)
¾" "T" connector
½" "T" connector
¾" to ½" reducer fitting
¾", 90-degree elbow
¼" eye bolt
¼" nut and washer
Scrap of sheet copper, 1/16" (1.6 mm) or thicker
Scrap of leather
Cable release, 18" (45.7 cm)
Epoxy glue
Silicone cement
Emery paper
Steel wool, fine and extra fine
Liver of sulphur
Glass or plastic container

TOOLS

Hacksaw
File, 8" (20.3 cm) half-round
Ball peen hammer
Center punch
Pliers
Razor knife
Drill and bits
Ruler

It's best to use a heavy-duty, very sturdy tripod when shooting with a long telephoto lens. This ensures the sharpest possible photos. Unfortunately, using a tripod isn't always feasible. When photographing birds or other fast-moving wildlife, a tripod isn't fast enough to follow the speedy subject. In sports photography, when in a crowd, or when the photographer has to move frequently, a tripod would be impractical. At these and other times, a riflestock can give the lens the additional support that it needs. A riflestock makes the camera and lens easier to handle and allows the use of slightly slower shutter speeds than are possible when just hand-holding the lens.

I want a riflestock that is sturdy, allows for taking vertical as well as horizontal photos, and can be used with a winder or motor drive. This doesn't seem to be a lot to ask for a riflestock, but I wasted a lot of time shopping for one that meets these specifications.

I finally decided to make a riflestock, which is what I should have done in the first place. You can make one like mine in less time than I spent shopping for one.

The list of materials seems long and complicated, but most of the materials are standard plumbing fittings that are easy to assemble. Begin by cutting short lengths of the ¾" (19.1 mm) pipe. You can cut the pipe with a hacksaw or a tubing cutter, if you have one. I cut two 3½" (8.9 cm) lengths, one 2" (5.1 cm) and one 1½" (3.8 cm) length, but these sizes can be changed to suit your equipment and personal preference. If you're unsure of what length you want to use, cut the pieces longer than needed. Assemble the riflestock, see how it fits together, and then shorten any pieces of pipe that are too long. Cut a 6½" (16.5 cm) length from the rigid ½" (12.7 mm) pipe. This length can vary to suit your needs.

Bend the flexible pipe into a curve 2½' (76 cm) to 3' (91 cm) in diameter. Trying to bend it tighter will only result in kinking of the pipe. Cut two lengths of the curved pipe, each approximately 3" (7.6 cm) long.

The next step is to modify the reducer fitting. Because it is crimped the ½" pipe will not slip through. Enlarge the crimped portion by filing with the half-round file from the ¾" end. Keep testing the size with the ½" pipe as you file. You want the pipe to slip through, but the fit should be tight. This modification will allow the riflestock to telescope in length.

Saw a piece for the base plate from the sheet copper. I cut mine 2½" × 1½" (6.4 × 3.8 cm). Small pieces of sheet copper are commonly sold as scrap metal. You can use them or substitute any other kind of metal you might happen to have.

Assemble the pieces of copper to form the riflestock as shown in the photo. Position your camera and lens next to it to determine where to put the hole for the eyebolt, which will attach the camera and lens to the riflestock. If more than one lens will be used with the riflestock, check these also. An additional hole or holes may have to be drilled.

Center punch the location for the holes. Drill a ¼" (6.4 mm) hole through the pipe and copper sheet. Then drill the hole for the cable release. Depending on the design of the cable release, two holes of different diameters may have to be drilled. First drill the smaller hole all the way through the metal. I angled the hole to put the trigger button under my index finger. Now drill the larger hole, which will house the button end of the cable release. Drilling is a lot easier if you have a vise or clamp to hold the metal.

I modified the cable release by removing the finger grip and the locking screw and then shortening the plunger travel to only the amount needed to trip the shutter. Use pliers to unscrew the button and saw off the extra length of the plunger if you wish to modify yours. Then file a taper on the end of the metal so it will fit inside the button. Epoxy is used to reattach the button to the end of the plunger.

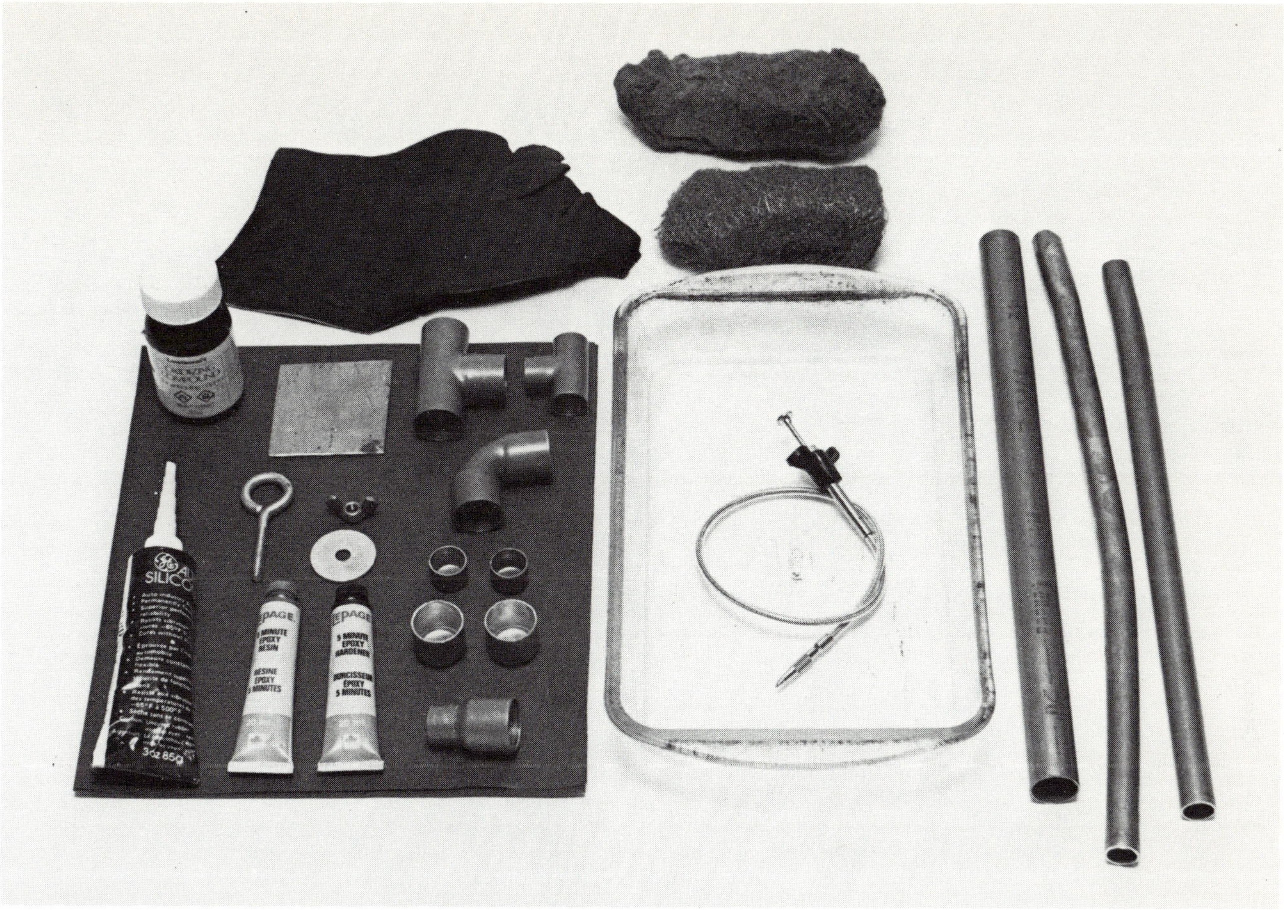

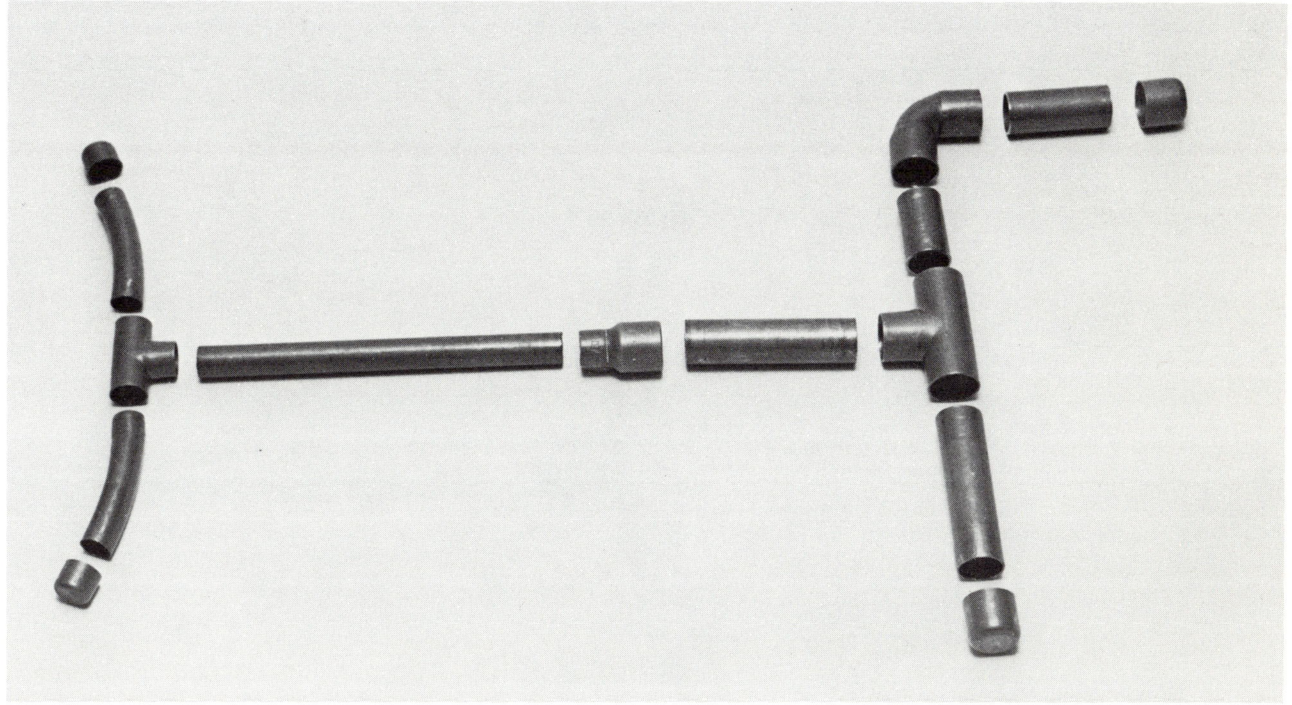

1. Copper pipe and fittings, sheet copper, leather, an "eye" bolt, and a cable release are the materials needed to make the rifle-stock. Epoxy and silicone hold everything together. A dark gunmetal finish can be produced with an oxidizing compound.

2. Here's how everything goes together. The curved "butt" pieces are ½" flexible pipe. The telescoping section is made of ½" rigid pipe. The rest of the riflestock is ¾" pipe.

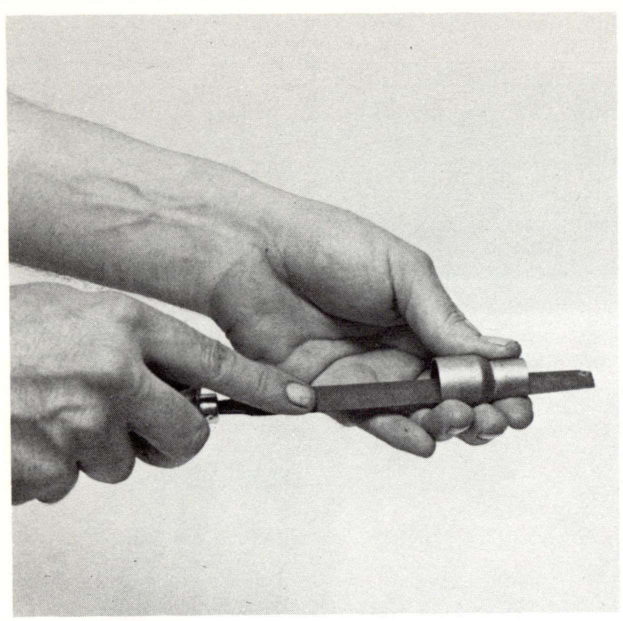 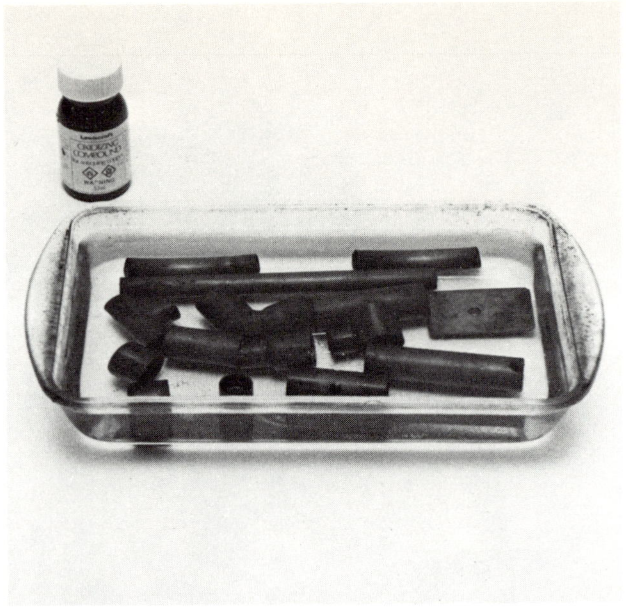

3. To make the riflestock telescope in length, use a half-round file to enlarge the crimped portion of the reducing fitting.

4. Antiquing compound (Liver of sulphur), bought in a craft shop, gives the copper a gunmetal finish.

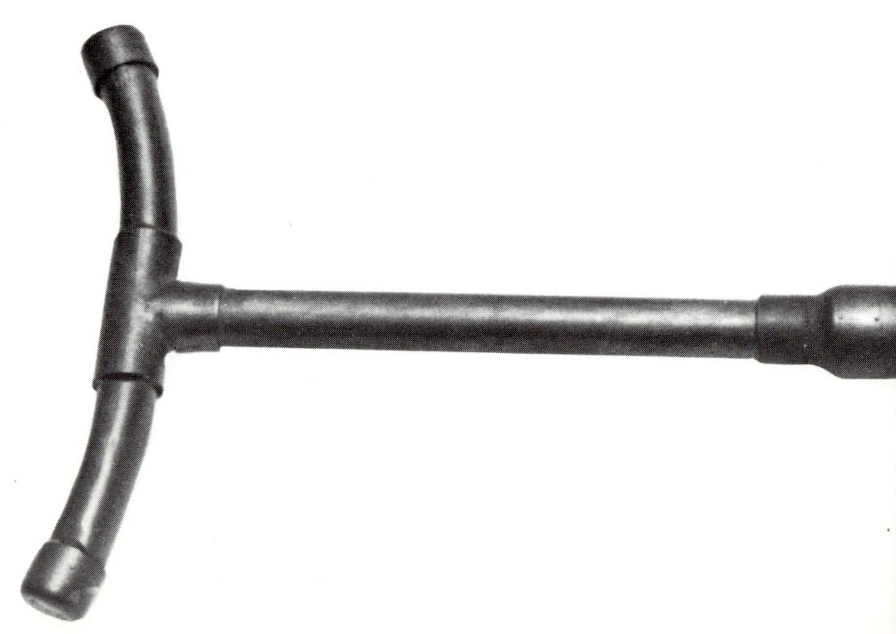

Use emery paper to remove any sharp edges and then clean the copper thoroughly with steel wool. The metal will be beautiful and shiny, but it will tarnish quickly. Rather than fight nature, you can speed up this oxidation process and produce a nice gunmetal finish. Liver of sulphur, sold in most craft shops, can be used as an oxidizing compound for antiquing copper. It is safe and simple to use if you follow the directions on the label. Mix as directed and place the copper into the solution. When the copper reaches the desired color, anything from gray to dark gray or almost black, rinse it clean. Wipe it dry with a paper towel to obtain a nice metallic luster. You may wish to experiment first with scraps of copper to see how they look after being in the oxidizing solution for different lengths of time.

When the metal is completely dry, it can be reassembled. This time, use epoxy to glue all the joints except the ½" (12.7 mm) end of the reducing fitting. This is left unglued so that the riflestock can be adjusted in length.

Cut a leather pad and punch a hole for the bolt. Use the nut and washer to clamp the leather and sheet copper to the pipe with the eye bolt. Use a generous amount of epoxy to glue the platform to the pipe. Be careful not to get any glue on the eye bolt. The cable release is also glued in place with epoxy. Do *not* oven dry the epoxy. The large amount of glue used will liquify and flow to places where you don't want it. Use silicone to glue the leather to the platform.

Shorten the eye bolt with the hacksaw so that only ¼" (6.4 mm) extends above the leather pad. File any rough edges smooth. The riflestock is now finished and ready to use. Some day, when I have the time, I plan to replace the metal grip with a hardwood grip. Drilling a hole the diameter of the pipe fitting and using epoxy to glue the metal to the wood would be very simple. The cable release could then be added like it was for the flash bracket. My only problem is finding the time to do it.

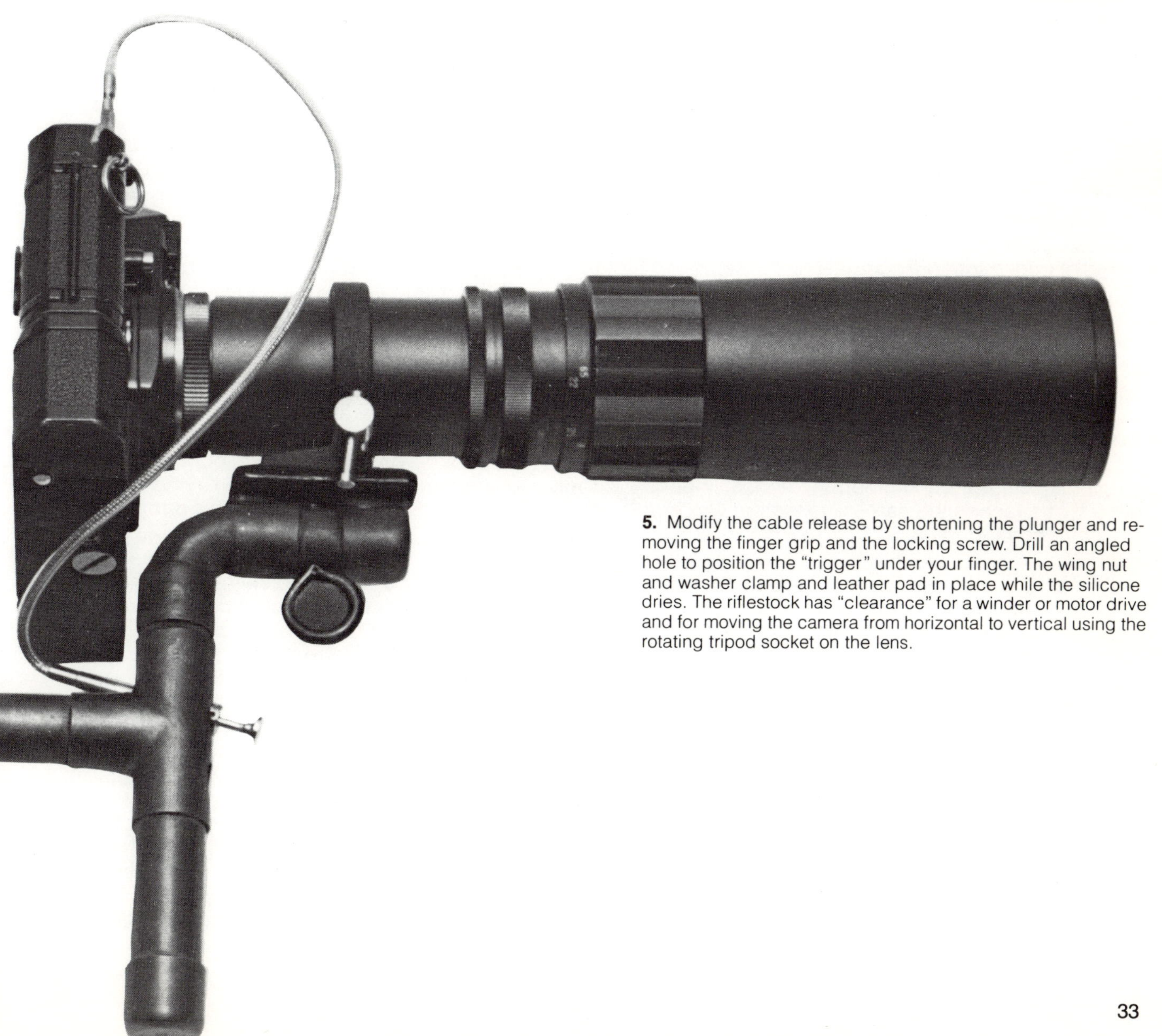

5. Modify the cable release by shortening the plunger and removing the finger grip and the locking screw. Drill an angled hole to position the "trigger" under your finger. The wing nut and washer clamp and leather pad in place while the silicone dries. The riflestock has "clearance" for a winder or motor drive and for moving the camera from horizontal to vertical using the rotating tripod socket on the lens.

Camera Support That Fits on a Car Window

MATERIALS

Large paper clamp (Double Clip No. 108)
Small ball-and-socket head that fits the clamp
¼" bolt ½" (12.7 mm) long, standard thread
Small scrap of leather
Small block of wood ¾" (19.1 mm) thick
Scrap of fiberboard or plywood ⅛" (3.2 mm) thick
Masking tape
Quick-drying epoxy
Clear silicone cement
Small piece of cardboard

TOOLS

Electric drill
Masonry drill bit, ¼" (6.4 mm)
Ball peen hammer
Metal punch
Leather punch
Razor knife

A car can be more than just a way of getting to where you're going. As a wildlife photographer, I often use my car as a mobile blind. Animals in national and state parks and in wildlife sanctuaries have become accustomed to the presence of vehicles. A photographer sitting quietly in a car or truck can get some excellent photos without the trouble of constructing a special blind.

The best photos are often taken early in the morning or late in the evening when the animals are most active. Unfortunately, this is also when the light is low and some kind of camera support is needed. A bean bag is one frequently used camera support in this situation. But a bean bag resting on the car door is too low to use comfortably and it is difficult to follow a moving subject when using one. To solve the problem, I made a small clamp that attaches the camera to the car window for a more comfortable and flexible camera support.

Begin by using the ball peen hammer and metal punch to make a small dent in the center top of the paper clamp. This will make drilling the center hole easier. Use the masonry bit to make the hole for the ¼" bolt that attaches the ball-and-socket head. Since the clamp is made of spring steel, which is too hard to be drilled with a regular drill bit, using the masonry bit is essential.

Cut a leather pad larger than the top of the clamp and punch a hole for the bolt in the center using the leather punch. The excess leather will be removed after the pad is glued to the top of the clamp. Glue the leather in place with a little silicone. This pad provides a cushion for the ball-and-socket head that will be added later.

Mix together a small amount of epoxy. From the inside of the clamp push the ¼" bolt through the center hole and glue the bolt head in place. Insert the small block of wood to hold the clamp open while applying the epoxy. Both the silicone and the quick-drying epoxy will set in about an hour in a warm (150F [66C]) oven.

When the glues are dry, test the strength of the epoxy bond by adding and removing the ball-and-socket head, using considerable force. Also spring the clamp fully open several times. If the bolt loosens, reglue it with more epoxy and try again. The spring is flexible and the epoxy isn't, so the bond may break when stressed. Once the clamp passes these tests, the glue will hold because the clamp will never be fully opened in normal use.

Next tightly fold a piece of leather over a small scrap of ⅛" (3.2 mm) fiberboard or plywood and insert everything into the clamp as far as possible. The leather should be large enough to completely line the inside of the clamp, with some extra left over. This excess will be trimmed off after the leather is glued in place.

Since the clamp is wedge-shaped, there will be gaps or openings between the leather and the clamp that should be filled with silicone. To keep the silicone in place while it is drying, cover one side of the clamp with masking tape. Add the silicone by inserting the applicator nozzle deep into the opening to ensure that the glue reaches the taped edge. After the bottom is filled, raise the level of the nozzle to fill the remainder of the opening. After all the openings are filled, smooth the silicone with a small piece of cardboard. Press down firmly to make sure that there are no air bubbles present.

Dry the silicone in a warm oven. Since the silicone is thick, oven-drying may take three or four hours. The silicone gives off a strong odor, which is similar to vinegar (acetic acid), while drying. The silicone will be completely dry when this odor is totally gone.

Once dry, remove the tape and fiberboard and trim the leather to the size of the clamp with a razor knife. Any excess silicone can also be pared off with the knife. Add the ball-and-socket head. The clamp is now finished and ready to use.

The ball-and-socket head must be the same size or smaller than the width of the top of the paper clamp so that the levers will open with the head in place. After you have used the levers to attach the clamp to the window, they can be lowered to keep them out of the way.

The leather and silicone inside the clamp serve a dual purpose. They protect the glass from the metal and they add stability. The ⅛" (3.2 mm) fiberboard inserted into the clamp during construction is slightly thinner than the car window glass. When the finished clamp is put on the window glass, the silicone and leather compress and apply pressure

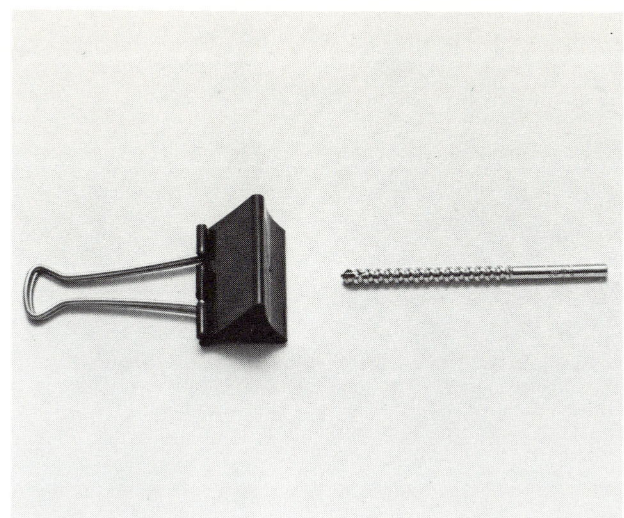

1. Spring steel is very hard, so use a masonry bit to make the hole for the ¼″ bolt.

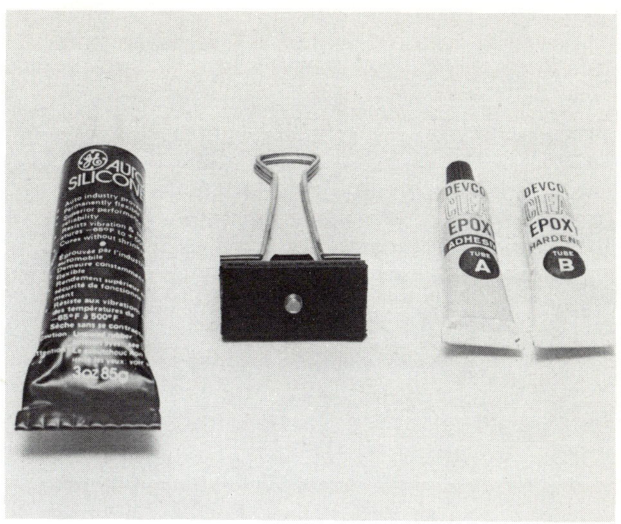

2. Epoxy glue and black silicone cement are used to make the car window clamp.

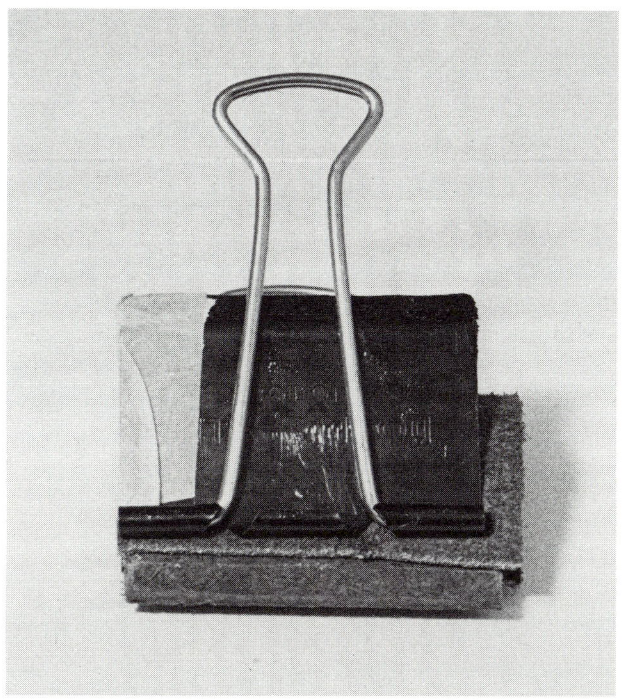

3. Fold the leather over a scrap of Masonite and insert them into the clamp. Cover one end of the clamp with masking tape to hold the silicone.

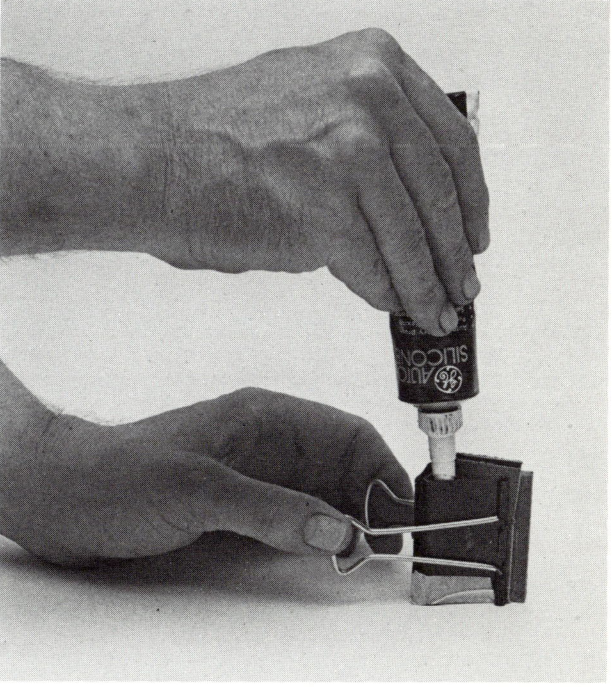

4. Stand the clamp on edge before adding the silicone. First add the silicone to the bottom and then raise the nozzle to fill the rest of the opening.

from the spring to a larger area of glass than would
be possible without this lining. The clamp wouldn't
be stable without the leather and silicone insert.

Despite its small size, the clamp is capable of
holding a heavy SLR and a telephoto lens. I know
that this clamp is nothing more than an overgrown
paper clip, but the spring is very strong, much
stronger than its size would indicate. The weight of
the camera and lens forces the clamp down. This
combined with the friction of the leather against
the glass makes the car window camera clamp a
strong and stable camera support.

When photographing with the clamp, turn off the
engine. Engine vibration can ruin image sharpness. At slower shutter speeds, a cable release
should be used as well.

The window clamp should also be used with
lenses 300mm or longer, even if there is plenty of
light. At faster shutter speeds, this camera support
will improve image sharpness. Long lenses need
all the support you can give them to obtain the
sharpest possible photos.

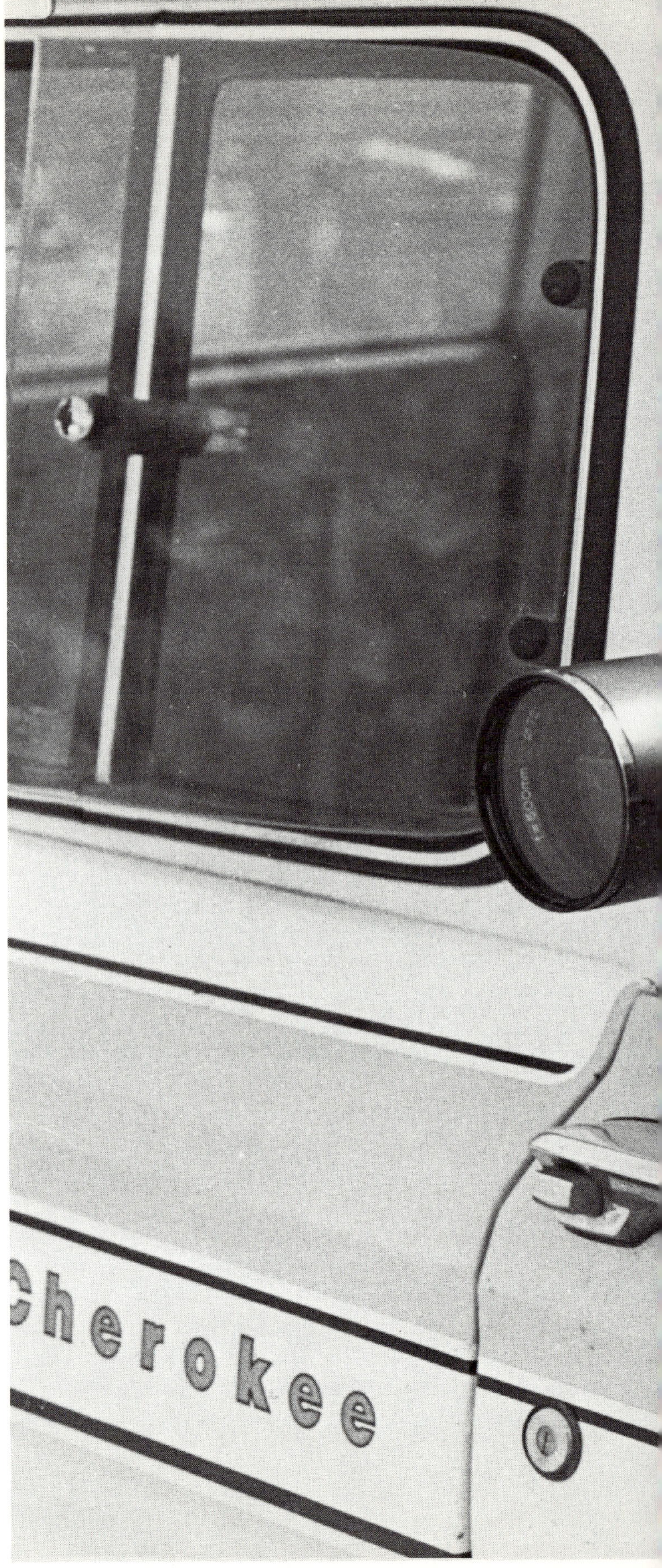

5. As small as it is, the clamp with a small ball-and-socket
head can hold a heavy SLR and telephoto lens.

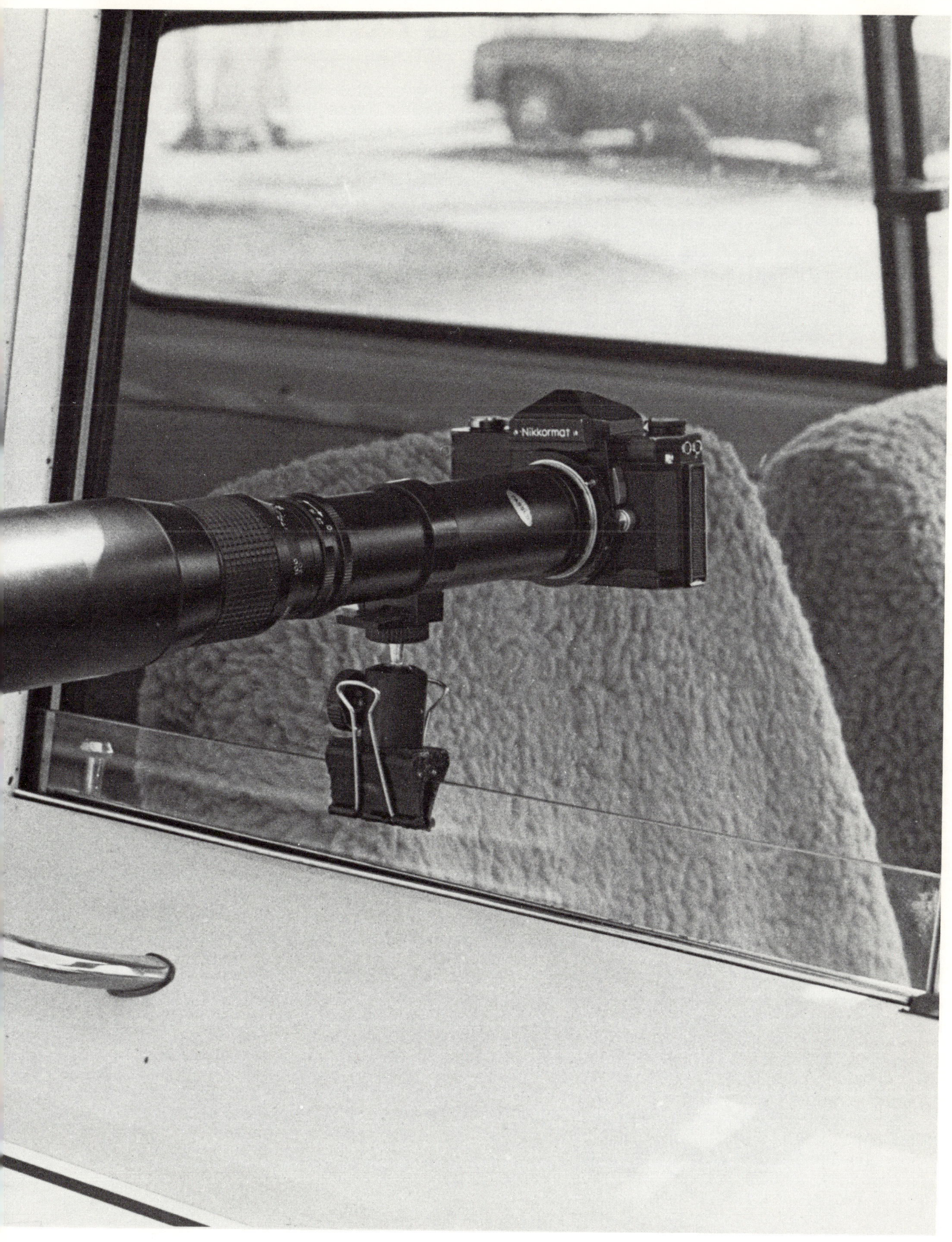
Nikkormat

Extra Long, Coiled PC Cord

Murphy's Law states that "Whatever can go wrong will go wrong." There should be a photographic corollary that says, "PC cords will always fail at the worst possible time." You should always carry spares to allow for any problems. But when a cord fails, it hurts to throw it away, especially if it was a long, expensive one.

I prefer using long coiled PC cords — when I need extra length, it's there. Until I do, the extra length stays neatly coiled and out of the way. However, these cords aren't always available for my flash and they are rather expensive. I am always on the lookout for any type of coiled cord that is sold at electrical supply houses, camera stores, and discount places. These cords may be made for guitars, stereos, microphones, or some other brand of flash, but all will work for this project.

A regular PC cord has only two wires. You may find many cords that have three or four wires, but they can still be used. If possible, test the cord's spring by stretching and releasing it and buy one that tends to keep its coiled shape. Some coiled cords will lose their spring and turn to mush with very little use. These are the ones to avoid. The length of the cord isn't important. Extra-long ones can be cut into more usable lengths for making several PC cords. These coiled cords can be inexpensive — I have purchased them on sale for as little as a dollar and a half, so some are really bargains.

The coiled cord shown in this project has three wires and is made for a stereo. The extra wire will provide insurance against one of the wires failing. For practice, begin by cutting the short PC cord in half. Use the razor knife to strip off 1″ (2.5 cm) of the outer insulation, but be sure to cut just barely through the rubber coating. This is done by rolling the cord on the table while gently pressing down on it with the blade of the knife. Take care not to cut through the wire that lies just below the insulation. When you have cut completely around the insulation, pull it off the wire.

Most PC cords are miniature coaxial cables — alternate layers of wire strands covered by insulation. Unravel the outer strands of wire and twist them between your fingers to make a single wire. The center insulation is now exposed. Use the knife to cut and remove ½″ (12.7 mm) of the insulation from the center wire. Now you know what to expect and how to strip the wire. You can practice again on the other half of the PC cord if you do not feel confident enough to proceed.

Plug in the soldering iron and let it heat while you are preparing the ends of the cords. To attach the PC cord ends to the coiled cord, all you need are the PC and flash unit plug, each with 1″ of its attached wire. Cut off the extra wire and strip the insulation from the two ends of the cord that hold the connectors.

Next cut off any unneeded connectors or excess length of wire from the coiled cord and strip off an inch of the insulation from each end. The wires in the coiled cord may be any color. Twist together the uninsulated portions of any two wires at one end of the coiled cord and repeat with the same color wires at the other end. These twisted wires are then soldered together. Use the soldering iron or gun to heat the bare wire and apply very little solder to the wire, *not* to the tip of the iron. The solder should melt instantly. If it doesn't, reheat the wire or allow more time for the soldering iron to reach its maximum temperature. A good solder joint should be bright, shiny metal. If you are using a four-strand coiled cord, solder two pairs of wires together. With a three-strand cord, solder two wires, leaving a single wire and a joined pair.

Cut four sections, two of each size, of heat-shrinkable tubing — about ½″ (12.7 mm) of the narrower tubing and about 2″ of the larger (¼″) tubing. Slip the larger tubing over the insulation on the coiled cord. Then push the smaller (⅛″) tubing over the soldered wires on the coiled cord, bending the single wire aside. There should be about ½″ of bare wire extending beyond the insulation.

Next, connect the wires from the center of the PC cord and the paired wires of the coiled cord. Cross the bare portions of the wires and hold them between your fingers. Twist the wires around each other in opposite directions. Repeat this with the similar wires on the other end of the cord.

Keep the heat-shrinkable tubing as far away from the soldering iron as possible and solder together the twisted wires. When the solder is cool, slip the insulating tubing down over the joint. Use the heat from a light bulb or a match to shrink the plastic to a tight fit. A light bulb is better for this — I used a match because it's easier to photograph. If you use a match, keep the flame at least ½″ from the plastic.

Join the outside wire of the PC cord and the remaining wire of the coiled cord by twisting the

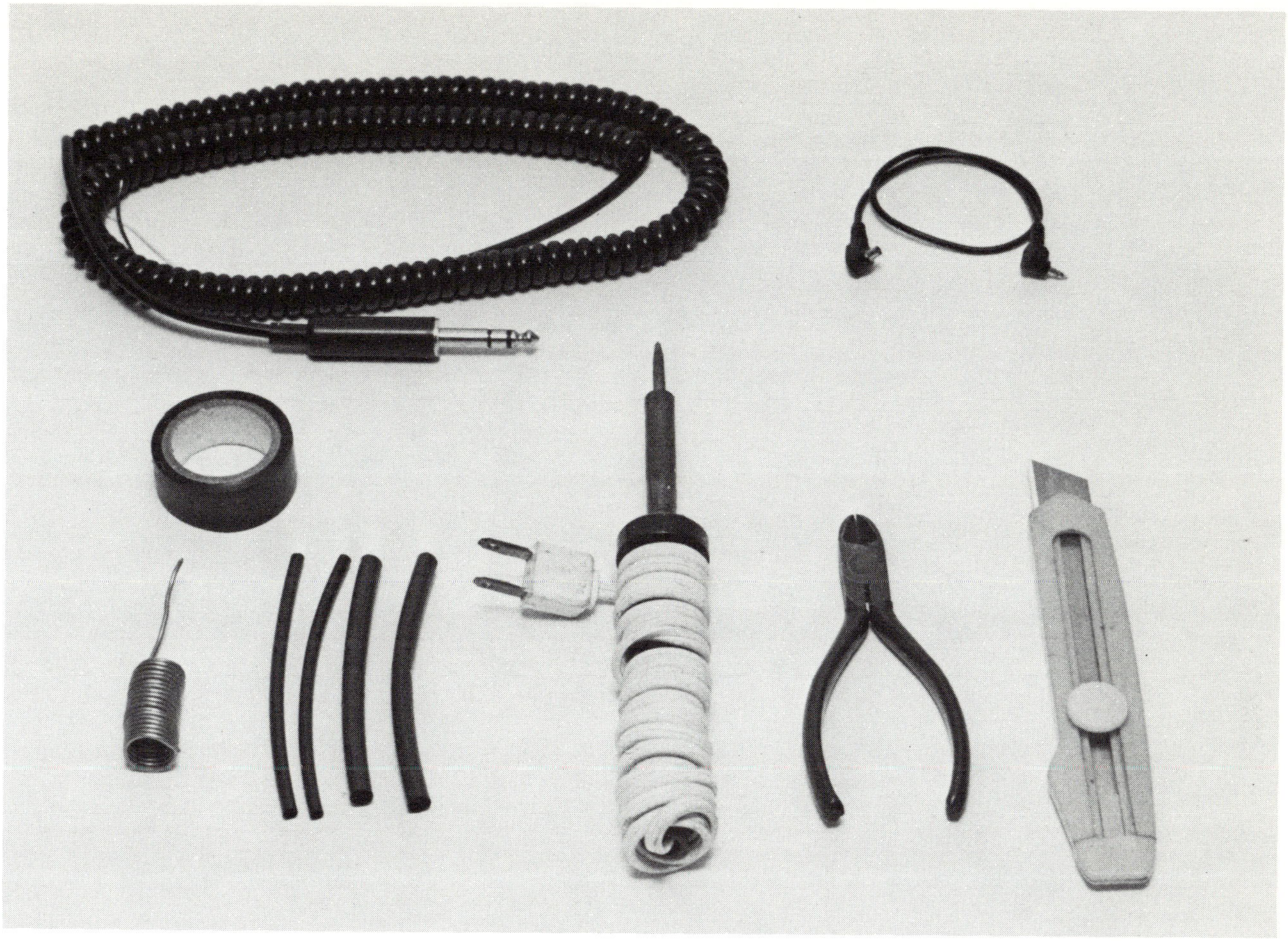

1. These are the tools and materials needed to make a long coiled PC cord from a coiled cord and a short PC cord.

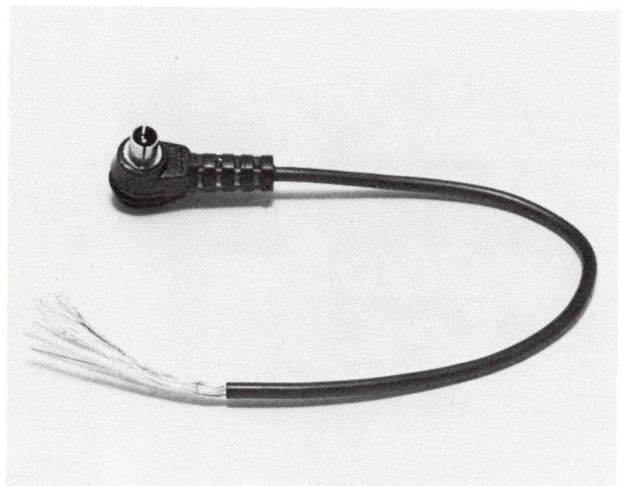

2. You can see what's inside a PC cord by cutting it in half and stripping off the outer insulation. The cord is a coaxial cable with alternating layers of wire covered with insulation.

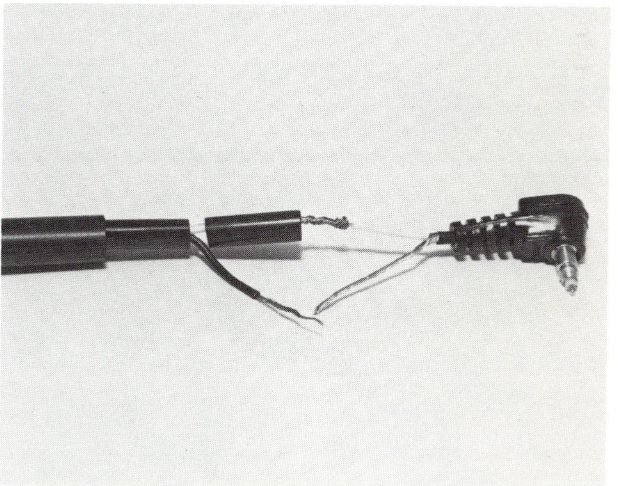

3. The heat-shrinkable insulation is positioned before soldering. The center wire is soldered first, then insulated with the heat-shrink.

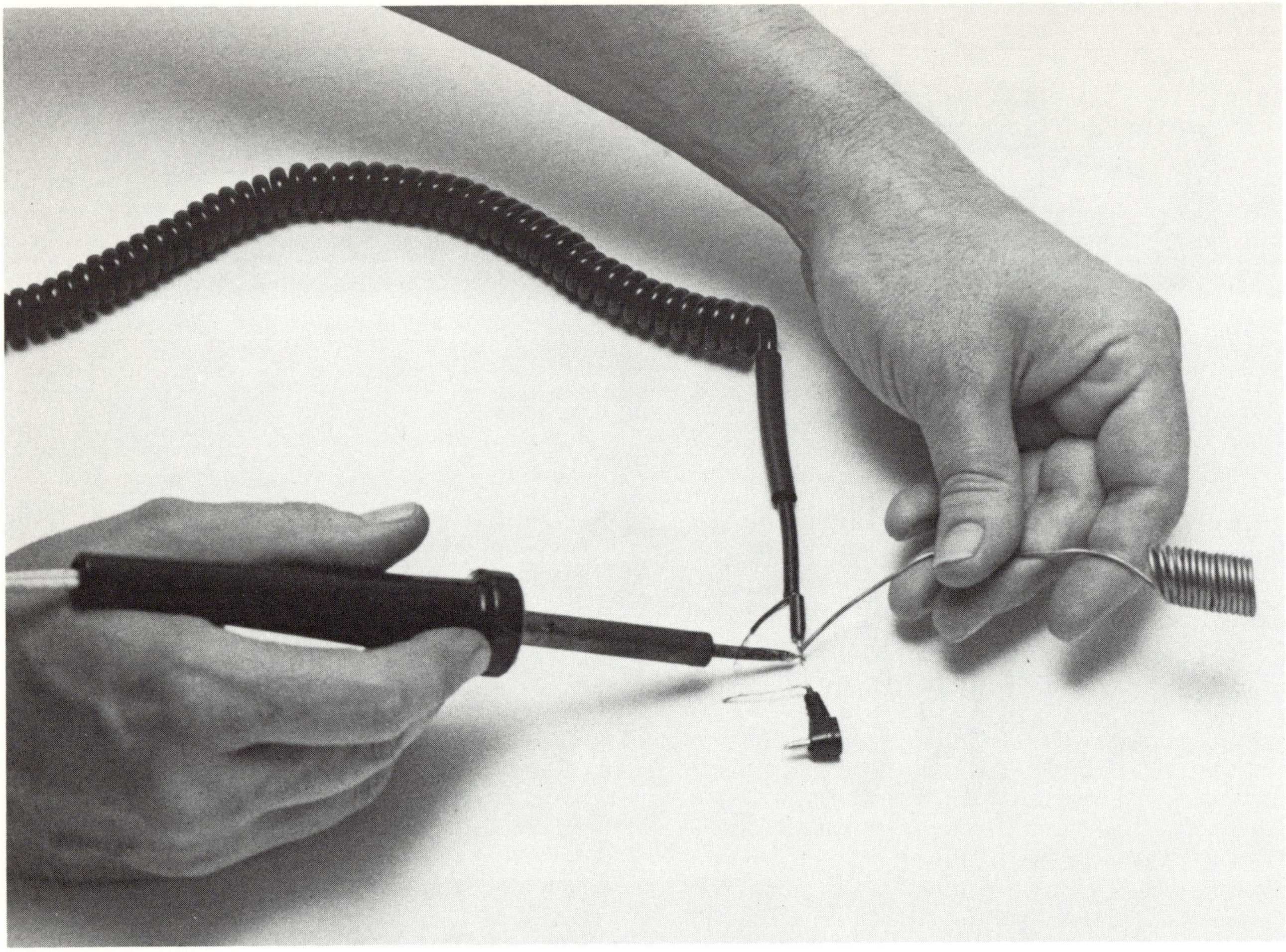

4. The solder point for the center wire must be made quickly before the heat from the soldering iron shrinks the tubing. Plastic tape can be used to cover this joint if you have problems.

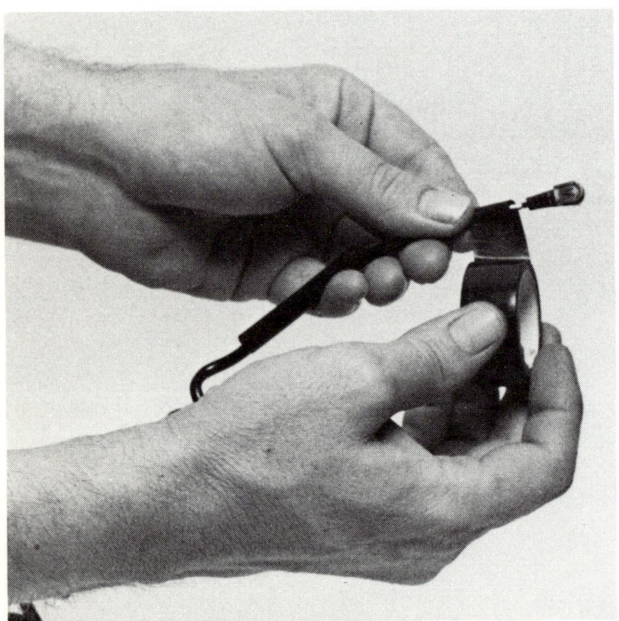

5. Plastic tape is used to increase the diameter of the joint before the larger tubing is positioned and shrunk.

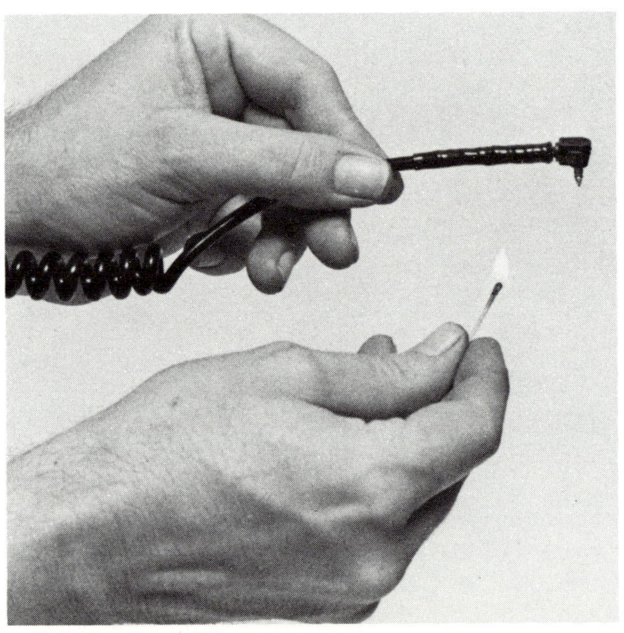

6. Almost any heat source can be used to shrink the insulation. Here I'm using a match but the heat from a light bulb will shrink the plastic without the danger of melting.

wires around each other in opposite directions like you did before. Solder these wires together using just a small amount of solder. When the solder is cool, wrap plastic electrical tape around the joint to increase its diameter to match that of the insulation on the coiled cord. Slip the larger tubing over the taped joint and use heat to shrink it to a tight fit. Repeat these steps with the wire at the other end. Using the heat-shrinkable tubing gives a very finished look to the joined cords and the finished joints should be barely noticeable.

The techniques outlined here will also enable you to salvage parts from the bad PC cords that are usually thrown away. Cord failure is most often due to a broken center wire. The flash won't fire or will only fire occasionally when the cord is bent a certain way. These breaks usually occur near the end of the cord where most bending occurs. By cutting off the end of the cord and stripping the insulation, you can pull on the center wire and often find the break. In this way, a portion of a bad cord can be salvaged to make a new PC cord. You can test defective cords with a multimeter.

Check your long coiled PC cord by using it to connect your camera to your electronic flash unit. Try firing the flash several times, off camera, with the cord stretched to different distances. Also try bending the soldered joints when using the flash. Your long coiled PC cord should pass this test with flying colors. It can then be put inside your camera bag, ready for use when you need it.

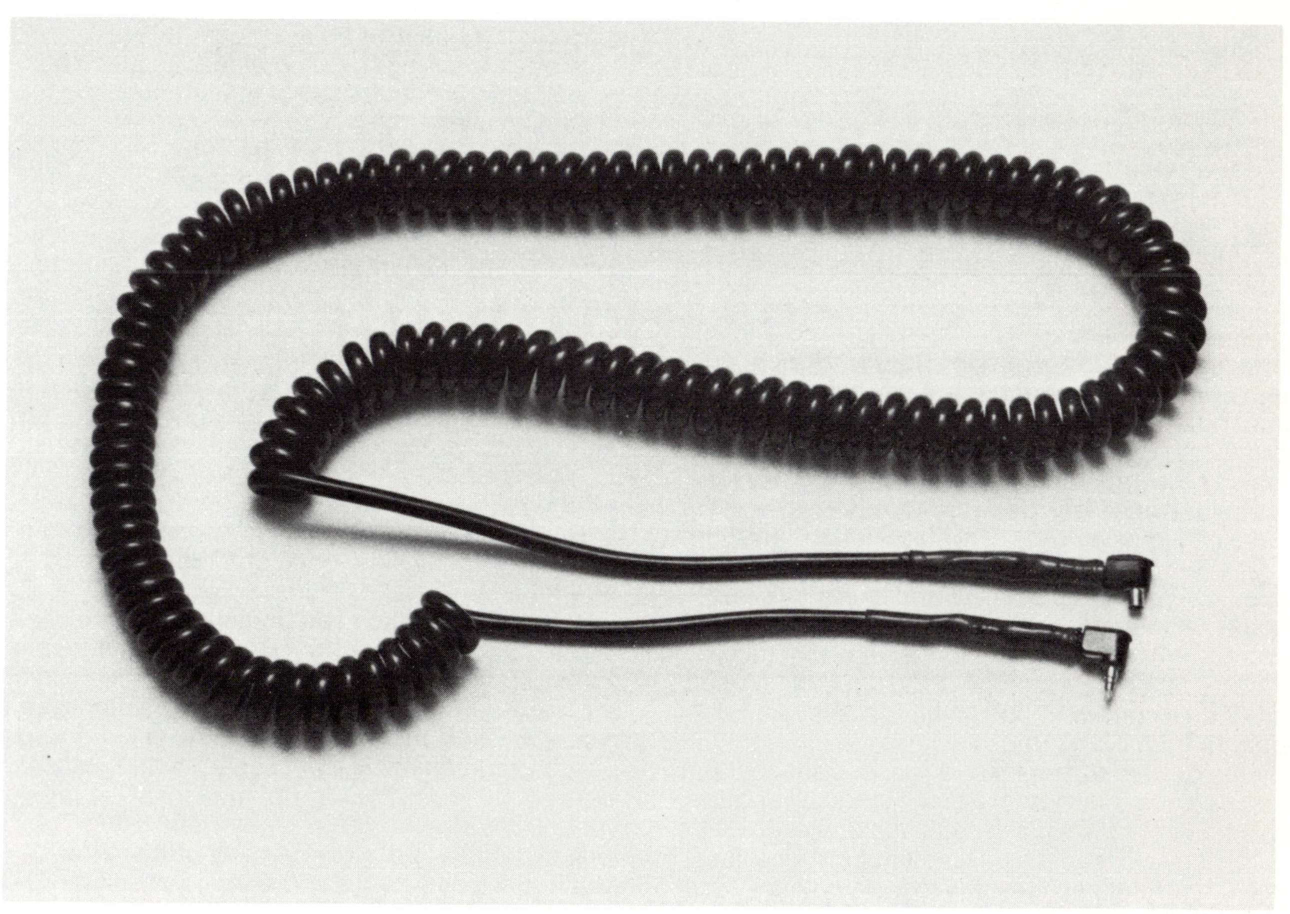

7. Here's the finished PC cord, ready to use. The shrinkable insulation makes a neat joint at the ends of the cord.

Soft Focus Lens

Lens designers spend a lot of time and effort
making the sharpest possible lenses. Spherical
and chromatic aberrations are minimized, multi-
coating is used to reduce flare, and distortions are
eliminated. Nothing is missed when it comes to
making the lens razor sharp. This project would
probably appall lens designers.

A soft focus lens has all types of lens aberrations
— these are what make the lens *soft*. This lens
uses a single glass element and its focus is very
soft. The element is 40mm in diameter and has a
focal length of about 85mm. Any lens that has a
focal length between 75 and 150mm can be used
(100 or 105mm would be ideal). Lenses can be
bought from Edmund Scientific in the United
States or from Efstonscience Inc. in Canada. Or
you can use a lens from a small magnifying glass
that has the right focal length. You can even use a
+10 close-up lens. The diameter of the lens isn't
very important and lenses with a diameter of 25 up
to 50mm can easily be used.

Finding the right sizes of tubing for the lens may
take a little searching. I used plastic tubing from a
telescopic fishing rod case. A few of the other things
you might use are plastic drinking cups, cardboard
mailing tubes, and plastic or aluminum pipes.

First you will need to cut two 1″ (2.5 cm) lengths
of the larger diameter tubing and one 2″ (5.1 cm)
length of the smaller tubing. Use a hacksaw with a
miter box to cut the tubing as square as possible.
Smooth the rough cut edges with sandpaper. If
you don't have a miter box, the plastic can be cut
with a razor knife. Use a book the right height to
support the knife handle, press the end of the tubing against the table, and rotate the tubing against
the knife blade. This method of cutting will make a
perpendicular cut.

Compare the diameter of the lens element to the
smaller tubing. If the lens is slightly smaller, the
diameter of the tubing can be reduced by adding
cardboard inside the tube. If the lens element is a
lot smaller, mount it in a cardboard or matte board
disc. Then the element with its cardboard holder
can be mounted inside the tubing.

From a heavy wire, make retaining rings to hold
the lens inside the tubing. Wrap the wire three full
times around the outside of the tubing. Then remove the wire from the tubing and cut circles from
the spiraled wire. Cut an additional ½″ (12.7 mm)
from each wire ring to reduce the diameter. These
retaining rings should now fit tightly inside the tubing's diameter.

Cover the inside and outside of the small tubing
with the flocked paper. (Self-adhesive flocked
paper is available from scientific suppliers and
from art supply stores.) This paper seals light leaks
and reduces flare. Place the lens element inside
the tubing, holding it in place with retaining rings
on both sides. Use lens tissue when handling the
lens to prevent fingerprints. Exactly where the lens
is placed in the tubing will depend on the focal
length. You will determine this by trial and error
after you have assembled the soft focus lens.

Set the tubing with the lens element aside to
work on the lens mount. I used a portion of extension tube to mount the lens. You can use one of
these short extension tubes or a lens reversing
ring for a lens mount. You could also modify a
camera body cap to make a mount for the lens.

With silicone, glue a 1″ piece of the larger diameter tubing to the lens mount. When the glue is dry,
slip the smaller tubing into the tubing on the lens
mount and test the fit. Use extra layers of flocked
paper to tighten the fit if necessary. Add another 1″
piece of tubing to the front of the lens. This prevents the tubing from slipping too far inside the
lens mount and possibly damaging the mirror.
Mount the lens on your camera and check the
focus, making sure that the lens can be focused
on a distant object, 50 feet (15.2 meters) or more
away. If the lens element doesn't focus at infinity,
reposition it by moving it closer to the camera
body. If the lens focuses past infinity, move the
element farther from the camera body. A little trial
and error will determine where the lens element
should be located. If the lens vignettes, the element is too deeply recessed, so part of the front
portion of the tubing must be removed.

After you're satisfied with the positioning of the
lens element, add a little silicone to the retaining
rings to hold them in place. Use the long nozzle to
add silicone to the rings inside the tubing. Use just

enough to prevent the rings from slipping. At the same time, glue the 1" piece of the large tubing to the inside tubing and allow both to dry.

As it is, the lens is probably softer than you would want. It can be made sharper by adding a diaphragm. Cut a circle from the black poster board that is the size of the inside tubing's diameter. Then cut a hole in the center of the circle, about one-half the diameter of the lens. This diaphragm, more correctly called a stop, is placed inside the tubing behind the lens element.

A circular opening is only one of many possibilities. Star-shaped openings with any number of points can be cut in the poster board discs, or a perforated stop with one central hole and several smaller holes surrounding it can be made. The shape of the stop determines the shape of the out-of-focus highlights. Cut several different types to find the ones you like the best.

The soft focus lens gives a misty romantic look to photographs — quite a change from the razor-sharp photos that regular lenses produce. Changing the size of the stop changes the degree of softness. A color filter can be used to sharpen the lens even more.

Exposure is best determined with a through-the-lens light meter and is controlled by changing the shutter speed. If you don't have through-the-lens metering, find the correct exposure by shooting a test roll of film.

This project is meant to be a lot of fun, so don't put too much work into the lens by making it too complex. If you have any problems in construction, they can usually be solved by cutting, gluing, or adding some cardboard. I couldn't resist the temptation of making the lens a little fancier, so I glued some black leather to the outside for a finishing touch.

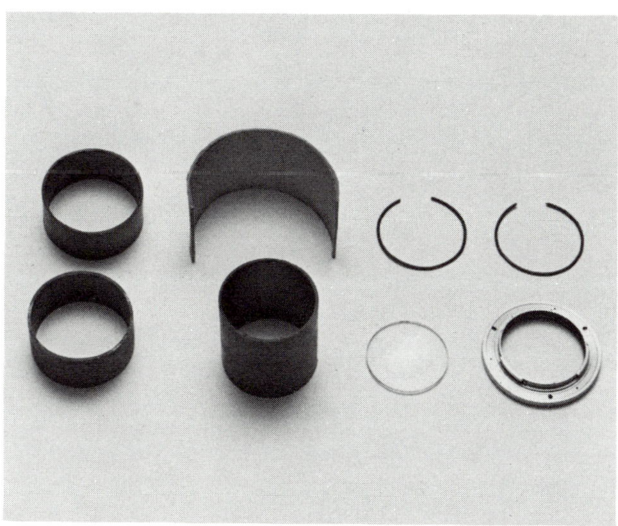

1. To make the soft focus lens, you'll need two different sizes of plastic tubing that nest inside one another, cardboard for a spacer or filler, a simple lens element, two wire retaining rings, and an extension tube segment or lens reversing ring that mounts on your camera.

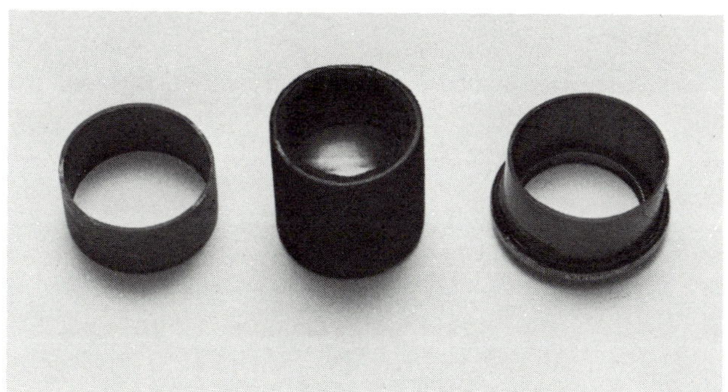

2. Black flocked paper is used to cover the smaller tubing, both inside and out. You can substitute black construction paper if you cannot locate the flocked paper. Wire retaining rings hold the lens element inside the tubing. If necessary, place cardboard inside the tubing to reduce its diameter to match the lens.

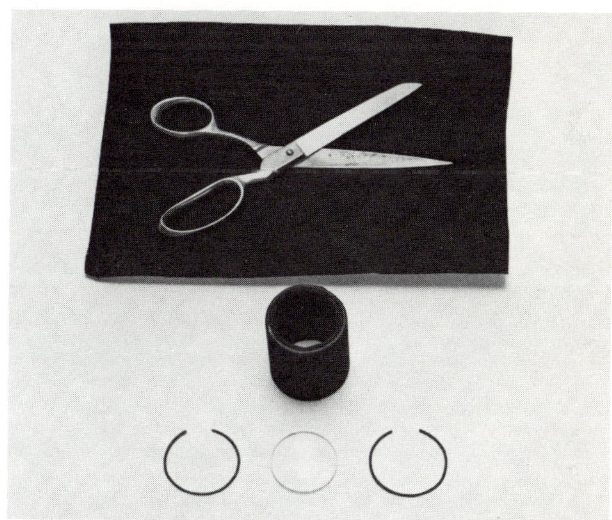

3. The lens is made of three parts. The center tubing contains the lens element and fits inside the other two tubes. The tubing on the left acts as a lens hood and the one on the right is glued to a lens mount. The lens slip focuses with the center section sliding inside the tubing glued to the lens mount.

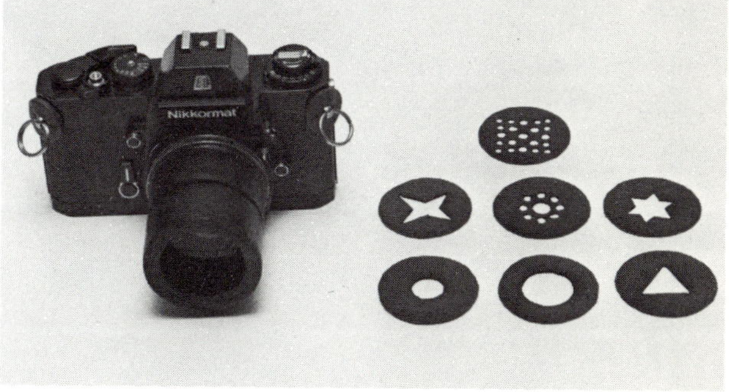

4. The finished soft focus lens can be made a little fancier by gluing leather to the outside. Cut diaphragms (more correctly called stops) from poster board. These stops make the lens sharper and can be used to control the shape of the out-of-focus highlights.

DARKROOM AIDS

High Quality Safelight

Quality safelights are expensive, but they are equipped with filters that transmit more light than the cheap ones. And the light is exactly the right color for the paper or film. Safelight filters deteriorate with use and the better filters will last longer than cheap ones.

One way to save money is to buy quality filters and make the rest of the safelight. An additional advantage to making your own safelight is that you can make a separate housing for each filter you use. This eliminates the need to change filters. All you have to do is switch on a different safelight.

Making the safelight is very simple. However, there is *only one safe way* of working on this and the other projects that use house current (AC). Leave it *unplugged* until the project is finished and the equipment is assembled and ready to use.

The best type of socket I could find for the safelight is the Leviton plastic socket with rotary switch. Having the switch built in makes wiring very simple. This switch has no exposed electrical contacts when assembled, which is important for safety. Other manufacturers may make similar switches.

Begin by drilling two ⅜″ (9.5 mm) holes in the bottom of the empty coffee can. Drill one of the holes in the center and the other 1½″ (3.8 cm) from the center of the can. Center punch the locations for the holes to make drilling easier.

Take the power cord and split a 2″ (5.1 cm) section at the end of the cord. Use the razor knife to strip off ½″ (12.7 mm) of insulation from the end of each wire. Twist the strands of wire together to make them compact.

Take apart the socket by unscrewing the finger screw around the switch and force out the center portion. Inside are two screws for attaching the power cord.

Run the power cord through the outside hole that was made in the coffee can and through the rectangular hole in the outside part of the socket. Twist together the insulated portions of the two wires as shown in the first photo. This acts as a shock absorber and prevents the wires from being accidentally pulled out of the socket. Attach the two wires to the screws. Wrap the uninsulated ends of the wire around the screws in a *clockwise* direction. When wrapped this way, the wires will stay neatly in place as the screws are tightened.

Put the two parts of the socket back together and push the switch through the center hole in the coffee can. Tighten the finger screw to hold the socket in place. Attach the shock-absorbing grommet to the cord. Grasp the grommet with pliers and force it into the hole in the coffee can. Use this or another type of grommet to protect the power cord from the sharp edge of the metal.

I made the bracket for the safelight from a copper strip 1″ wide. Aluminum or steel could be used instead, if that is what you happen to have. The metal should be about 14″ (35.6 cm) long and 1″ (2.5 cm) or 1 ½″ wide. Bend the metal into a "U" shape with a flat base the width of the coffee can (about 5″ [12.7 cm]). Drill 3/16″ (4.8 mm) holes where the bracket attaches to the can and two more holes for attachment to the wall. Add the bracket using the 3/16″ nuts, bolts, and washers. It's a good idea to use two nuts inside the coffee can so the bolts won't loosen. Paint the outside of the can and the bracket, if you wish.

Sheet metal screws and mirror holders are used to attach the filter. The filter is 5 ½″ (14 cm) in diameter while the coffee can is just 5″ wide, so the clips need to be modified to adjust for the difference. Grasp ¼″ (6.4 mm) of the clip's end with a pair of pliers and tap the metal with a ball peen hammer to start the bend. Once you have the bend started, it can be completed by squeezing the metal with a pair of pliers. The "U"-shaped channel is the same width as the thickness of the filter. Bend four clips into the shape shown in the photo on page 48. Position the filter on the coffee can and mark where the holes should be drilled. Drill a 1/16″ (1.6 mm) hole to start the screws. They will enlarge the hole as they are screwed into the metal.

Install the correct size of light bulb before attaching the filter. This bulb should be 7 ½ watts or 15 watts, depending on the type of filter. Don't use bulbs of higher wattage as the heat they generate can damage the filter.

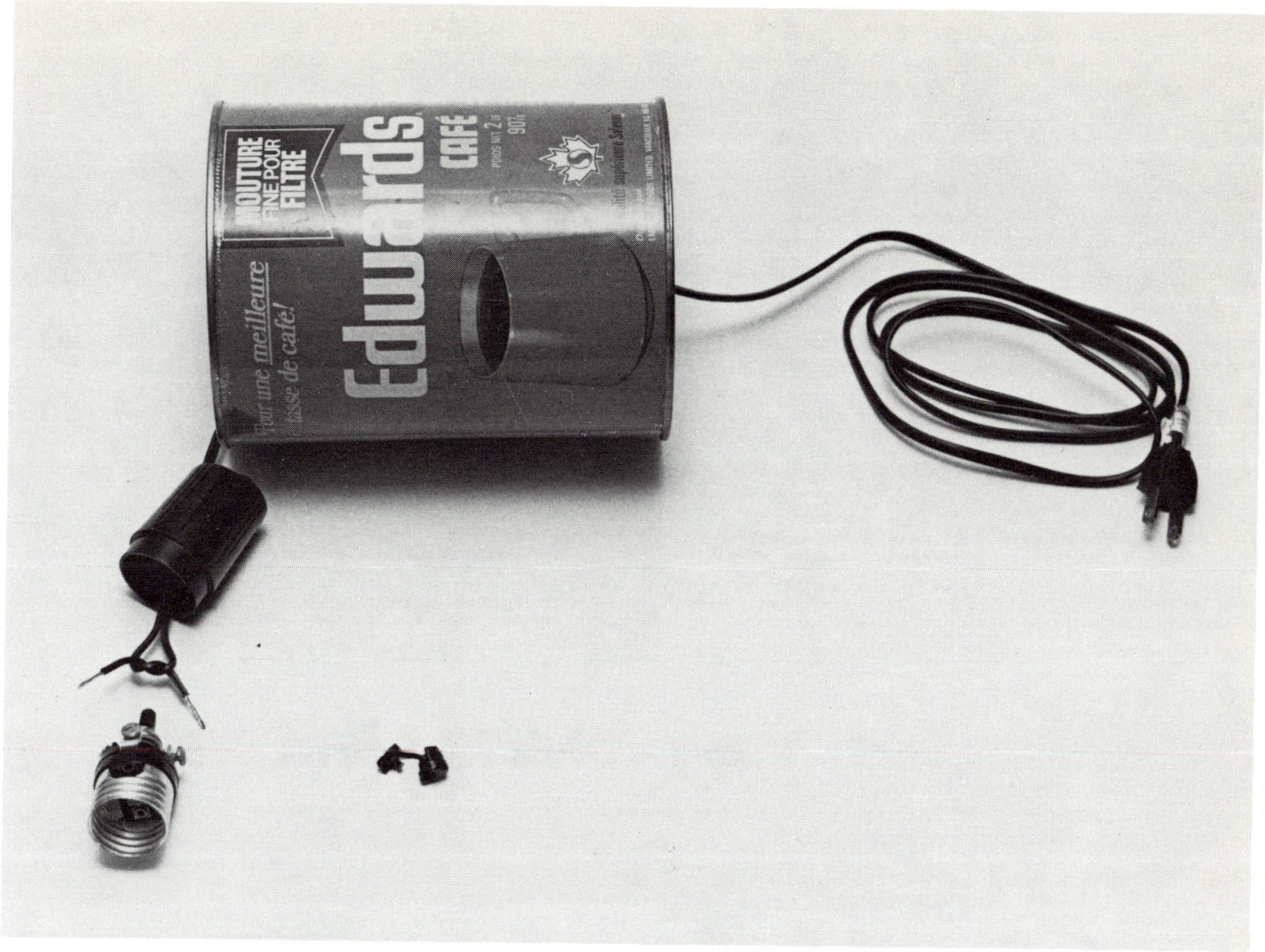

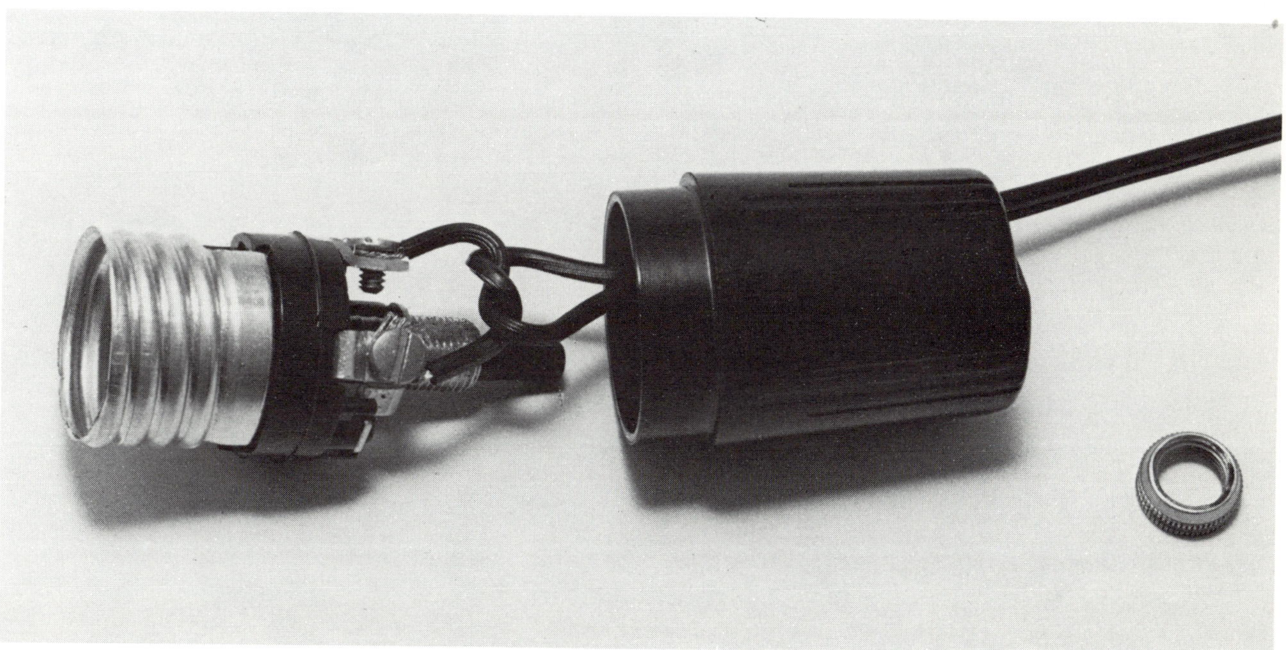

1. The power cord is put through the outside hole in the coffee can, then through the rectangular hole in the rear of the socket. Then the insulated split ends are tied in an overhand knot, as shown.

2. The stripped ends of the power cord are attached to the screws in the socket. Wrap the wires around the screws in a clockwise direction so they will stay in place as the screws are tightened. Only work on the wiring when the cord is unplugged.

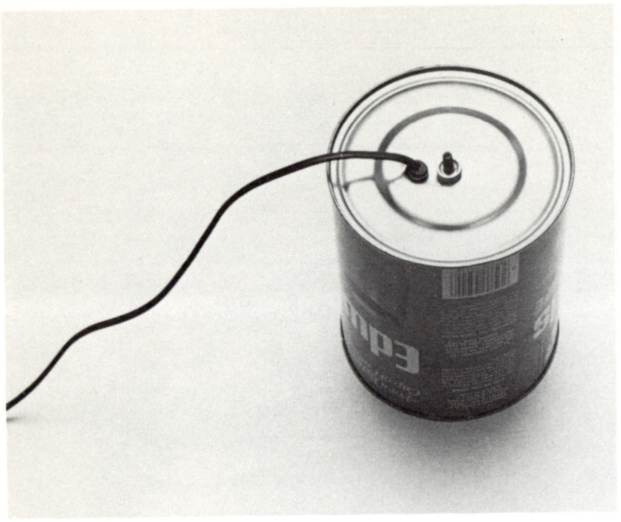

3. The screw that goes around the switch holds the lamp socket in place. The power cord must be protected from the sharp edge of the metal with a grommet.

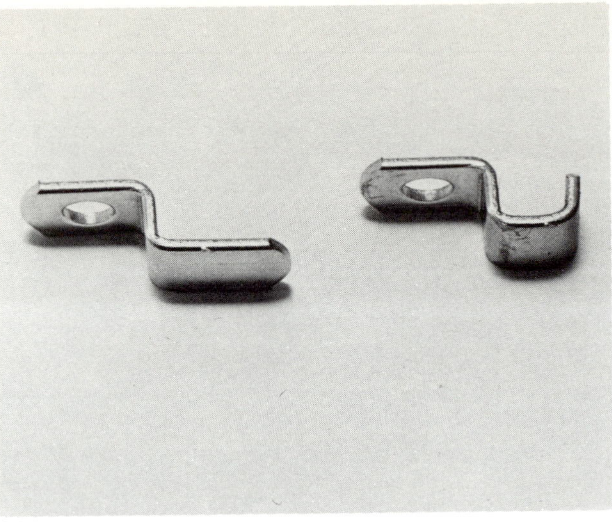

4. Modify the mirror holders by bending them with pliers. The modified holder is on the right. The "U" portion is the same width as the thickness of the glass filter.

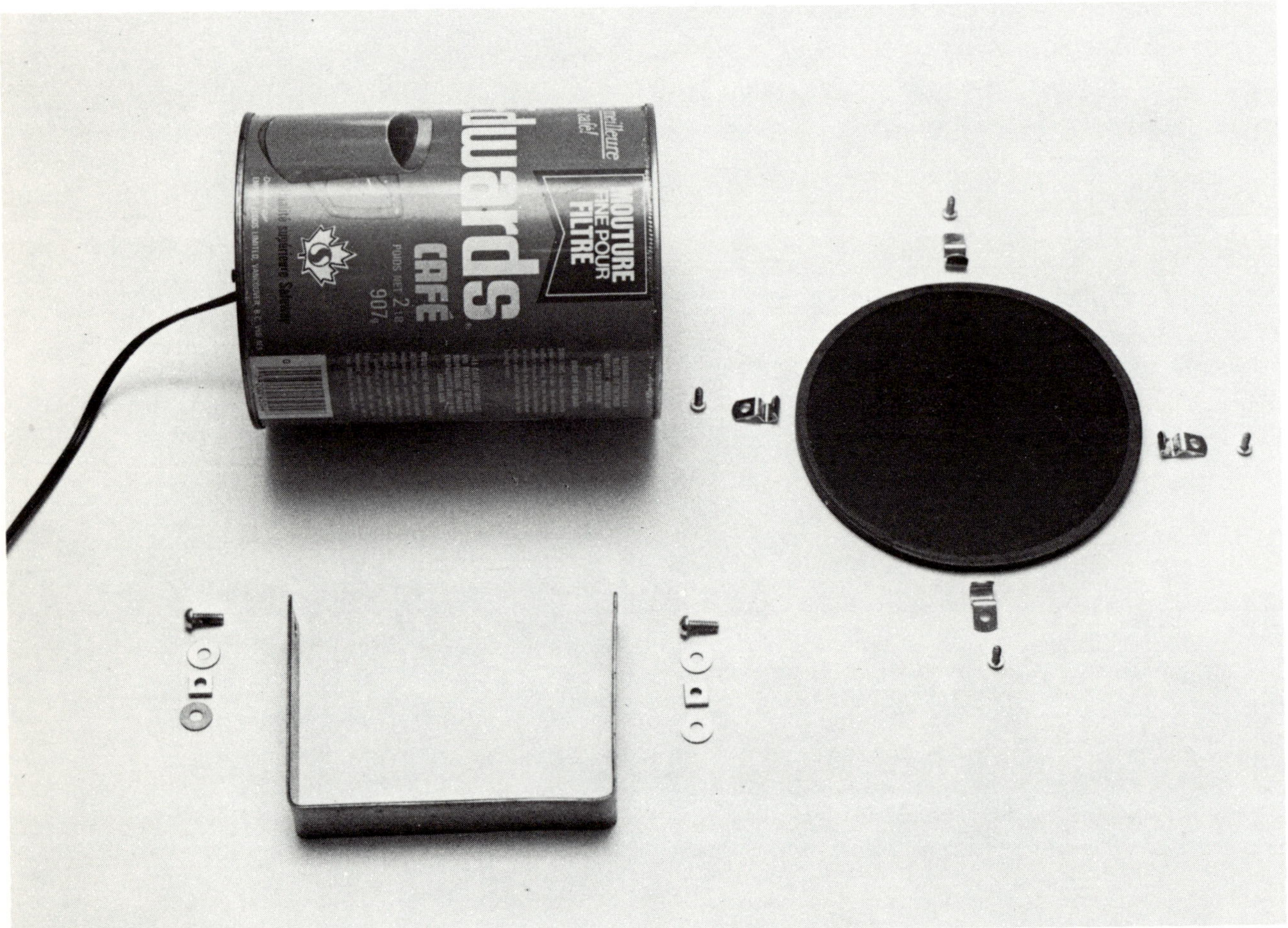

5. Make a bracket from sheet metal so the safelight can be mounted on the wall. Here are the metal parts ready to be added to the coffee can.

Now that everything is assembled, you can plug in the safelight and see how it works. Take the safelight into the darkroom and turn it on. If there are any leaks of white light, these can be sealed with black silicone cement. The safelight can be mounted on the darkroom wall with whatever type of screws are appropriate. For plaster board, use molly screws or hollow wall anchors. For concrete walls, use lag shields and screws.

Kodak safelight filters come with detailed instructions for testing the light. It's a good idea to complete this test to see if the safelight is truly safe. Then your safelight is ready to use.

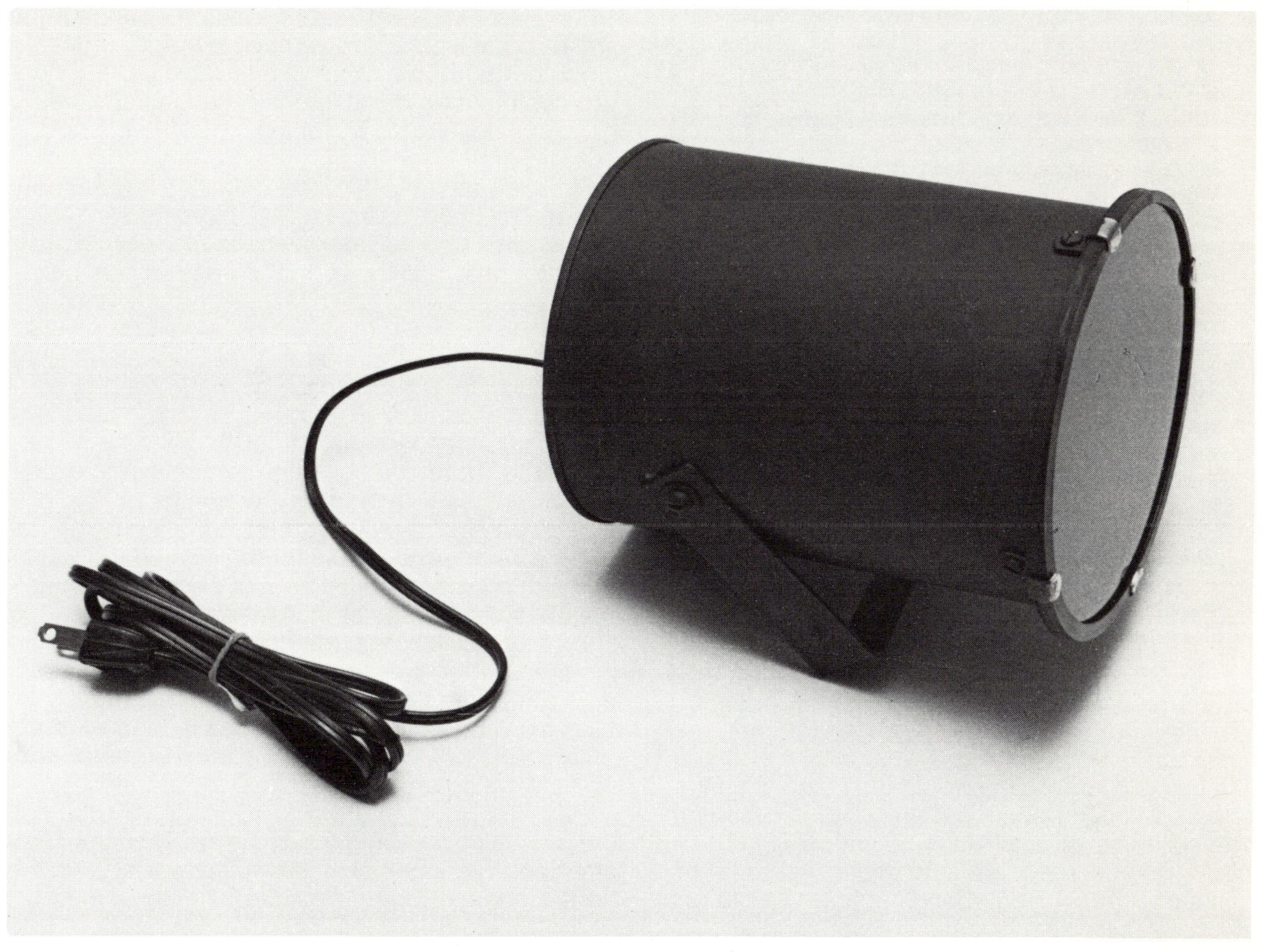

6. The appearance of the finished safelight can be improved with a coat or two of enamel paint.

Custom Darkroom Sink

MATERIALS

36″ × 72″ (91.5 × 183 cm) sheet styrene, 2 mm thick
24″ × 48″ (61 × 122 cm) sheet styrene, 2 mm thick
Two 12″ × 72″ (30.5 × 183 cm) particle board shelves,
 ¾″ (1.9 cm) thick
12′ (3.7 m) of fir, 2″ × 4″ (3.8 × 8.9 cm)
8′ (2.4 m) of fir, 1″ × 2″ (1.9 × 3.8 cm)
12″ × 24″ (30.5 × 61 cm) fiberboard or plywood, ⅛″
 (3.2 mm) thick
Silicone cement (clear or white), 12 oz. (340 g)
White latex paint, one quart or liter
Gaffer's tape
Mirror clips, size 1×
Nails
Sandpaper
White weather stripping, ⁵/₁₆″ × ⅜″ (7.9 × 9.4 mm)
Marble

TOOLS

Hammer
Saw
Razor knife
Metal yardstick or meter stick
Screwdriver
Wrench
Pliers
Paintbrush
File
Wood rasp
Caulking gun

Many photographers who do their own printing try to do without a darkroom sink. This is because large sinks are expensive to buy and difficult to build. Being basically lazy and cheap, I spent a lot of time designing and figuring out how to build a darkroom sink with a minimum of work and expense. I found a method of construction for making a large sink easily and inexpensively.

The sink is designed around a table and a laundry tub with a stand. The working surface is wood-based and waterproofed with sheet plastic and silicone cement. This method of construction takes little time.

The plumbing should be the first consideration when planning a darkroom sink. Design your sink around the available plumbing. Installing a new drain or faucet is expensive and should be avoided whenever possible. The location of the drain and the plumbing should determine the size and location of the sink. Most photographers work from left to right in the darkroom — that is, the developer, stop bath, and fix are ordered from left to right, and the deep tank for the wash would therefore be on the right end of the sink. (My sink is reversed because of the placement of the plumbing.)

In general, the larger the darkroom sink, the better. A sink that can hold six of the largest trays that you would want to use would be ideal. The size of my sink was limited by the space available. It has a 21″ (53 cm) square deep tank, a flat working area of 21″ × 70″ (53.3 × 177.8 cm) inside, and it is designed to hold 11″ × 14″ (27.9 × 35.6 cm) trays. If you use 16″ × 20″ (40.6 × 50.8 cm) trays, the working area should be at least 26″ (66 cm) wide inside.

You probably already have a suitable table. If not, you can buy an old one from a secondhand store, garage sale, and so on for less than the cost of building one.

First saw the rails from the 2″ × 4″ (3.8 × 8.9 cm) board. Cut the 1″ × 2″ (1.9 × 3.8 cm) into 24″ (61 cm) lengths and the fiberboard into 2″ × 24″ (5.1 × 61 cm) strips. Nail the 2″ × 4″ pieces together to make the rails and then nail the two particle board shelves to the rails. The shelves should be nailed only on one side and the two ends.

The laundry tub may have a small raised ridge around the edge. If so, trim this off with a razor knife so that the rails will sit flat. Position the tub and table. The height of the two must match and can be adjusted by adding the lengths of 1″ × 2″ boards and strips of fiberboard to the top of the table. Place the wood base for the sink on the table and make the fine adjustment of the height using the bolts on the legs of the laundry tub.

Use a marble to test the drainage of the working area. When the marble rolls toward the drain from the far end of the working area, the one-by-twos and fiberboard can be nailed in place. About an extra ¼″ (6.4 mm) must be added to the far end of the working area to make it drain properly.

Paint the wood, and while it is drying you can cut the plastic lining using a razor knife. Tape the straight edge to the plastic with gaffer's tape to hold it in place. Deeply scribe a line in the plastic

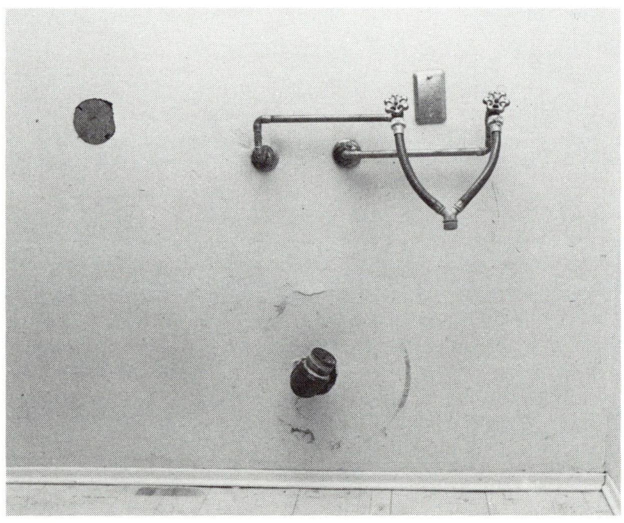

1. I moved the faucets over slightly and covered the electrical outlet in preparation for making the sink. The wall drain is located below the faucets.

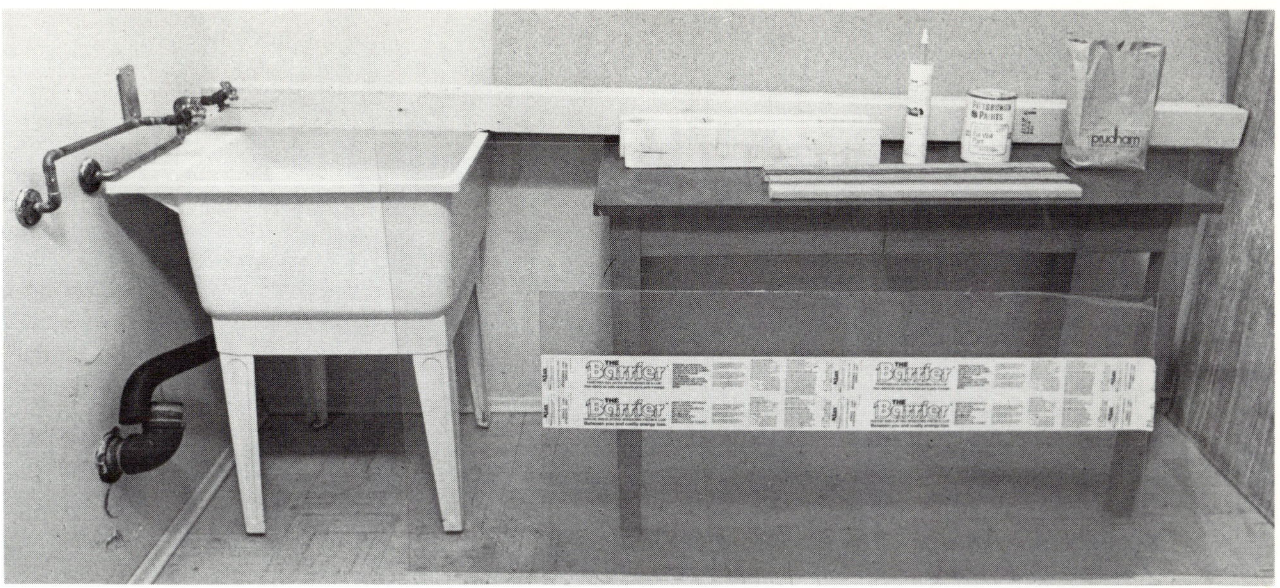

2. A plastic laundry tub and a table are the frame that the sink is built around. The rest of the materials include particle board shelving, sheet styrene, silicone cement, 2″ × 4″s, 1″ × 2″s, white latex paint, fiberboard, nails, and other hardware.

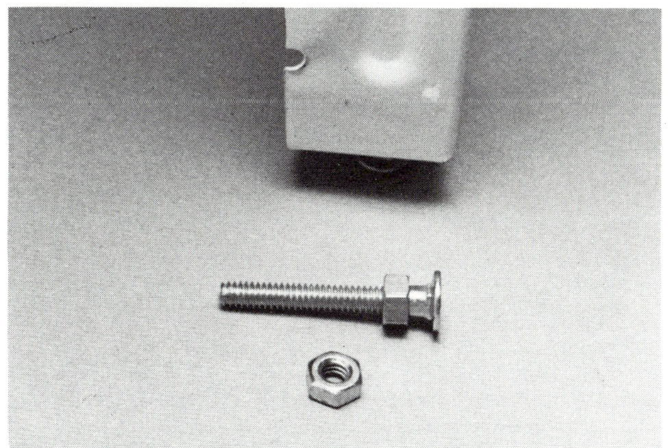

3. A bolt and nut like these are on the legs of the laundry tub. They are used to make fine height adjustments and to level the laundry tub.

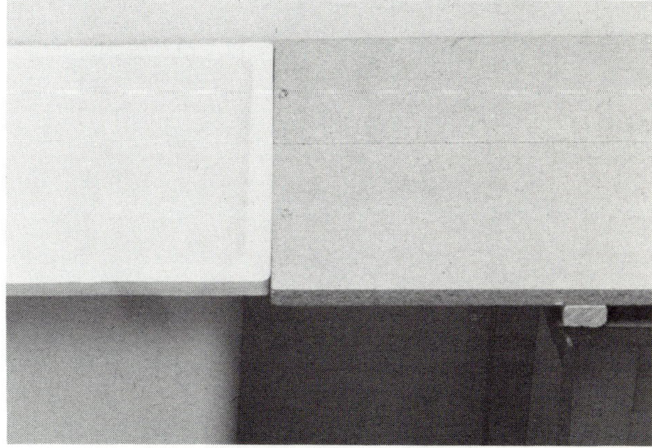

4. The height of the tub and table are made to match by adding 1″ × 2″s and strips of fiberboard to the top of the table. The particle board shelving must match up with the edge of the laundry tub.

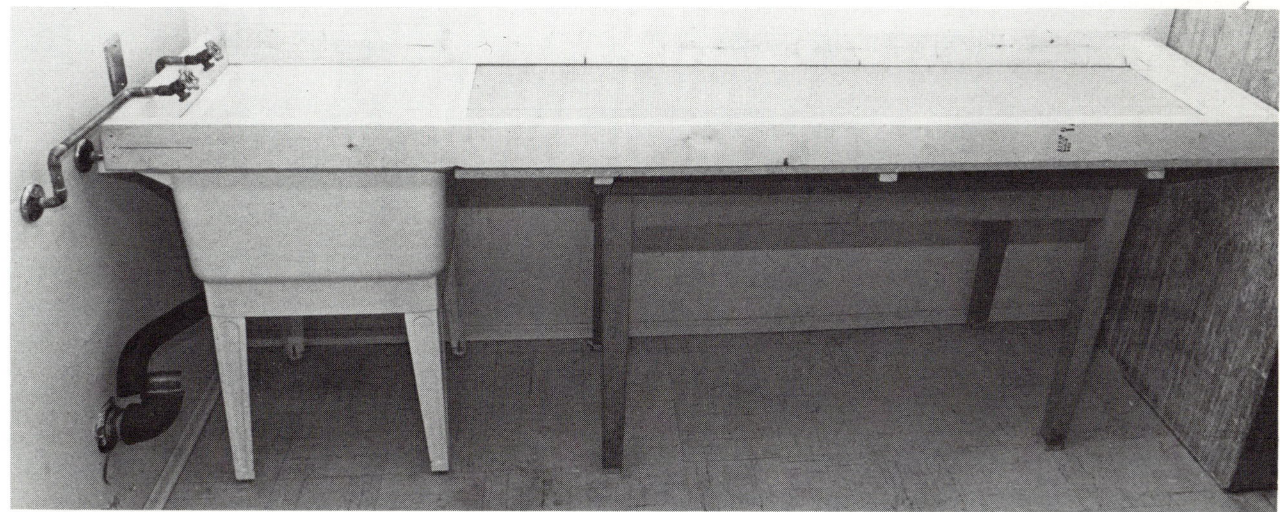

5. Particle board shelving and 2″ × 4″s are nailed together to make the working area of the darkroom sink. It must slope slightly to drain into the laundry tub. Add fiberboard to make it slope. A marble is useful to test the drainage.

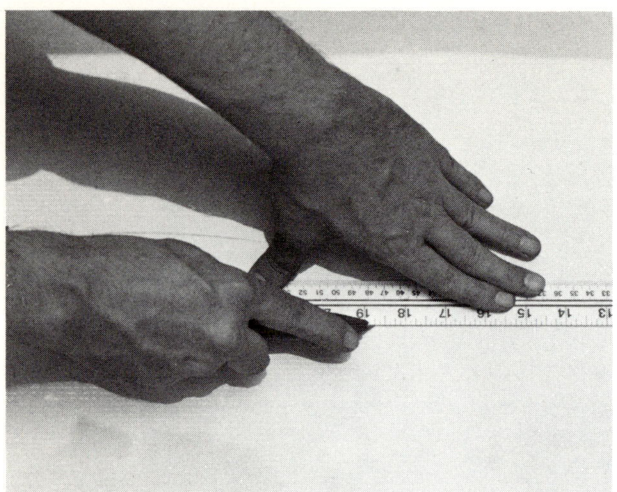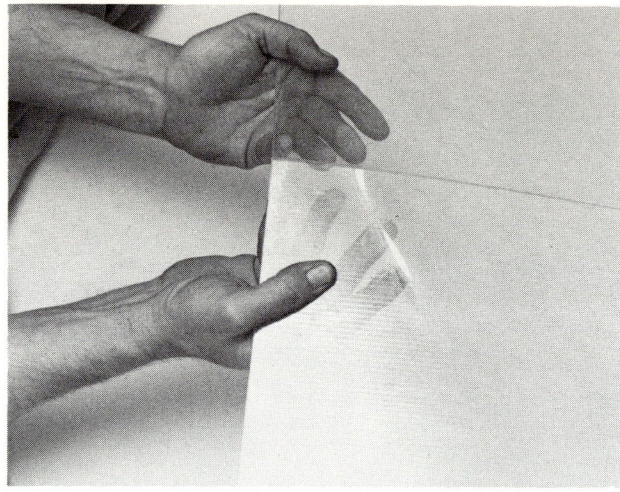

6. Tape a metal yardstick or meterstick to the plastic when making a cut. Use a special razor knife like the Olfa P-Cutter or a regular razor knife to score a line in the plastic.

7. After scoring a deep line in the plastic, bend it to break it. The plastic has a protective film over it that can be left in place until the plastic is ready to be glued.

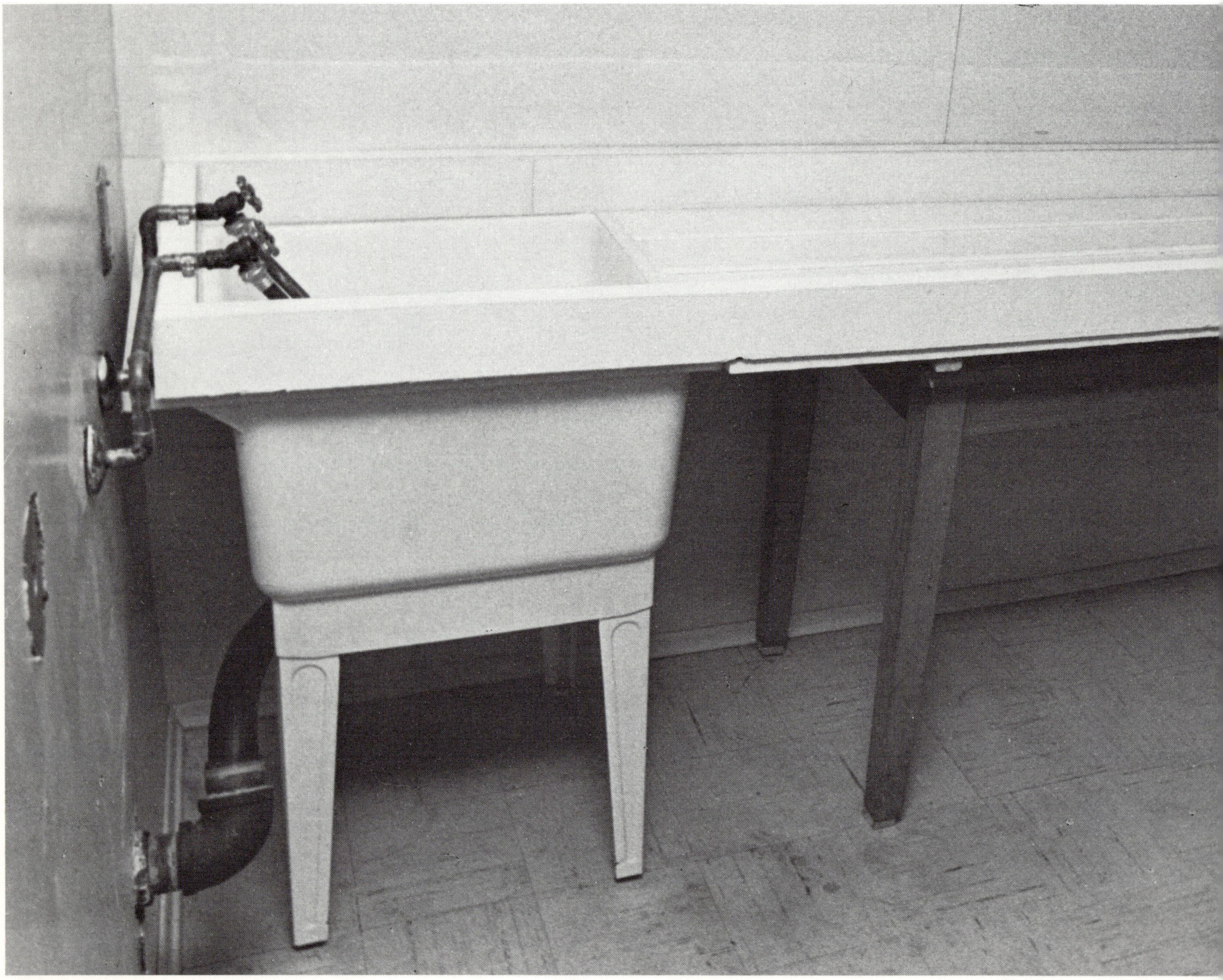

9. Plastic splash panels held in place with mirror clips protect the back wall. An old radiator hose attaches the sink to the wall drain. Wait 24 hours for the silicone to dry before you use your darkroom sink.

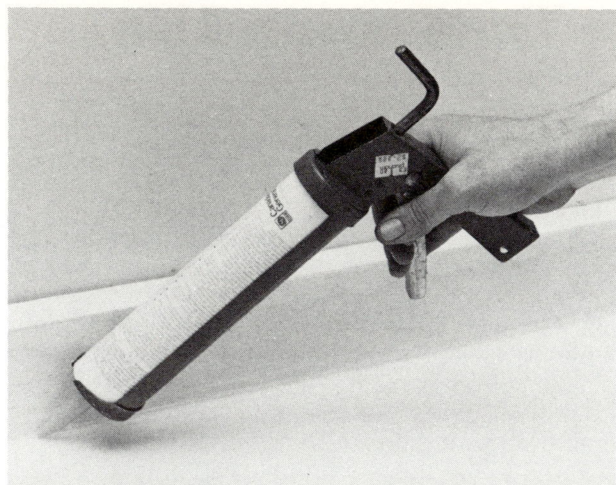

8. Use clear or white silicone to glue the plastic to the wood. When the plastic has been attached to the wood, run a ribbon of silicone into all the corners.

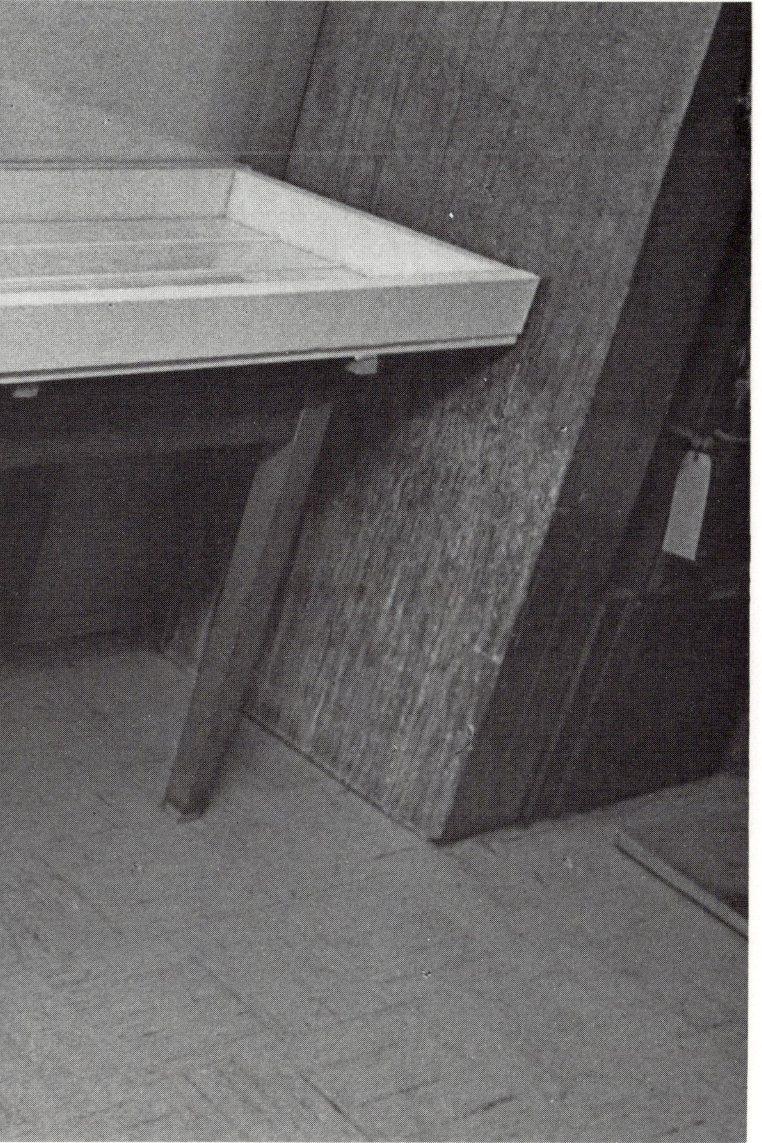

with the knife. Three or four firm strokes should be sufficient. Face the line away from you and gently bend the plastic, which should break cleanly along the line. If it doesn't break, cut the line deeper and try again.

To make the long cuts, start breaking the plastic at one end and continue bending and breaking until the pieces separate. To trim a small amount from a sheet, use pliers to bend the plastic and break it along the scribed line.

First add the plastic bottom of the sink over the particle board. Cut the plastic piece for the bottom longer than the wood base so it extends over the edge of the laundry tub. Squeeze silicone around the outside of the plastic bottom and the edge of the tub. Use silicone to glue the rails around the tub. Press the plastic firmly in place. Glue the plastic lining for the rails next, squeezing additional silicone into the corners and seams.

Mechanics' waterless hand cleaner will remove silicone from your hands. Any silicone that accidentally gets on the wood or plastic should be left to dry. When it's dry, it can be easily peeled or rubbed off.

Now cut the plastic for the splash panels that will protect the walls. The top of the panel is fastened to the wall with mirror clips and the bottom is glued to the rail.

Use three strips of self-adhesive white weather stripping to hold the trays off the bottom of the sink and let you wash the sink with the trays in place. The weather stripping comes in many different thicknesses. The 5/16" (7.9 mm) is thick enough, but you may wish to use one that is thicker. The weather stripping also acts to cushion the trays and prevents them from scratching the plastic.

The working area and deep tank are not nailed to the table, so the darkroom sink can be separated into three easy-to-move pieces. The top of the back rail is covered with plastic to catch the water running down the splash panel, but the top of the front rail is not covered. I find this is a good place to thump developing tanks to dislodge air bubbles.

The plastic has a sharp edge that should be smoothed with a file or sandpaper when the silicone is dry. If you wish to trim more plastic, a wood rasp can be used.

Various plumbing fittings may be needed to attach the sink to the drain. My drain was very close to the sink. I used an old radiator hose and clamp to make the connection. Instead of using an expensive mixing faucet, I used the existing faucets and added a mixing hose. If the mixing hose is too long, it can be shortened by cutting the hose and adding female replacement fittings to the cut ends.

Allow the silicone to dry for 24 hours before using the darkroom sink.

Flashlights Safe for Darkroom Use

A flashlight can be very useful in photography with only a little modification. Fitted with an appropriate filter, it can be used as a portable safelight for your darkroom. Add a white diffuser, and it becomes a printing aid. If you add colored filters, it can even be a creative tool for taking photographs.

If you've been doing your own printing for some time you probably have some unused plastic safelight filters that can be used to make filters for the flashlight. If not, common items can provide the appropriate color. A plastic flower pot is just about the right shade of dark green for the filter needed during processing of black-and-white film. The golden plastic often used for margarine containers can be used as a filter when you are using black-and-white printing paper.

The reason why these colors (which are only close to being correct) can be used as filters is that the light is never allowed to strike film or paper. Every effort is made to prevent this from happening. The flashlight with its safelight filter is used to find things and to read instructions and labels when the white light should not be turned on.

Take a flashlight apart. Remove the glass or plastic that covers the bulb. This will be the pattern, or template, for cutting your filters. Place the cover on the filter material and mark around the pattern with a scribe or a pencil. Then cut the filter out with a razor knife, staying slightly inside the line so the filter won't be too large.

Reassemble the flashlight with the filter and take it into your darkroom. The color and intensity of the light from the flashlight should be almost identical to that of the darkroom safelight. If the flashlight is too bright, reduce the intensity by adding a second layer of the same plastic or a neutral-density filter. Uniformly exposed black-and-white film makes an excellent ND filter for this use.

For the next modification, begin with a flashlight that has a shape different from the first one's. If the shapes are different, then the flashlights can be identified by feel when the lights are out. Again, remove the glass or plastic covering the bulb and use it for a template. This time, cut white filters from a plastic disposable container. Two layers of the plastic will probably be needed to reduce the light from the flashlight sufficiently. The white plastic acts both as a diffuser and as a ND filter.

You can use this second flashlight as a burning tool for black-and-white enlarging. Suppose you have a distracting highlight in a print and want to darken it, but giving it additional exposure with the enlarger takes too long — even a minute or two of exposure won't darken it sufficiently. For a case like this, cut a mask with the shape of opening needed and give the paper a brief exposure with the flashlight. (The black paper used to wrap enlarging paper is excellent for making masks.) A few seconds of exposure will burn the area black. With experience and practice, you can learn to darken such areas to the desired shade of gray by holding the flashlight different distances from the mask opening or by exposing the paper for different amounts of time.

The corners or edges of a print can be darkened without having to cut a mask by carefully aiming the flashlight.

During development, use this flashlight to expose the print and produce solarization on a part or all of the print.

A flashlight with colored filters is even useful for making photographs. The plastic from the flash filters project can be used with the flashlight. Suspend the flashlight from the ceiling with a string and swing it over a camera during a long time exposure. This produces complex patterns. Use different colors of filters and multiple exposures to make intriguing abstractions.

Use the flashlight when photographing people or objects. Make a time exposure in a darkened room and trigger an electronic flash to light the subjects normally. With the camera's shutter still open, move around the room with a flashlight. Use the flashlight to outline the subject with colored light or to add streaks of color to the photo. These are just some of the ways you can use these flashlights in photography.

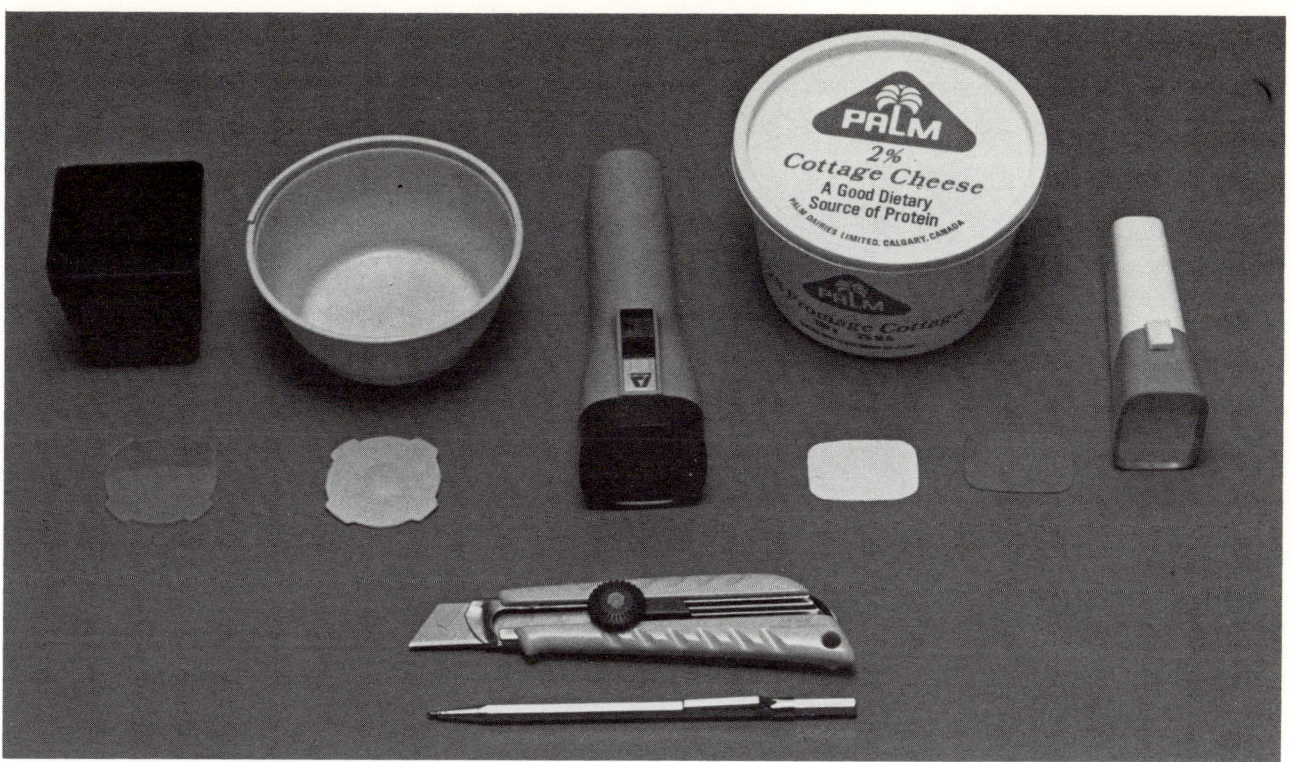

1. Use plastic from a gold margarine container and a green plastic flower pot as filters for the safelight flashlight. Cut sections of white plastic from a disposable container to make a flashlight into an enlarging tool.

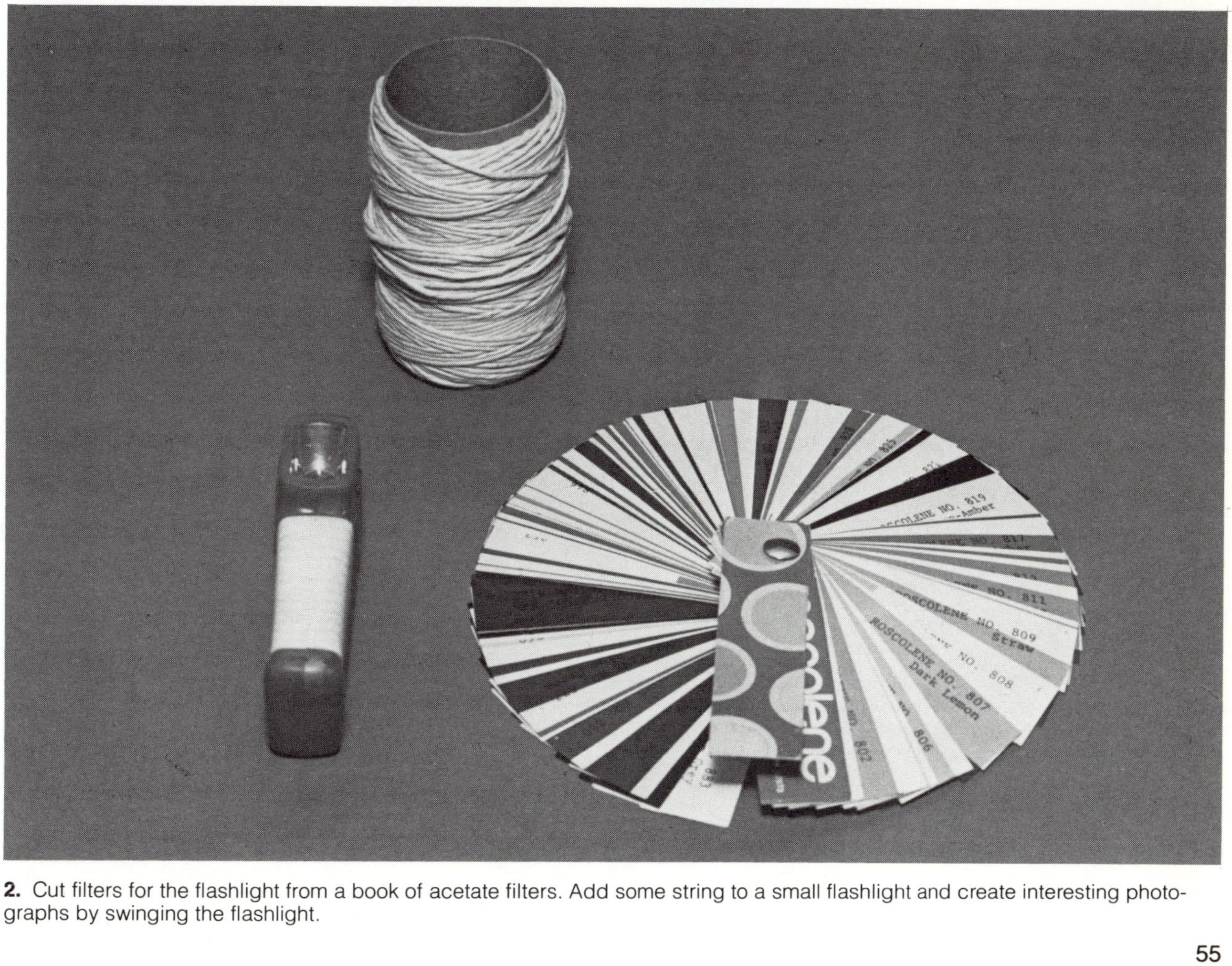

2. Cut filters for the flashlight from a book of acetate filters. Add some string to a small flashlight and create interesting photographs by swinging the flashlight.

Long and Narrow Trays for Processing Large Prints

MATERIALS

Three wallpaper trays
6' of 1" (1.8 m of 2.5 cm) dowel rod
Wood screws and washers
White paint
Silicone

TOOLS

Saw
Drill and bits
Screwdriver
Small paintbrush

It is embarrassing to admit, but I have never made very large prints. I frequently make 11" × 14" (27.9 × 35.6 cm) prints, but since I don't have any large developing trays, I have never made any 16" × 20" (40.6 × 50.8 cm) or 20" × 24" (50.8 × 61 cm) prints. I checked the price of the trays several times but never did buy any, as I didn't think I would make enough large prints to justify the cost.

Besides the cost of the trays themselves, filling them with chemicals can also be rather expensive. Each tray will hold 1 gallon (3.8 liters) or more of chemicals before you have a reasonable level for developing.

I recently found some trays for 79 cents each and that was too good a price to pass up. The trays I found are made of plastic and are used for wallpapering. You can find them in paint and wallpaper stores. These trays are 4" × 5" × 24" (10.2 × 12.7 × 61 cm). Trays 36" (91 cm) long are also sold if you wish to make some really giant prints. With a little minor modification, these trays can be used for printing with a minimum amount of chemicals.

To modify the trays for printing, all you have to do is place a dowel rod across the bottom. The rod will hold the paper submerged so it can be seesawed through the chemicals. Measure the width of the tray and cut a length of the dowel rod to fit across the bottom. I used a 1" (2.5 cm) dowel so the paper wouldn't make a sharp bend that might damage the emulsion. To attach the dowel rod, I used wood screws and washers, and to waterproof the trays, I used black silicone to make a seal around the screws.

To prevent the wood from splitting, drill holes slightly smaller than the screws in the ends of the dowel. The holes should only be about half as deep as the screws are long. Next drill holes for the screws in the plastic. These holes should be centered about 1" from the bottom of the tray. This way, there will be a ½" (1.3 cm) gap between the bottom of the tray and the dowel to allow room for the insertion of the paper. Smear some silicone on the end of the wood and the outside of the plastic and use the screws and washers to attach the dowel rods.

The wood will absorb some chemicals, even after the tray is washed and dried, so it's important to label each tray to avoid mixing chemicals. I labeled the trays with white latex paint. A single letter on each tray is adequate. To identify mine, I painted the letters D, S, and F.

As soon as the paint and silicone are dry, the trays are ready to use. Insert one end of the paper into the chemicals and under the dowel rod. If you wish, you can wear rubber gloves to protect your hands from the chemicals. The emulsion side of the paper should face away from the dowel. Only the base of the paper should come in contact with the wood. This protects the emulsion from being scratched. Seesaw the paper through the chemicals, making sure that all the paper is wetted. Time each step to ensure proper developing and fixing.

To obtain uniform development at the edges, keep changing the location of your fingers. The heat from your fingers can increase development, or if they are kept in one place, your fingers can block the flow of chemicals to the paper.

Wet the entire paper with developer as soon as possible. However, once the paper is wet, it can be moved through at a more leisurely pace. Make some long thin test strips to get experience in using the trays before you make your first print.

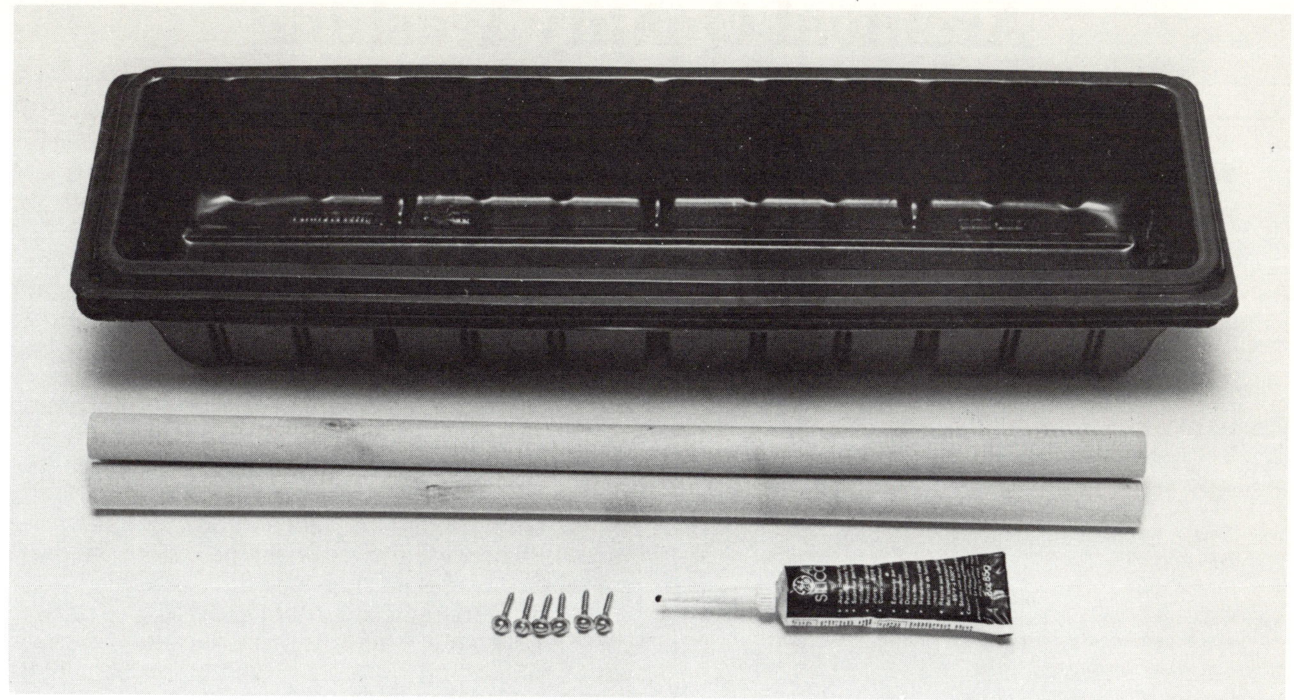

1. Wallpaper trays like these can be bought in paint and wallpaper stores for very little. Add a length of dowel rod across the bottom of each tray and you can use them to develop large prints.

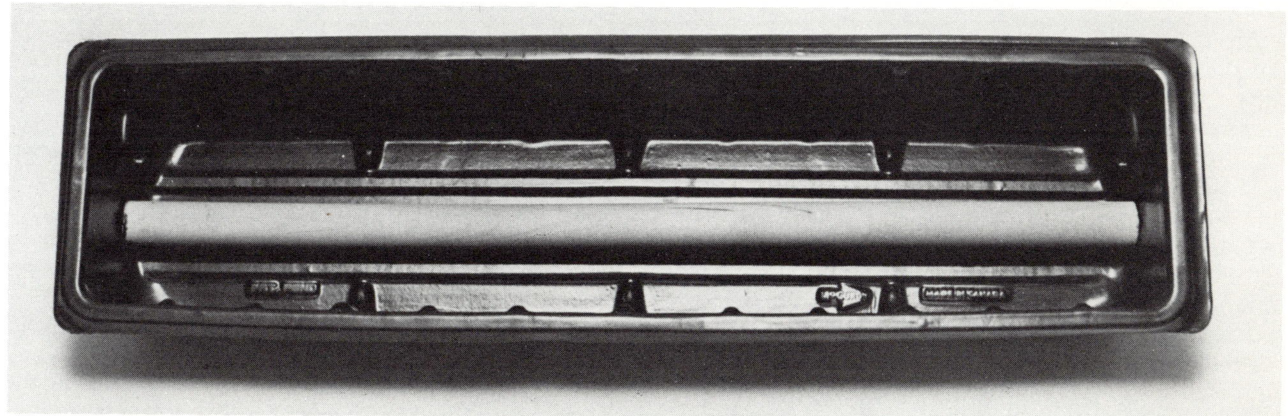

2. Above. A ½″ gap between the bottom of the dowel rod and the tray allows you to insert the paper. Wood screws, washers, and silicone hold the dowel rod in place and keep the trays waterproof.

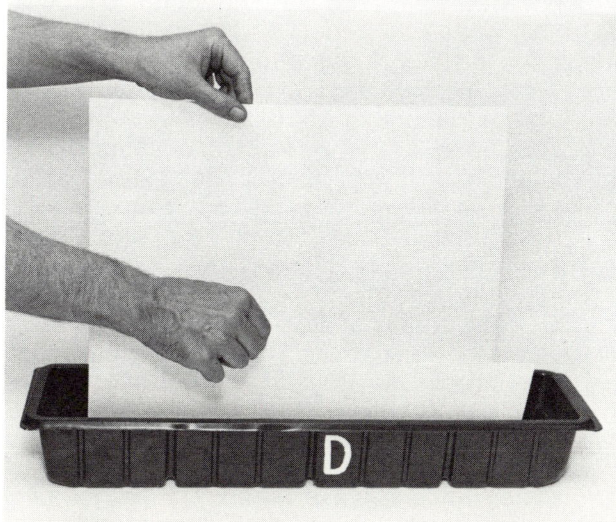

3. Left. Mark each tray with white paint — one letter on each will do. This way, you will know which tray to use for developer, stop bath, or fixer and can avoid mixing chemicals. Seesaw the paper through the chemicals to ensure uniform development.

Print Washer for Archival Quality Washing

MATERIALS

Transparent styrene; 2 sheets 24″ × 48″ (61 × 122 cm), 2 mm thick
16′ (5 m) of 1″ × 4″ (1.9 × 8.9 cm) redwood
16′ (5 m) of 1″ × 1″ (1.9 × 1.9 cm) fir
Utility hose or shampoo hose
Clear silicone cement, two 3 oz. (85 g) or one 11 oz. (315 ml) tube
1½″ (3.8 cm) nails
Masking tape
Sandpaper

TOOLS

Saw
Drill and bits
Razor knife
Claw hammer
Metal yardstick or meter stick
Carpenter's square
Grease pencil
Wood rasps, round and flat (optional)
Calking gun (optional)

Are the prints you make going to last? Look at old photographs and you'll see prints that are faded, stained, and yellowed. Making photos that can stand the test of time requires careful processing during development, fixing, washing, drying, and storage. One critical step is the washing. Archival print washing requires that the prints be kept separated and immersed in a uniform flow of water. Prints must be washed for a long time to remove residual hypo that will cause the image to gradually deteriorate.

As simple as these requirements are, few print washers are capable of archival washing. You can make an archival print washer from sheet styrene, silicone cement, and redwood. This print washer is designed for prints as large as 11″ × 14″ (27.9 × 35.6 cm) but the design can easily be modified for prints of any size.

Begin by sawing sixteen 1′ (30.5 cm) lengths of the 1″ × 1″ (1.9 × 1.9 cm) wood. These serve as the spacers used to separate the sheets of plastic during gluing. They will not be part of the finished washer. These boards are actually ¾″ (1.9 cm) square and can be used to make the paper safe, which is another project, after being used here. After all pieces are cut, set the wood aside and prepare to cut the plastic.

To cut the plastic you will need only a razor knife, metal yardstick, and gaffer's tape. First tape the yardstick in position and scribe a line in the plastic with the razor knife, using three or four firm strokes. Face this line away from you and bent the plastic to break it. Only gentle bending is needed if the cut is deep enough. Always bend the plastic away from your body so the pieces won't pop at you when it breaks.

Cut the first sheet into three 16″ × 24″ (40.6 × 61 cm) pieces and then cut each piece in half. You will now have six 12″ × 16″ (30.5 × 40.6 cm) rectangles that will be the dividers in the washer. Next, cut two 13″ × 16″ (33 × 40.6 cm) pieces from the second sheet of plastic. These will go on the outside of the washer.

Stack the wood spacers and sheets of plastic. Start with two boards and place a 13″ long sheet on top. Alternate the spacers and the plastic sheets, finishing with the other 13″ sheet on top. Once they are stacked, use a carpenter's square to align them. On the base, the top and bottom sheets should extend 1″ (2.5 cm past the others. All the other edges should be aligned.

Measure the stacked sheet's width. It should be about 5 ¾″ (14.6 cm). Cut two end pieces measuring 5 ¾″ × 13″ (14.6 × 33 cm) from the remaining plastic. Place a cut end against the stack. With a grease pencil mark lines where the dividers will be. (Only fine marks are necessary. I used dark lines so they would show clearly in the photos.)

When marking with the grease pencil, make all the marks on what will be the outside of the plastic and put the glue on the other side. This way the marks can be washed off when they're no longer needed.

I glued the entire length with silicone. The dividers can be held in place with very little glue.

Squeeze approximately a ⅛″ (3.2 mm) wide ribbon of silicone where the end piece has been marked. Press the end piece in place and position it without sliding it. Try not to smear the glue. Use masking tape to hold the plastic in place while the silicone dries. Repeat the process on the second side and tape this end in place as well. Let the silicone dry for at least eight hours before proceeding to the next step.

I chose redwood because of its tolerance for water. Other woods would quickly rot from the moisture. Measure the stack of plastic to find the lengths needed for the redwood frame. I sawed four 18″ (45.7 cm) and four 5 ¾″ (14.6 cm) lengths. Next place the wood around the top and bottom of the plastic and align it with the ends. Before nailing, apply silicone between the wood and plastic and between the abutted wood ends at the joints. Use two nails in each corner to hold everything in place. Allow the nail heads to protrude slightly so that they can be removed easily after the glue dries. If they were left in they would rust. The nail holes can then be filled with silicone. After the frame is in place, remove the wood spacers. The frame strengthens the print washer so it will withstand the weight of the water when full.

Measure the inside of the bottom where the outside sheets of plastic extend 1″ (2.5 cm) beyond the

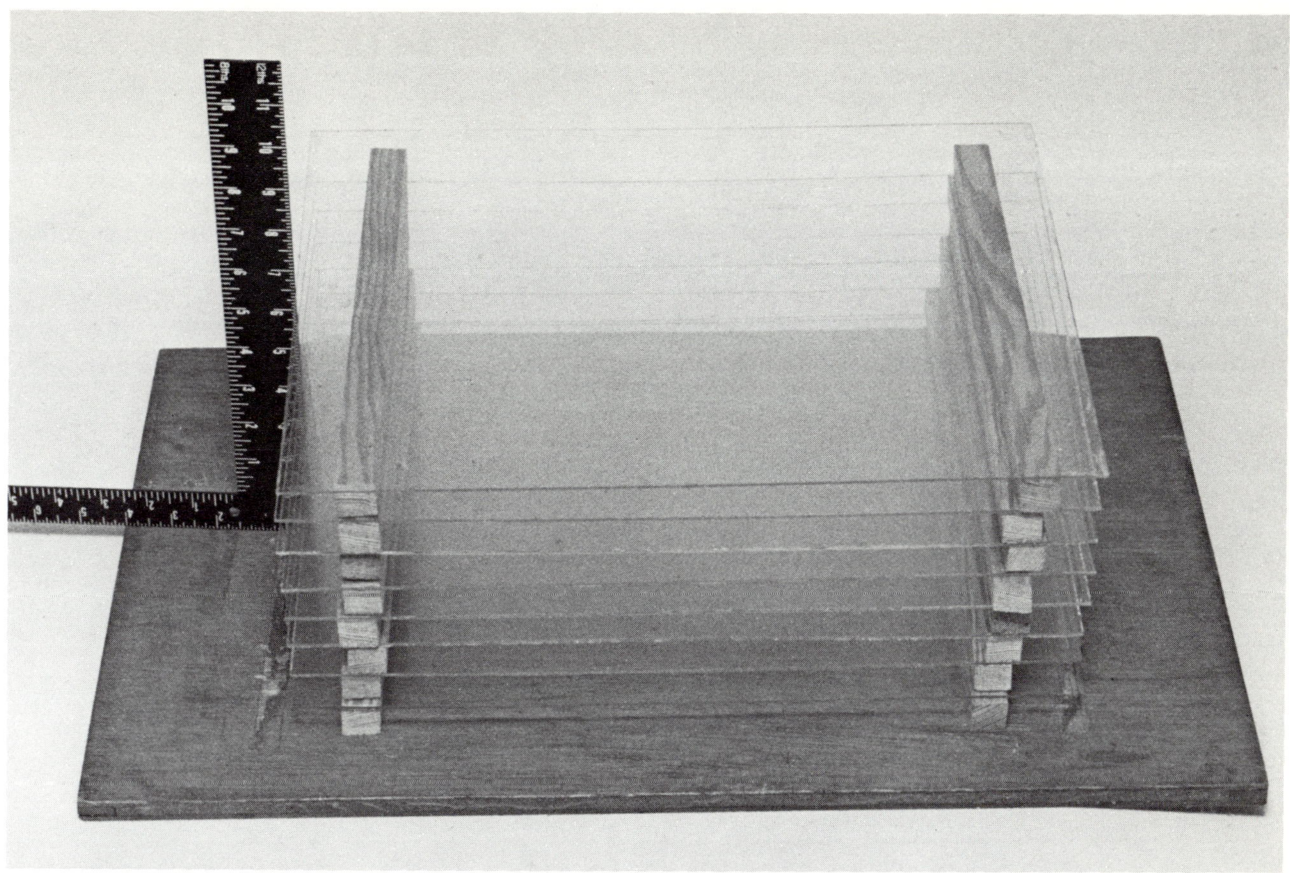

1. Stack the sheets of plastic using the spacers as shown. Then align the sheets with a carpenter's square.

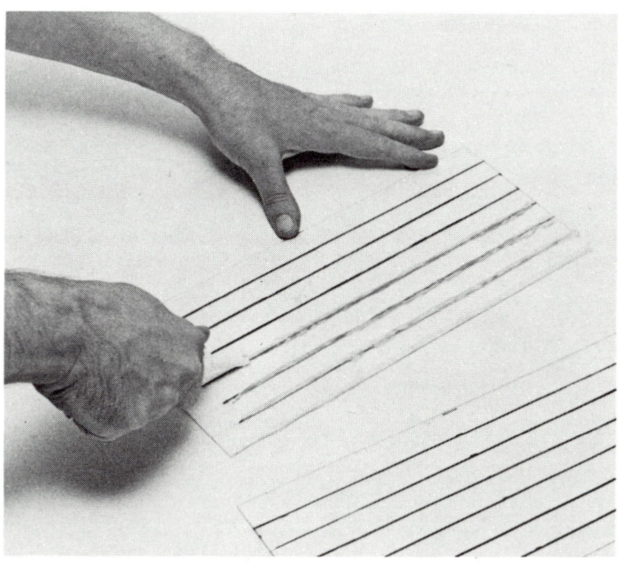

2. Apply glue to the ends where the dividers will be located. Only a small amount of silicone at the top and bottom is required for the dividers. But, the outside corners of the plastic must be glued the full length.

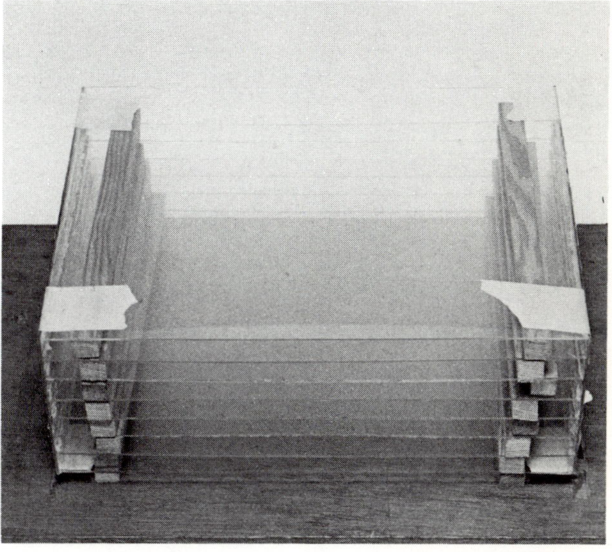

3. Press the ends against the stack of plastic and hold them in place with masking tape.

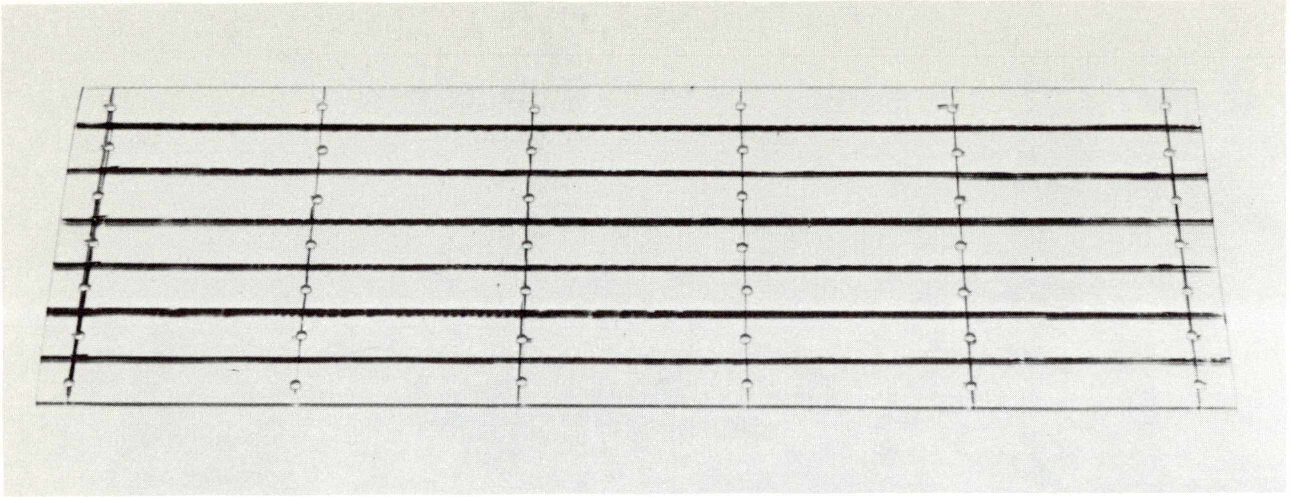

4. Use a grease pencil to mark holes in the sheet of plastic that fits against the dividers. Drill 42 holes to ensure uniform circulation of the water.

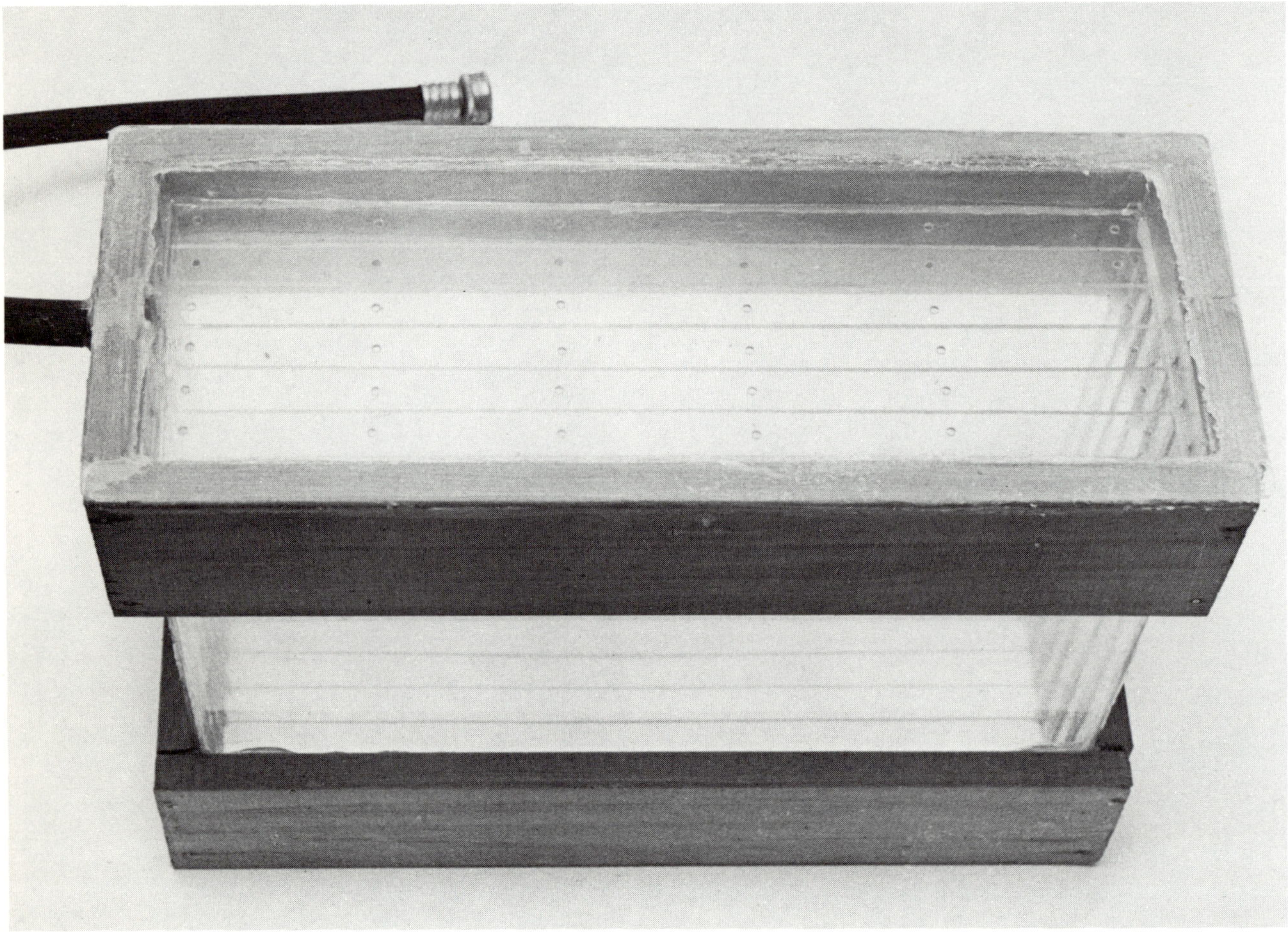

5. After the wood frame is nailed in place, glue the perforated sheet against the dividers and glue another sheet of plastic across the bottom.

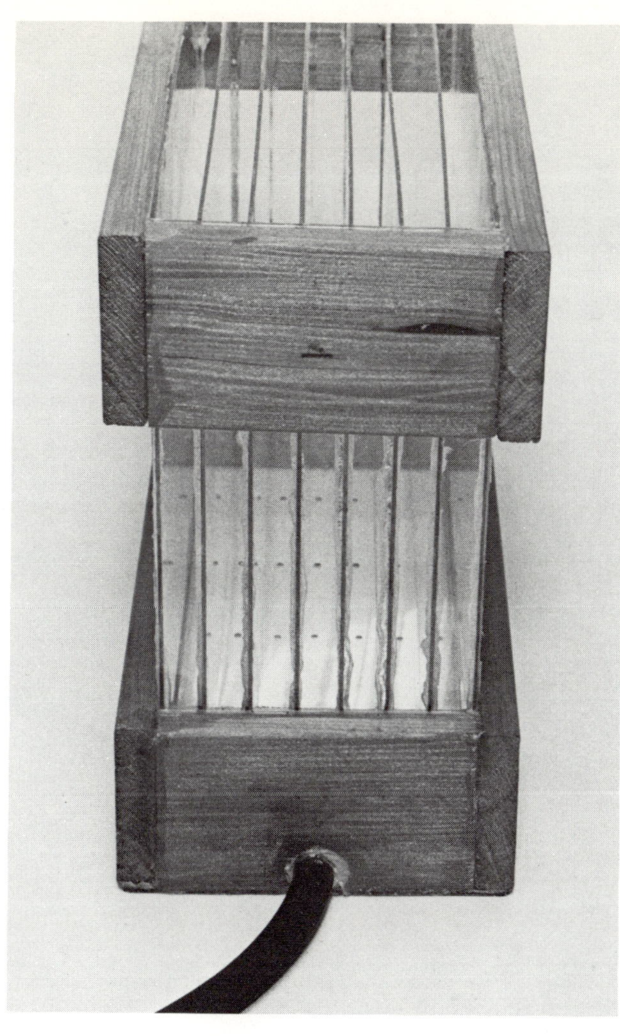

6. Left. I used silicone the full length of each divider edge. Using only a little at the top and bottom will give your washer a neater appearance.

7. Below. Two redwood boards are glued to the bottom to protect and strengthen the plastic.

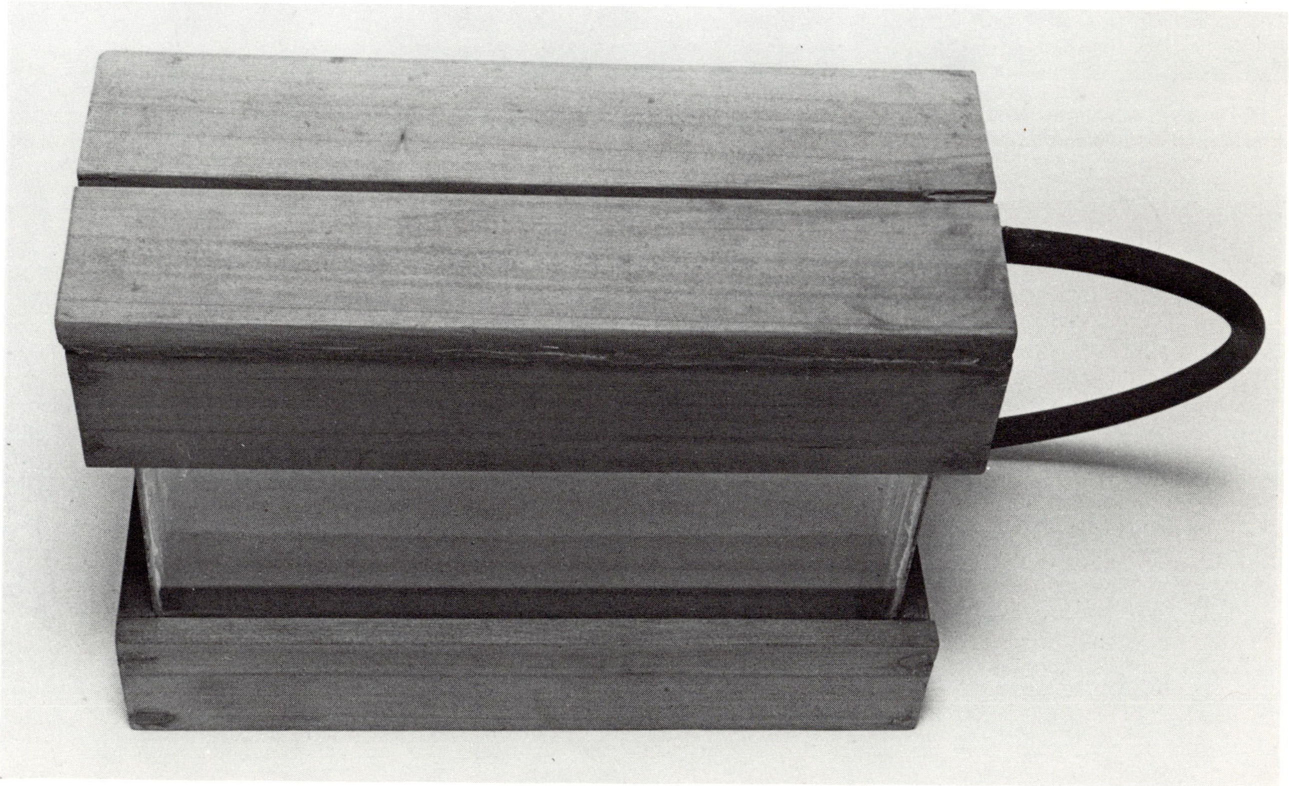

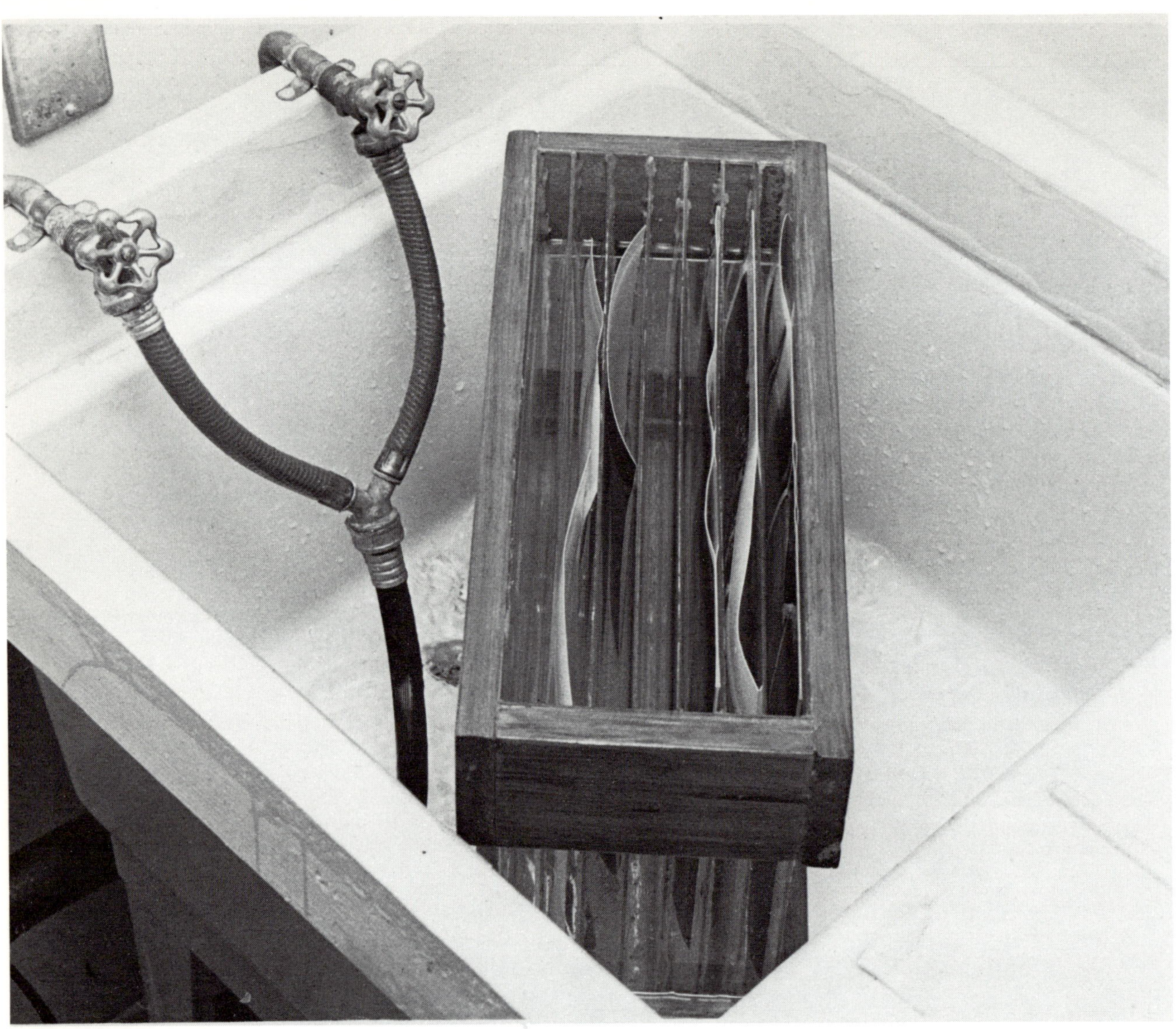

8. The finished washer will hold seven 11″ × 14″ prints and fourteen 8″ × 10″ prints. When in use, the washer holds the prints in a separate compartment and prevents them from sticking together.

dividers. Cut a sheet of plastic that will fit inside the extension, flush with the dividers. You will need to drill 42 holes 3/16" (4.8 mm) in diameter in this sheet to ensure an even flow of water through each compartment. Align the six holes in each compartment so they will be centered between the dividers. Mark the position for the holes with the grease pencil and then drill.

Next drill the holes for the hose and bottom drainage. Center a hole the diameter of the hose at the bottom of one end of the washer. Place the hole between the bottom of the washer and where the perforated plate will fit against the dividers. If you don't have a drill the correct size, you can either drill a hole that is too small and enlarge it with a round wood rasp, or you can taper the end of the hose with the razor knife so it will fit tightly in the hole. Glue the hose in place with silicone.

I used a short length of utility hose that fits a standard threaded faucet. You could use a hose and rubber fitting from a shampoo and bath hose to attach the washer to a bathtub faucet.

Then drill a ⅛" (3.2 mm) hole through the wood and plastic opposite the hose. This hole provides bottom drainage, which is necessary because hypo is heavier than water and tends to collect at the bottom of the washer.

Position the perforated sheet against the dividers and glue it in place. Measure the bottom dimensions of the outside of the wood frame and cut a sheet to fit. Glue this sheet to the frame and let the silicone dry overnight before testing. Don't try to speed the drying in the oven, as the plastic expands from the heat and the joints will fail. (I tried this and made a real mess.)

The important place to use a lot of silicone is at the bottom, especially between the wood and the plastic and between the outer corner pieces of the plastic. Only a little silicone is needed to attach the dividers and the upper wood frame.

From the remaining wood, cut two boards the length of the washer's bottom and glue these to the plastic sheet that covers the bottom. This wood protects and strengthens the washer bottom. Leave a small gap between the boards so the wood can be flush with the outer frame.

When the silicone is dry, use a wood rasp and sandpaper to smooth the edges and corners of the wood and plastic. The grease pencil marks that are visible on the outside of the plastic can then be removed with spray cleaner and a paper towel.

Now is the time to test the washer. Set it in the darkroom sink or bathtub, hook it up, and turn on the water. Watch for leaks as the water level rises. A few small leaks are to be expected. Mark their location with the grease pencil and then seal them from the outside with silicone. If you have a major leak at a corner, don't despair. Another wood frame can be glued around the middle of the washer and will seal any leaks, no matter how bad. Brass screws can be used to strengthen the wood corners if the joint doesn't hold. I left the center of the washer transparent so I could see the prints that are washing and because I thought it looked better. But a washer entirely enclosed by wood would work just as well.

When using the washer, make sure that the bottom is resting on a flat surface. And *don't* pick up or move the washer when it is full of water. The washer will weigh almost 50 pounds (22.7 kg) when full and the unsupported weight could crack the plastic or pop a seam. Another thing — avoid accidentally filling the washer with only hot water. Hot water will cause the plastic to buckle and bend. Always start filling with cold water and then add some hot to obtain the desired temperature.

The washer can hold seven 11" × 14" (27.9 × 35.6 cm) prints or fourteen 8" × 10" (20.3 × 25.4 cm) prints with two prints in each of the compartments.

A description of effective print washing and testing prints for permanence is given in *Kodak Black-and-White Darkroom Dataguide*.

Compact Print Drying Rolls

MATERIALS

Fiberglas window screen 2′ × 18′ (.6 × 5.5 m)
Two rolls of foam tape, 3/16″ × 1¼″ × 30′ (4.8 mm ×
   31.9 mm × 9.2 m)
Clear silicone cement, 3 oz. or 12 oz. (85 gm or
   340.2 gm)
Gaffer's (duct) tape
Indelible marker
Two pairs of cloth shoe strings, 60″ to 72″ (152.2 to
   182.9 cm)

TOOLS

Scissors
Ruler
Caulking gun (if you use the 12 oz. tube of silicone)
A Popsicle stick or two

When doing some cleaning, I found the old blotter roll that I used to dry prints when I first got started in photography, over 20 years ago. It was stained yellow and I'm sure that it was saturated with fixer. Back then, I washed prints by dropping them in a bucket of water. Finding this old blotter roll gave me the idea for making a better drying roll.

Today there are many types of paper — fiber-based, resin-coated, stabilized, and color. Print drying has also become very complicated. The color and stabilized prints are saturated with chemicals that are damaging to regular black-and-white prints. Add to this the problems of archival processing and it's no wonder that some photographers have resorted to using a different dryer for each type of paper. Making print drying rolls that can dry all types of paper is the simplest way I know to solve print drying problems.

Fiberglas window screen and foam tape are used to make the rolls. This screen is also used to make print drying racks, but racks and the cabinet to hold them are a lot of work to make and take up valuable space in the darkroom. With drying rolls, prints are put on the screen and rolled up in the same way they were with the blotter roll. Foam tape, normally used for weather stripping, is used to keep the prints separated and allows air to circulate.

All the materials, except the shoe strings, can be bought in a building supply store. Self-adhesive foam tape is sold in many different widths and thicknesses. A 1″ (2.5 cm) tape will work as well as the 1¼″ tape I used, and a tape slightly thicker than 3/16″ could also be used. Don't use very thin or very narrow tape, as these won't provide adequate spacing. A 3-oz. tube of silicone, if used sparingly, is enough to make the drying rolls, but the 12-oz. tube used with a caulking gun is a more economical investment.

Begin by finding a place on the floor where you can work and where the screens can be left to dry overnight without being in the way. Sweep the floor or, if need be, mop it to get it clean. Cut the screen in half to make two 9′ (2.7 m) lengths. Lay these pieces on the floor and tape the ends down with gaffer's tape, stretching the screen to keep it flat. Taping the screen to the floor is important, because if you don't, the screen will wrinkle as you apply the foam tape.

The foam tape has a memory and tends to stay coiled when it is unrolled, but after it has been glued to the screen and taped to the floor overnight it will have lost this tendency. Cut four 9 ½′ (2.9 m) lengths of tape. The extra 6″ (15.2 cm) length holds the tape and the screen to the floor while you apply the tape strip to the edge of the screen. Cut four 2′ (.6 m) lengths for the ends of the screen. Allow an extra 2″ (5.1 cm) of tape to hold the screen to the floor. It will be cut off later. When all pieces are cut, set them around the screen.

Remove the backing from a 9 ½′ length of tape. (Finding the starting point to peel off the backing may be the hardest part of this project.) Tape a 3″ (7.6 cm) length to the floor at one end of the screen. Then go to the other end, line up the tape with the edge of the screen, and tape the other 3″ piece to the floor. Do not stretch the tape when doing this, as it will cause the screen to wrinkle later. Press the foam tape onto the screen, being careful to line up the edge of the foam tape with the edge of the screen. The tape is easy to remove and reposition if you make a mistake. Put tape on all the long edges. The gaffer's tape, which was used to tape the screen to the floor, can now be removed and the end pieces pressed into place.

When all the foam edging is in place, remove the screen and foam from the floor and turn it over. Add a little silicone at corners where the tape strips meet. Tape the screen to the floor with gaffer's tape. Use small pieces of gaffer's tape at the corners. Squeeze a small amount of silicone on the back of the foam and smooth it with the wooden stick. Work only on a bit at a time and add more silicone as you need it. Coat all of the screen that is over the tape. Be careful not to get any silicone on the untaped part of the screen. When you finish one side of the screen, hold the stick at an angle and scrape it over the entire glued length. This will pick up any excess silicone, which can be used to glue some of the rest of the foam.

Silicone is used because the tape's self-adhesive alone is not sufficient to make a permanent bond. If any silicone gets on the floor, let it dry and it will be easy to peel or rub off later. The floor could also be protected with newspaper or a plastic drop cloth. Repeat the steps for the second screen. Allow the screens to dry overnight.

The next day, remove the screens from the floor.

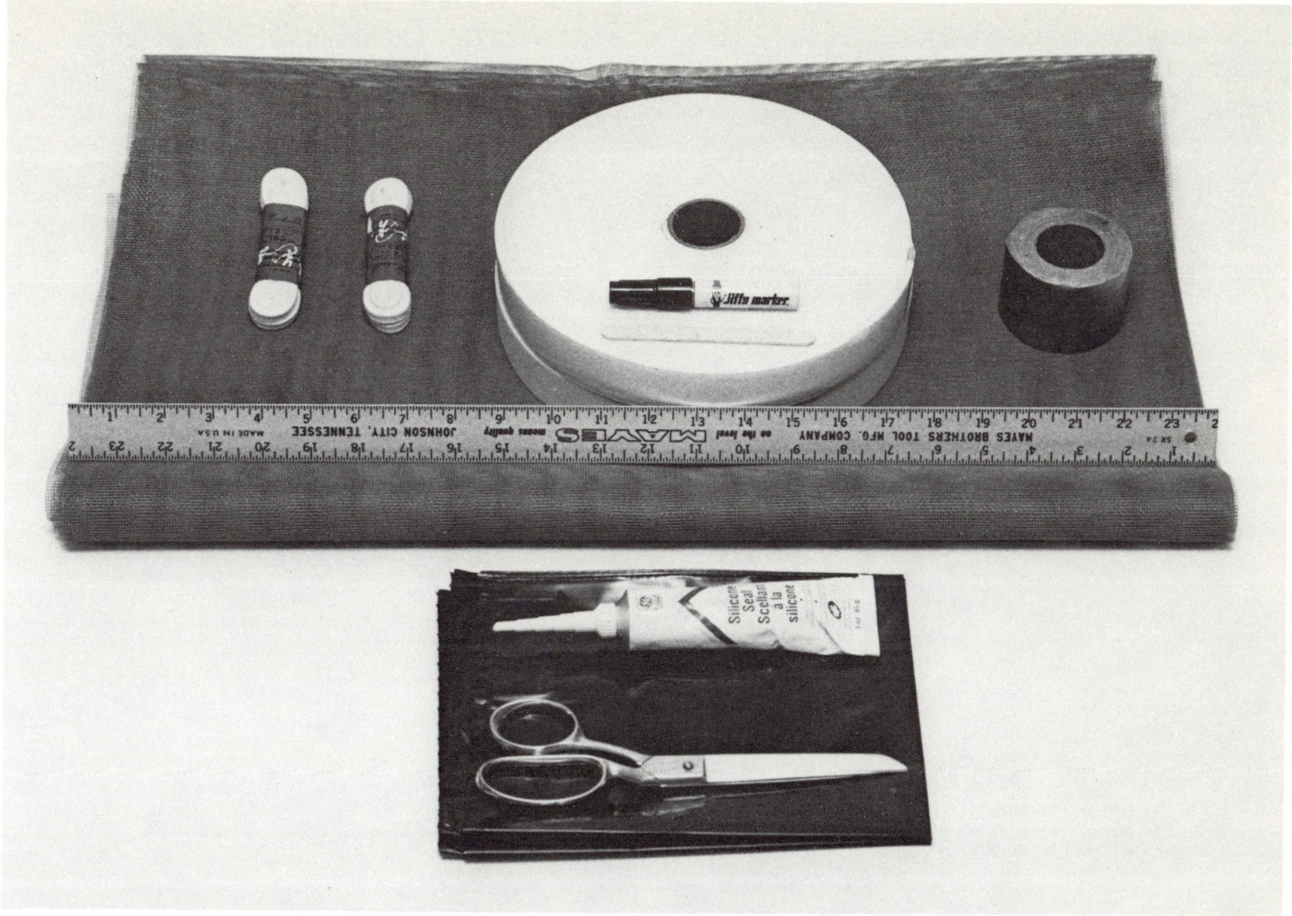

1. Print drying rolls are made from Fiberglas window screen. Foam tape is used for spacing. Other tools and materials needed are shoe strings, clear silicone, gaffer's tape, a marker, scissors, a ruler, plastic bags, and a Popsicle stick.

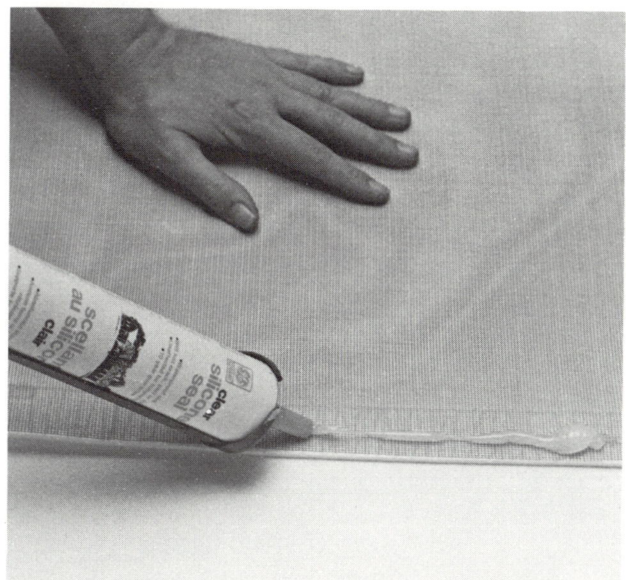

2. Apply clear silicone sparingly to only the back of the foam-covered edge.

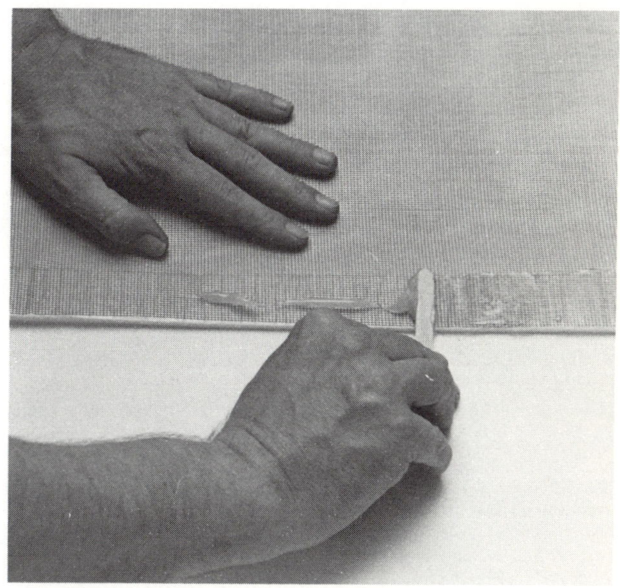

3. Spread the silicone with a wooden stick and then run the stick along the back of the tape to remove the excess silicone.

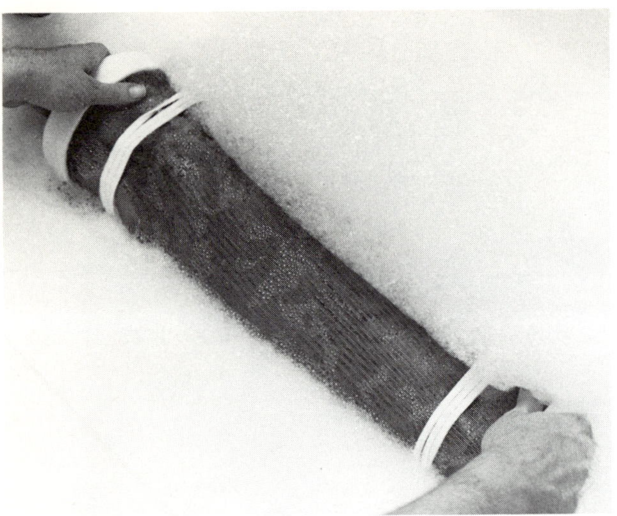

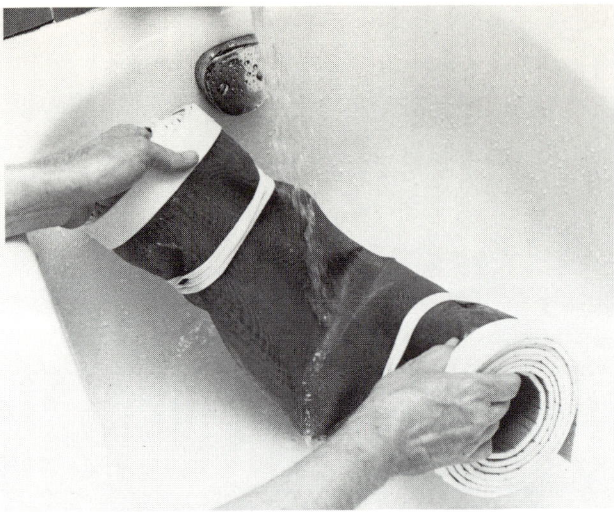

4. Wash the roll in warm soapy water.

5. Rinse the roll in running water. Be sure to remove all the soap. If there is a convenient place, hang the screens to dry.

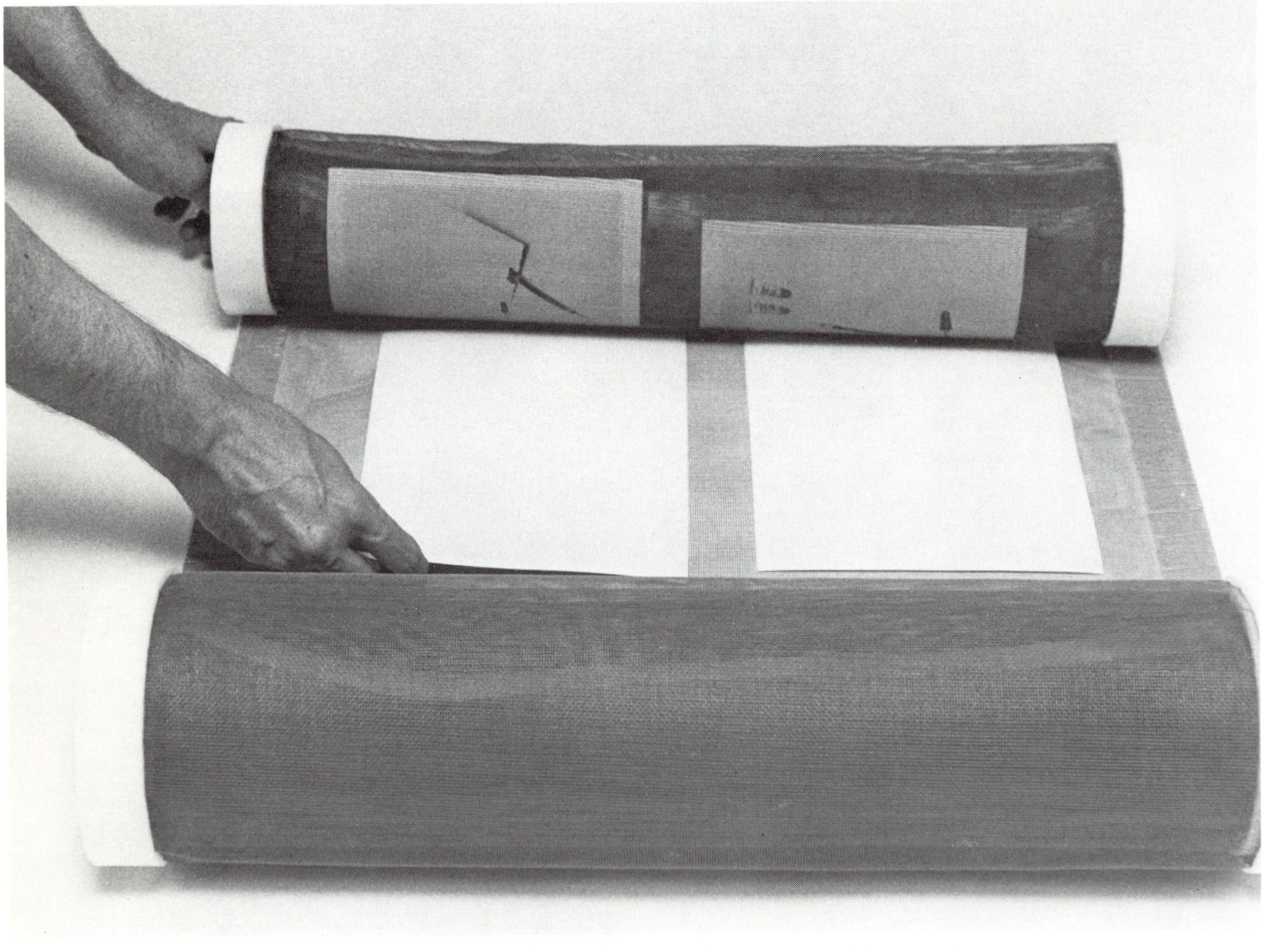

6. The rolls are used like a scroll. Prints are already rolled up in one section as more prints are added.

Use the scissors to trim off any part of the screens that extends past the edge of the foam tape. Also cut off the ends of the foam tape that once held the screens to the floor. Any silicone that accidentally got on the screens can be rubbed and peeled off. Also clean off any silicone that got on the outside edges of the foam.

When everything is clean and trimmed, roll up the drying roll with the foam strip on the outside. This is the opposite direction to the way the foam tape was rolled originally, but it will soon take to its new curl.

Tie the drying roll with the shoe strings, one at each end. Wash the rolls in the bathtub or in a large sink using warm soapy water. Rinse the screens thoroughly under warm running water, then shake the rolls to remove most of the excess water. Washing removes any dirt or chemicals that might be on the screens or foam tape.

Allow the screens to dry at room temperature, as drying in the oven would probably crinkle the foam. Foam tape is easier to dry than most foam because it tends to repel water instead of absorbing it.

When the screens are dry, use the indelible marker to label each roll for the process intended. Label the foam strip on both ends of each roll so a label will always be visible. I labeled mine "color" and "black-and-white."

The 9′ drying roll is easy to handle if used like a scroll. Unroll 2′ or 3′ and place the prints face down on the screen. Then roll up the section with the prints and unroll more screen to add more prints. The scroll can even be tied together with the shoe strings while you are doing more printing. This way it will open to the place where you inserted the last print. Keep the foam-covered edges of the roll aligned to maintain the spacing between the coils of screen.

One print drying roll will hold sixteen 8″ × 10″ (20.3 × 25.4 cm) prints, ten 11″ × 14″ (27.9 × 35.6 cm), or five 16″ × 20″ (40.6 × 50.8 cm) prints and still allow plenty of room for air circulation. The rolls could hold more prints, but overloading would only slow the drying time.

Drying prints curved with the emulsion side stretched facing outward counteracts their normal tendency to curl towards the emulsion. Double-weight and RC papers will be flat when removed from the roll. Single-weight paper won't come out of the drying roll flat, but at least it won't be as tightly curled as it is when dried on drying racks.

Drying times depend on the type of paper and the room's humidity. RC paper may dry in two hours, while a double-weight paper may take a day or more.

Don't roll the drying rolls too tightly when drying prints. Start with a 4″ or 5″ diameter curl and roll from there. This way the entire roll will only be about 7″ or 8″ (17.8 cm) in diameter. Rolling tighter would only slow the drying. Two drying rolls will be adequate for most people but you can always make more rolls if you need them.

If a roll accidentally becomes contaminated with chemicals, wash it again with soap and water. It is a good idea to wash the rolls occasionally, even if you think they don't need it, just to be sure they are free from contamination. When not in use, your print drying rolls can be kept in plastic garbage bags to protect them from dust.

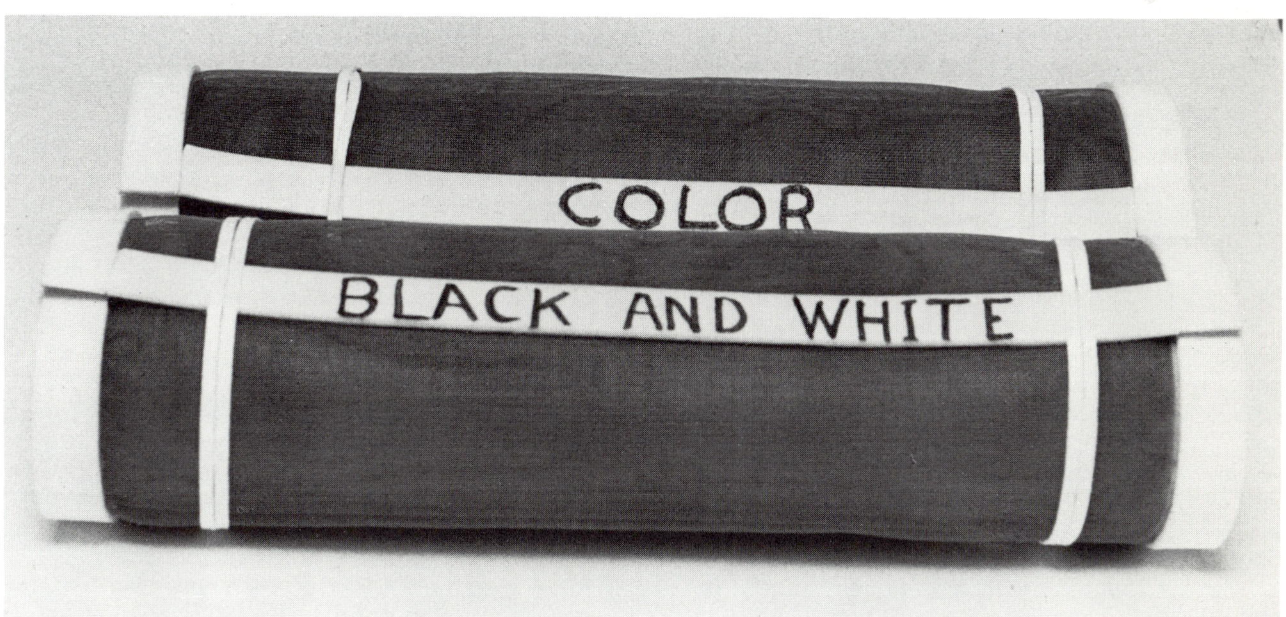

7. Label both ends of each roll if you are using different and incompatible types of paper. Two drying rolls are sufficient for most home darkrooms.

Vacuum Brush for Cleaning Equipment and Film

When canned air was first sold, I used it faithfully. I would blow dust off of slides and negatives as a routine part of editing and printing. I used it so much that I often bought three or four cans at a time. Then I realized how expensive this air is and started searching for an alternative. A refillable air tank was too expensive, so I decided to use a vacuum cleaner as a source for the air. I first planned to use the exhaust air to blow off the dust, but quickly realized that the vacuum was a better method.

Blowing the dust only moves it around and may even send it to another place where it's not wanted. With the vacuum, the dust is trapped where it can't cause any more problems. When you blow the dust from slides, it frequently lodges in the seams between the slide and the mount. When the slide is jarred in the projector, the dust may reappear on the surface of the slide. Cardboard mounts are plagued by paper dust and the vacuum brush is an excellent way of cleaning them. The vacuum brush also works well at cleaning cameras, lenses, enlargers, and much more.

You can buy a used vacuum cleaner very cheaply at an auction, or at a garage or rummage sale — especially if it is old, the attachments are missing, and it doesn't have much vacuum left. When you get it home, give it a thorough cleaning inside and out, change the bag, and clean or replace the filter. Cleaning or replacing the filter will often greatly improve the performance of an old machine. Cleaning the flexible hose is almost impossible, so I removed it from the metal fitting.

Using the regular household vacuum cleaner for this project isn't a good idea. Adding the small tubing restricts the flow of air and places an extra strain on the motor. Using the machine intermittently keeps this strain to a minimum, but there is no point taking a chance on damaging an expensive machine.

Use flexible tubing that has a ½″ (12.7 mm) outer diameter to replace the flexible hose that was on the vacuum cleaner. A portion of a flattened funnel serves to spread the flow of air across the width of the brush. Use an adapter made from a plastic cap to attach the small tubing to the cleaner.

Begin by flattening the plastic funnel. To do this, place the funnel on a foil-lined cookie sheet in a warm oven (250 F or 121 C). Watch the funnel carefully — as it starts to collapse or change its shape, remove it from the oven using hot pads or kitchen mitts. Hold the funnel with the hot pad and squeeze the softened plastic flat using pliers. Cool the funnel under cold running water.

Use a hacksaw to trim the funnel to make it only 2″ (5.1 cm) wide at the widest part. This is the same width as the brush. Attach the funnel to the end of the tubing to check the fit. If there are plastic ridges on the small end of the funnel, remove these with a razor knife.

Attach the funnel part and the tubing to the brush with bands made from ¾″ (19.1 mm) elastic. Wrap the plastic around the parts to find the correct length, making sure it fits tightly. Use either a needle and thread or a sewing machine to sew the ends together.

Use a plastic cap to attach the tubing to the metal fitting of the vacuum cleaner. I used the inner portion of the cap from a can of spray paint. Plastic caps come in so many different sizes, it shouldn't be hard to find one that fits. Drill a hole slightly smaller than the tubing in the center of the cap. Drill four additional ⅛″ (3.2 mm) holes around the outside of the cap. These holes decrease the pressure so the brush bristles won't be sucked into the tubing and also allow more air to circulate through the vacuum cleaner, which is needed to keep the motor cool.

Add the tubing to the cap, enlarging the hole slightly with a file if need be. Use plastic cement or an instant glue to hold the tubing in place, and with gaffer's tape attach the cap to the metal fitting.

I didn't want a noisy vacuum cleaner in the darkroom, so I ran both the power cord and the tubing under the door and taped them down with gaffer's tape to keep them out of the way. Most doors have a ½″ (12.7 mm) or so gap to allow for the installation of rugs, so running the power cord and tubing under the door shouldn't be a problem.

I use an outlet controlled by a wall switch to turn the vacuum cleaner on and off. If this isn't possible, you can add an in-line switch to the power cord, or the cleaner can be turned on and off using the plug. Make sure your hands are dry before handling this or any other electrical equipment.

About 10′ (3.1 m) is the longest length of tubing

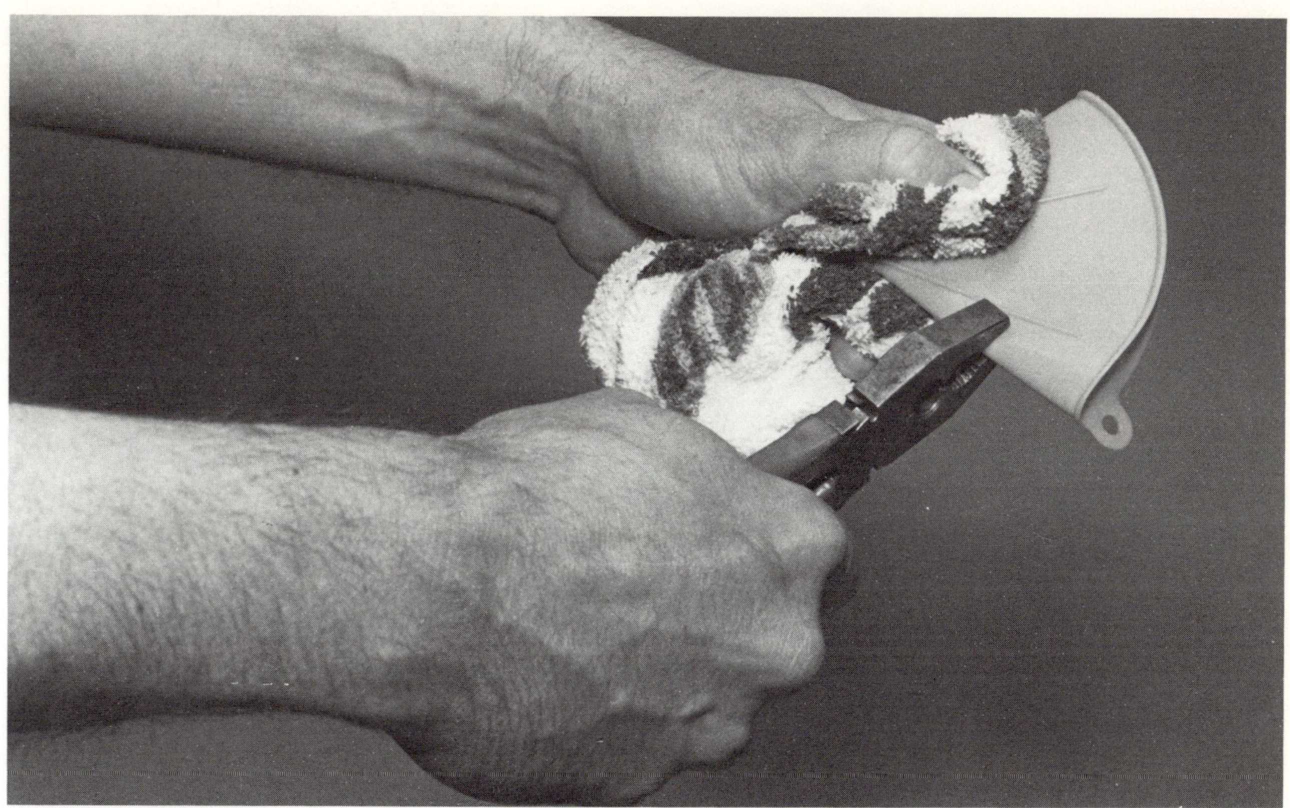

1. First heat the plastic funnel in the oven and then flatten it with pliers. Use a hot pad to protect your hand.

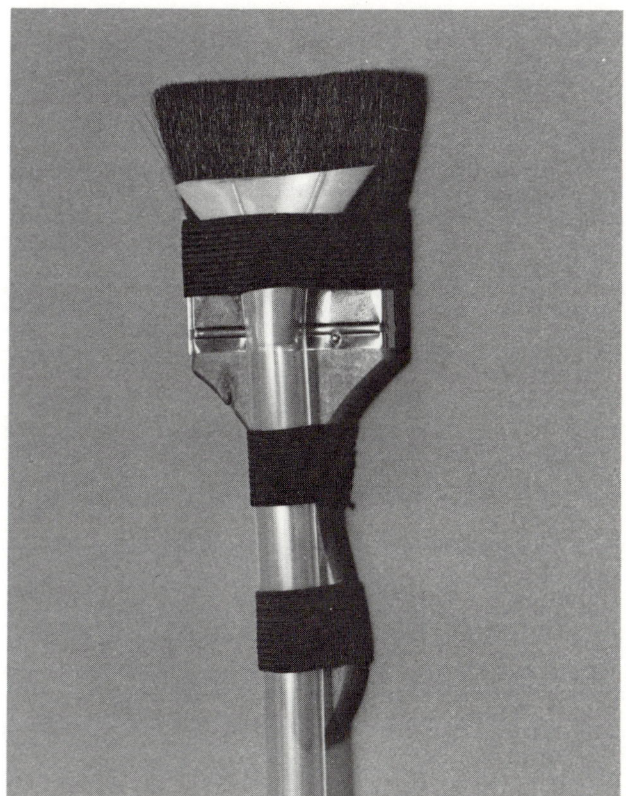

2. Three elastic bands securely attach the vacuum hose and the small portion of the flattened funnel to the brush. The flattened funnel spreads the flow of air across the width of the brush.

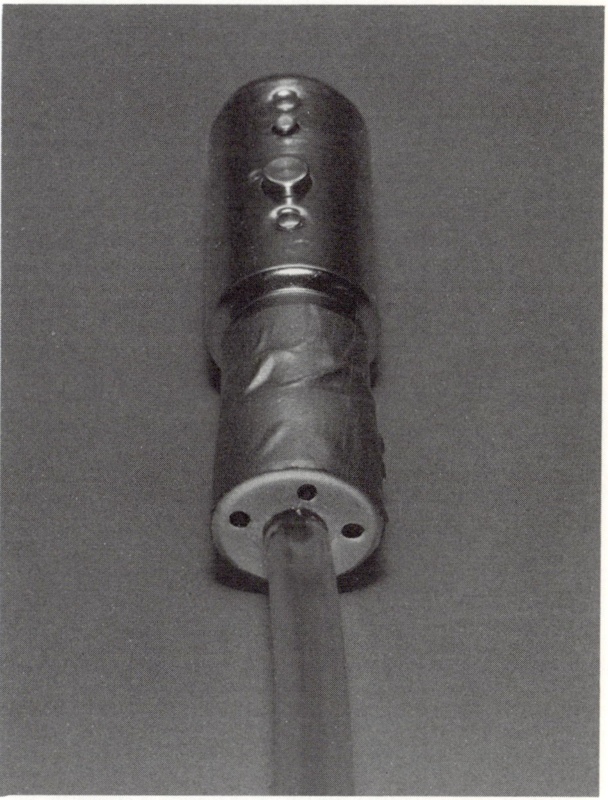

3. The tubing is attached to the metal fitting of the vacuum cleaner with a plastic cap and gaffer's tape. The small holes around the tubing reduce the pressure and provide additional air to cool the motor. Use the vacuum brush only intermittently to prevent the vacuum cleaner's motor from overheating.

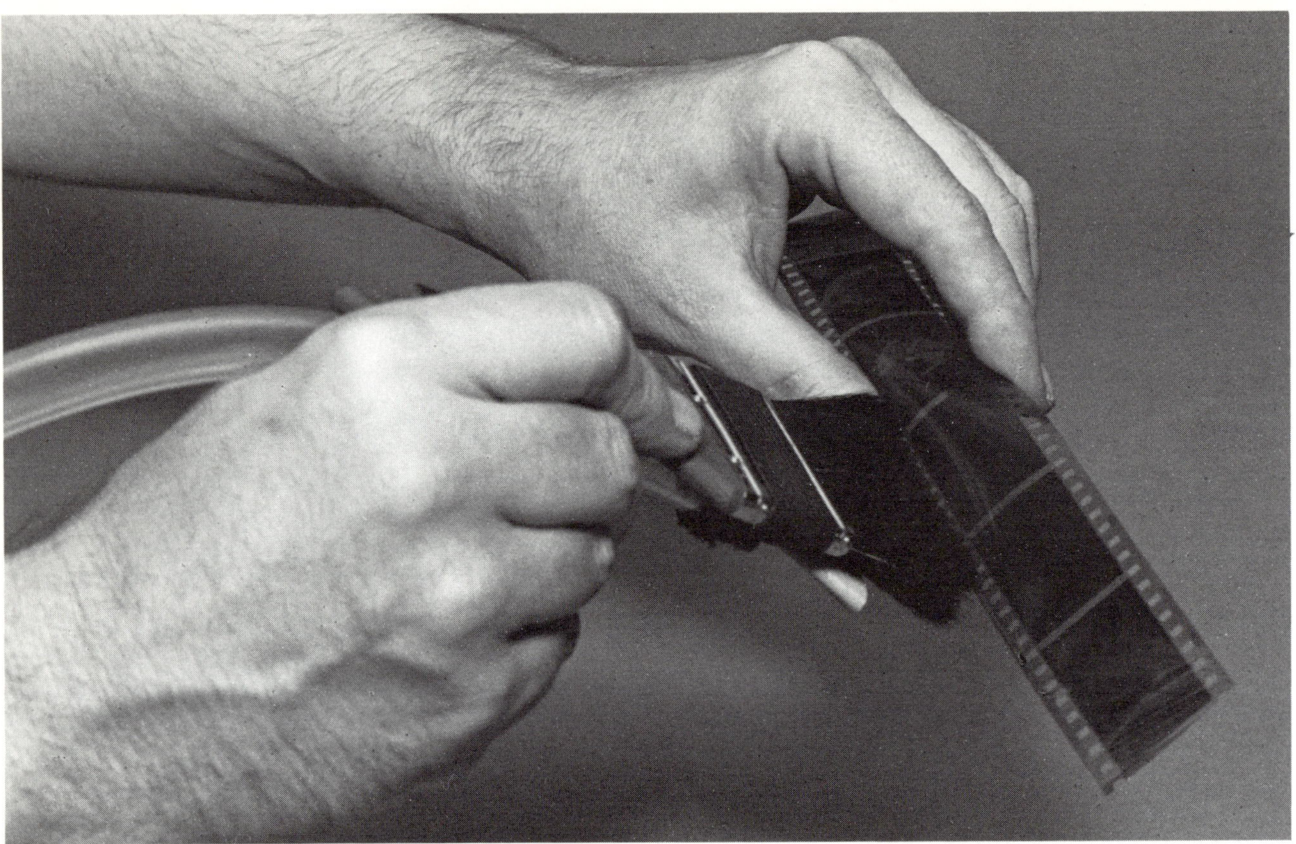

4. The vacuum brush cleans negatives much better than the brush alone.

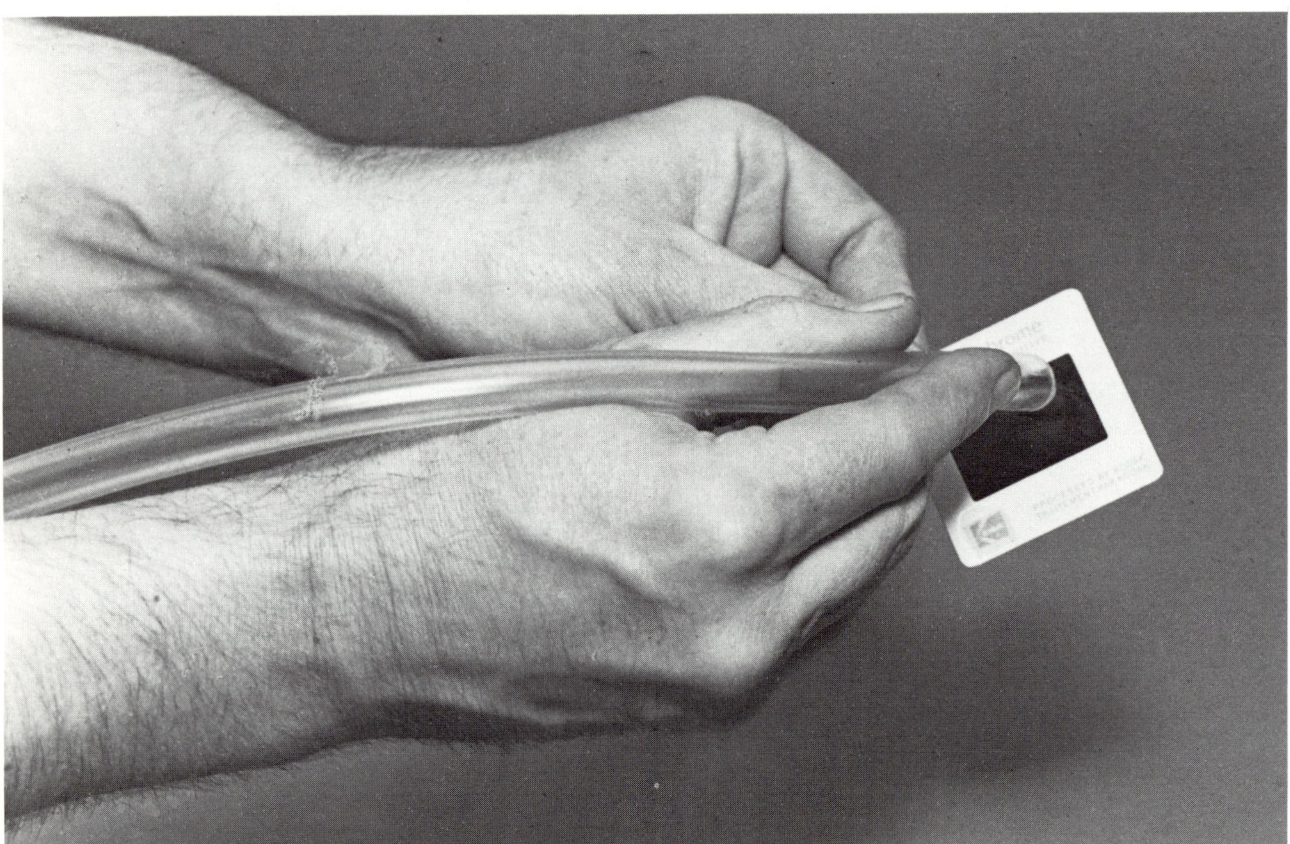

5. Cardboard-mounted slides are plagued by paper dust. The vacuum tubing can be used to remove the dust from the seams between the slide and the mount. It is also useful for cleaning hard-to-reach parts of the enlarger, cameras, and other equipment.

that will work. Anything longer will have too little vacuum. A hose 6′ (1.8 m) or 8′ (2.4 m) works about the best. The plastic tubing easily detaches from the brush so the tubing can be used alone to clean slides, cameras, enlargers, and other equipment with hard-to-clean places. By switching the metal fitting to the exhaust outlet of the cleaner, the tubing can be used as a blower as well. When used this way, the hose will provide a strong flow of clean air.

If you use the vacuum to clean the inside of your camera, don't let the hose come in contact with the blades of the shutter. Pulling the hose free could pull the blades of the shutter from the rails, resulting in an expensive repair bill. For the same reason, don't blow air from the vacuum cleaner or from canned air on the shutter as you could blow the blades loose.

Between printing or cleaning sessions, store the brush in a plastic bag so it won't get dirty.

Film Washer-Dryer

MATERIALS

Hose-type hair dryer or vacuum cleaner
1' (.3 m) of plastic pipe 4" (6.4 mm) in diameter
End cap for the pipe 4" in diameter
Two plastic hose couplers
A chrome-plated round lifter-drainer, larger than 4"
Silicone cement (black or clear)
Utility or shampoo hose, depending on the type of
  faucet

TOOLS

Hacksaw
Metal shears
Drill and 3/16" (4.8 mm) bit
Saw-type large-diameter drill bits
Ball peen hammer
Metal punch
Pocket knife
Thermometer

I recently bought a large stainless steel developing tank and some extra film reels. When I got them home, I realized that I didn't have any way of washing all the rolls of film the tank could develop, at least not all at once. My first idea was to make a large-capacity film washer and then I decided to make a dual-purpose washer-dryer instead. This way I would have one piece of equipment to both wash and dry film. With it, processing a large amount of film can be a snap, even in the smallest home darkroom.

The plastic pipe, water hose, and fittings can be bought in a plumbing supply store. Take the hose from the hair dryer or vacuum cleaner with you and choose a coupler that fits inside the hose. Select another coupler that fits the water hose (either inside or outside) and also fits tightly inside the large coupler. Hose couplers come in many sizes, both straight and reducing, and fit inside one another for further reduction. There shouldn't be any problem finding two that are the right sizes. A lifter-drainer, which costs about a dollar, can be purchased at any store that has a large selection of kitchen utensils. I used one made by Ekco, but there are other suitable brands. Buy a chrome-plated one as it will be easier to modify later on. If a utensil is not marked stainless steel, it is probably plated.

Use a hacksaw to cut the two couplers in half. Only half of each one will be used. Place the end cap on the pipe, forcing the pipe all the way to the bottom. Drill a hole the size of the large coupler through both the end cap and the pipe. The inexpensive, large-diameter drill bit easily drills through the plastic. The bottom of the hole should be about ¼" (6.4 mm) above the base of the end cap to leave room to attach the air hose to the

coupler. You can trim all the rough edges with a pocket knife.

Next take the lifter-drainer and center-punch the rivets that attach the handle. Center-punching prevents the drill bit from slipping when you drill through the rivets. Use metal shears to trim about ⅛" (3.2 mm) from the circumference of the perforated metal plate so it will fit inside the pipe. This round plate will allow an even flow of air and water through the pipe.

Use silicone to cement the plate inside the pipe just above the hole drilled for the coupler. Glue the large half-coupler into the pipe and glue the smaller one to the water hose. You can use a warm, 150 F (66C) oven to speed the drying. In the oven, the silicone will set in about an hour. Allow it to dry overnight if you air-dry it.

When the silicone is dry, check the fit of the water hose. A tight fit is necessary to hold under the pressure of the water. To tighten the fit, a little silicone can be added to the outside of the coupler (allow it to dry). This portion of the washer-dryer is now ready to use.

Note Using a hair dryer to dry film or prints was a standard and uncomplicated darkroom practice until it was discovered that some hair dryers contained asbestos. Asbestos in the dryers is a potential health hazard and the fibers can also lodge on the film.

If you have a hair dryer that you *know* doesn't contain asbestos, there is no problem using it. If you are uncertain, you can check the dryer yourself or take it to a small appliance repair shop. With the dryer *unplugged*, remove the plastic case. Usually only three or four screws hold it on. Look at the wires leading to the heating element. If the wires have a white or light-gray fibrous coating that looks like paper, this is asbestos. If the wires are plastic-coated or covered with woven cloth over plastic, they are okay and you can reassemble the dryer. If there is asbestos present, the wires should be replaced. The type and positioning of the wires is important, so I strongly recommend that the replacement be done by a small appliance repairperson.

An alternative to using the hair dryer is to use a vacuum cleaner with its suction providing the flow of air. Since the air is not heated, drying will take longer, but the problem of asbestos will be avoided.

Film should be washed at or near the processing temperature with a generous flow of water and with a complete water change at least every five minutes. Black-and-white film should be washed for 20 minutes or longer for maximum permanence. For color film, follow the time and temperature specified on the instruction sheet that comes with the film. Be certain to *drain all* the water from the

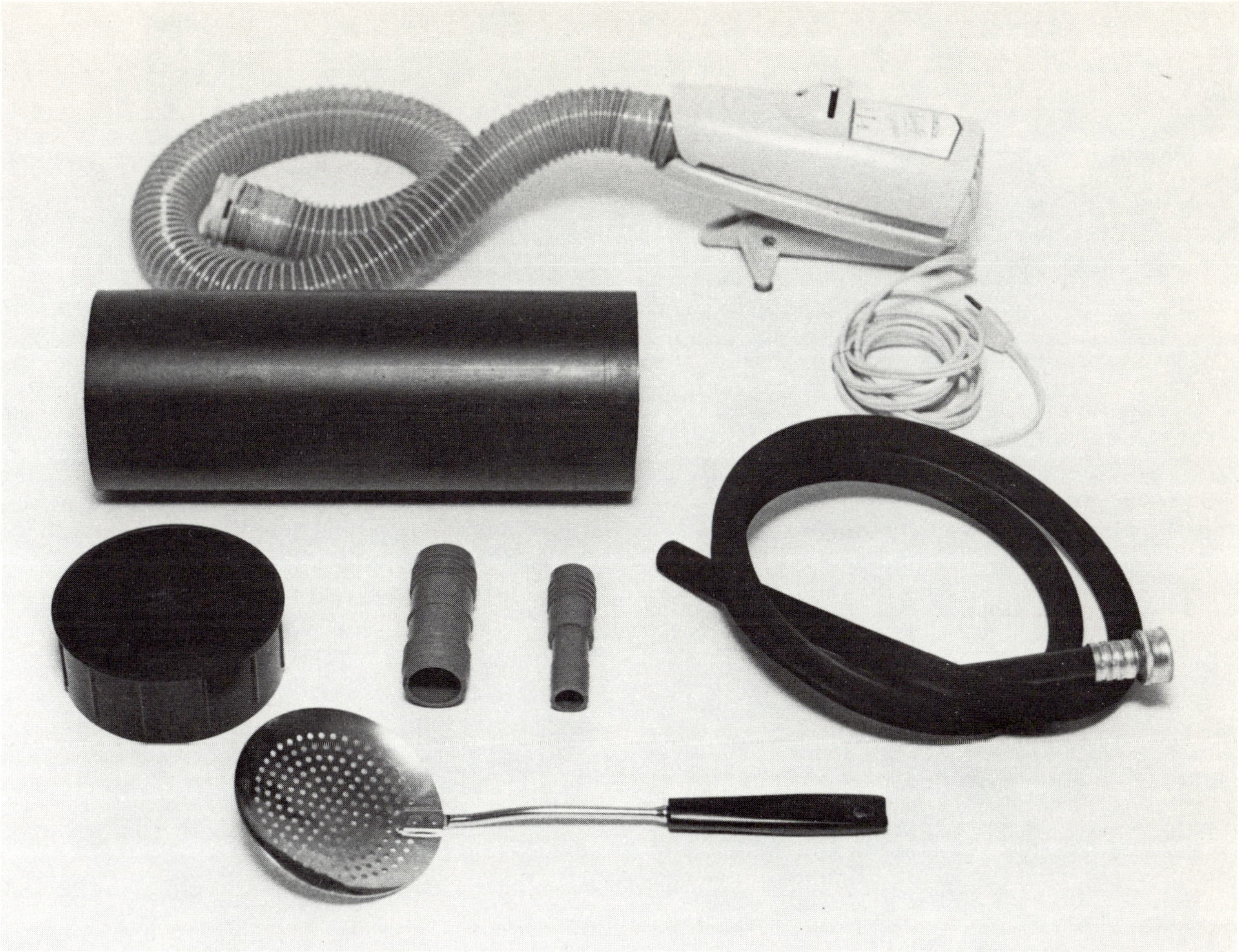

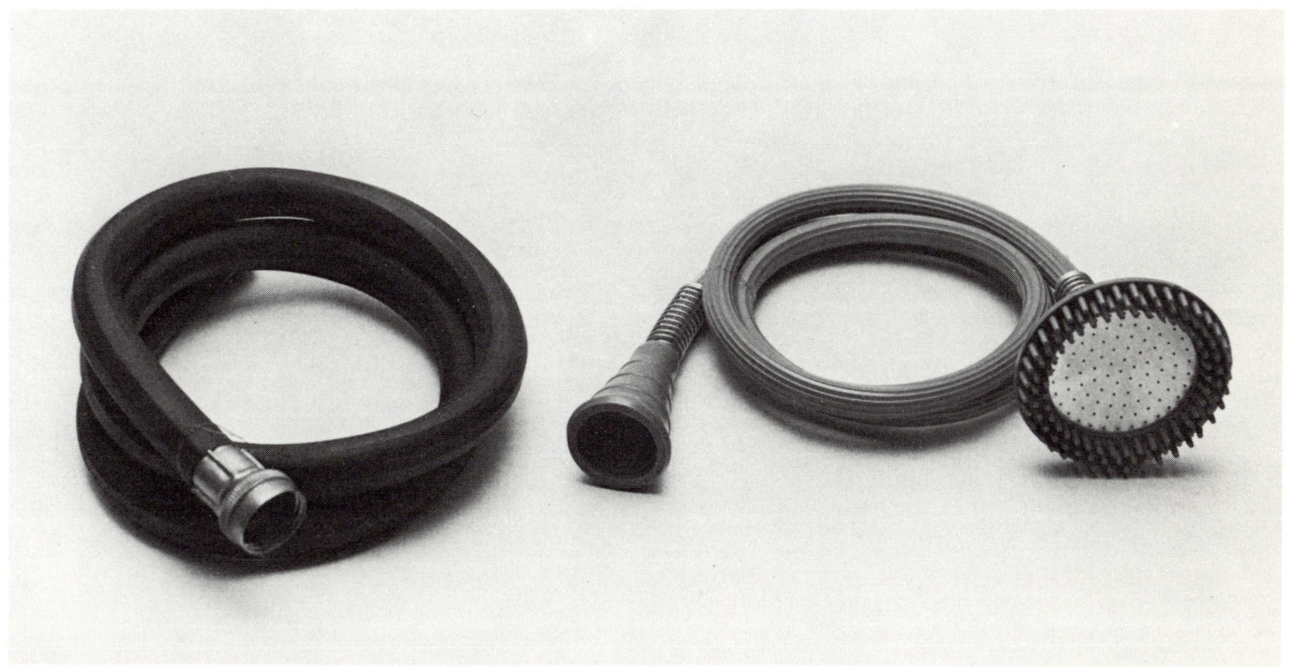

1. Here are the materials I used to make my combination film washer and dryer. A vacuum cleaner could be used instead of the hair dryer.

2. The shampoo hose on the right has a hose and rubber fitting that can be used to attach the film washer to a bathtub faucet. The utility hose on the left has a standard hose fitting.

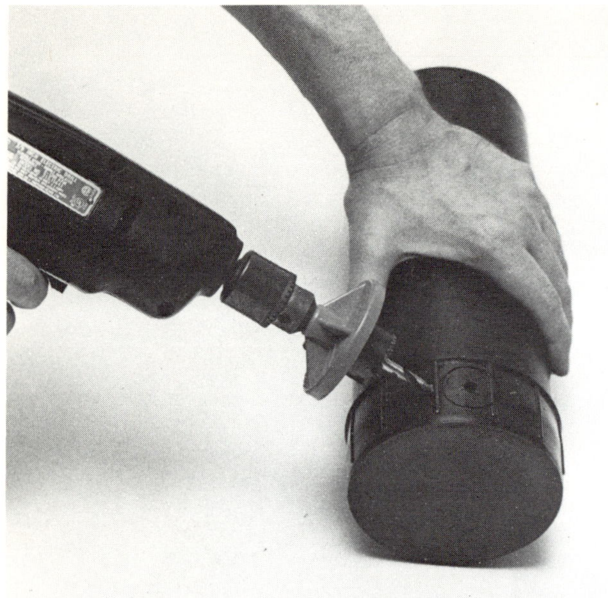

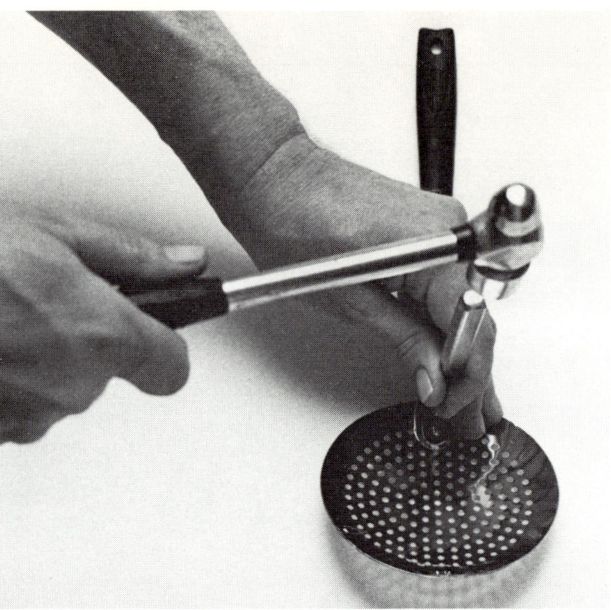

3. A saw-style of drill bit makes a hole for the hose coupler in the pipe and end cap. Here the hole is only partly drilled.

4. A ball peen hammer and a metal punch are used to center-punch the rivets that attach the handle of the drainer. This prevents the drill bit from slipping on the metal.

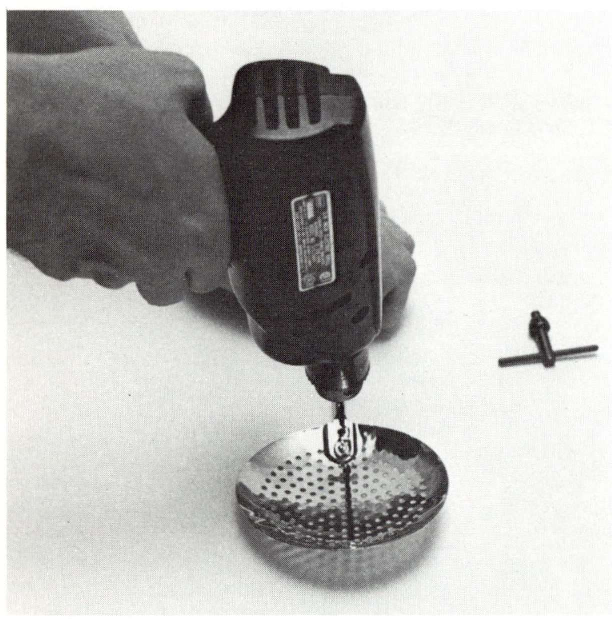

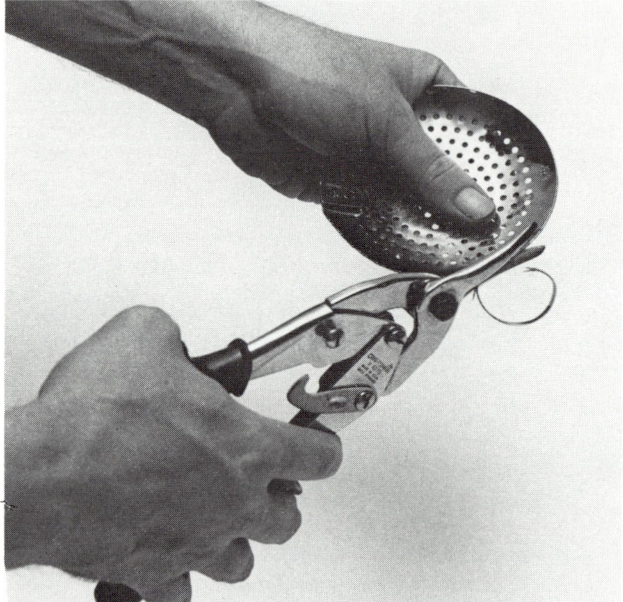

5. Drill out the rivets using a 3/16″ bit. If you have a variable-speed drill, use a slow speed to drill metal.

6. Use metal shears to reduce the diameter of the perforated plate to 4″ so it can fit inside the pipe. The chrome-plated metal is easy to cut.

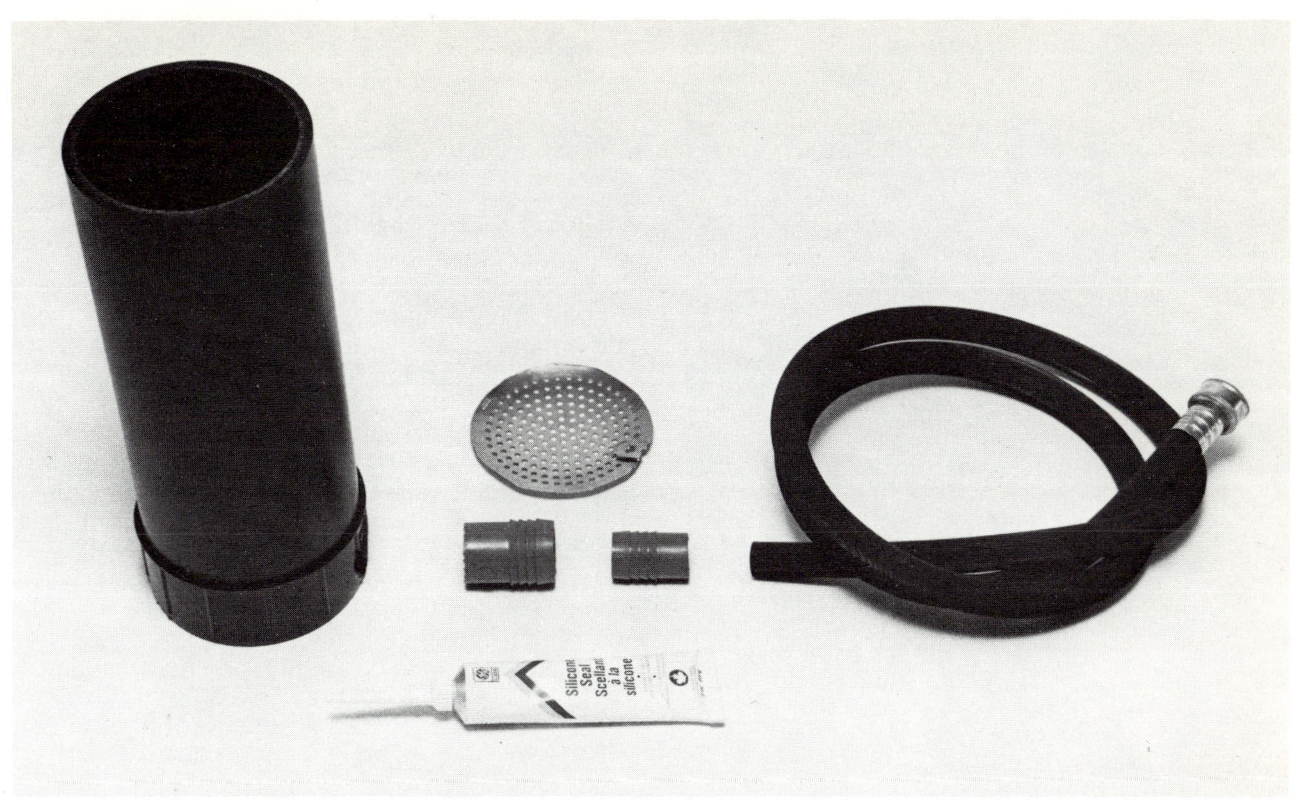

7. All the different pieces are now ready to glue in place with silicone cement.

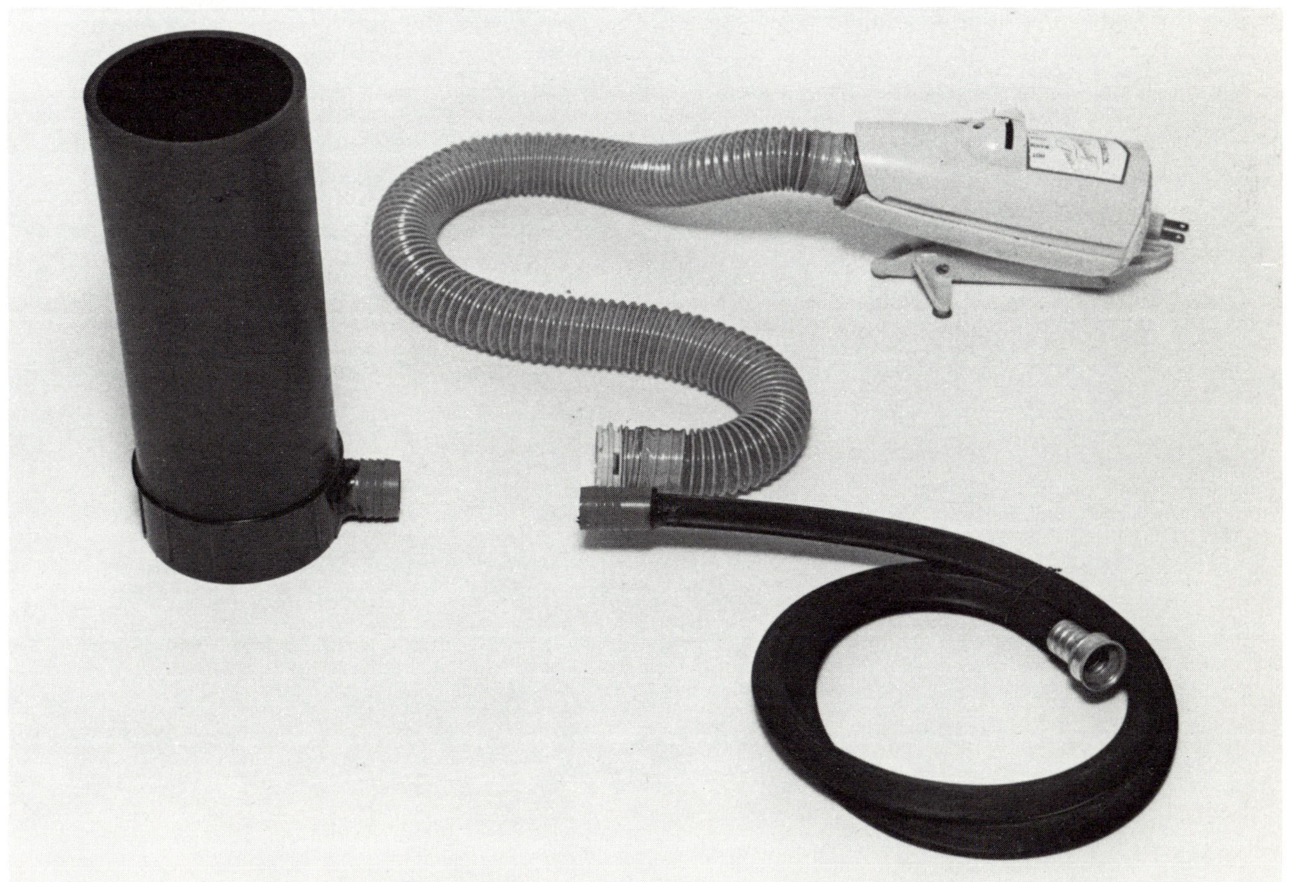

8. The air hose attaches to the outside of the large hose coupler while the water hose with its small coupler fits tightly inside the large coupler.

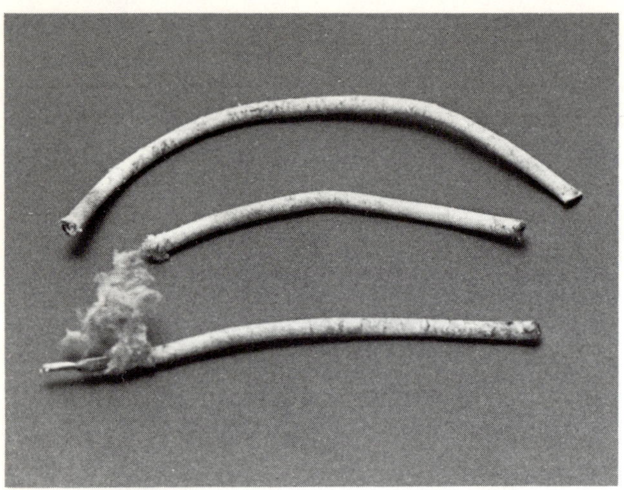

9. Asbestos wire found in some hair dryers has a white or light gray fibrous coating that looks like paper. On one wire, the asbestos has been frayed to show its texture.

pipe after the washing is completed.

After washing black-and-white film, I return the reels to the developing tank for a quick rinse in Photo-Flo. I squeegee the film between my fingers one roll at a time and put the film back on the reels and into the washer-dryer for drying. When loading the reels into the empty pipe, tilt the pipe slightly so that the reels slide inside. Dropping the reels could damage them or the metal plate.

If you are using a hair dryer to dry the film, check its operating temperature. You can do this by placing a thermometer inside with the film for 10 minutes. The temperature should not exceed 110 F (43 C), as a higher temperature can damage the film. If the temperature goes too high, the heat setting can be switched to warm or cool. With a hair dryer, it should take about 10 minutes to dry the film. With the vacuum cleaner, the drying time will be 20 or 30 minutes.

Over-drying causes film to curl and should be avoided. Frequently check the film. Once you know how long drying takes, a timer can be used. If a roll of film does curl, it can be straightened by hanging it with a weighted film clamp.

The washer-dryer has a capacity of three 120 or six 35mm stainless steel reels. It can also hold most plastic film reels. The capacity can easily be increased or decreased by using a different length of pipe.

I even use my washer-dryer to quick-dry resin-coated prints. Curl the print and slip it into the pipe with the emulsion side facing outward. The print dries quickly in the hot air and when removed from the pipe, it flattens nicely.

This washer-dryer is a good addition to the home darkroom as it makes washing and drying a number of rolls very simple.

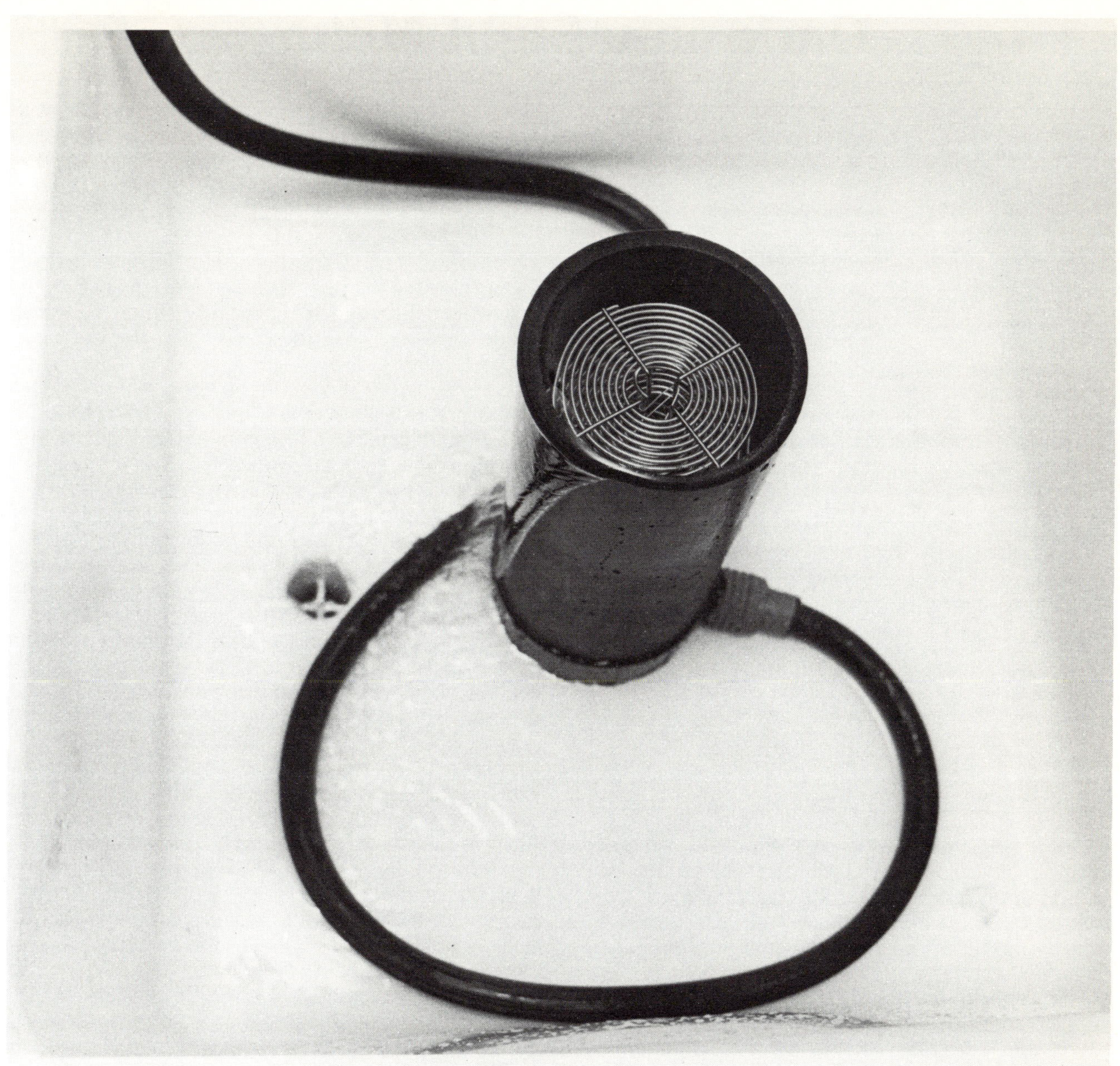

10. When washing film, use a generous flow of water. The perforated metal plate distributes the water flow evenly.

Darkroom Light Meter

Photographic paper is a major expense. Using an enlarging meter is one way you can save money by saving paper. Unfortunately, the cost of a good enlarging meter is considerable, and months or years will go by before the meter pays for itself. Making an enlarging meter saves money two ways — on the cost of the meter and then on the cost of the photographic paper.

A multimeter (multitester) is the main component of this enlarging meter. A multimeter has many photographic uses — testing batteries, checking PC cords, and monitoring line voltage fluctuation, just to name a few. It's almost an essential tool for the do-it-yourselfer. All that needs to be added to the multimeter is a light-sensitive probe and you will have an enlarging meter.

The photoresistor has a range of resistance from 500,000 ohms in total darkness to 100 ohms in bright light. All you have to do to make a light probe is attach the photoresistor to the multimeter leads and switch the meter to the R × 1000 position. The photoresistor costs about $2. If you already have a multimeter, this $2 could be your only expense. The rest of the materials only make the light probe a little fancier and easier to use. This fancy probe is easy to make and looks a lot more professional.

To make the probe, begin by sawing a ¾" (19 mm) piece of wood to approximately 2" × 3" (5.1 × 7.6 cm). Next cover one face of the wood with white plastic. I used the scraps of plastic left over from making the flash reflector, but you could also use white plastic from a disposable container. Glue the plastic to the wood with silicone or instant glue.

When the glue is dry, drill a ½" (12.7 mm) hole in the center of the plastic-covered face. Drill only deep enough to seat the cell, approximately ⅜" (9.5 mm). Drill two small holes 1/16" (1.6 mm) through the wood, inside the large hole, to hold the wires of the photo-resistor cell.

Cut a Y-shaped groove in the bottom of the block of wood. This will hold the wires so the probe will sit flat on the easel. Make the groove with a razor knife. Trim the plastic to fit the wood and sand the edges.

Next, make a leather slip case to cover the probe and to protect the photo cell from the bright light when the white light is turned on in your darkroom. Without a case or cover of some kind, the cell would retain a memory of the bright light and be inaccurate for 1 or 2 minutes. I glued the case with an instant glue made for wood and leather. Be careful with this glue — it really does bond to skin.

Cover the block of wood with wax paper, holding it in place with cellophane tape. Next wrap a scrap of leather around the block of wood as if you were wrapping a package. You can use overlapping joints, which is simpler, or do as I did and trim off the excess leather for butt joints. Glue the long joint first. Add the glue to the seam and hold the leather in place as the glue dries. The wax paper prevents the leather from being glued to the wood. Next cut the end flap and fold it over to cover one end, leaving a little excess leather. This makes the gluing easier and the excess can be cut off when the glue is dry. If the black leather shows a light color edge where it has been cut, this can be dyed with a black indelible marker.

This method is a quick and easy way to make small leather cases for photo accessories. If you wish, the seams could be sewn instead of glued, but this would take longer.

Slip off the leather case and remove the wax paper from the block of wood. Place the photo cell in the block, and run the wires through the small holes. Cut two 12" (30.5 cm) pieces of insulated wire and strip ½" of insulation off of both ends of each wire. Add the meter tip plugs to one end of the wires. No soldering is necessary — just insert the wires and twist the nuts tight to hold them in place. Slip a short length, 1" (2.5 cm), of the heat-shrinkable tubing over each wire. Twist one wire from the photoresistor with an insulated wire and solder them together. Repeat with the remaining wires. Slip the insulation over the solder joint and shrink the tubing with heat. The heat from a light bulb works best. You could use plastic electrical tape as a substitute for the heat-shrinkable insulation.

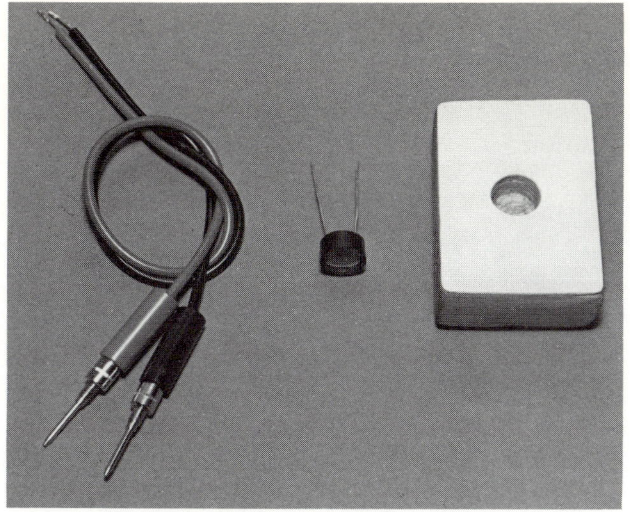

1. The light probe is made from a plastic-faced wood block, lead wires with tip plugs, and a photoresistor.

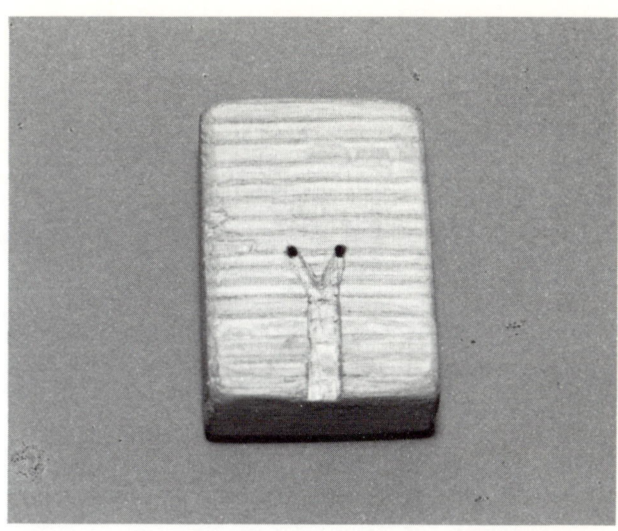

2. Cut a Y-shaped groove in the back of the wood block. This holds the wire so the probe will sit flat.

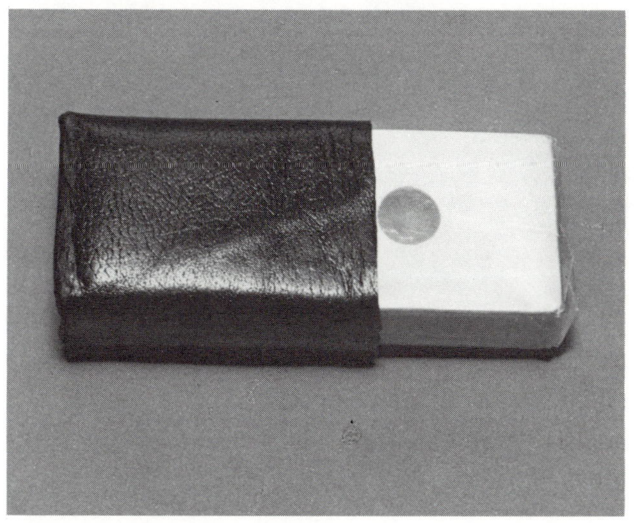

3. Wrap the plastic-faced wood block with wax paper and then with leather. Trim off the excess leather and glue the seams with instant glue for wood and leather.

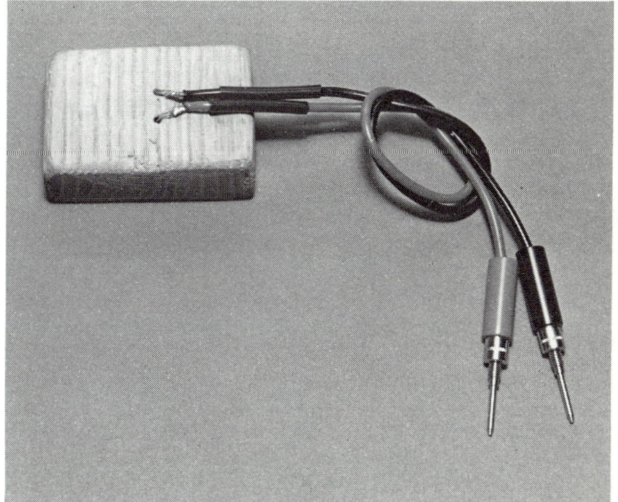

4. Insulate the solder joint with heat-shrinkable tubing. Shrink the tubing with heat from a light bulb, then force the wire into the Y-shaped groove cut in the wood.

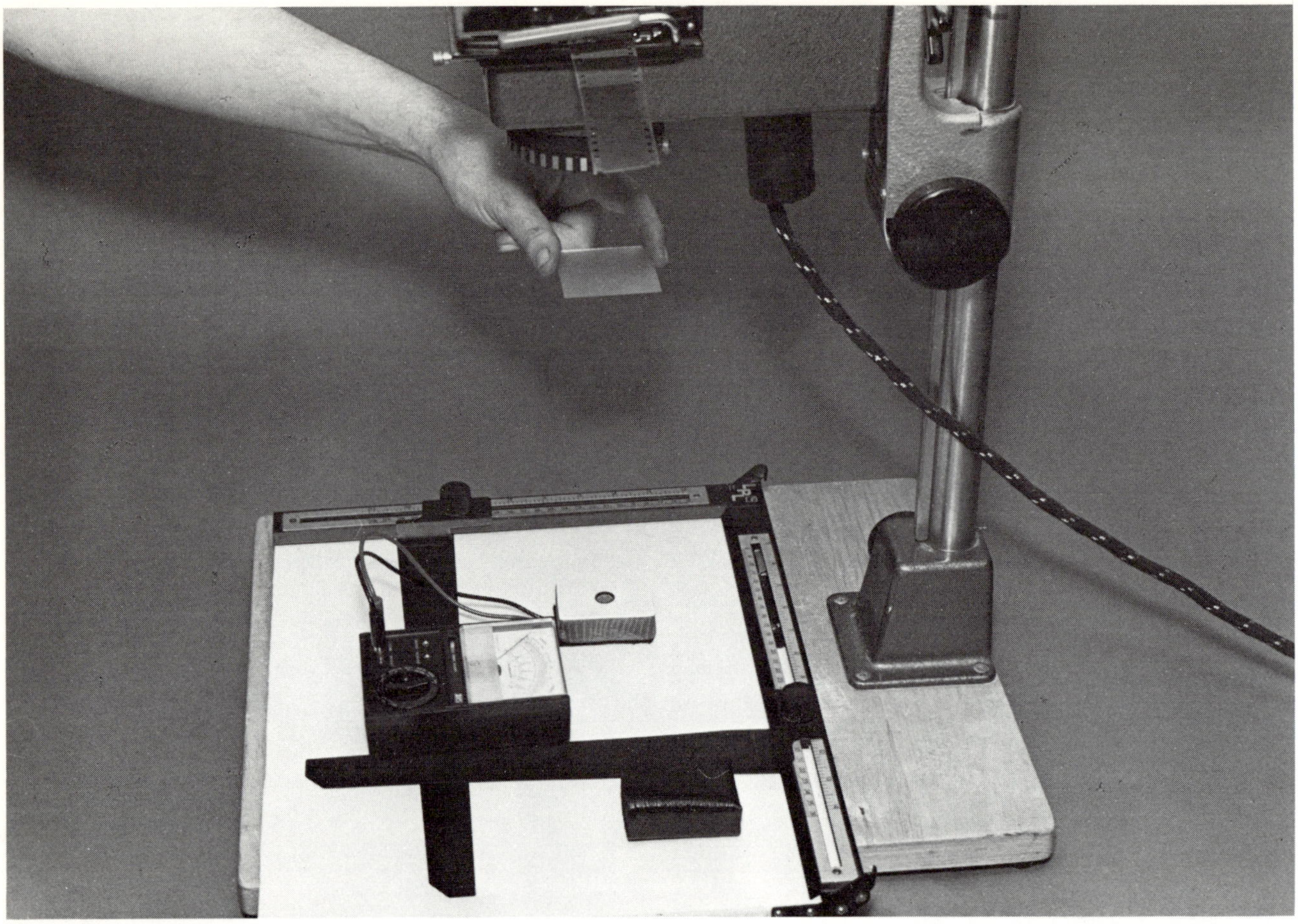

5. A mixture of light values can be integrated with ground glass to an average gray. This works well for average negatives with equal amounts of light and dark areas. Other techniques are used for negatives where dark or light values predominate.

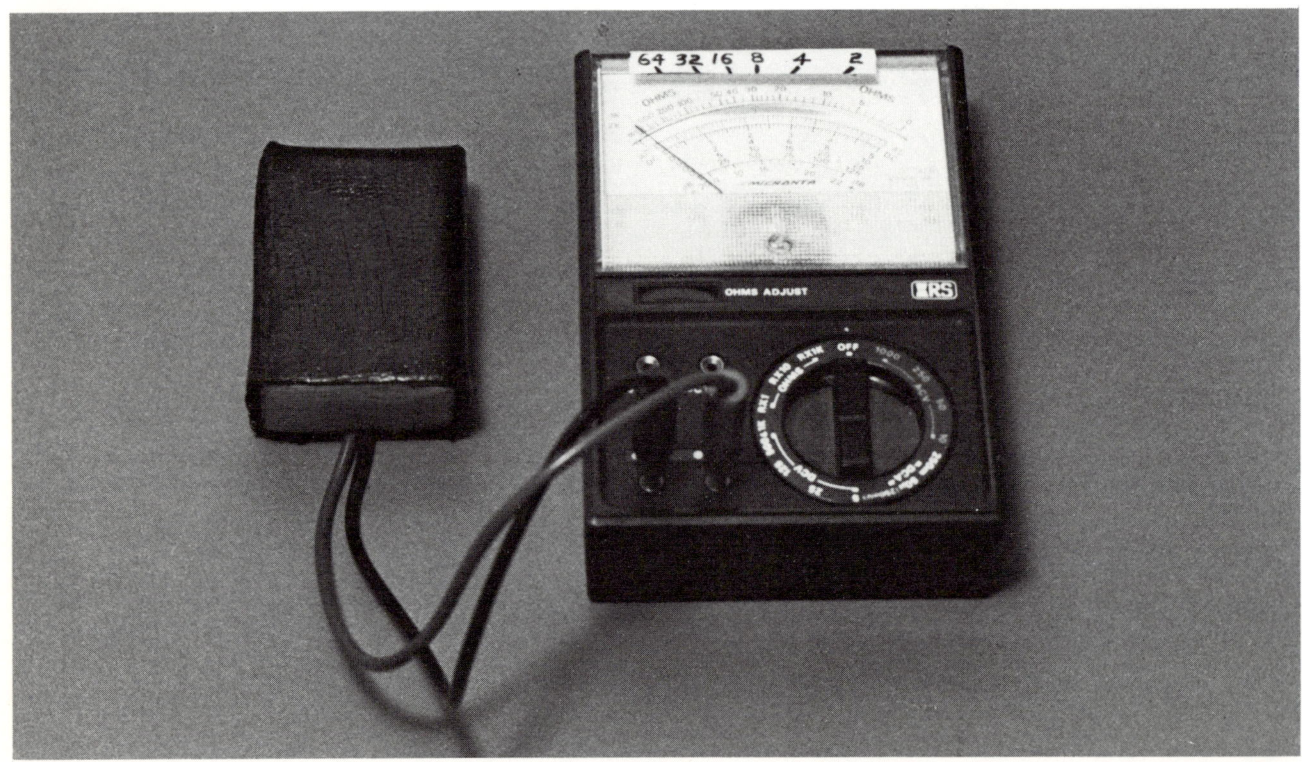

6. Mark the label on the meter with the times that produced a good print at the *f*-stops tested.

After the leads are soldered and insulated, place the wires coming from the photo cell in the Y-shaped groove and smear some silicone on the bottom of your probe. Press a small piece of felt on the bottom of the wood and let the silicone air-dry. The felt protects the easel from getting scratched. When dry, trim the felt to size with scissors. The enlarging meter is now ready to be calibrated.

Take a typical negative and put it in the enlarger. This negative should have equal amounts of light and dark areas and a wide range of grays in between. Adjust the enlarger to make a print and set the enlarging lens to $f/8$.

Hold a small piece of ground glass between the lens and the probe. This can be real ground glass or frosted plastic cut from a disposable plastic container. Take a meter reading using the ground glass to integrate the light and make a note of the reading. Turn off the safelight or shade the probe, as this meter can read even the dimmest safelight. Also allow at least one minute for the probe to lose the memory of the bright light to which it has been exposed. Your reading should be somewhere in the middle of the scale when the multimeter is set to R × 1000. If it is not, change the height of the enlarger so that the needle reaches the middle of the scale.

Without using the ground glass, position the probe on a middle gray value and take another light reading. This reading should be about the same as the first. If it isn't, select another gray value and find one that matches the integrated reading. Remember this tone of gray.

Next make a highlight and a shadow reading. Add these two readings together and divide by 2 to find the average. This answer should be close to the other two readings.

I have just described three different ways the meter can be used. One of these methods will be suitable for any negative.

Make a series of test strips and note the exposure time that produces the best print. Cut a self-adhesive label and stick it on the face of the meter where it won't block the other scales. Mark the position for the middle gray reading and label it with the exposure time of the best looking print (for example, "8 seconds").

Take additional readings at different f-stops with the probe. At $f/5.6$ mark the time on the scale one-half that of the $f/8$ reading. Using the 8 seconds example, this would be 4 seconds. At $f/11$, the time for a correct exposure would be twice as long. Again using the example it would be 16 seconds. Continue marking the label on the meter until you have run out of f-stops.

Once marked this way, the meter will give you the exposure time in seconds, no matter what size of print you are making. With experience, the highlight and shadow reading will indicate the grade of enlarging paper that should be used for the print.

The *Kodak Black-and-White Darkroom DataGuide* gives you the information needed and has an enlarging computer that is helpful when using polycontrast filters or changing from one type of Kodak paper to another. When printing color, take a reading without filters and use the information in the *Kodak Color DataGuide* to correct the exposure for the filters being used.

Once it's properly calibrated, this enlarging meter works just as well as the expensive meters you could buy.

Deluxe Contact Printer
(for 2¼-Square and 35mm Negatives)

MATERIALS

Two sheets of ¼" (6.4 mm) plate glass, 9" × 12" (22.9
   × 30.5 cm)
Heavy leather, 2½" × 11" (6.4 × 27.9 cm)
Two pieces of felt, 9" × 12"
Vinyl report cover
Sheets of paper
Copper pipe or pipe connector
Clear silicone cement
Scraps of fiberboard or Masonite

TOOLS

Spring clamps or "C" clamps
Hobby knife or razor blade
Ruler
Ball peen hammer
File
Emery paper, 220 grit

Most homemade contact printers are nothing
more than a sheet of glass with taped edges. I
used one like that for years. You can tell when contact sheets are made with this type. The strips of
negatives are never straight and evenly spaced.
The negatives always move as the glass is being
lowered. I got tired of this and decided to make a
better contact printer. I made one that would ac-
commodate both 35mm and 2¼-square negatives,
since I use both of these formats.

When you buy the plate glass, ask for two pieces
without flaws and about the same size. Be careful
when handling the glass — the edges are very
sharp.

The leather can be bought either dyed or undyed. You may wish to buy undyed leather and dye
it yourself. Leather dye is easy to use and comes in
many colors. I used black, but I have a conserva-
tive side to my nature. Nine inches (22.9 cm) of the
leather is used as a hinge for the glass and the rest
to make pads that level the contact printer. Felt can
be bought in craft shops in 9" × 12" (22.9 ×
30.5 cm) sheets or in fabric shops by fractions of a
yard or meter. Again, I used black but many colors
are available. Any place that has school supplies
will carry vinyl report covers. These are available in
clear and several transparent colors. I used a light
blue to make photographing the vinyl a little easier,
but clear vinyl would give the contact printer a
more professional appearance.

Begin by removing the sharp edges and corners
from the glass. Tear narrow (2" to 3" [5.1 × 7.6 cm]
wide) strips from a sheet of emery paper (220 grit),
and use these to sand the edges of the glass. It's
easiest to hold the glass between your knees and
sand with a seesaw motion like you're polishing
shoes. Sand all the edges and don't forget to do

the corners. When you're finished, the glass
should be free from sharp edges and safe for you
to handle.

Next, cut two 9" × 12" pieces of felt and a 9" strip
of leather. With the silicone, glue about ½"
(12.7 mm) of the edge of each felt piece inside the
9" side of the glass sheets. Glue it just below the
location for the hinge. Place a sheet of paper between the pieces of felt to prevent them from being
glued together. Glue the leather hinge to the outside of the 9" edge of the glass at the same time
you glue the felt. Use clamps to ensure a tight
bond. To protect the leather from being marred
and to create a more evenly distributed pressure,
place strips of wood or fiberboard over the leather.
Either spring clamps or "C" clamps will work. At
room temperature, the silicone will dry overnight
but drying can be speeded up by placing everything in a warm oven (150 F to 170 F [66 C to 77 C]).
In the oven, the glue will set in about an hour.

While the silicone is drying, mark and cut the
vinyl. Begin by cutting the report cover in half to
get two 8 ½" × 11" (21.6 × 27.9 cm) sheets. Use
the grease pencil to mark the openings that will
hold the negatives. For 35mm, the openings are 1
1/16" (18.4 cm) wide by 9½" (49.5 cm) long. Between the openings, leave strips that are 5/16"
(7.9 mm) wide. For 2¼-square format, the openings should be 2¼" × 9¾" (5.7 × 24.8 cm) with
9/16" (14.3 mm) strips in between. Once the openings that will hold the negatives are marked, carefully cut them out with a razor knife.

Be careful when gluing the vinyl sheets to the
glass to make sure that excess glue doesn't
spread where it's not wanted. Extremely small
amounts of glue should be used. To accomplish
this, use the smallest opening on the applicator
nozzle. This small amount is reduced even further
by wiping off excess silicone with a paper towel.
Not all of the vinyl strip is glued to the glass. The
upper half of each horizontal strip is left unglued
so it can hold the negatives.

Position the vinyl on the inside of the glass and
press it onto place. So little glue is used that it
shouldn't spread, even when pressed down. Place
a sheet of paper between the vinyl and felt to prevent these from being glued together.

When both sheets of vinyl are in place, you can cut
some pads from the remaining scrap of leather.
These pads keep the contact printer level and also
prevent the glass from being scratched. To make
round pads, file a sharp edge on a short piece of
copper pipe or a copper pipe connector. A ball peen
hammer can then be used to punch out four round
pads. Glue these pads to the outside corners of both
glass sheets. A warm oven can be used to quick-dry
the silicone.

When the glue is dry, remove the sheets of paper

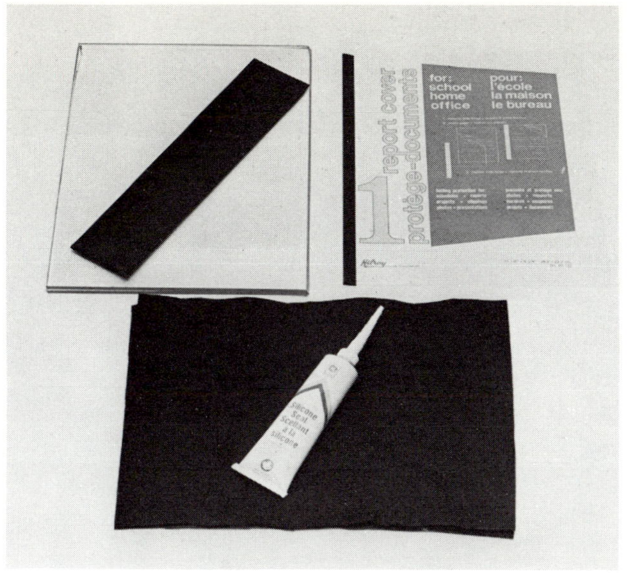

1. The contact printer is made from glass, felt, leather, and a vinyl report cover.

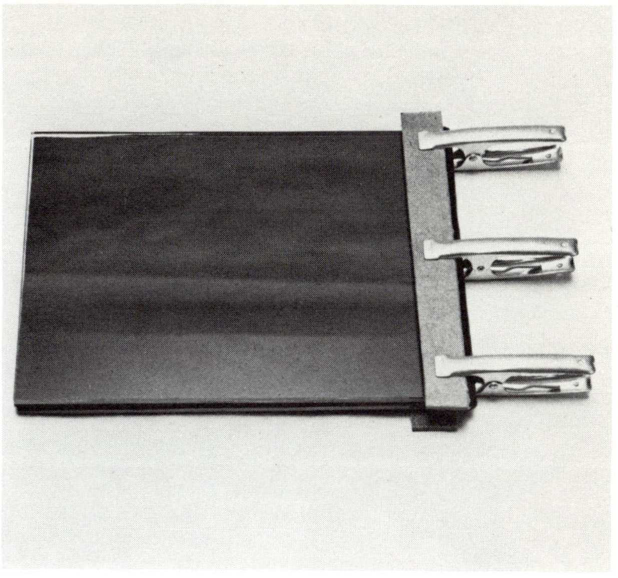

2. Use spring clamps to hold the leather hinge to the glass while the glue sets. Glue the felt pad inside at the same time. Place fiberboard or wood over the leather so the clamps won't mar the surface.

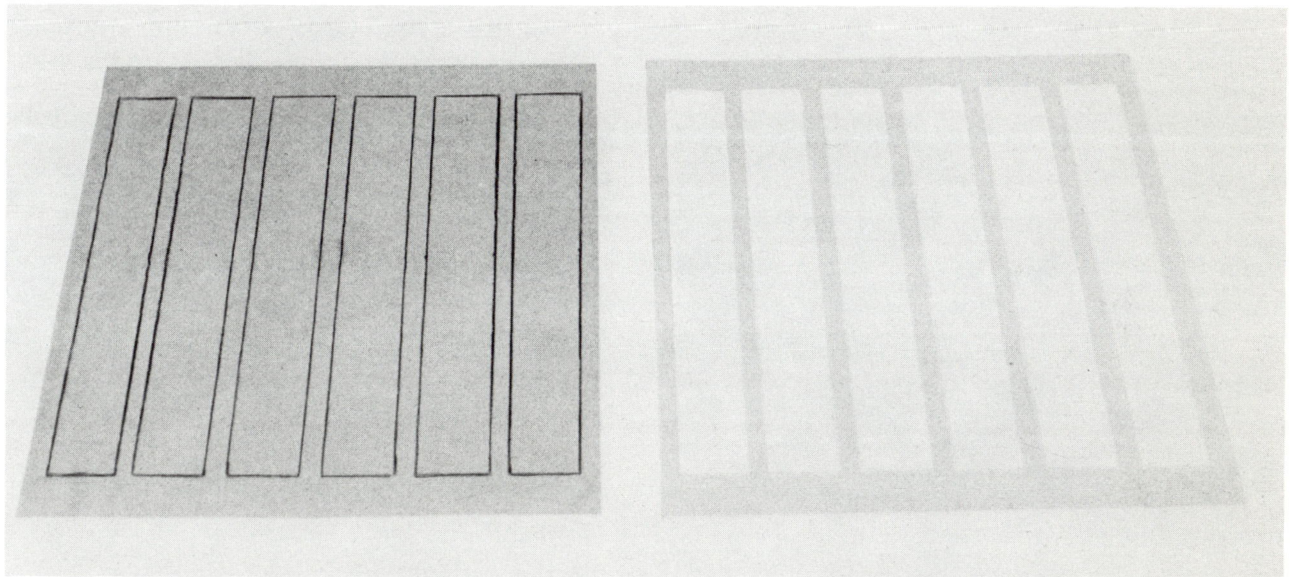

3. Cut openings in the vinyl to hold the negatives. Mark cutting lines on the vinyl with a grease pencil.

4. Glue the vinyl to the glass with a very small amount of silicone. Place paper between the felt and vinyl to prevent gluing them together.

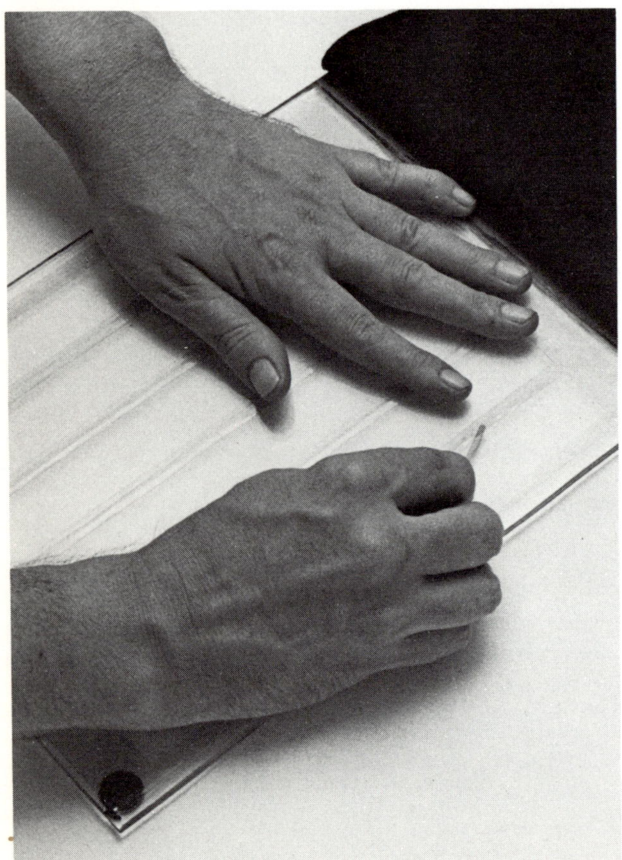

5. Carefully remove the excess silicone with a hobby knife or razor blade.

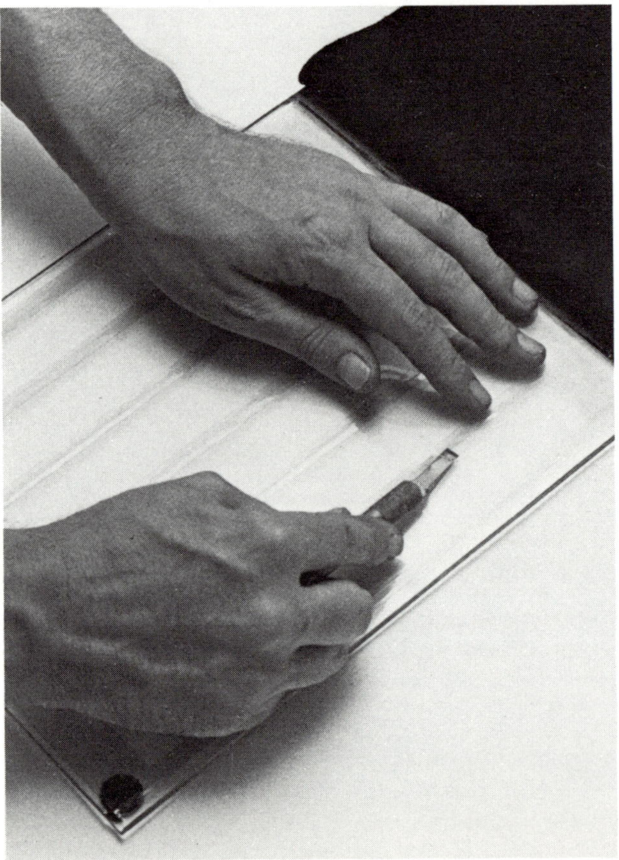

6. Only the bottom of each vinyl strip is glued to the glass. Use a toothpick or your fingernail to open the unglued part of the vinyl. Considerable pressure can be used, as the tough vinyl won't tear.

and check your work. Some glue may have spread where it's not wanted. Remove this and any excess glue with a razor blade or a hobby knife with a square blade. Do this carefully. Only remove the unwanted silicone after it is dry — trying to remove the wet glue will only make things worse.

If some of the vinyl isn't glued, you can apply more silicone with a toothpick. With your fingernail or a toothpick, check the section of the vinyl that will hold the negatives. If some of it has been accidentally glued, it can be cut free using the knife. Be careful not to cut the vinyl.

Bend open the channels that hold the negatives.

The vinyl is tough, so considerable force can be used. These channels should stay open slightly when released, so that you can easily insert the negatives.

Now you can clean all of the glass surfaces using your favorite glass cleaner. The inner surfaces can be cleaned because silicone is waterproof. When the glass is clean, the contact printer is ready to use.

The design for this contact printer is easily modified. If you use only one size of film, you can use only one sheet of glass and the base can be plywood or fiberboard. If you use other sizes of film, cut the vinyl sheets to fit your film's dimensions.

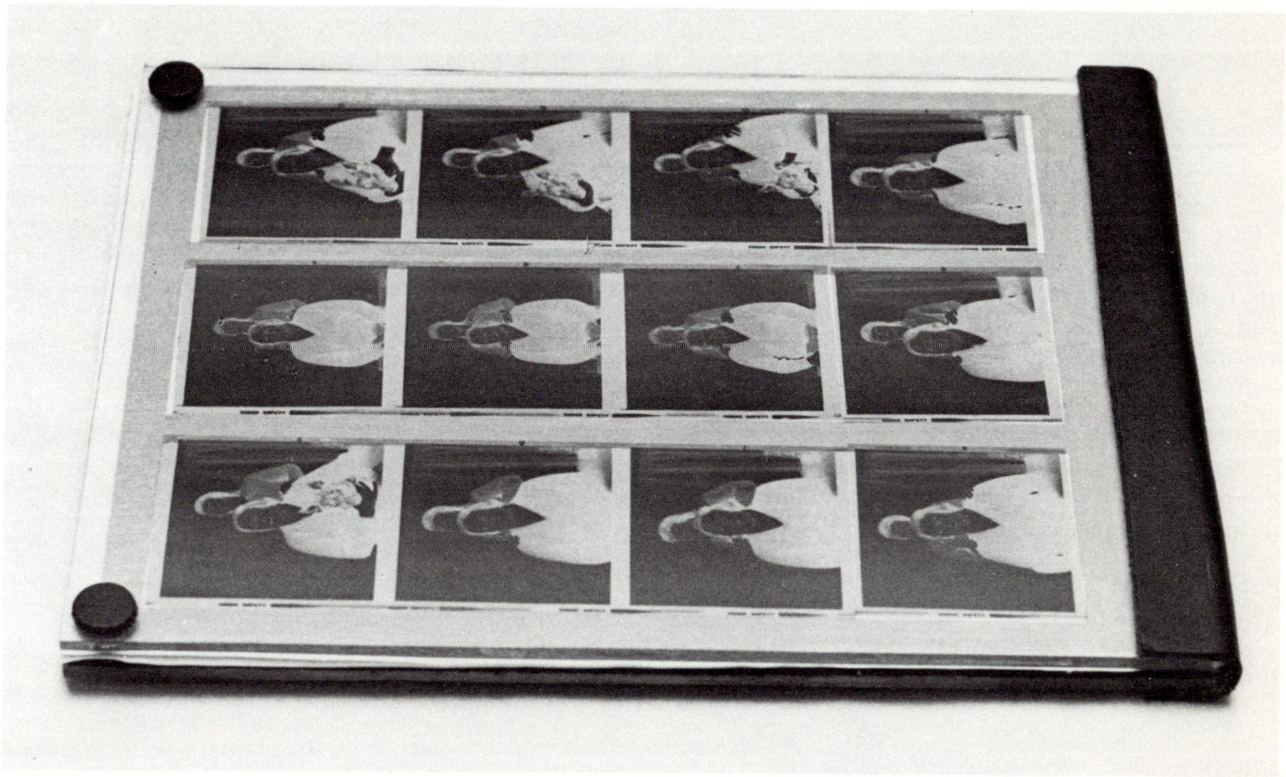

7. This is the finished contact printer showing the 2¼"-square side holding negatives. Round leather pads are glued to the corners on both sides opposite the hinge. This protects the glass from being scratched and keeps the contact printer level.

Mini Light Box
for Viewing Slides and Negatives

MATERIALS

Mini fluorescent lantern, Radio Shack No. 61-2733
5 "C" batteries for the lantern
Translucent white plastic
Plastic cement or instant glue
Sandpaper

TOOLS

Razor knife (regular or plastic-cutting)
Ruler
File
Scribe
Pencil

If you have a large number of slides or negatives, one convenient way to store them is in plastic sheets. The sheets can be kept in binders or a filing cabinet. One problem with this method of storage is finding the slides or negatives you want. Usually the sheets have to be taken out and held up to a light to view them properly. A better way is to have a small light that can be slipped between the plastic pages without having to remove them from the binder or files.

I found a battery-operated mini fluorescent lantern at Radio Shack. It's not very bright, but it's just about the correct brightness for locating slides or negatives. All that needs to be added to the mini lantern is a translucent plastic, wedge-shaped cover to convert it into a light wedge.

Fluorescent light can fool your eyes and make the color of slides appear just as natural as incandescent light does. The small fluorescent tube is a soft and even source of light. Since it's battery operated, the light wedge is a truly portable slide sorter — one that can be used almost anywhere.

You can use the scraps of plastic left over from making the large slide sorter to make the light wedge, or you can buy a plain white fluorescent lighting panel. I've used this plastic in several projects and am always finding new uses for it.

Use a special plastic-cutting razor knife or a regular razor knife to cut the plastic. Begin by cutting two pieces for the face of the wedge. I cut mine 5½" × 6¼" (14 × 15.9 cm). The longer side is the same width as the mini lantern. Scratch a deep line in the plastic where you wish to make the cut. Use two or three strokes of the knife to make the line deep enough. Face the scribed line away from your body and bend the plastic to break it. When the line is cut deeply enough, the plastic will break cleanly with just gentle bending.

Glue these two pieces of plastic to the sides of the lantern, even with the ends of the clear plastic shield that covers the fluorescent tube. Attach the plastic with a plastic cement or an instant glue — a drop in each corner will do. Hold the plastic in place until the glue dries. When the glue is dry, bend the free edges of the plastic until they meet to form the end of the wedge. Add glue along the seam and hold the plastic together until the glue is dry.

To determine the shape needed for the sides of the wedge, place the mini lantern on its side and trace around the added pieces of plastic with a scribe or pencil. Mark this shape on another piece of the translucent white plastic. The scribe works better because it makes a scratch in the plastic that won't rub off. Repeat this procedure for the other side.

Use the razor knife to cut the plastic following the marked lines. Break apart the plastic and glue the end pieces in place. When the glue is dry, file and sand the edges and corners of the plastic smooth. After this is done, the light wedge is ready to use.

Just slip the light wedge between the plastic slide pages in the binder or files so you can see the slides or negatives. This is a much simpler way to find what you're looking for. The light wedge can also be used to edit a few loose slides or to examine negatives carefully. I'll often do this with the light wedge in my lap while I'm watching television.

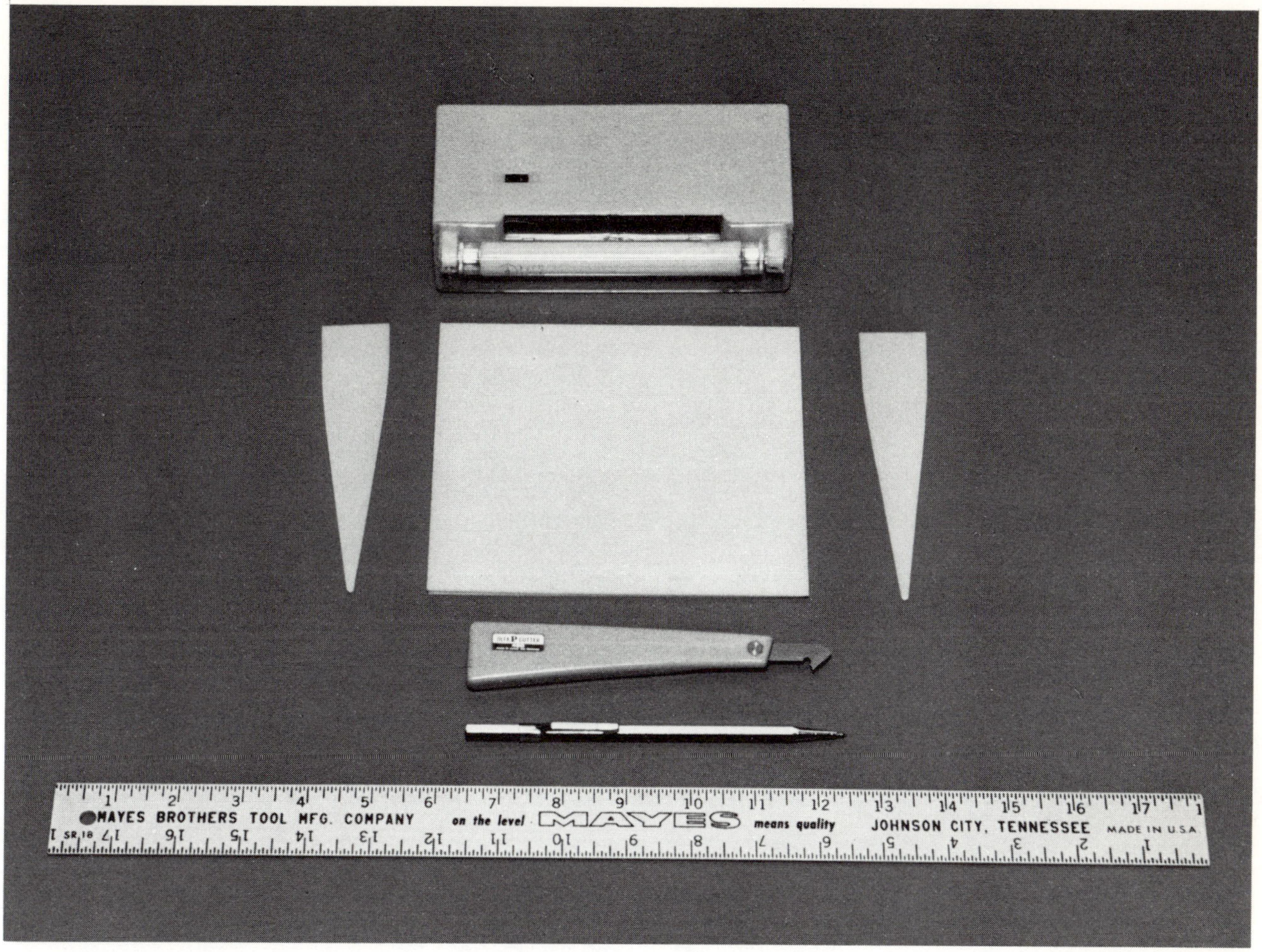

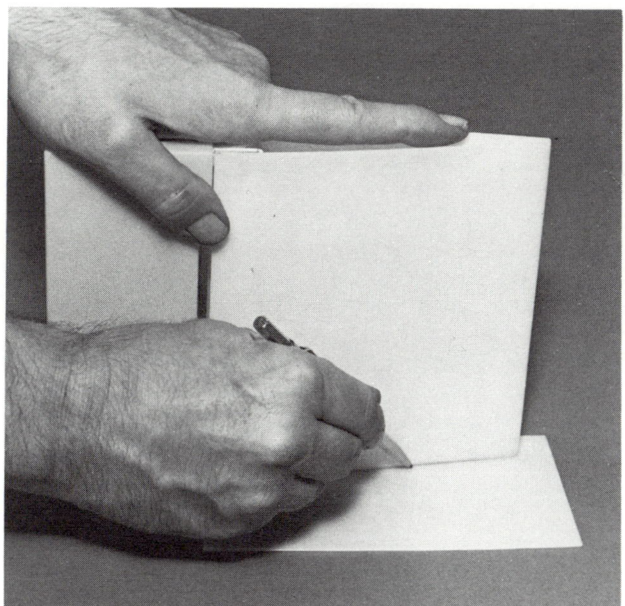

1. A mini fluorescent lantern is the light source for the light wedge. Make a wedge-shaped translucent plastic cover for the lantern, using a ruler, scribe, and razor knife. The plastic is held together with plastic cement or instant glue.

2. Mark around the outside of the attached pieces of plastic with a scribe. Cut out the side pieces, following the lines, with a razor knife and attach them with plastic cement or instant glue.

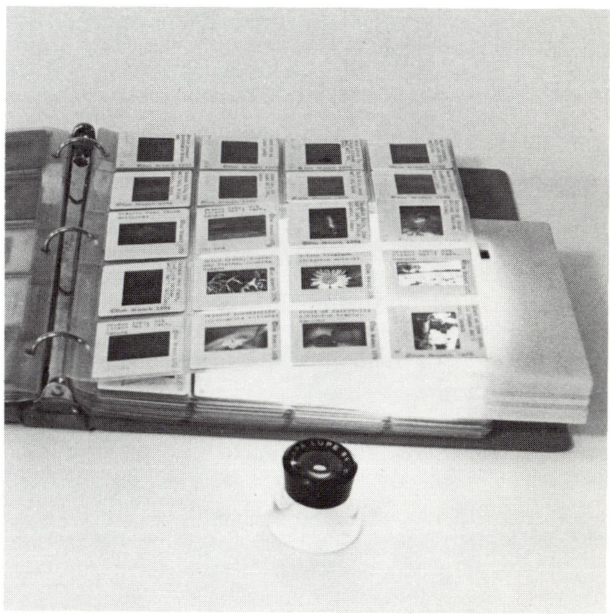

3. The shape of the light wedge allows it to be inserted between the slide pages in a binder or in files. It is also useful as a mini slide sorter or for examining negatives.

Paper Safe for Five Varieties of Paper

MATERIALS

24″ × 48″ × ⅛″ (0.6 m × 1.2 m × 3.2 mm) fiberboard
1″ × 1″ (19 × 19 mm) boards, 12′ (3.7 m)
Black felt, 1 sq. ft. (30.5 sq. cm)
Black leather, 4″ × 16″ (10.2 × 40.6 cm)
Black elastic, ¾″ × 4′ (19.1 mm × 1.2 m)
Black silicone
Instant glue
Sandpaper
Black or dark color of paint (optional)
Nails, 1½″ (3.8 cm) finishing
Brads, ½″ (12.7 mm) or ½″ cigar box nails

TOOLS

Miter box
Finishing saw or hacksaw
Coping saw or sabre (jig) saw
Carpenter's square
Razor knife
Scissors
Claw hammer
Ruler
Caulking gun (optional)

I wanted a better way to organize photographic paper. Opening a box of paper every time I needed a sheet and then rewrapping the paper and closing the box was becoming an annoyance. What I needed was a paper safe that could hold five or six different types of paper, protect them from light, and make the paper easily available. I use mostly 8″ × 10″ (20.3 × 25.4 cm) paper but I use different grades, surfaces, and weights — so I made a paper safe with six compartments to hold the different types of paper.

A paper safe should have a self-closing door to prevent accidental exposure. Originally, I had planned to use a spring to close the door, but after several design changes, I decided on elastic instead. The elastic provides a simple yet secure way to keep the door of the paper safe closed but still easy to open. The door and front of the paper safe are lined with felt to provide a lighttight seal.

The first step is to cut the boards for the spacers between the shelves. The 1″ × 1″ boards used for temporary spacers in the print washer project can be used here. These boards actually measure ¾″ × ¾″ (19 × 19 mm), so each shelf can hold about 50 sheets of single-weight paper. Saw 12 boards 10¾″ (27.3 cm) long. Use a miter box to cut the wood so the ends will be perpendicular. Be careful to cut the boards to exactly the same lengths.

Next cut the fiberboard into seven 10″ × 10¾″ (25.4 × 27.3 cm) rectangular sheets. Use a carpenter's square to be sure that cuts are made at right angles. Five of these sheets are for the inner

shelves and the other two will become the top and bottom of the paper safe.

Nail the five sheets for the shelves together with three or four nails. This makes it possible to cut the shape shown for the front of the shelves all at the same time. The front edge of the shelves must be inset ¼″ (6.4 mm) to make room for the light trap that is part of the door. The semicircular cutout in the center makes pulling out the paper easier. The rectangular extensions in the front corners are ¾″ (19.1 mm) wide and ¼″ deep and fit below the 1″ × 1″ boards used to space the shelves. Use a coping saw or saber (jig) saw to shape the front of the shelves. Remove the nails and begin assembling the parts of the paper safe.

If you have a table saw, the paper safe could be made by sawing grooves for the shelves in ¾″ boards. Without a table saw, do as I did and make the body by nailing together the fiberboard shelves and the 1″ × 1″ spacers. Squeeze black silicone onto the base where the spacers will be located, and then use small nails to attach the first pair of spacers. The silicone acts both as a light seal and a glue.

Add shelves and spacers to this base, using the silicone and nails in the manner described before. Finishing nails 1¼″ (3.2 cm) long are a sufficient length to nail one spacer and a shelf to the next spacer. Use the carpenter's square to keep the boards aligned. Be especially careful of the alignment of the front of the box where the door will be. Irregularities in the back are less important.

After the top is nailed and glued in place, measure the outside of the front and back of the paper safe. Mine measures 5½″ × 10″ (14 × 25.4 cm). Saw two sheets of fiberboard to these dimensions. Next measure the inside of the front of the paper safe. This should be about 5¼″ × 8¼″ (13.3 × 21 cm), so you'll need to saw a fiberboard sheet 5″ × 8″ (12.7 × 20.3 cm). The sheet is ¼″ shorter to allow for the felt and silicone that is used for a light seal.

Cut a piece of felt larger than needed to line the door. The excess can be trimmed off after the felt is glued in place. Smear a thin coat of silicone on the inside of the door and press the small sheet of fiberboard to it. Coat the inside of the two pieces of fiberboard with silicone and glue the black felt to it. Position the felt-lined door in place on the front of the paper safe and align the light trap so it fits properly. The silicone is slow to dry so the parts of the light trap can still be moved to correct their position.

Next cut the hinge from the leather. I cut mine 4″ × 10″ (10.2 × 25.4 cm). Also cut four 1½″ × 2″ (3.8 × 5.1 cm) and two 1½″ × 1½″ (3.8 × 3.8 cm) leather pads. These level the bottom of the paper safe. Attach the larger pads to the rear of the paper safe with silicone, using a double thickness of leather. Glue on the leather hinge with the leather lying flat and the

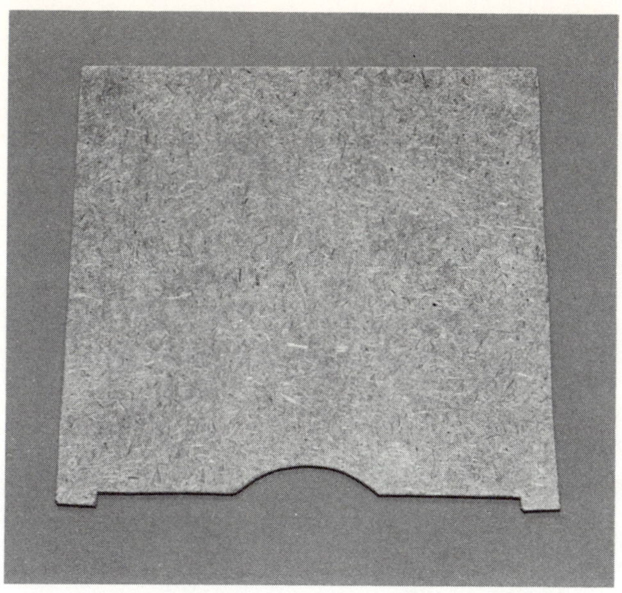

1. Cut the five shelves in this shape. Nail the shelves together so they can all be cut at the same time.

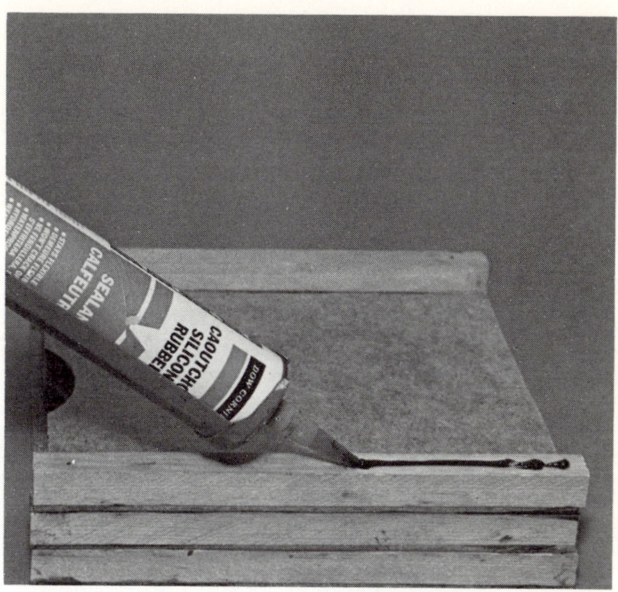

2. Squeeze black silicone into all the seams to seal out light.

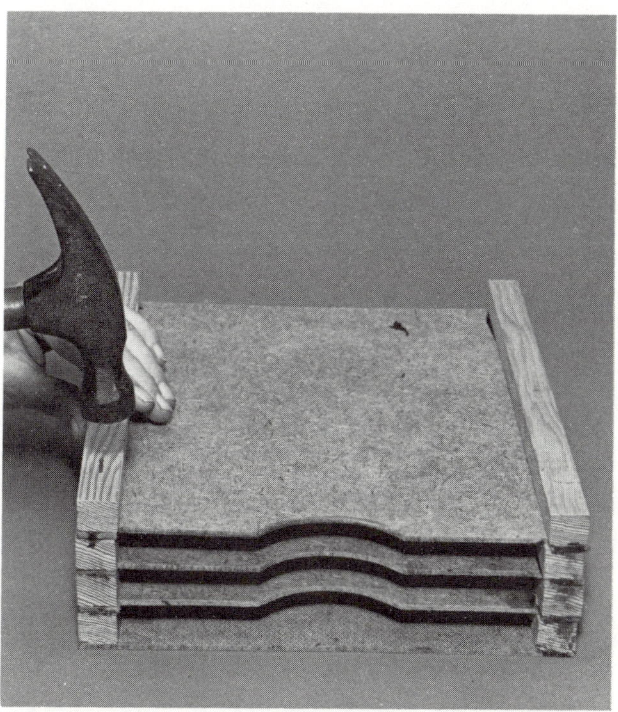

3. Use two or three 1¼″ finishing nails on each side to nail the layers of the paper safe together. Align the front of the spacers and shelves as closely as possible so the door will fit properly.

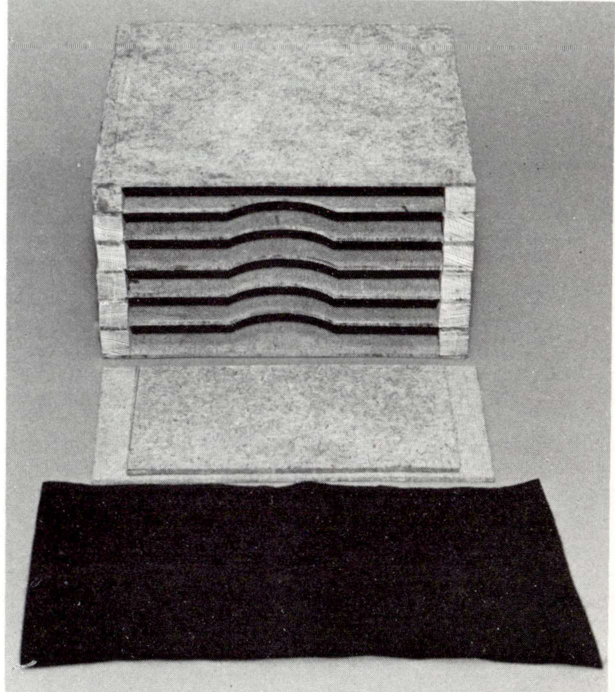

4. Measure and cut two sheets of fiberboard for the door — one to fit inside the opening, the other outside. Cover these with black felt to make the light trap door.

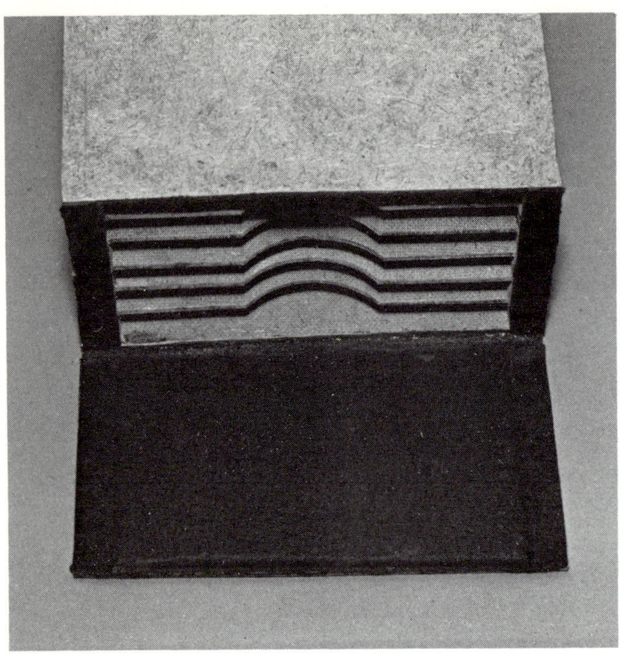

5. Glue felt to the edges of the door opening and the inside of the door.

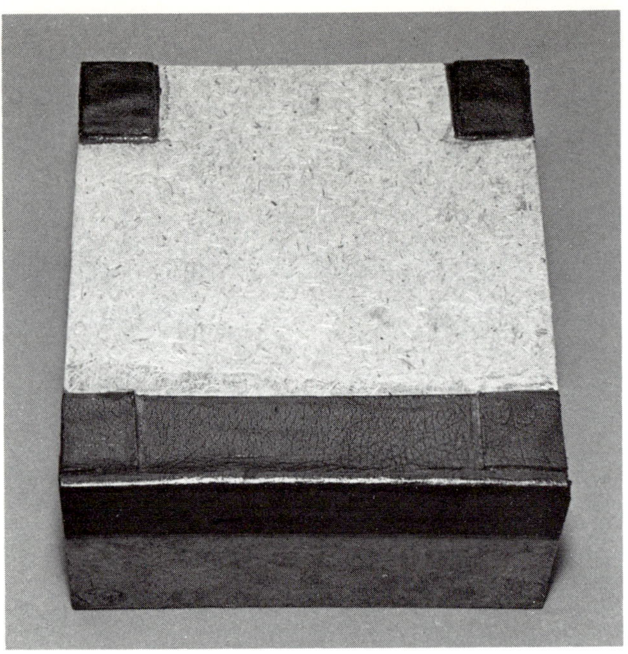

6. Level the bottom of the paper safe with leather pads — a double thickness of leather in back, and single pads glued to the leather hinge.

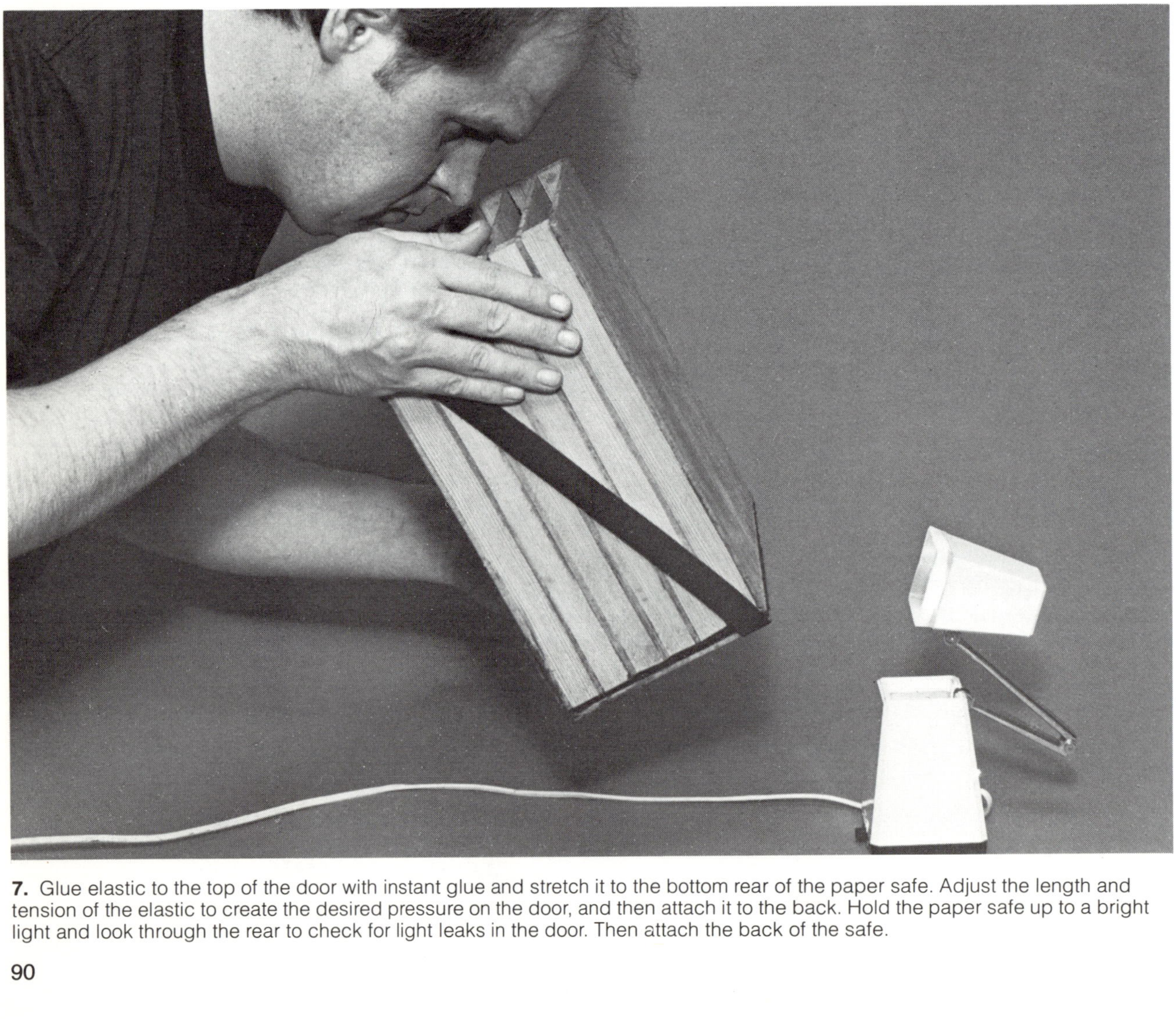

7. Glue elastic to the top of the door with instant glue and stretch it to the bottom rear of the paper safe. Adjust the length and tension of the elastic to create the desired pressure on the door, and then attach it to the back. Hold the paper safe up to a bright light and look through the rear to check for light leaks in the door. Then attach the back of the safe.

safe door on top. Leave a ¼" gap between the bottom of the light trap door and the bottom of the paper safe. This gap allows for the bend in the hinge. Glue the small leather pads to the back part of the hinge so the safe will sit level.

Cover the front edges of the paper safe with strips of felt, gluing them in place with silicone. These should be cut too large and then trimmed to fit after the silicone is dry. Add books or other heavy objects to the top of the safe and the door to press everything in place while the silicone is drying. Let the silicone set overnight so it will be thoroughly dry.

After the silicone is dry, test the leather hinge and the fit of the light trap door. If there are any gaps, you can glue extra felt where needed. Test the light seal by holding the paper safe up to a bright light and looking through the rear. Use felt and silicone to seal any leaks you find.

When you are sure that the light trap on the door is working properly, experiment with the length of elastic needed for the desired tension on the door. The elastic should snap the door securely shut. When you've determined the length, glue the elastic to the rear of the safe and to the door with instant glue. This glue works better than silicone for attaching the elastic. Be careful not to glue any of your fingers together.

When the glue is set, trim off the excess elastic.

Use silicone and small nails to attach the back of the paper safe. After this is completed, hold the back of the safe up to a bright light with the door open. Look inside to check for light leaks in the back or sides. If any are present, they can be sealed with silicone.

I didn't paint the paper safe before adding the felt, leather, and elastic in order to make photographing it easier — I didn't want to have to photograph a black-on-black object. If you wish, you can paint it a dark color to make it look more finished.

The positioning of the elastic for the door allows it to be opened without the paper safe tipping or sliding about. The door slams shut with a pronounced thud, letting you know that it is closed.

To be completely sure of the safety of the paper safe, fill it with one or two sheets of paper per shelf and use it for a printing session or two. Any light leaks will show up as fogged areas on prints. This should not happen if you have carefully checked the safe for light leaks. But it's best to double-check before trusting it with a lot of valuable paper.

I store only a few weeks worth of paper at a time in the paper safe and store the rest in the refrigerator in the original box, which keeps the paper fresh longer.

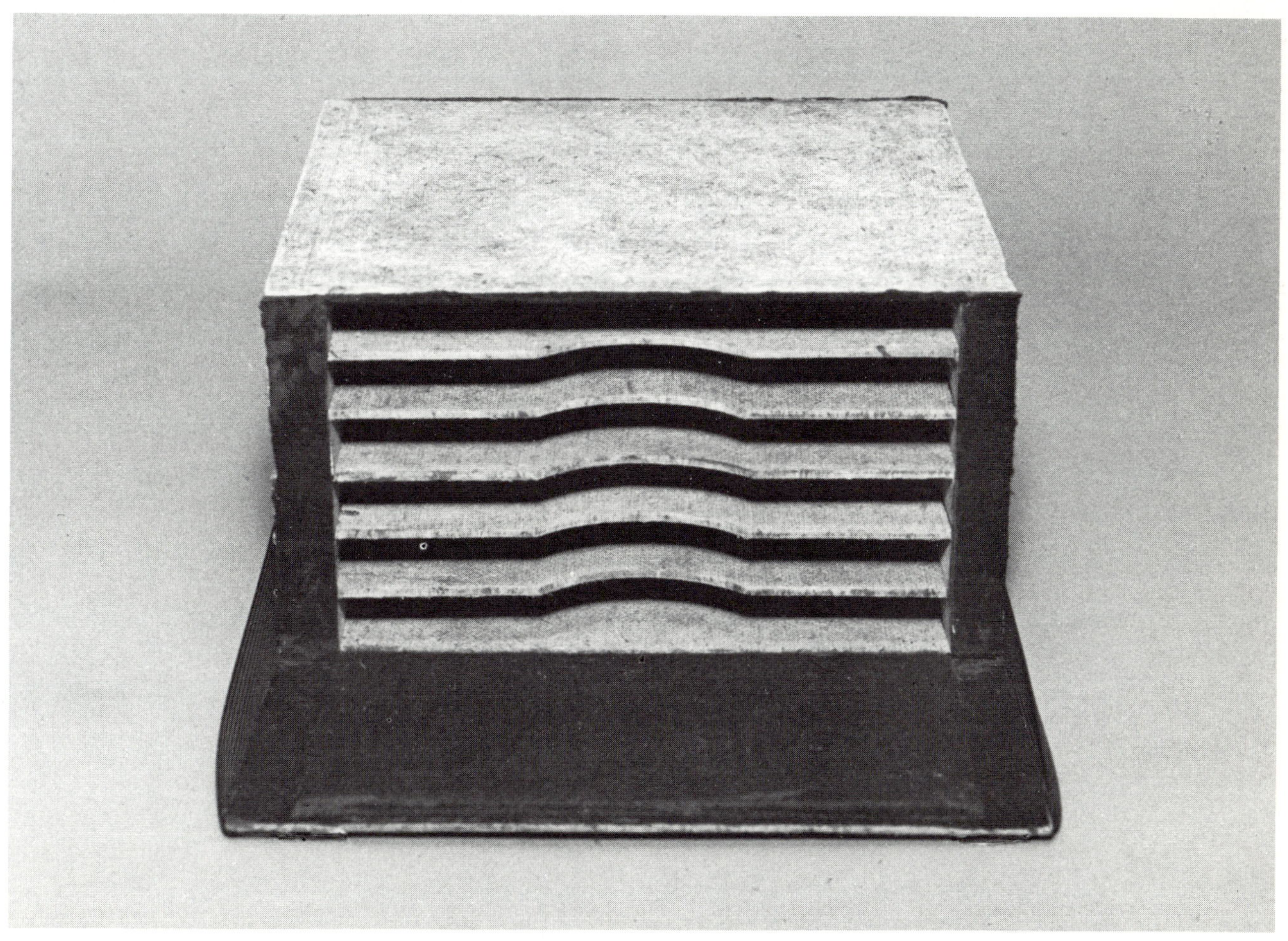

8. The finished paper safe holds about 50 single-weight sheets of paper in each shelf. The six shelves provide storage space for different grades, surfaces, and weights of paper.

Dodging and Burning Tools

<table>
<tr><td>

MATERIALS

Scraps of cardboard and mat board
Stiff wire or a coathanger
Wine cork

TOOLS

Needle-nosed pliers
Wire cutters
Razor knife
Ruler
Scissors

</td></tr>
</table>

Dodging and burning tools and cropping "L"s are the basic darkroom devices that most photographers make for themselves. Each is simple to make and requires the use of only a few tools.

Begin by making some cropping "L"s. These are "L"-shaped pieces cut from cardboard or mat board. If you have matted your own prints, you probably have some of the cutout rectangles left over and this is a chance to use them. Other cardboard will do also. The "L" can be any size you wish — small for small format negatives, large for large format negatives. I use two kinds of "L"s. One with wide sides is used as a burning tool, and one with narrow sides is for examining a contact sheet. Use a razor knife and ruler to cut the "L" shapes from mat board squares. The wider pair is about 6" (15.2 cm) on the sides and 2½" (6.4 cm) wide. The smaller pair is about 4" (10.2 cm) on a side and 1" (2.5 cm) wide.

Cropping "L"s are helpful in examining individual frames on a contact sheet. Make an opening the size of the format and place the "L"s on the contact sheet. It is amazing how different an individual frame can look when separated from the others. Another use for the "L"s is to see how a photo will look when cropped. Make a square or narrow rectangular opening with the cardboard and you can see how a print will look with a different shape. Occasionally proper cropping of a print can turn a mediocre one into one that is truly exceptional.

You can also use the wide "L"s as a burning tool. You can position the cardboard to make various-shaped openings that allow some light to strike the print and block the rest. Place the pieces of cardboard between the enlarger lens and the paper. Keep them moving during the exposure, so hard lines will not be formed by the dodging tool's shadow.

Dodging tools are almost as easy to make as the cropping "L"s. The traditional material for the handle of the dodging tool is coat hanger wire. It's traditional because authors recommend it and they recommend it because it's a stiff wire that everyone has. This wire is hard to cut and even harder to bend, but you can use it if you wish. I used some thick copper wire that I had on hand, but any stiff wire would do.

Cut a 12" (30.5 cm) piece of wire and use needle-nosed pliers to twist a tight coil of 1½ or 2 turns on one end. Leave a gap between the loops to hold the pieces of cardboard that will be the dodging shapes. For a handle I added a wine cork to the wire.

Cut the cardboard shapes with scissors or a razor knife. The cardboard sheet that comes in boxes and packages of photographic paper is the proper thickness. Commercial dodging kits have all kinds of shapes: star, oval, square, L-shaped, and others. To begin with, just cut a large and a small oval. These will take care of 90 percent of the dodging you will do. Keep the scissors and cardboard handy so you can cut out special shapes as you need them.

A burning tool other than the wide "L" isn't really necessary. Many experienced photographers will just cup their hands to produce the desired size and shape for burning a selected area of the print. But if desired, you can make a burning tool by using a sharp pencil to punch a hole in a piece of cardboard or mat board. The hole should be about ⅛" (3.2 mm) to ¼" (6.4 mm) in diameter. By varying the distance between the hole and the print, different-sized areas can be darkened.

It is best to keep these tools organized in some specific place near the enlarger so you can find them when you need them.

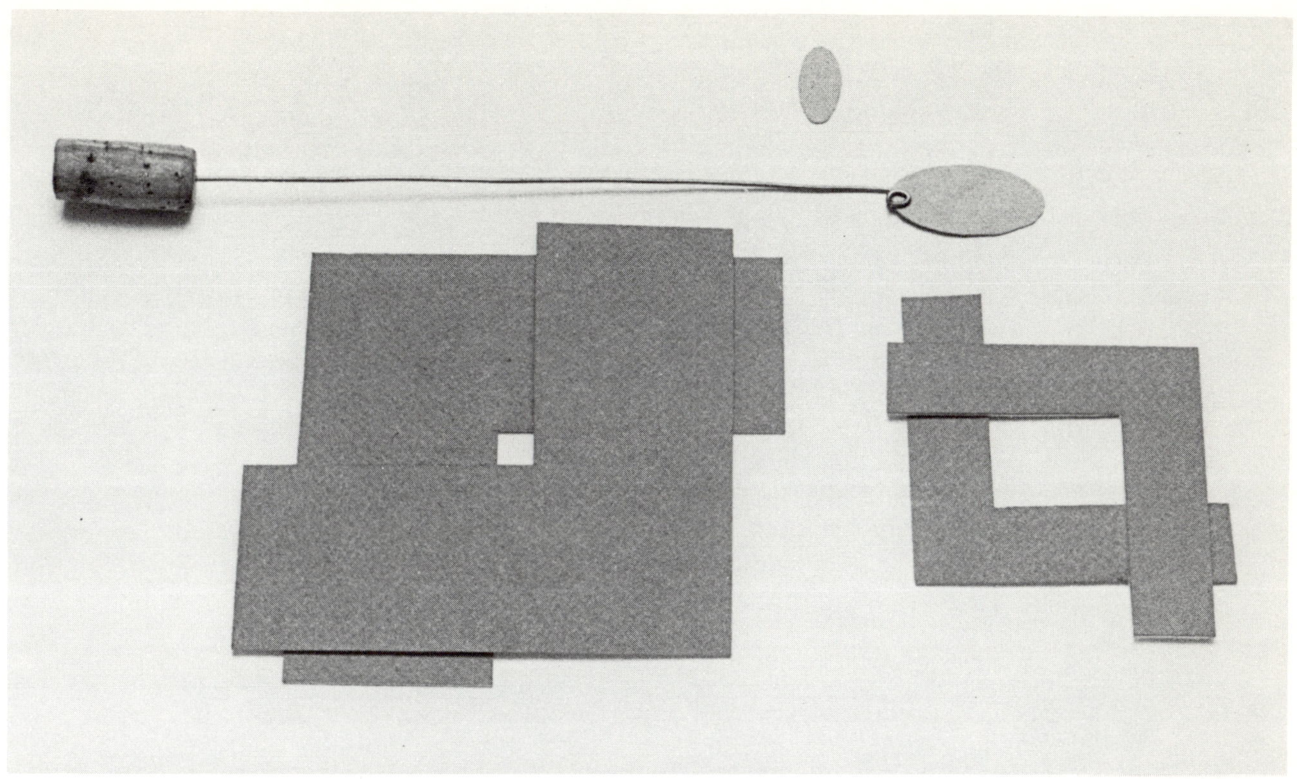

1. These are the basic printing tools that most photographers make for themselves. The cropping Ls are cut from mat board and the dodging tool is a stiff piece of wire with a coil on one end and a wine cork handle on the other.

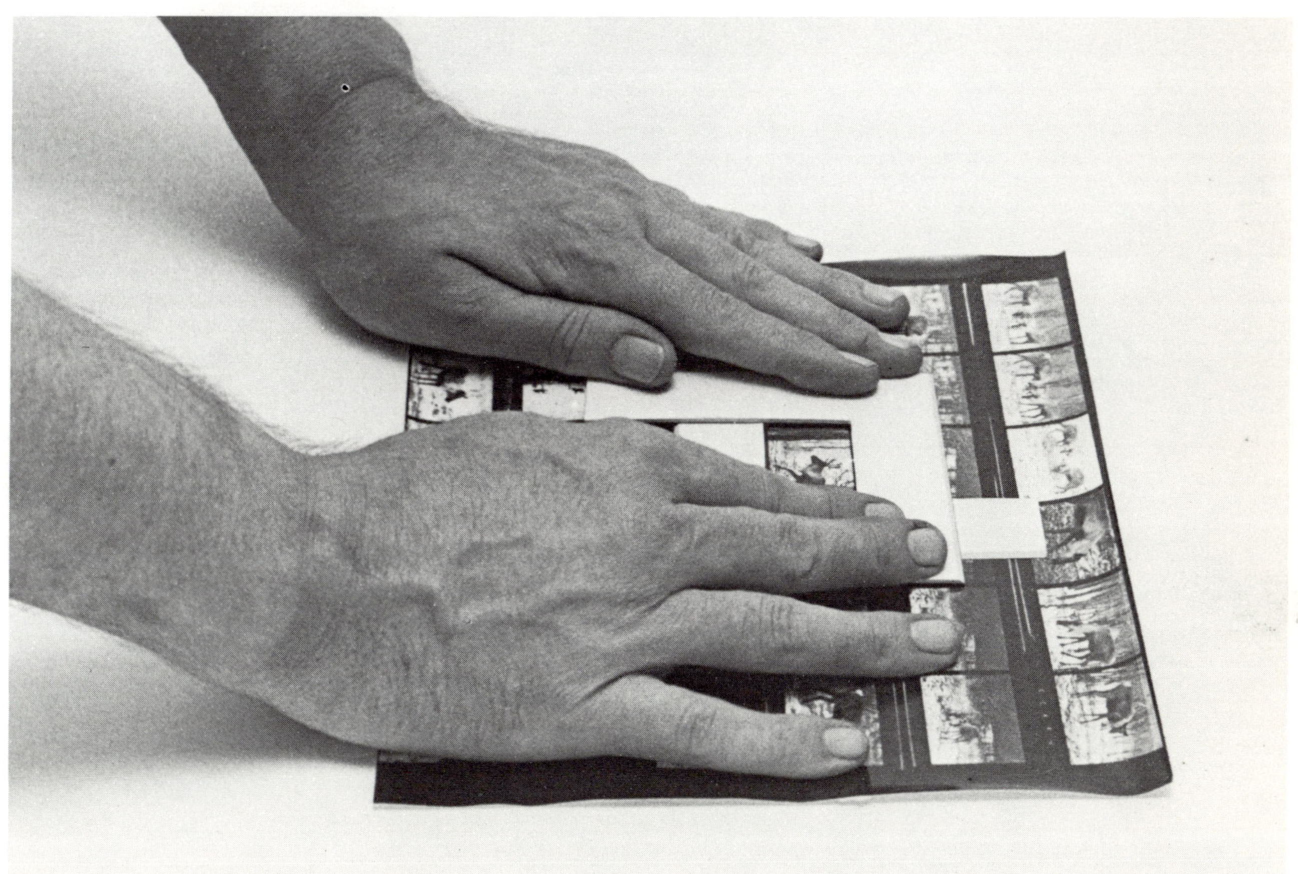

2. Cropping Ls are useful for examining contact sheets. They can isolate an individual frame from the rest and show you how a print will look with a different shape.

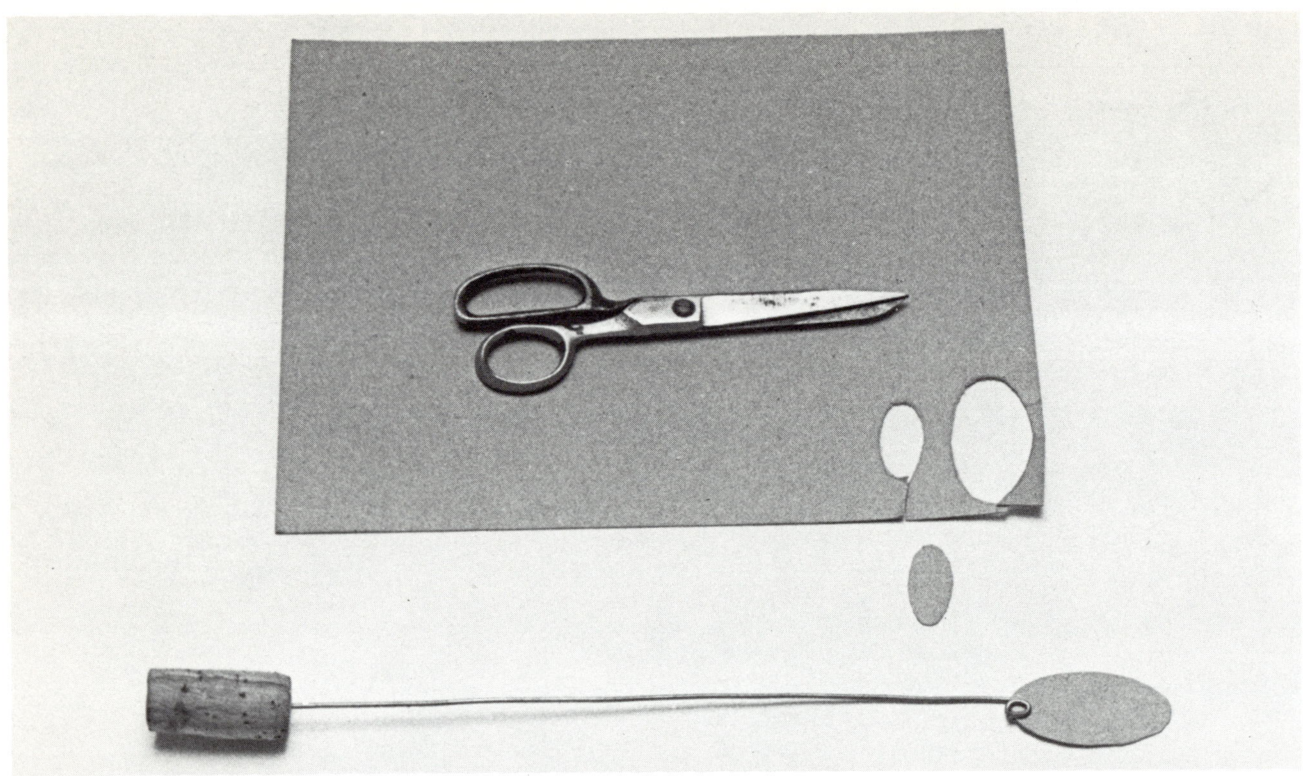

3. Two basic shapes will do for most dodging — a large (2″ [5.1 cm]) and a small (1″[2.5 cm]) oval. Keep thin cardboard and your scissors near the enlarger so additional shapes can be cut out as they are needed.

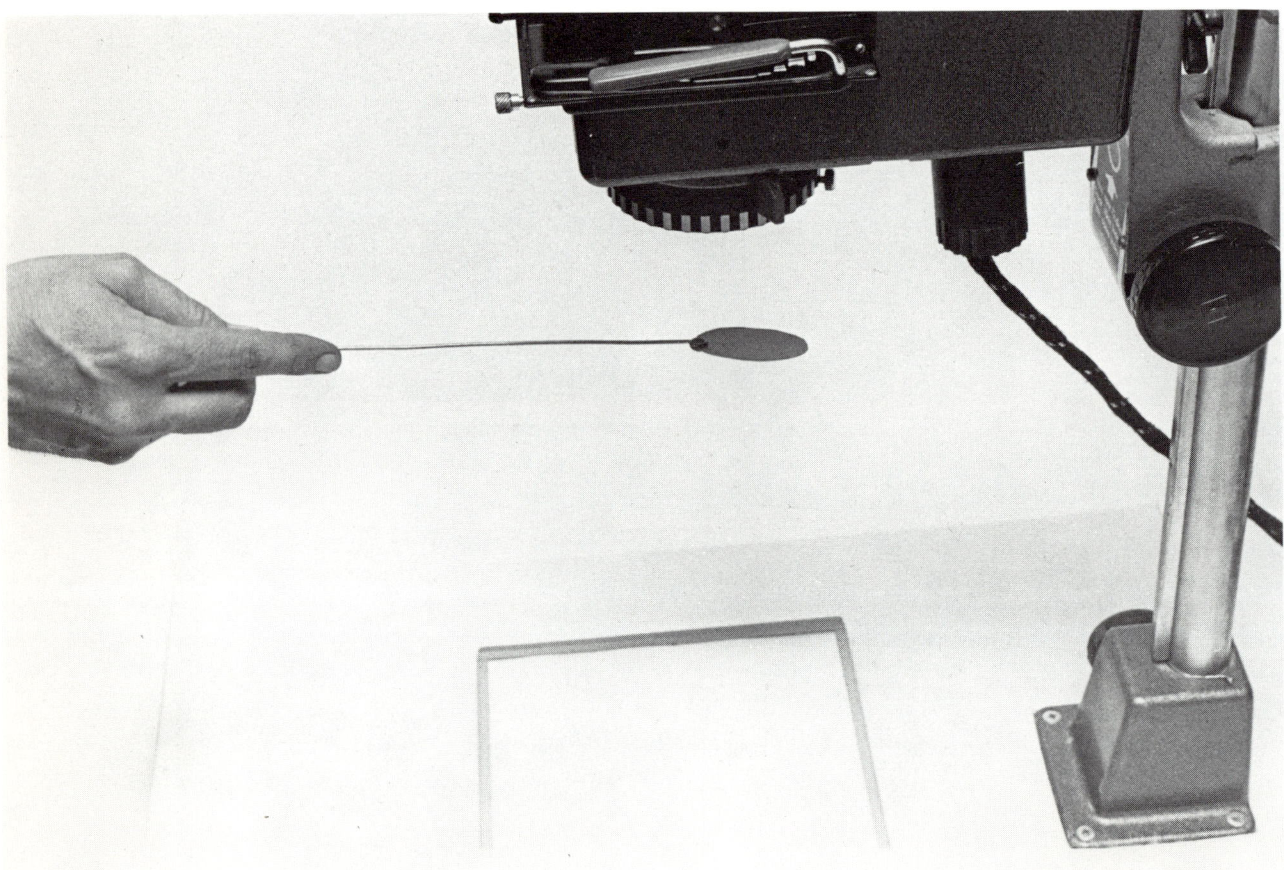

4. The dodging tool is positioned between the enlarging lens and the paper and keeps the light from striking the paper. Keeping the wire handle moving prevents it from forming a light line in the print.

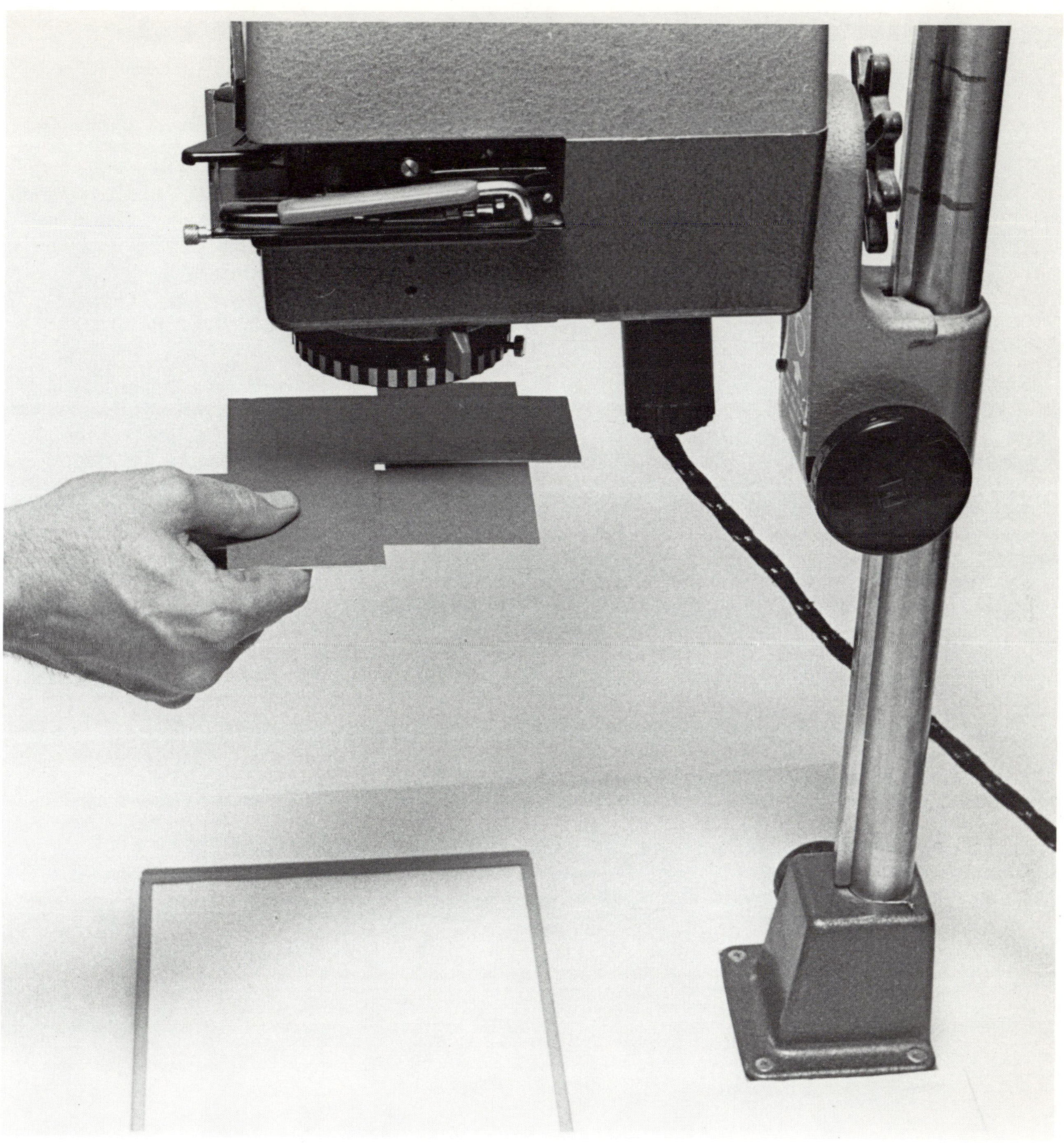

5. The wide pair of Ls makes an excellent burning tool. The cardboard can be positioned to make openings that are different sizes and shapes.

Quick and Easy Diffusion Screens

Almost everyone who prints his or her own photos has made diffusion screens by stretching some kind of fabric over a small frame. Forty years ago the favorite material was silk stockings. Thirty or so years ago nylon stockings were used. Today people cut up panty hose to make diffusion screens. I wonder if the trend will continue. In the distant future some new kind of leg covering may be used as a diffusion screen.

Small embroidery hoops have always been a popular means of stretching the fabric for diffusion screens. My wife started asking embarrassing questions about where hers were, so I had to find a quick substitute. The rimmed top from disposable plastic containers can be used instead. Margarine, ice cream, yogurt, and cottage cheese containers would all be of suitable size.

From one leg of the panty hose, cut a piece slightly larger than the container that you are going to use. Stretch the fabric across the mouth of the container and hold it in place with a rubber band. If the band seems too loose or too tight, try using another one. If you are using colored ones remember that different colors have a different amount of stretch.

After the rubber band is in place, stretch the fabric tight. Use some rubber cement to coat the rubber band and the fabric around the edge of the container. Set everything aside and let the glue dry. When dry, use the scissors to trim off the excess fabric and then use the razor knife to cut off the upper part of the plastic container. The diffusion screen is now ready to use.

Panty hose differ in amount of diffusion they provide. Flesh or nude shades will probably provide the least, while dark support hose provide the most. You can judge the amount of diffusion by just looking through the stretched fabric. Mount two or three different types of materials and give them a try in the darkroom to see which you like best.

Another favorite material for making diffusion screens is crinkled cellophane. Just crinkle and flatten the cellophane before adding it to the mouth of a plastic container with a rubber band and glue. Other found materials can also be used to make diffusion screens. Experiment to see which you like the best.

Diffusion screens can give a photo a romantic, misty look when used during the entire exposure. When used only for a part of the exposure, they can produce a more flattering portrait.

Another use for the diffusion screens is to smooth out the grain. In a 20-second exposure, for example, just use the screen for 3 seconds or so. This will mellow the grain with a minimal effect on the overall sharpness.

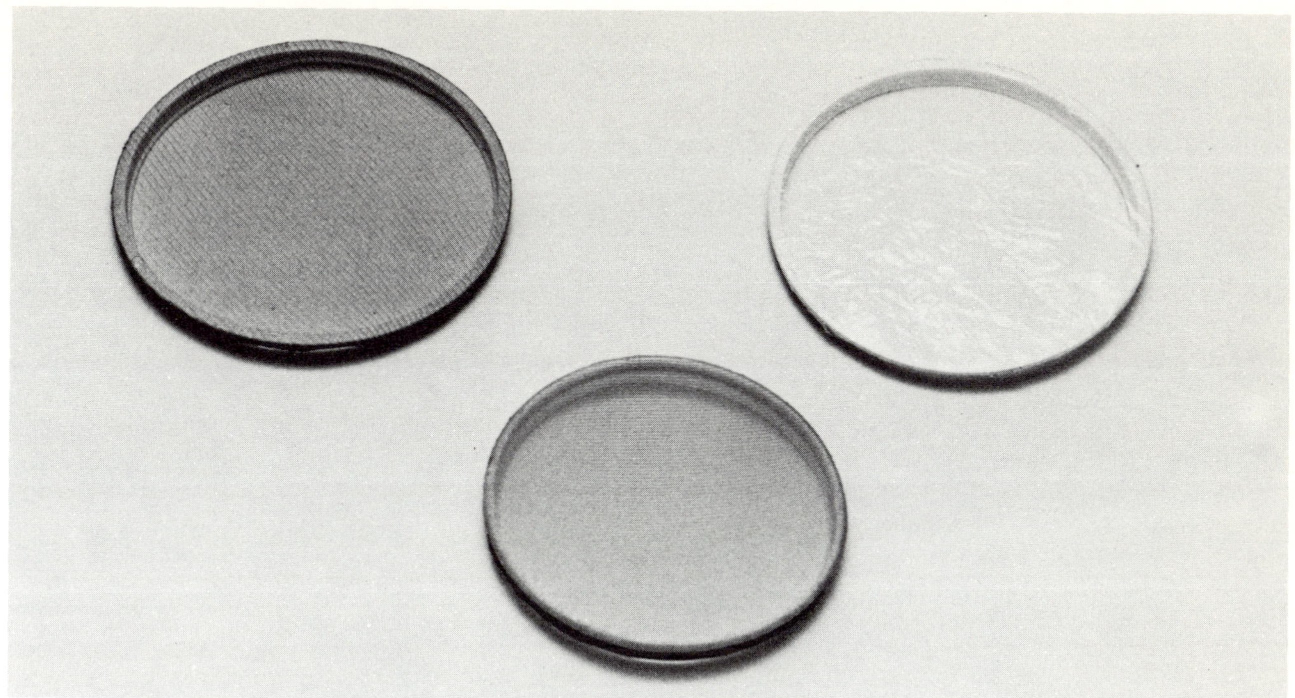

1. Excellent diffusion screens for enlarging can be made by stretching panty hose or crinkled cellophane over the rimmed top of a plastic container. The diffusion screen on the right was made with the cellophane.

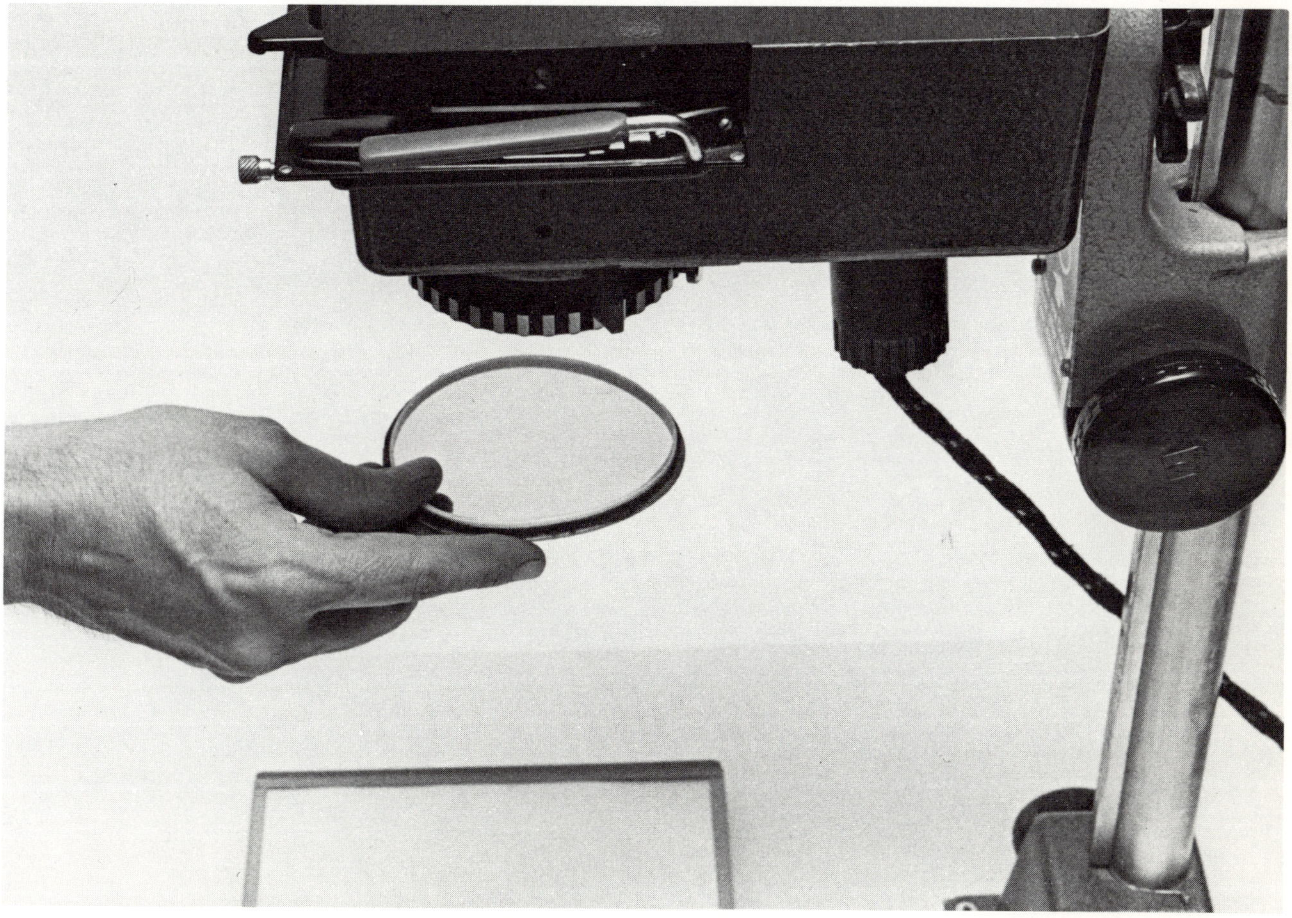

2. Using a diffusion screen during a part of the exposure can produce a wide range of different effects, everything from a romantic misty look to a subtle smoothing of the grain. Experiment with using the diffusers to see which produces the amount of softness you like best.

PART THREE

LIGHTING AND STUDIO ACCESSORIES

Light Stand with Adjustable Boom

MATERIALS

Plant pole or other tension pole
Dowel rod, 6' (1.8 m) long, 1" (2.5 cm) in diameter
6" × 6" × 1" (15.2 × 15.2 × 2.5 cm) hardwood board,
   or larger
4 "U" bolts, 1" (2.5 cm) with ¼" threads
9 wing nuts, ¼"
¼" hanger bolt
2 fender washers, ¼"
Scrap of leather
Solder (resin core 4 percent silver) or epoxy glue
Sandpaper, 180 grit or medium

TOOLS

Drill and bits
Round or half-round wood rasp
Saw
Pliers
Razor knife
Propane torch for soldering (optional)

Using a tension pole for a light stand has only one drawback — repositioning the lights is awkward. It would be nice to leave the pole in one place and still be able to get a variety of lighting effects. To make this possible, all that needs to be added to the tension pole is a boom. Professional photographers frequently use lighting stands with booms. Unfortunately professional stands are too expensive for the average photographer. When you build things for yourself, most of the expense is eliminated and it is possible to have the convenience of easy-to-position lights.

If the hardwood board is too large, cut it to a 6" (15.2 cm) square. I used oak, but other hardwoods would also work. A soft wood isn't suitable because it might crack under stress. Hardwood has a lot more strength and can withstand the pressure of the "U" bolts without cracking.

Position the "U" bolts on the wood block to allow for the following positions. Two vertically placed bolts attach the block to the tension pole. Horizontally placed bolts hold the boom at a right angle. Diagonally placed bolts allow the boom to be angled upward. The second photo shows the position of the holes to be drilled. Try to keep the holes about ½" (12.7 mm) from the edge of the wood. Drill 5/16" (7.9 mm) holes so that the "U" bolts will slip in and out easily.

After the holes are drilled, use a round or half-round wood rasp to make shallow grooves where the tension pole and boom will contact the wood. These grooves need to be only about 1/16" (1.6 mm) deep. They increase the area of contact between the dowel rods, tension pole, and wood. They are also needed because the "U" bolts aren't quite long enough. The removal of this small amount of wood makes the bolt

ends protrude just enough for easy attachment of the wing nuts. Metal braces come with the "U" bolts. These braces are used under the wing nuts and prevent the nuts from gouging the wood.

I used only four "U" bolts with the block of wood. The diagonal holes are usually empty, as they are only used when the boom needs to be positioned at an angle.

To prevent splinters, smooth the surfaces and edges of the wood block with sandpaper. Then set the block aside while you work on the boom.

Add a hanger bolt to the end of the boom. This bolt is half wood screw and half machine screw. The ¼" size will fit the threaded socket used for camera accessories. Drill a hole slightly smaller than the hanger bolt in the end of the dowel and about two-thirds as deep as the length of the bolt's wood screw portion. This hole prevents the wood from splitting. Screw in the bolt by using pliers to grasp the machine threads just above where the wood screw ends. This way you won't damage the important end of the machine threads.

A thumb nut (finger nut) fits the hanger bolt. This nut locks the electronic flash in the desired position. In many ways, it is like the tripod screw commonly used with photo accessories, but it has a female thread instead of a male thread. This allows it to be added to the bolt in the end of the boom.

A fender washer is a large washer with a small hole in the center. To make the thumb screw solder a wing nut to the washer. Add a leather pad to cushion the equipment. If you don't have a propane torch for soldering, you can attach the wing nut with epoxy (as in the pole clamp project).

Use a resin-core solder with a 4 percent silver content because it is much stronger than regular solder and only costs a little more. Find a fireproof place to work. Fire brick or asbestos pads are normally used for torch soldering but you can also use concrete, cinder blocks, brick, sand, or gravel, if they are dry. Position the wing nut on the washer, light the torch, and heat the washer and wing nut. Remove the flame from the metal and apply the solder to the edge of the nut. If the metal is hot enough, the solder should melt immediately on contact. Completely circle the wing nut with solder. Then turn off the torch and wait for the metal to cool.

When the metal is cool, punch a hole in a scrap of leather slightly larger than the washer. Glue the leather to the washer with silicone. It can be clamped in place with another washer and bolt. Wait until the silicone is dry and then use a razor knife to trim the leather to the size of the washer.

Now that all the parts are ready, your light stand can be assembled. Put up the tension pole and add the hardwood block. Tighten the wing nuts to hold the block in place. Use two more "U" bolts to attach the boom. Practice changing the position of the boom, raising and lowering it, and locking it into position. The wood block and "U" bolts form a strong connection between the tension pole and the boom, yet it is easy to change the boom's position.

Add an electronic flash to the hanger bolt using a tripod adapter on the base of the flash. The thumb nut allows you to lock the flash in the desired position. Using a small ball-and-socket head on the hanger nut makes aiming the flash even easier. You can also attach a clamp-on modeling light to the boom. A 100-watt bulb is bright enough to demonstrate to you the effect of the flash without changing the color balance of the photo.

If you place the tension pole in a central location, you can position the lights just about anywhere you might wish without having to move the pole. For a really complete lighting system, you might want to employ two lighting stands with booms.

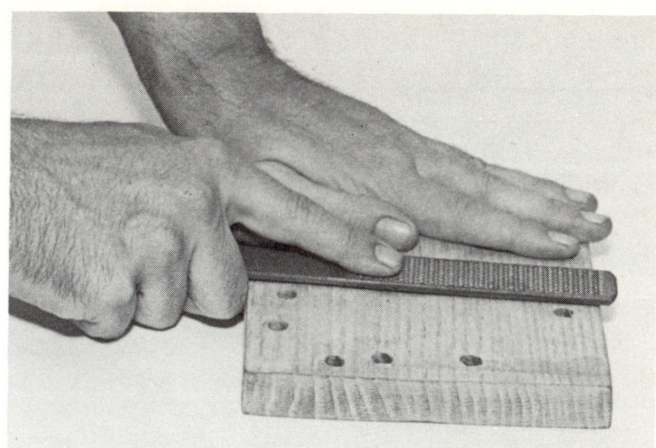

1. Make shallow grooves in the wood where the boom and tension pole will be placed. The grooves are required so that the "U" bolts will fit through the block.

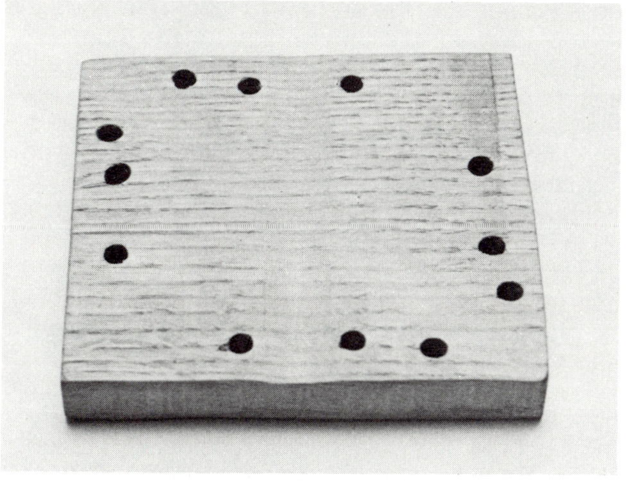

2. Drill holes in the hardwood for the "U" bolts. Twelve holes are positioned in this way so that the boom can be placed either horizontally or angled upward. Try to keep the holes ½" (12.7 mm) from the edge of the wood.

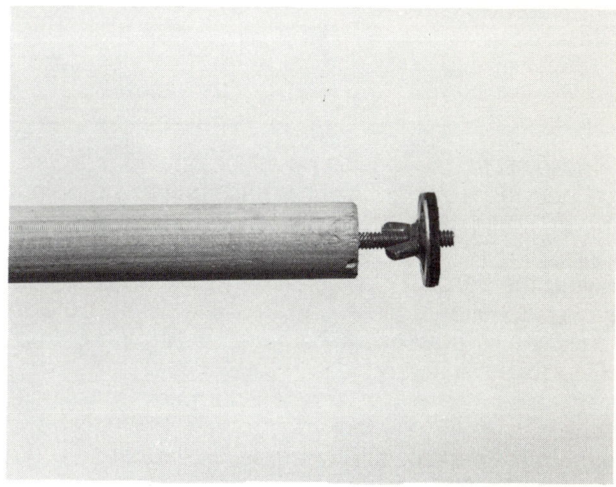

3. On the end of the dowel rod are a finger nut and a hanger bolt. The hanger bolt is half wood screw and half machine screw. The finger nut is made from a fender washer, a wing nut, and a leather pad. The hanger bolt, fender washers, and wing nuts can be purchased in any large hardware store.

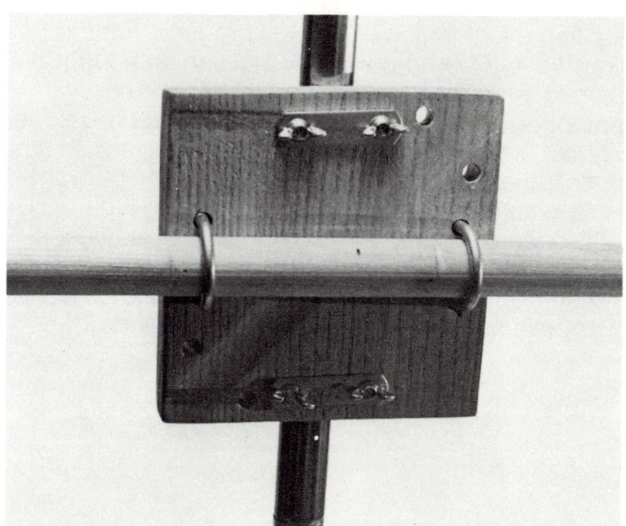

4. Attach the boom to the tension pole with "U" bolts. The hardwood block can hold the boom horizontally or at an angle. This method of attachment is very strong and stable.

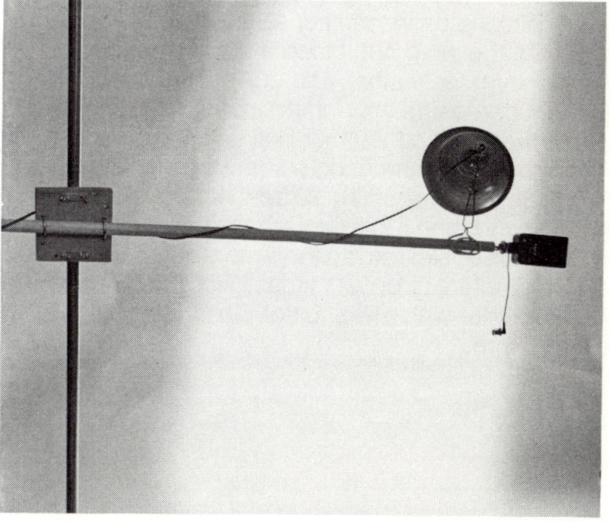

5. The lighting stand with boom makes it easy to change the position of the lights. A clamp-on light serves as a modeling light for the flash.

Pole Clamp for Cameras, Flash Units, or Lights

I wanted to use tension poles for lighting stands, so I needed a way to attach a flash unit to the pole. The best thing I could find was a 2″ (5.1 cm) No. 2 spring clamp, which is sold in hardware stores. Avoid buying the bargain clamps — they don't have enough tension in the spring. Test the clamp before you buy it by squeezing the handles. A good clamp will require considerable pressure to open the jaws.

A fender washer is a large washer with a small hole in the center. A well-stocked hardware store will have them in several sizes. Buy extras, as they are handy to have around.

Begin by making the thumb screw from the wing nut, fender washer, and a leather scrap. Cut a piece of leather larger than the washer and punch a hole in the center. Mix some epoxy and glue the wing nut to the washer. Apply the epoxy to the outside of the wing nut so you won't get any on the threads. Smear some silicone on the leather and glue it to the washer opposite the wing nut. Place a second fender washer over the leather, and bolt everything together. Set this part aside and let the epoxy dry.

Cut the head off another bolt using the hacksaw. Place the bolt in the handle of the clamp with about ¾″ (19.1 mm) protruding. Wrap the black wire around the bolt and then run it through the hole in the handle of the clamp. Next, wrap the wire around the outside of the handle a couple of times. Twist the ends of the wire together with pliers to tighten it, then cut off the excess wire.

Run the last bolt through the hole in the other handle and use a nut to keep it in place. Tighten the nut with a screwdriver and pliers.

Mix up some more epoxy and apply a generous amount inside the handle that has the wire and bolt. Also add some epoxy to the nut holding the other bolt to the handle. This will keep the nut from loosening. The epoxy is strong enough to hold the bolt to the handle, but the wire provides an extra amount of security. It can prevent an expensive flash unit from falling if the the glue joint should fail. A warm oven (150 F or 66 C) can be used to speed the drying. When the epoxy is applied very thick, as it is in this project, a quick-drying epoxy works best.

When the epoxy and silicone are dry, trim the excess leather from the pad with a razor knife. Add the thumb screw to a bolt on the clamp. The thumb screw lets you lock a flash unit in the desired position. I usually use a small ball-and-socket head on the clamp for greater flexibility. A tripod adapter is used on the base of the flash so it can be screwed onto the bolt or the ball-and-socket head.

The clamp is also strong enough to hold a camera. It can be used to clamp a camera to the leg of a tripod for low-level shooting or to a door or table for available-light shooting inside. Leather pads should be glued to the jaws of the clamp so it won't mar the surface.

Epoxy isn't the best way of adding the bolts to the handles of the clamp — it's just the easiest way for most people. The bolts could be soldered, brazed, or welded to the handles. These methods of attachment are much stronger than the glue, so wrapping the wire wouldn't be necessary. A welding shop would attach the bolts to the clamp for you at very little cost.

When using the tension pole and pole clamp with electronic flash, I need a modeling light to see the lighting effect that the flash will produce. For this light, I use a clamp-on variety that can be bought in a camera store or a hardware store and comes equipped with or without a reflector. If you have one without a reflector, you can use a floodlight bulb that directs the light with a built-in reflector. A 100-watt bulb is sufficient for use as the modeling light.

Two tension poles and two or three pole clamps are needed for more complex lighting arrangements. These clamps and the tension poles make up a complete and versatile set of lighting stands.

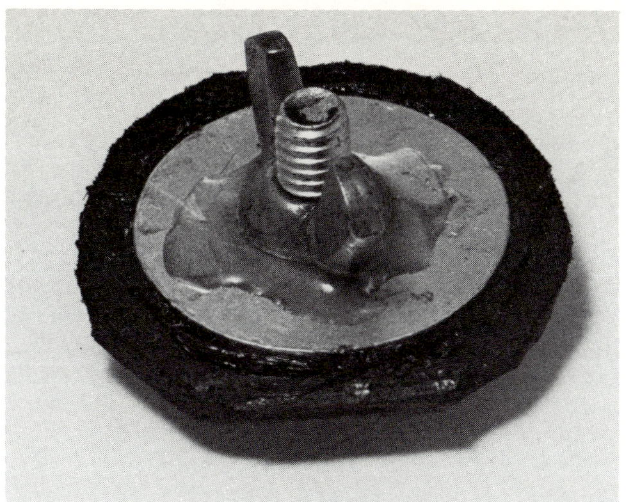

1. The thumb nut is made up of a wing nut and fender washer glued together with epoxy. A leather pad acts as a cushion and is glued to the washer with silicone. Trim the leather to size when the glues are dry.

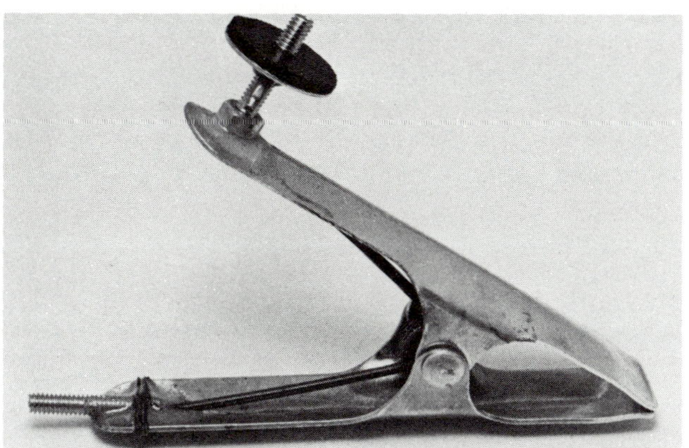

2. The pole clamp has a bolt added to each handle. One bolt is at a right angle to the handle and is held in place with a nut. The other bolt is first wired to the handle and then is glued with epoxy to hold it in place.

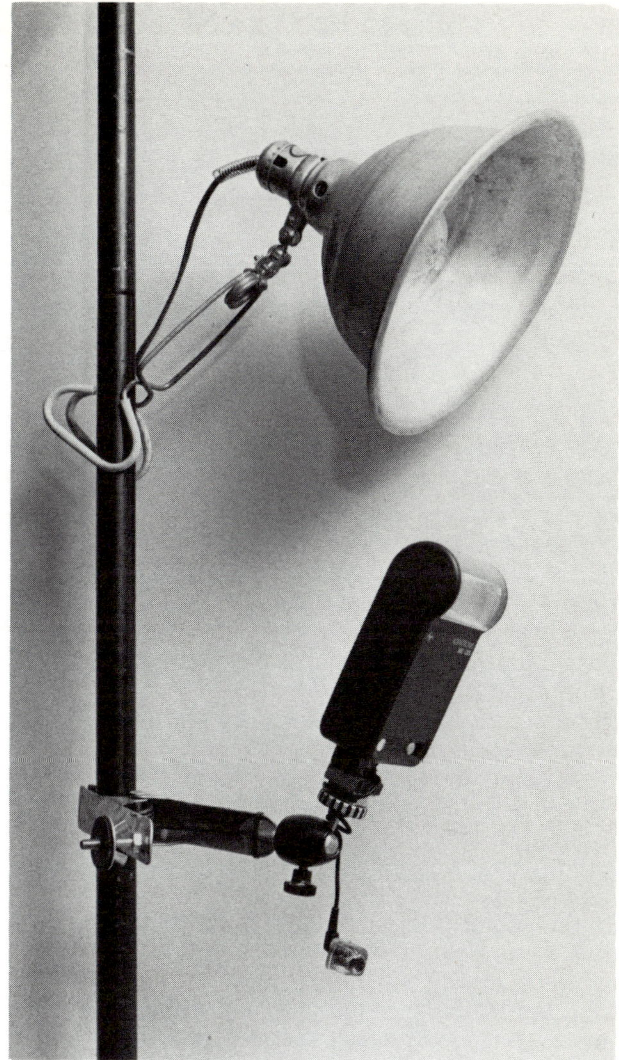

3. The pole clamp allows you to add an electronic flash to a tension-pole light stand. A small tripod head makes the clamp more flexible. A tripod adapter must be used on the base of the flash. A clamp-on light serves as a modeling light.

Panel for Soft Lighting Effects

In lighting, size counts—the larger the light source, the softer the light. The small diffusers, reflectors, and attachments usually used with electronic flash just can't produce truly soft light. This is why professionals use giant reflectors, diffusers, and photographic umbrellas when they want soft lighting. Unfortunately, the larger the equipment, the more expensive it is.

You can make an inexpensive lighting accessory that provides truly soft lighting. At a building supply store, buy a plain white fluorescent lighting panel. This 2' × 4' (0.6 × 1.2 m) sheet of flexible plastic is 1 mm thick and is normally used to soften the light from fluorescent tubes. Larger sheets of translucent plastic are also available.

The rope controls the shape of the plastic and provides a means of hanging it. Drill ⅛" (3 mm) holes in each corner of the sheet about ½" (12.7 mm) from the edge. Next make a pair of holes in the center of one side and another pair in the center of one end. These holes should be about 1" (2.5 cm) apart.

Run a 12' (3.7 m) piece of rope through the holes in the corners. Tie the ends of the rope together and cut off the excess. You might use the excess to make small rope loops and add them to the pairs of side and end holes. Nylon rope frays easily, so melt each end with a match to prevent it from fraying.

Bend the plastic sheet into a U-shape and pull up the slack from the long rope. Tie an overhand knot in the rope to hold the plastic in the U-shape. Turn the "U" over and place it on a table covered with seamless paper. Cut a piece of poster board the size and shape needed to fill the open ends of the plastic. Cut a hole for the camera's lens in one sheet of the poster board. Tape these ends in place with masking or gaffer's tape.

Now the plastic sheet can be used as a light tent. Objects inside the light tent will be completely surrounded by white. One or two electronic flash units aimed at the plastic from outside provide the light. The light tent provides the softest possible kind of lighting. This is an ideal way of photographing glassware and shiny metal objects.

Remove the poster board ends and loosen the rope a little to change the shape of the plastic from a "U" to an "L". Support the plastic between two chairs, using gaffer's tape to hold the plastic in place. Now you can use the plastic for a light table by aiming flash units at it from behind and below. A light table provides a shadowless white background. Color filters used over the flash units can render the plastic any color. Using this light table eases the problems of photographing glass and transparent plastic.

Untie the knot in the rope and let the plastic straighten. Hang the sheet of plastic from a tension pole or light stand and aim an electronic flash at it. Now the sheet can be used as a soft light for portraiture. The flash should be positioned so the light strikes the entire sheet. With the translucent plastic between the flash and the subject, the plastic becomes the source of the light. It's a large light source so the light it produces is very soft. Keep the subject close to the plastic for the softest possible effect.

The plastic can also be used as a substitute for a photographic umbrella. Bend the plastic into a U-shape and use the rope loop on the side to hang the plastic from a lighting stand, tripod, or tension pole. Aim a flash unit into the "U" and use the plastic as a reflector. This kind of use will provide lighting that is not quite as soft as the lighting from the flat sheet. It is more directional and intense.

Two, three, or four *f*-stops more exposure are required when using the plastic as opposed to direct flash. With a powerful electronic flash, this loss hardly matters. With smaller units, the light loss can be counteracted by using a high-speed film. Correct exposure is best determined by shooting a test roll or by using an electronic flash meter. Remember that the amount of light can always be increased by moving the plastic and the flash closer to the subject.

All of these different uses for the plastic will also work with incandescent light. The plastic has only a moderate tolerance for heat, so photo floods should be kept 2 to 3' (0.6 to 0.9 m) from the plastic. Frequently check the plastic to see how hot it's getting.

This plastic sheet is a very versatile lighting accessory. I've only mentioned the uses I've found—I'm sure that you'll find even more.

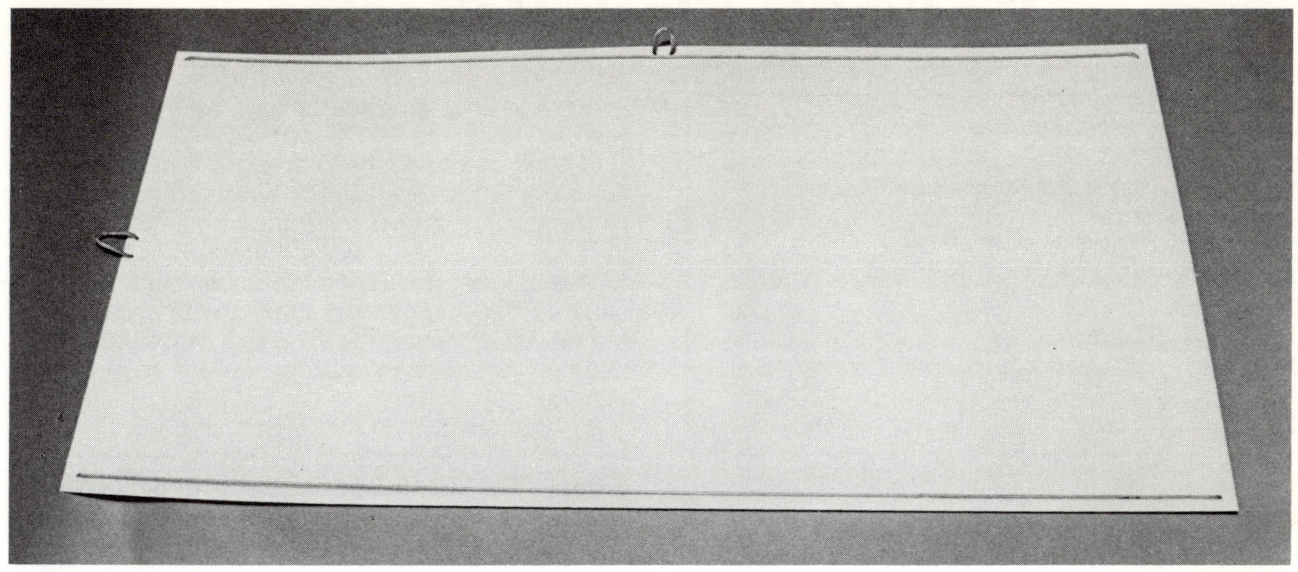

1. Thread a nylon rope through holes made in the corners of a plastic lighting panel. Add rope loops to one end and one side of the plastic. Adjusting the rope changes the shape of the plastic so it can be used as a lighting accessory.

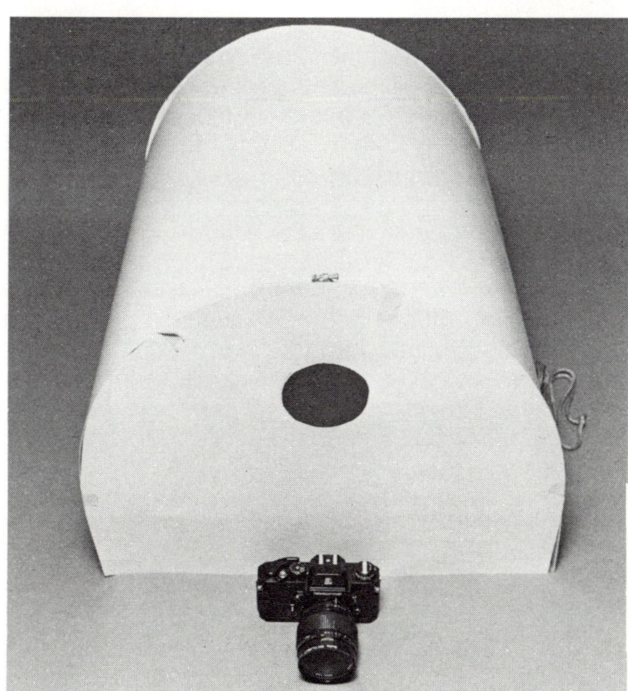

2. To make a light tent, bend the plastic into a U-shape, holding it in place with the rope, and tape white poster board to the ends. Cut a hole for the camera lens in one of the ends.

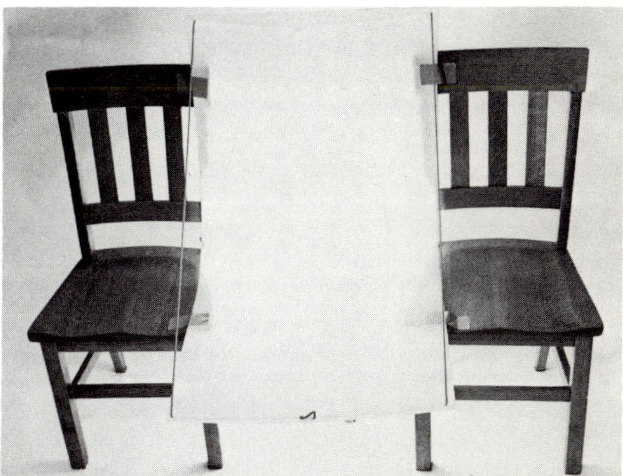

3. Use the rope to change the shape of the plastic to an "L" and support the plastic between two chairs. Hold it in place with gaffer's tape. Flash units aimed at the plastic from behind and below will provide a shadowless white background, which is ideal for photographing glassware and small objects.

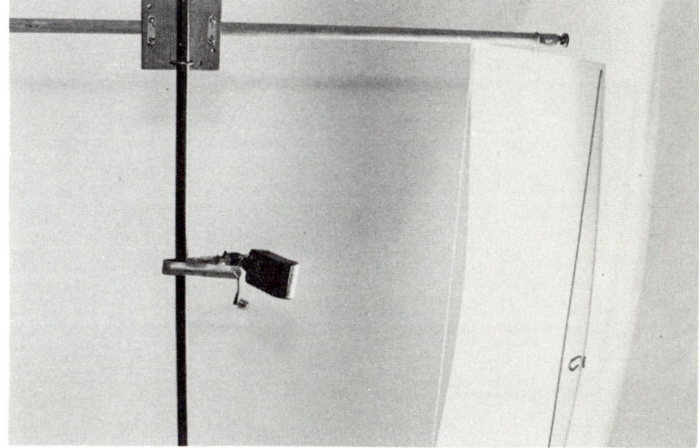

4. Here the tension pole is being used with a boom and the pole clamp to hold the plastic and the flash. This sheet of plastic is large enough to make an excellent reflector and transmits enough light so that it can also be used as a diffuser.

Washable Flash Reflector

MATERIALS

12″ × 24″ (30.5 × 35.6 cm) opaque white plastic,
   1 mm thick
1″ (2.5 cm) wide black elastic, 12″ long
Black thread

TOOLS

Razor knife
Needle or sewing machine

Bounce lighting is usually done by bouncing the light of the flash from ceilings or walls. But often the ceiling and walls aren't white (the necessary color) or they aren't in the correct location. A flash reflector that is mounted on the flash is like having a wall that you can carry with you—a portable means of providing a soft light from an electronic flash. The light from the flash is bounced from the reflector to the subject. The reflector becomes the light source and because of its larger size, the light is softer.

Many photographers make flash reflectors from a mat board cutout leftover from matting a print. Unfortunately the mat board reflector quickly gets dirty and has to be replaced.

A better material for the reflector is opaque plastic. Unlike the mat board, if the plastic gets dirty, it can be washed. Sheets of opaque white plastic can be bought at either a plastic dealer or at a hobby shop that sells model-making supplies. It's important that the plastic be opaque so most of the light will be reflected and none of it wasted by going through the plastic. Buy a sheet at least 12″ × 14″ (30.5 × 35.6 cm) and 1 mm thick. This is enough for a medium-sized flash reflector. Both larger and smaller reflectors can be made, if you wish.

Cut the plastic to the shape shown and then cut two slots for the elastic. The slots should be 1″ (2.5 cm) apart and 1″ long. Insert the elastic through the slots and wrap it around the flash unit to find the length needed for a correct fit. Allow an extra inch for the overlap; then cut the elastic. Sew the elastic ends together. You can use a sewing machine or sew the elastic by hand in several minutes.

Put the reflector on the flash and make a slight bend in it so the plastic is angled over the flash window. This way the entire light output of the flash will strike the reflector. If the reflector isn't bent, a large portion of the light would miss it.

If your flash unit has a wide-angle attachment, use it with the reflector. This attachment will ensure that the light strikes the largest possible area of the reflector.

Determine the correct exposure by shooting a test roll and establishing a new guide number for the flash with reflector. This process is described in many photography books, but I'll give a brief description here. Take test photos from a set distance and keep a record of the *f*-stops used. Bracket your exposures widely. It's best to use a color slide film, as it has less latitude than black-and-white and color print films. Check the slides and find the one that has the best exposure. Multiply the *f*-stop by the distance—this is a guide number for the flash with reflector. For more information on how to find and use guide numbers, consult the Kodak publications *Exposure with Portable Electronic Flash Units*-AC-37 and *Kodak Master Photoguide*-AR-21 and the *Amphoto Guide to Flash Photography.*

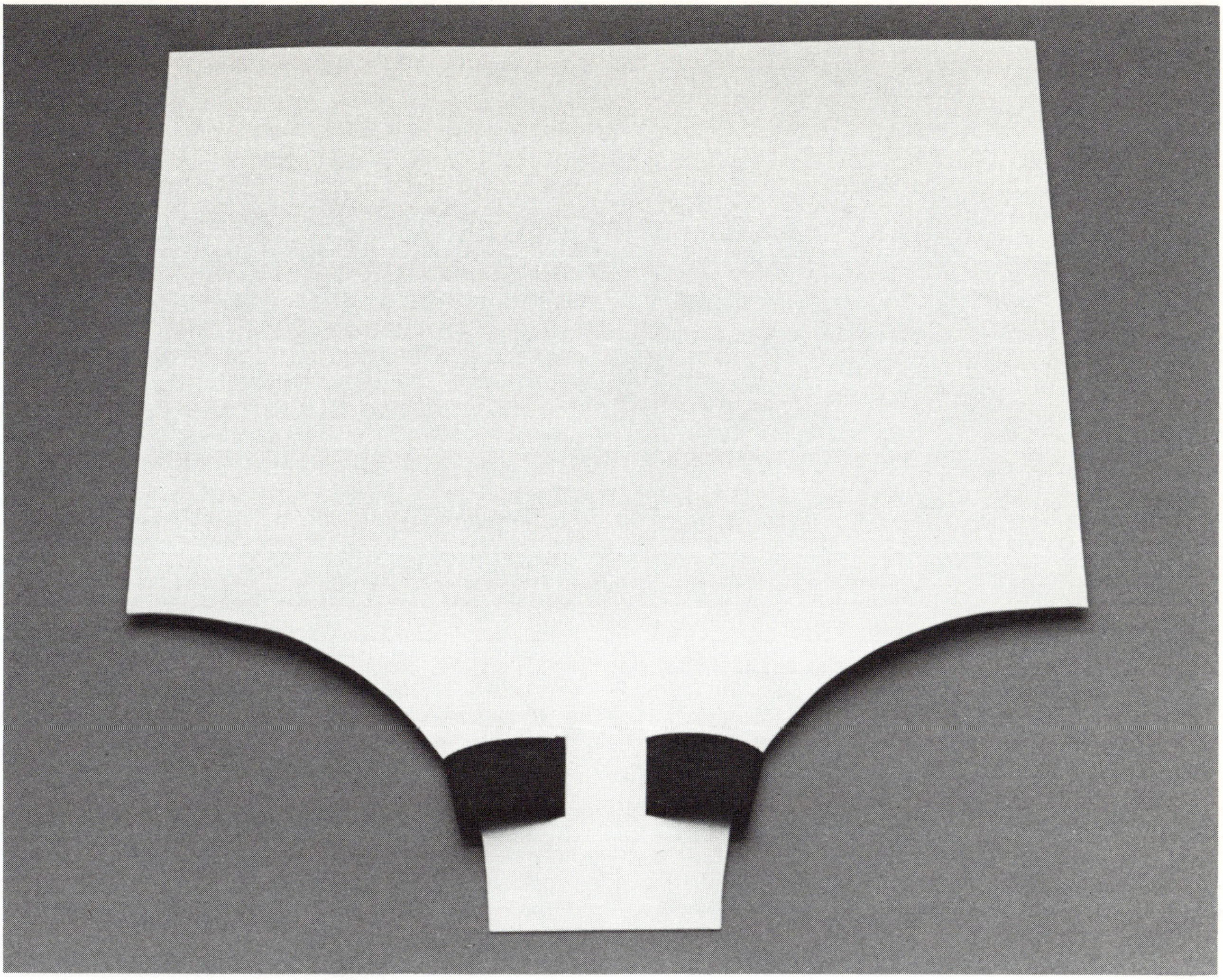

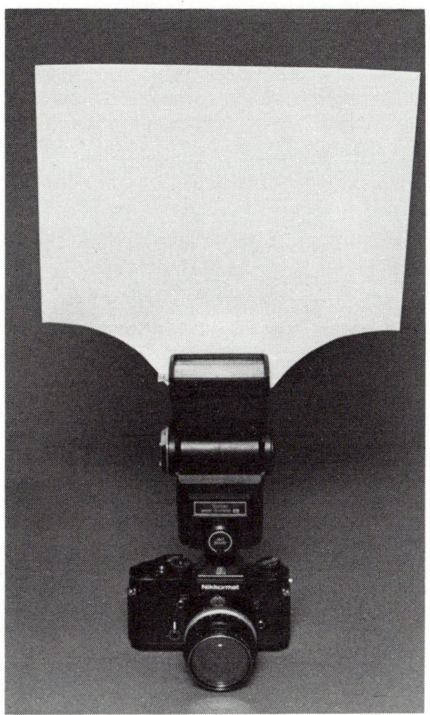 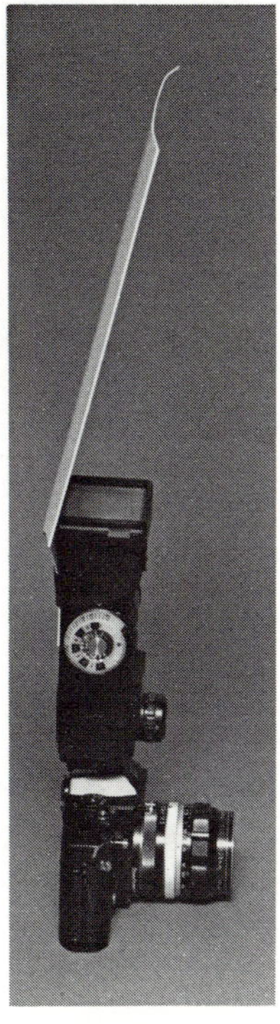

1. Above. A sheet of plastic shaped like this makes an excellent reflector for your flash. It is held in place with a 1″ (2.5 cm) wide elastic strip. The ends are inserted through the slits in the plastic and then sewn together.

2. Left. This is a medium-sized reflector. Larger or smaller ones can be made — the larger the reflector, the softer the lighting. Attach it to your flash with the elastic band. This type of reflector softens the light and is excellent for close-up portraits. Bend the plastic so all the light from the flash will strike its surface. Curve the plastic a little to strengthen it. A similar reflector could be made from mat board.

Oversized Reflector for Group or Full-length Portraits

A reflector is an easy way to provide fill light. It can fill in, or lighten, the shadows created by the main light and so keep contrast low. To work properly, a reflector should be placed close to the subject, just out of view of the camera. For best results, it should be about the same size as the subject. For a tightly framed portrait it could be small or medium sized, but for a full-length or group portrait it must be very large.

For a very large reflector to be practical, it must be inexpensive, easy to make, and easy to store. The one in this project is all of these things. The frame is made like a kite and can be set up and taken down easily. For storage, the reflecting sheet is rolled around the rods that are used for support. The cost to make it was only about $8.00.

An excellent light reflector is aluminized plastic film. This can be found in the sporting goods section of most stores in the form of a disposable emergency blanket, also called a space blanket. These blankets are made from a very tough, thin plastic film, and are available in gold and silver. If you shop around a bit, you may be able to find one with both a gold and a silver side. This would be ideal for a light reflector. The sporting goods department also sells plastic grommets for canvas and plastic sheets. The grommets are used to prevent the corners of the plastic sheet from tearing.

Begin by making the X-shaped center bracket that is used to hold the dowel rods. Cut two 6" (15.2 cm) lengths of pipe. If you use a tubing cutter, it will make a rim inside of the pipe. This rim will

have to be removed either with a file or with the triangular flaring tool found on some tubing cutters. This removal is necessary so that the dowel will fit inside the pipe.

Use a hammer to flatten the center of both pipe pieces so they will bolt together better. Next use the hammer and center punch to punch the location for the holes. Drill a ¼" (6.4 mm) hole through the middle of each pipe. Run the bolt through the holes and tighten the pipes together with the regular nut. Add a ¼" connecting nut on top of the regular nut. A connecting nut is simply an extra long nut and can be bought in most well-stocked hardware stores. This nut is used to attach the reflector to a tripod.

If you plan to use the reflector with a lighting stand that has a different size of thread, use bolts and nuts that will fit the stand.

Set aside the pipes and begin working on the plastic film. Unfold the plastic and lay it out on the floor. The folds will stay in the plastic, but they won't affect its use as a reflector. Add two short pieces of gaffer's tape to each corner of the plastic, one in front and one in back. The tape strengthens the film. In each corner, cut a hole the size required and add the two-part grommets. Then set the grommets by pounding on them with a hammer. Add a rubber band to each grommet by tying a slip knot.

Next, saw the dowel rods to the size you need. It is best to lay the dowel and pipe frame on the plastic and mark the required length on the dowel because the plastic may not be exactly the size marked on the package. After you have cut the dowels, saw a shallow notch in the end of each dowel. The notch will help when attaching the rubber bands.

Attach the plastic to the frame by making a slip knot in the rubber band, slipping it around the dowel, then putting the band into the notch cut in the end. The band tension can be adjusted to stretch the plastic and keep it as flat as possible. Use the connecting nut to attach the "kite" to the tripod or lighting stand. The reflector can also be supported with a tension pole, using the pole clamp made in another project.

The full-size (80" × 52" or 203.2 × 132.1 cm) may be larger than you want or need. The plastic can be cut to a smaller size to make a smaller "kite" and the leftover plastic can be glued to cardboard to make other reflectors. This giant reflector softens the light from a single flash unit or photo flood. It increases the lighting possibilities and lets you create professional-looking lighting.

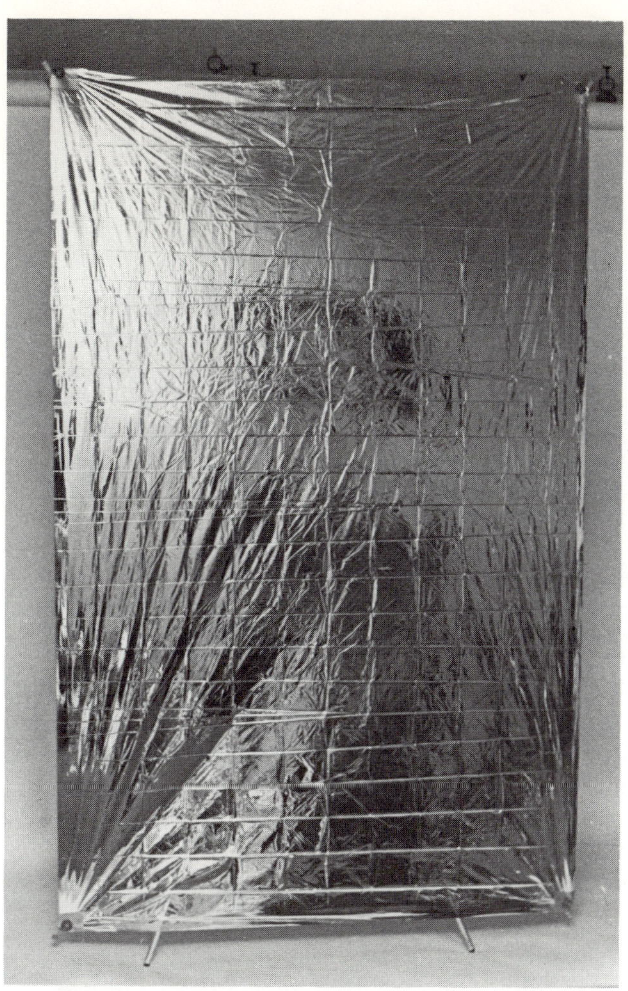

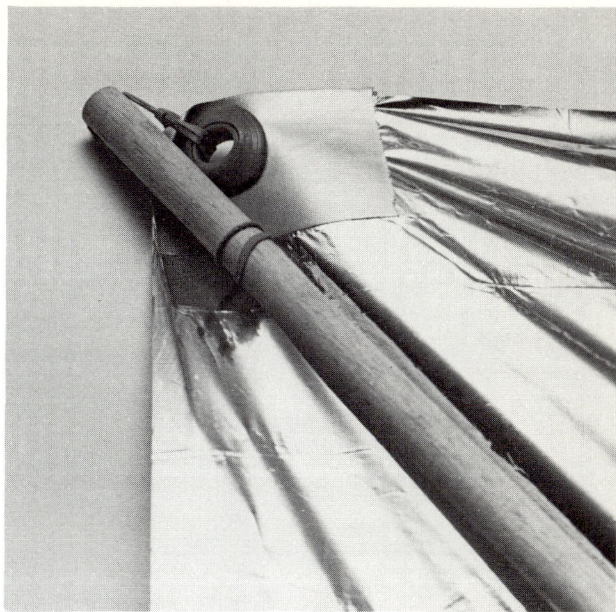

1. Left. It's easy to make a giant reflector like this one. Stretch a disposable emergency blanket on a dowel rod frame — like making a kite.

2. Above. Reinforce each corner of the plastic on both sides with gaffer's tape, then add plastic grommets. Use rubber bands to attach the plastic blanket to the dowel rods, which have grooves sawed in the ends.

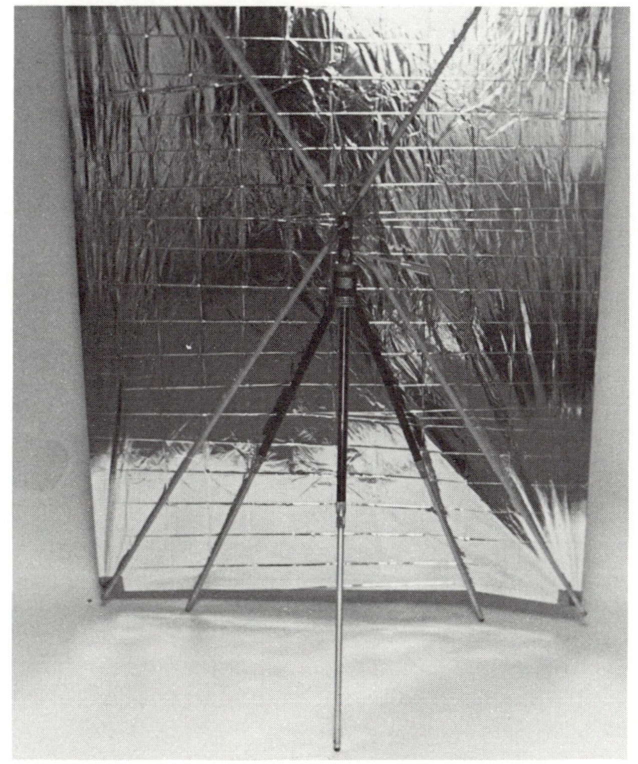

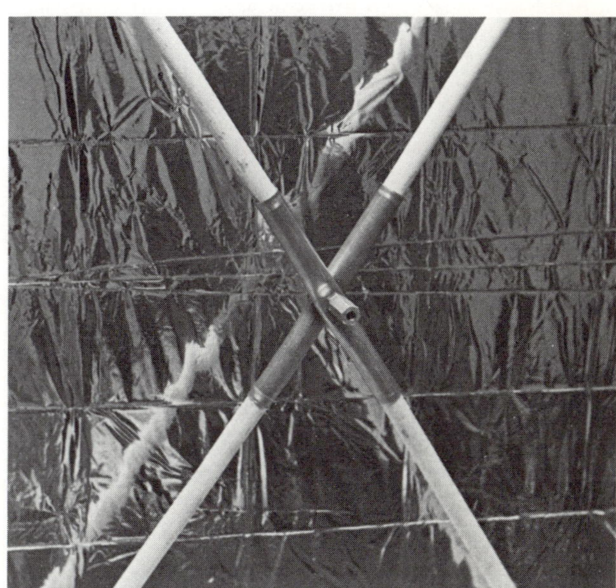

3. Above. The center bracket is two pieces of copper pipe bolted together. A connecting nut allows the bracket to be attached to a tripod or lighting stand.

4. Left. This is the rear of the reflector and its stand. A lightweight tripod or lighting stand can hold it easily. Or, if you wish, it can also be positioned with a pole clamp and tension pole.

Half-Ring Flash for Natural Lighting in Macrophotography

MATERIALS

Frig-O-Seal Mini Food Savers
Margarine or other white translucent plastic container
Aluminum foil
Black flocked paper or flat black paint
¾" (19.1 mm) black elastic, 12" (30.5 cm) long
Black thread
Clear silicone cement

TOOLS

Razor knife
Scissors
Needle or sewing machine

A ring flash provides soft lighting for close-up and macrophotography. Ring flashes are designed for use by doctors, dentists, and scientists to provide a shadowless lighting for medical and scientific illustration. This soft lighting isn't very dramatic, so when the ring flash is used for close-ups of flowers, insects, and other small subjects, nonscientist photographers frequently use black tape to cover a portion of the flash. This changes the lighting, making it uneven, directional, and much more natural in appearance.

There is a contradiction here. Manufacturers make the ring flash to provide perfectly even, flat lighting and then the photographers subvert all their efforts, using tape to make the lighting uneven. This is because the real advantage of a ring flash isn't the flat, shadowless lighting. Its ease of use and the location on the lens front are the real advantages of the ring flash for most photographers.

A half-ring flash has all the advantages of a regular ring flash and it produces natural-looking lighting. A half-ring that goes around the top of the lens mimics the light from an overcast sky. The little light that comes out of the bottom acts as fill light, which minimizes contrast. A half-ring flash makes more sense than a regular ring flash that has to have part of its light blocked off with tape.

If you have a small flash unit, you can make a half-ring flash for a couple of dollars. Small flash units are frequently on sale for less than $10.00. So even if you have to buy a flash, the cost of the project is much less than the cost of a ring flash.

I used plastic refrigerator jars for the ring parts. These small containers (Frig-O-Seal Mini Food Savers) fit snugly around the outside of my macro lens so a special mounting ring isn't needed. Your lens may have a different diameter, so find a plastic container that fits. A plastic drinking glass, caps from spray cans, or other plastic containers may work for you. With a little searching, you should be able to find something the right diameter. As a last resort, an adapter ring for your lens can be glued to the plastic to make a mount.

The largest container from the set will become the outside ring. The margarine or other white translucent plastic container is used to make a diffuser, which softens the light from the flash.

Begin by cutting the bottom from the small container. The plastic is quite stiff and a little hard to cut. Don't try cutting all the way through on the first cut. Scribe a line where you wish to make the cut and then go over the line another time or two with the knife. Now the plastic should be easy to cut through. A regular razor knife works best to make the small circular cuts. The special plastic cutting knives are for cutting straight lines.

Using the top of the small container as a pattern, mark a circle on the bottom of the large container. Cut along the circle, staying inside the marked line. Test the fit of the small container inside the large one. If need be, shave off more plastic to get a tight fit. Thin shavings can be cut from the edge of the plastic with a single stroke of the razor knife.

Position the flash unit on the outside of the large container to determine where you want to mount it. Cut an opening for the flash window in the side of the container. If your flash is irregular in shape like mine is, cut an opening that is too small and enlarge it a little at a time until the flash fits tightly inside.

After the opening is made, cover the outside of the small ring and the inside of the large ring with aluminum foil. Use silicone to glue the foil in place and the two rings together. To soften the light, add a diffuser to the top of the rings. Cut this from the bottom of the margarine container. Trace around the outside of the large ring to mark the outside curve and around the inside of the inner ring for the smaller curve. Cut a half-doughnut shape from the white translucent plastic and glue it inside the upper part of the rings with silicone. The silicone can be dried in the oven if you keep the temperature low (150 F or 66 C). If the oven is too warm, the plastic will melt. If you dry the silicone at room temperature, allow it to set overnight.

I lined the inside of the inner ring with a black flocked paper. This ring acts as a lens hood and the paper is an excellent material for eliminating reflections. A flat black paint could be used instead if you have trouble locating the flocked paper. This paper is sometimes available in craft shops, art supply shops, or can be bought from Edmund Scientific Products in the United States or Efstonscience Inc. in Canada.

Hold the flash against the rings and wrap the elastic around the flash unit and rings to find the length needed. The elastic should fit snugly, but not so tightly that it bends the plastic. Allow 1" (2.5 cm) of overlap, then cut the elastic, sewing the ends together. The sewing can be done with needle and thread or with a sewing machine.

Attach the flash to the rings and test fire the flash to see how the rings work. The flash is best observed by watching its reflection in a window. The light bounces around inside the light chamber and is emitted as a neat ring of light, brighter at the top than at the bottom. The half-ring flash can be rotated on the lens to create top right, top left, or straight top lighting, all with some fill light from the bottom of the rings.

With a 55mm macro lens, the rings vignette (darken at the corners) when the subject is farther than 4′ (1.2 m) away. This doesn't really matter since the ring flash is intended for much closer shooting. The vignetting doesn't happen when the flash is used on a 90mm lens.

You will have to determine a new guide number for the half-ring flash. Shoot a test roll of color slide film, keeping a record of the *f*-stop used and the distance from the flash to the subject. Bracket your exposures widely. Find the guide number by multiplying the *f*-stop by the distance. Since the half-ring flash is used very close to the subject, it's best to calculate the guide number in inches or centimeters rather than in the normal feet or meters.

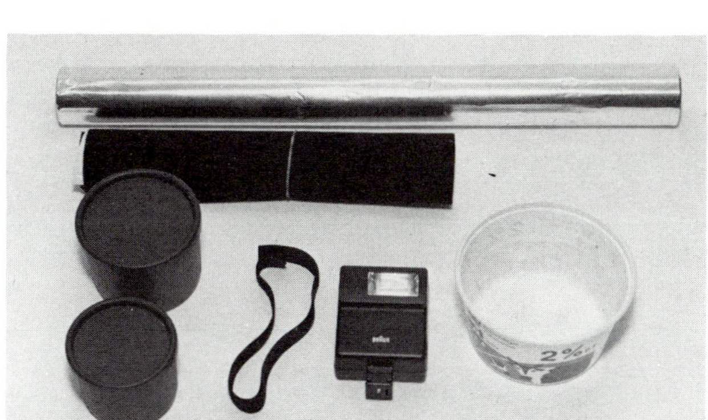

1. To make the half-ring flash, you'll need a small electronic flash unit, elastic band, two different diameters of plastic containers, black flocked paper, aluminum foil, and white plastic from a container — and of course silicone to hold everything together.

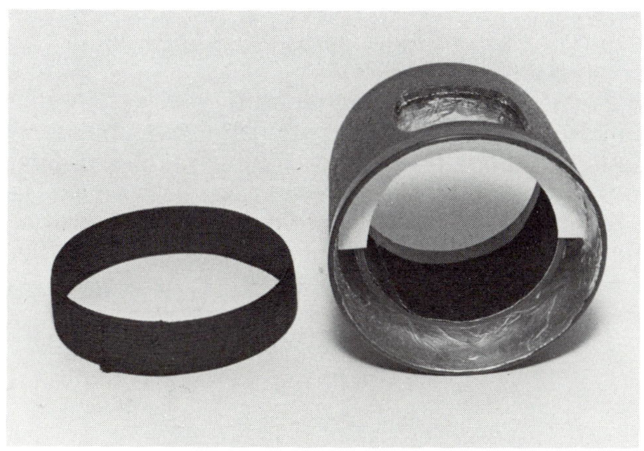

2. Make the light chamber from two sizes of plastic cylinders and line it with aluminum foil. The inside of the smaller cylinder acts as a lens hood, so it is lined with black flocked paper to eliminate reflections.

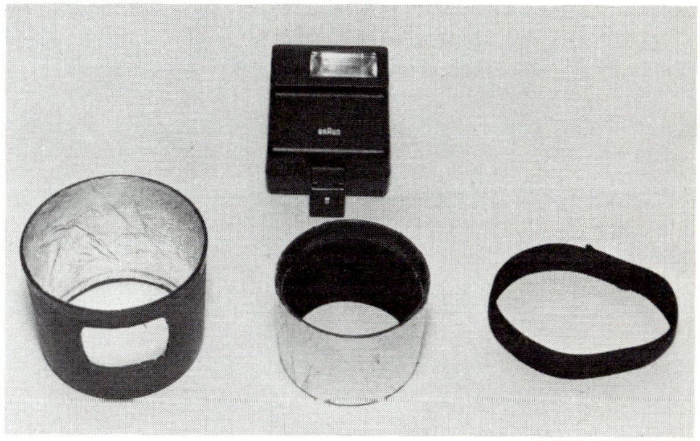

3. Glue the half-doughnut shape of white translucent plastic in position with silicone. It softens the light and makes it more even. Attach the flash unit with the elastic band.

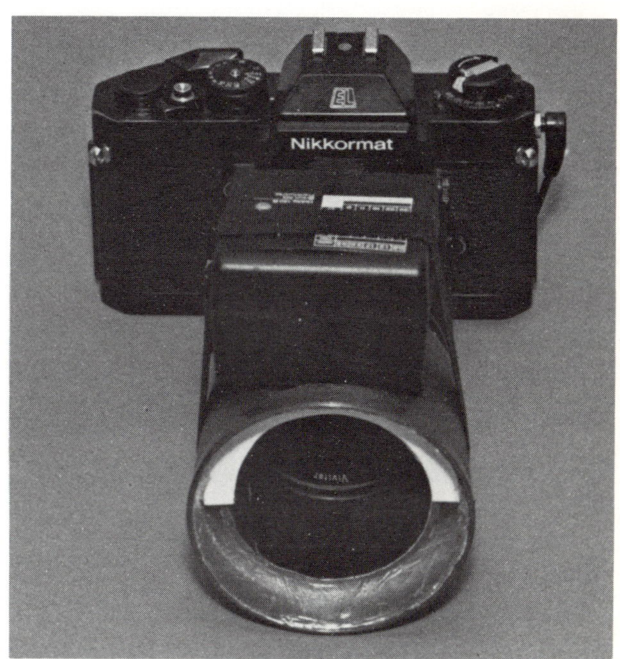

4. When mounted on a macro lens, the extra length of the ring flash will darken the corners of the photo if the lens is focused on a subject more than about a meter away. Since the ring flash is meant for use with much closer subjects, this doesn't matter. This darkening won't happen when the flash is used on a non-macro lens or one of longer focal length. Calculate a new guide number for the ring attachment using inches or centimeters, since the flash will be used very close to the subject.

Colored Filters for Flash

MATERIALS

Book of 44 color filters, 1" × 4" (2.5 × 10.1 cm)
Report cover with plastic clamp
Plastic cement or silicone cement
Transparent tape

TOOLS

Razor knife or heavy-duty scissors

Systems are popular these days—camera systems, enlarger systems, and flash systems. *System* is an advertising word for all the things that you can buy to add onto the basic piece of equipment. With many popular electronic flash systems, color filters that can be added to the flash are part of the system. These are expensive pieces of plastic that usually only come in three or four colors and are used for special effects.

You can add filters to any electronic flash very easily, for less cost, *and* have a larger variety of colors. A good source for these filters is Edmund Scientific in the United States and Efstonscience Inc. in Canada. Each sells a book of 1" × 4" (2.5 × 10.2 cm) filters, in 44 different colors, for less than $5.00. These filters are also available in larger sizes as is a booklet on spectral absorption curves for the filters.

Before ordering a book of filters, measure your electronic flash (window) reflector to see if it is small enough to be covered by a single filter. Most small units have a reflector that is easily covered with a portion of the 1" wide filter. Medium and large units may present a problem. Many medium-sized flash units have a window that can be covered with a 2" × 2" (5.1 × 5.1 cm) filter, made by cutting the 1" filter in half and taping the two pieces together with cellophane tape. Very large flash units have windows too large to be covered with a single filter. You will have to buy two books of filters and use transparent tape to tape two filters together to cover the window. Butt the edges closely together. This is less expensive than buying the larger filters.

Once you have the filters, the flash unit can be modified to hold them by the addition of a small filter holder. Report covers have a plastic clamp along the edge that holds the paper in place. This plastic clamp is sold separately in office supply stores. You can buy the entire report cover in almost any store that has school supplies.

Cut a piece of the plastic clamp the size needed for your flash. The plastic can be cut with heavy-duty scissors or a razor knife. Glue the clamp to the flash with plastic cement or silicone. Manufacturers are not very understanding about even such a simple modification as this, and may consider it voiding the warranty. You may wish to wait until the equipment is no longer under warranty to make this change.

Small pieces of the filter are rigid enough to stay in place just using the clamp. Large pieces of filter may need additional support. This can be provided by cutting a piece from a clear report cover. Cut this portion from the folded edge so that the double thickness of clear plastic can be used with the clamp to hold the filters in place.

If 44 colors aren't enough variety, you can combine filters to create new colors. Using three filters together can produce almost 80,000 possible combinations.

Exposure is best determined by experimentation. But as a rule you can open the lens a half stop for the light colors, one stop for the medium colors, and two stops for the darker colors. This would be a good starting point for bracketing your exposures. These filters are a lot of fun to use, even with a single flash unit. But the real fun begins when you use filters with multiple flash.

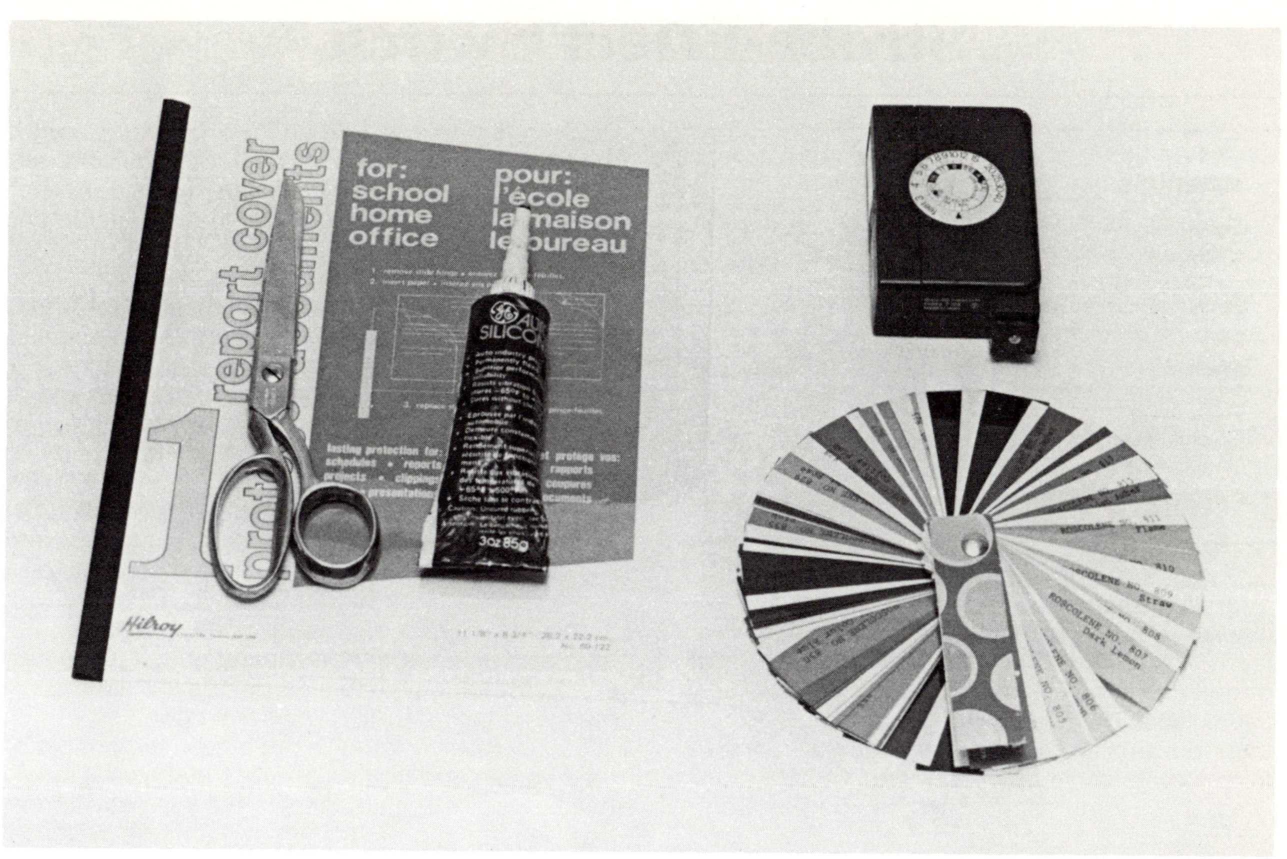

1. This is what you need to make flash filters: a book of plastic filters, a report cover, silicone, and scissors.

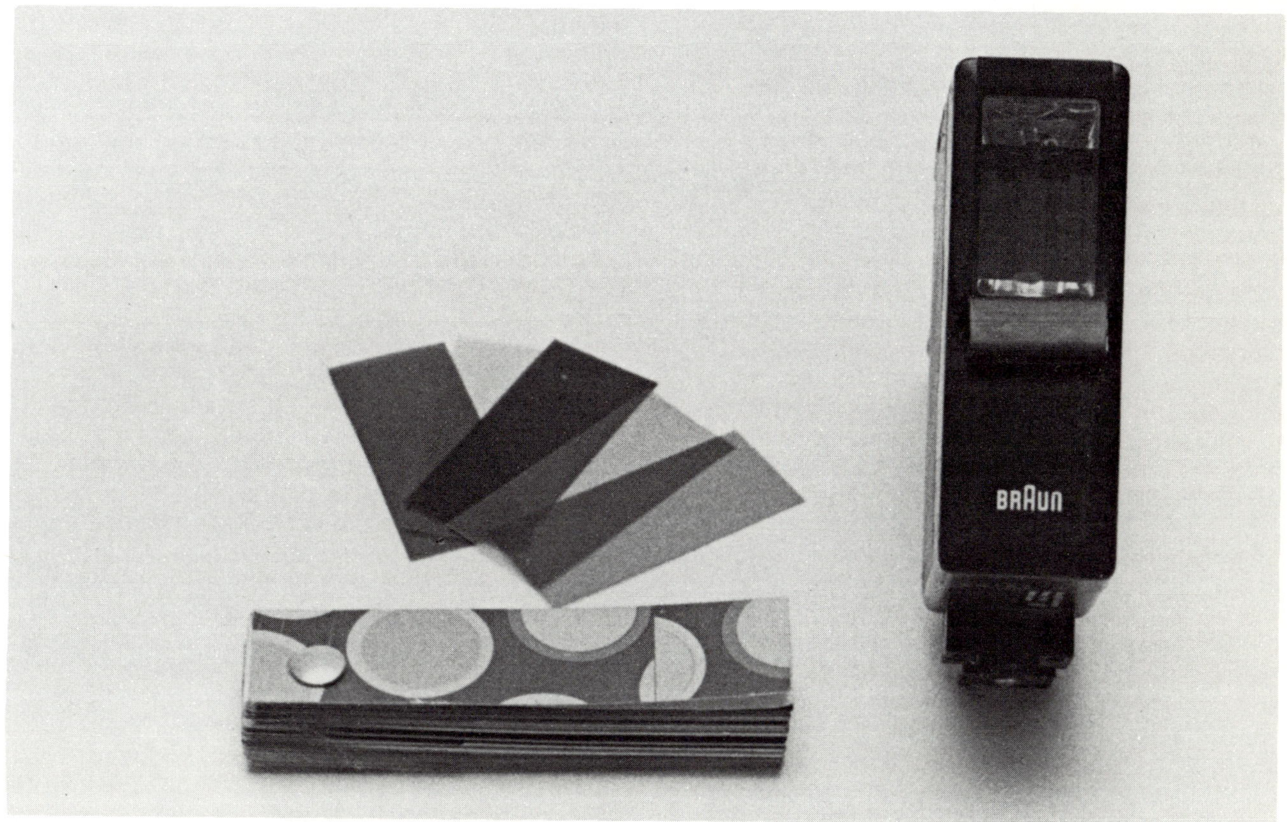

2. The book of 44 filters provide an almost endless variety of colors. At first just cut a few from the book and leave the rest stapled together for easy storage. Use the silicone to glue a small section of the plastic clamp from the report cover to the flash unit to hold the plastic filters.

Strobe-Effect Switch

Many popular electronic flash units are automatic and have an energy-saving thyristor. This means that the flash fires only the amount of light needed and stores the rest for the next shot. These flash units also often have a 1/2, 1/4, and 1/16 power position. Some units continue this range to include even a 1/64 power position.

With these features, the flash can be fired several times without pausing for the batteries to recharge the capacitor. If there is a way to fire the flash several times during one exposure, a strobe effect can be obtained. An easy way to achieve this strobing is to add a simple momentary-on pushbutton switch to the flash.

If you decide to make a switch like this one, there is one thing you should keep in mind. These flash units aren't designed to handle all the heat that this type of use can generate. Only flash the unit three, four, or five times and then let it rest for a minute or two so the heat can dissipate. Otherwise, enough heat can be created to damage the unit.

You can buy the momentary-on pushbutton switch in any electronics supply house. Use the standard size because it is larger and easier to handle than the miniature switches. When the button on this switch is pushed, contact is made and the flash is triggered. When the button is released, contact is broken. This allows the switch to be pushed quickly to repeatedly trigger the flash unit.

The coiled PC extension cord has one male and one female PC connector. Cut off the female end, the one that fits into a camera. Leave 1″ (2.5 cm) or so of wire attached to this end and you may be able to use it for some other project in the future. The male PC connector left on the coiled cord will fit into the PC fitting on any flash cord.

Strip the outer insulation (½″ or 12.7 mm) from the end of the coiled cord. This is best accomplished by placing the wire on a table and rolling it beneath the razor knife blade while applying gentle pressure. Pull off the insulation and separate the metal strands. Inside is another insulated wire.

Pull this wire to one side and roll the metal strands together to make a tight bundle. Strip ¼″ (6.4 mm) of insulation off the inner wire and twist together the strands that are inside. Set the cord aside and begin working on the plastic film can.

Use the soldering iron to melt a hole in the film can's cap for the coiled wire. Make a larger hole in the bottom of the can for the switch. You could also cut or drill these holes instead of melting them.

Insert the wire through the hole in the cap and tie an overhand knot in it. The knot prevents the wire from accidentally being pulled from the switch. Leave enough wire to attach to the switch. Slip the thin nuts that hold the switch in place over the wires. Pull the end of the wire through the hole for the switch and solder the wire to the contacts on the bottom of the switch. Most switches have two contacts—one for each wire. Some will have three—two that are identical and one that is different. Solder one wire to either of the identical contacts and the other to the different contact.

Slip the switch through the hole in the bottom of the film can and tighten the nuts that hold it in place. Needle-nosed pliers make this easy to do. Replace the cap on the film can and the switch is finished.

Connect the male PC cord end to the female PC end on the flash cord and turn on the flash. Switch the flash to a partial-power or automatic position and test it by pushing the button to fire the flash two or three times in rapid succession. The switch should work like a charm. Disconnect the switch and practice with it. Hold the switch in one hand and a cable release in the other. First trip the shutter with the cable release. Then push the button on the switch two, three, and even five times in rapid succession while the shutter trips only once. The purpose of this practice with the flash disconnected is to sharpen your coordination. With a little practice, you should be able to trip the switch four or five times in a second.

For taking strobe photos, the room should be almost dark to prevent the ambient light from adding to the exposure. An exception would be if you wish to have the subject blurred for part of the exposure and sharp in the flash portions of the exposure. Connect the switch and set the camera on one-second exposure, or for a time exposure. Take your strobe-effect photos. The background must be dark to prevent its overexposure. A high-speed film works best because of the greatly reduced output of the flash. Remember to rest the flash periodically to prevent heat buildup.

The flash duration will be greatly reduced. The flash will only last perhaps 1/10,000 or 1/25,000 of a second. With some flash units, the duration may be as short as 1/50,000 of a second. This makes it possible to freeze very high-speed action.

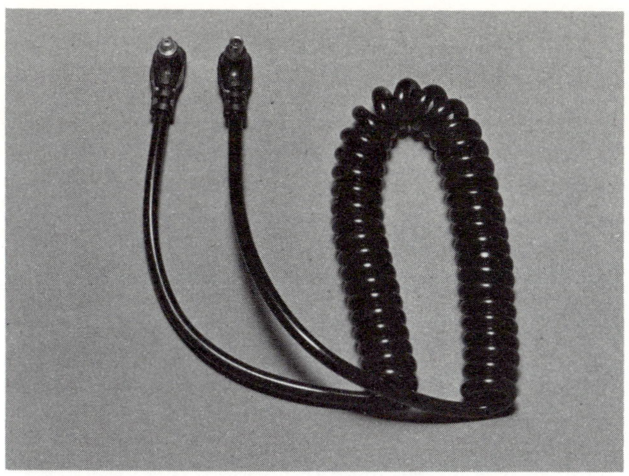

1. A PC-to-PC extension cord has a male and a female PC connection. The male connector is on the left. The female connector is cut off and replaced with a momentary-on switch.

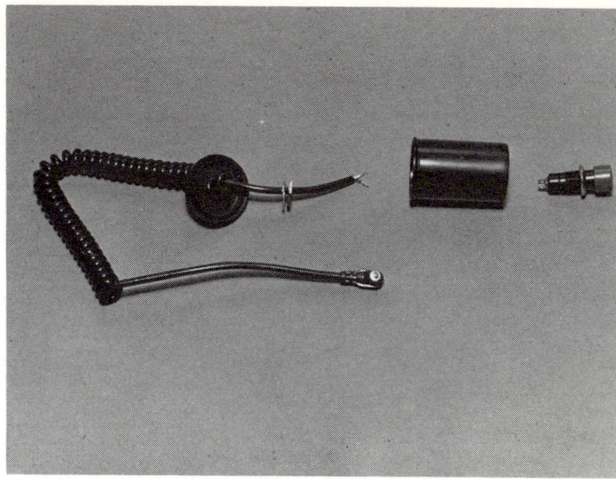

2. First slip the lid on the cord, tie a knot, and slip on the nuts that hold the switch. Then run the wire through the hole that has been cut in the bottom of the film can.

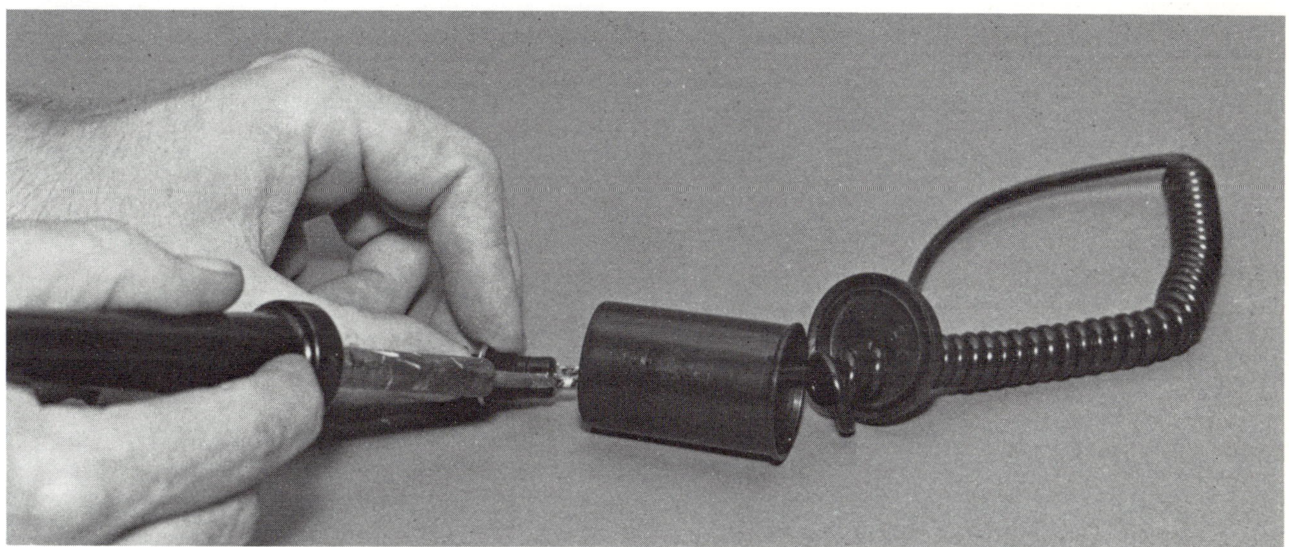

3. Solder the wires to the contacts on the switch. This is easiest if you insert the wires through the holes in the switch contacts and bend them over to hold them in place.

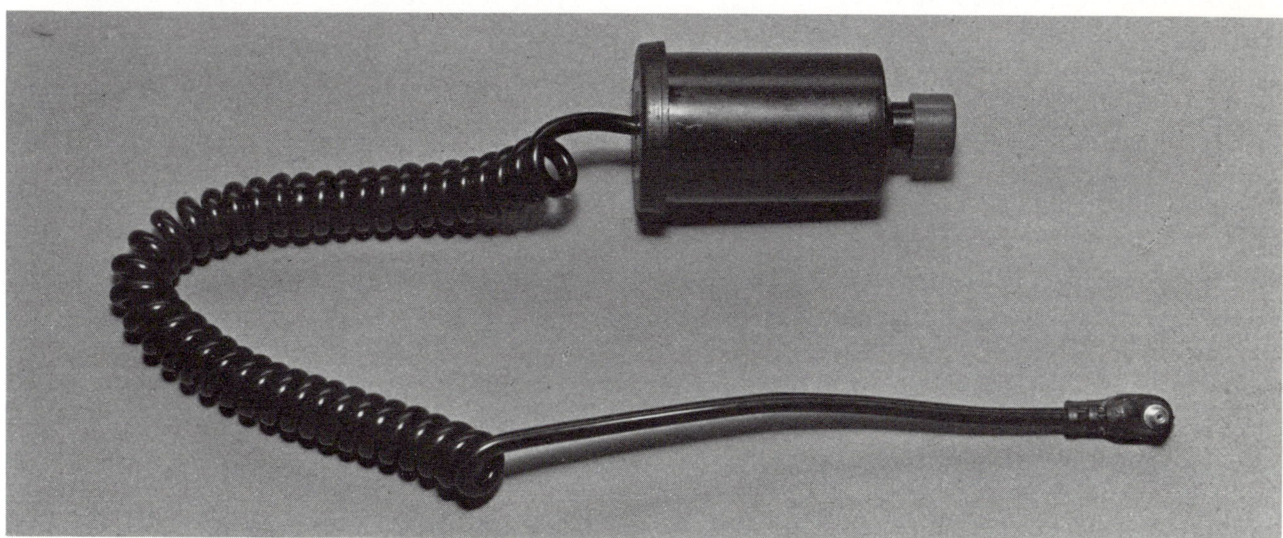

4. This is the finished strobe switch, ready to be attached to your automatic flash.

Low Voltage Battery Pack for Faster Flash Recycling and More Flashes

A low voltage battery pack (LVBP) uses two "D" in place of the two "AA" batteries normally used to power an electronic flash. The voltage is the same—it's the amount of current that the batteries deliver that is different.

With the LVBP, a flash unit will recycle faster and get many more flashes from a set of batteries. A unit that gets 30 to 40 flashes with "AA"s will get 300 to 400 flashes with the "D"s. The flash will also recycle faster. Initial recycling will be cut from perhaps a five-second period to three or four seconds. Even after a hundred flashes with the LVBP, the flash will still recycle in five or six seconds. This makes a world of difference, because you can eliminate some of the time spent waiting for recharging. I normally replace the batteries when recharging has begun to take eight or ten seconds. I usually get 200 or more flashes from a set of batteries. There is still enough power left in the used batteries to operate a flashlight or toy.

The advantages are extensive, but there is also a risk—the LVBP may ruin your flash unit. Some flash units can even be ruined by using nickel cadmium instead of alkaline batteries. Each make and model of flash is different, and it is hard to say which can be used with a LVBP. If your flash can take nickel cadmium batteries, the chances are good that you can use a LVBP.

Perhaps you have an old, infrequently used unit that takes longer to charge than it should, or maybe it just hums but the ready light never goes on. This kind of flash is a good candidate for the LVBP. The extra energy in the "D" batteries may bring the flash back to life. Disuse of a flash unit results in a deformed capacitor (one that doesn't hold a full charge). Repeated charging and flashing will usually reform the capacitor and make it work like it should. In order to keep a capacitor from becoming deformed, the unit should be flashed several times a month.

The capacitor in even the smallest electronic flash holds a potentially lethal charge. *Never* dismantle an electronic flash unless you're trained and know *exactly* what you are doing. This project is safe because only the battery compartment of the flash is opened, not the case.

To construct the adapter for the LVBP, begin by cutting the wires from the battery holder with the wire cutters. Split the two wires of the power cord apart for a distance of about 1″ (2.5 cm). Remove ¼″ (6.4 mm) of insulation from the end of each wire. This can be done with the razor knife or with a wire stripping tool. Now examine the power cord. One wire will be marked with printing or numbers at intervals along its length. Use the marked wire for the positive (+) battery contact, which is marked in both the battery holder and inside the battery compartment of the flash.

Push the two wires of the power cord through the holes in the battery holder. Solder these wires to the metal contacts inside, at the same place where you cut off the leads. At the other end of each wire, split the insulation connecting the wires for a distance of 1″ and strip off ¼″ of the insulation. Attach a metal thumbtack to the end of each wire by soldering the wire to the underside of the tack near its point.

Cut two pieces of ½″ (12.7 mm) dowel rod—one 1⅞″ (47.6 mm) and the other 1¾″ (44.5 mm). These dowel rods act as adapters and replace the "AA" batteries, which are 2″ (5.1 cm) long. The thumbtacks pushed into one end of each dowel increase its length by about ⅛″ (3.2 mm) and make it fit snugly into the compartment. The power cord bent over the end of the shorter dowel provides the additional length needed so the dowel will fit tightly into the compartment.

Push the thumbtacks into the ends of the dowels and place the two dowels side by side. Position the power cord in the groove between the dowels and tape everything together. Check which dowel is connected to the marked wire of the power cord. Mark a plus on the end of this dowel with a pen and mark the other dowel with a minus.

The cover on the battery compartment will not close completely because of the power cord, so you must cut a notch on the end of the cover to hold the cord. It is easiest to melt the notch with the soldering iron and then trim off some of the melted plastic with the razor knife. Make the notch in the end of the cover just large enough to hold the power cord.

Check the polarity of the contacts inside the flash. Then insert the dowel and thumbtack adapter into the battery compartment. Make sure the thumbtack contacts of the adapter are pressed against the electrical contacts inside the flash, with the (+) contact of the adapter going to the one marked (+) inside the flash unit. Close the cover on the battery compartment and add the "D" batteries to the battery holder. Turn on the flash to test if everything works. If it doesn't seem to be working, recheck the polarity of the batteries and make sure that the adapter is pressed firmly against the battery contacts inside the flash unit. This should correct any problem.

When using the LVBP some flash units may recycle with amazing speed. Avoid taking lots of flashes in rapid succession, though, as the rapid use will cause damaging heat buildup. Take only three or four quick flashes and then allow the unit to rest so the heat can dissipate.

The LVBP can be carried in a pocket where it will hardly be noticed. If the flash is going to be used primarily as a slave for off-camera flash, the long power cord isn't necessary. It's a good idea to keep an extra piece or two of tape on the battery pack to cover the thumbtack electrical contacts when the LVBP isn't in use.

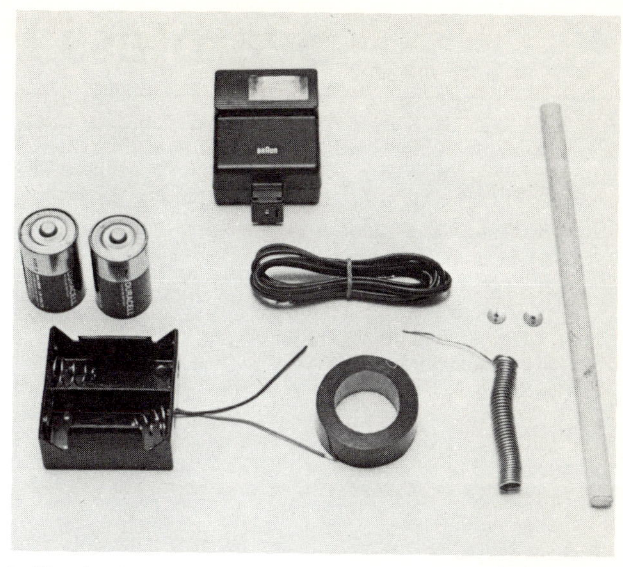

1. Here's what you'll need to make a low voltage battery pack.

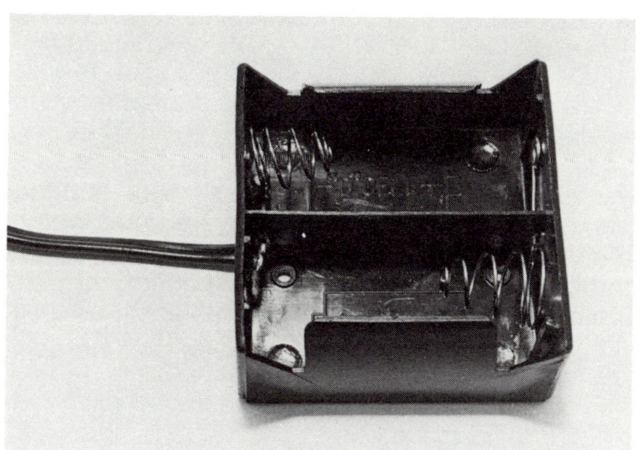

2. Solder the power cord to the metal contacts inside the battery holder.

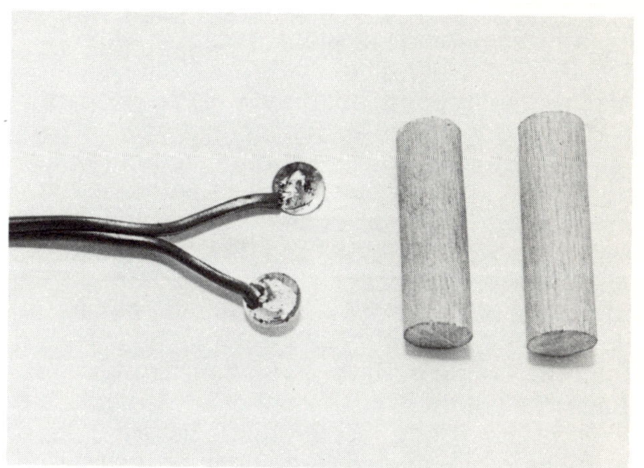

3. Solder thumbtacks to the ends of the power cord. Push these into lengths of dowel rod.

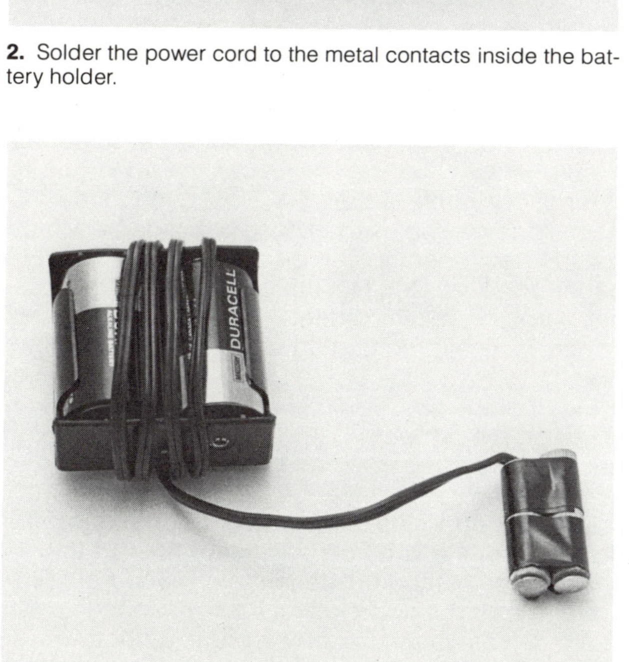

4. This is the finished LVBP. Make sure that the thumbtack electrical contacts are separated by a gap so they cannot touch.

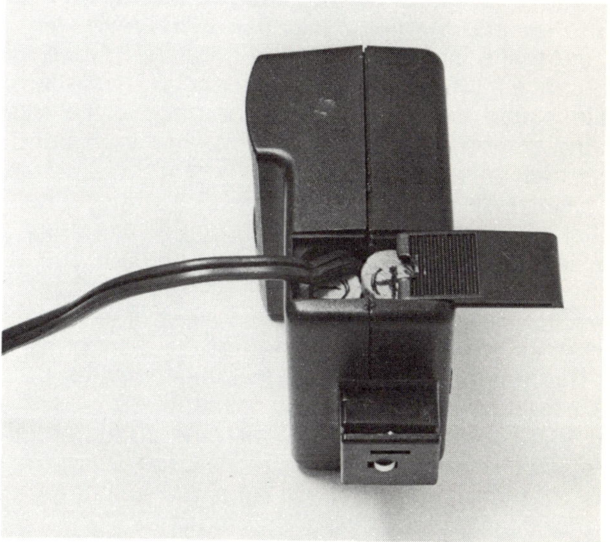

5. The power cord goes over the end of the short dowel and out through the notch made in the cover of the battery compartment.

Seamless Paper Stand

Seamless paper is available in black, white, gray, and fifty other different colors. White is the most frequently used, but gray is also a good choice. Changing the amount of light that strikes the paper can change its appearance from white to very dark. Use a color filter over an electronic flash and the paper takes on the color of the filter. A separate light (or lights) can give the subject a more natural appearance.

The rolls of paper come in several different widths from 53″ to 140″ (1.3 – 3.6 m). The standard is 107″ (2.7 m), almost 9′. If you have limited space, the 53″ roll is the best choice. Most rolls are 12 yards (11 m) long. Some brands have a rigid cardboard core, and some come in boxes for protection. So there are many possibilities for you to choose from.

Seamless paper is not expensive. My 107″ roll cost less than $20, but you need a stand to hold it. Buying a stand was too expensive, so I made a stand that cost less than the roll of paper. Once you have all the materials, this stand can be made in less than an hour. Best of all, perhaps, is that the stand can be put up or taken down in minutes and stored in very little space.

Using tension poles for the end supports makes all of this possible. Suitable plant poles are often on sale, or if you go to garage and rummage sales, you may be able to buy a bathroom space saver for a few dollars. Space savers have two tension poles that can be used instead of the plant poles.

The materials needed are two tension poles, 12′ (3.7 m) of ⅛″ (3.2 mm) nylon rope, two "S" hooks (2″ or 5.1 cm), and an old inner tube from a tire, which can still be found at the local garage. In addition you'll need a sharp knife, a wet sponge, gaffer's tape, instant glue, and matches.

Begin by cutting two rubber bands about 1″ (2.5 cm) wide from the inner tube. Use the sponge to wet the rubber, making it easier to cut. Then set up the tension poles a few inches farther apart

than the length of the paper. Place the rubber bands behind the pole at the desired height, holding both loop ends toward you. Insert one loop through the other and pull tight. This is a simple knot, easy to release, and is secured by the weight attached to it. Next attach the "S" hooks to the free loop in the rubber bands.

Place the seamless paper roll on the floor between the poles and run the rope through the center of the roll, leaving a portion extending from each end. Tie a loop in each end of the rope at a point slightly farther apart than the length of the paper. Lift one end of the roll and slip the rope loop over the "S" hook. Rest the roll of paper at an angle against the tension pole and then lift and attach the other side. Cut off any excess rope. The ends of the nylon rope fray easily, so melt them with a match.

To level the paper or change its height, simply pull on the rope to release the tension and reposition the rubber bands. This can be done without detaching the rope or the "S" hook. The weight of the paper prevents the rubber bands from slipping. The ⅛″ rope and rubber bands are much stronger than they look and can hold many times the weight of the paper. If your paper doesn't have a cardboard core, electrical conduit or copper pipe can be used as a crossbar. Use gaffer's tape to attach the paper securely to the pipe. The paper rolls easily with or without a crossbar.

If you use a pipe for the crossbar, you will need to file or sand the inside edges of the pipe ends smooth so it won't cut into the rope. A crossbar slightly longer than the paper works best.

A drop of instant glue can be put on each joint in the tension poles. This will keep the poles from coming apart and make the stand easier to put up or take down.

A roll of seamless paper will last a long time. Both sides can be used in case one side becomes soiled. A torn portion can be cut off and more paper unrolled. Don't just throw away the torn paper. It can be cut into sheets and used for drawing paper. The children and artists in the family will love it.

Much of the time your subjects won't have to stand on the paper to be photographed. For a background the paper can be unrolled behind. This saves wear and tear on the paper. When the paper is used for an infinite background (one with no horizon), the subjects can either take off their shoes or can stand on a sheet of plywood placed under the paper to prevent it from tearing.

A seamless background provides a photographer with more complete control of the appearance of his or her photographs. Once you start using yours, you'll wonder how you ever got along without it.

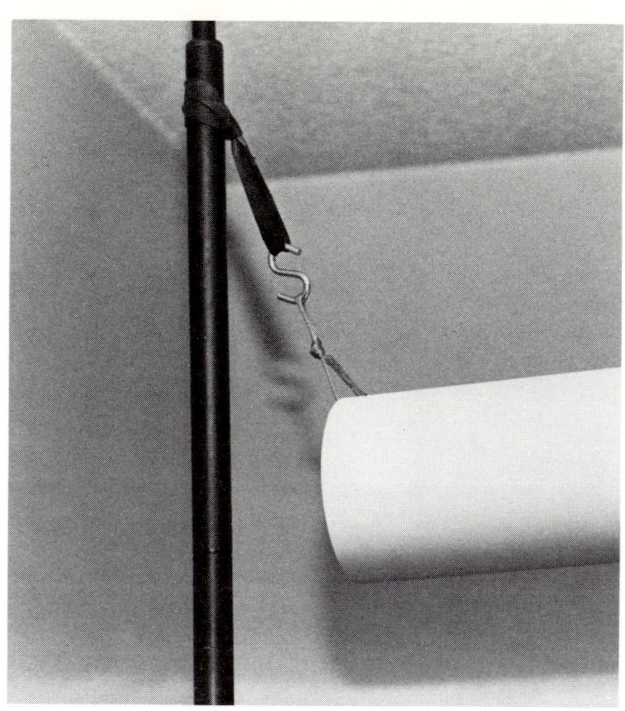

1. Left. First put the rubber band behind the pole. Pull the ends toward you, putting one end through the other and then pulling tight. The "S" hook attaches the loop in the rope to the rubber band.

2. Below. Rubber bands cut from an old inner tube, "S" hooks, and rope suspend the roll of seamless paper between two tension poles. The setup can be put up and taken down quickly.

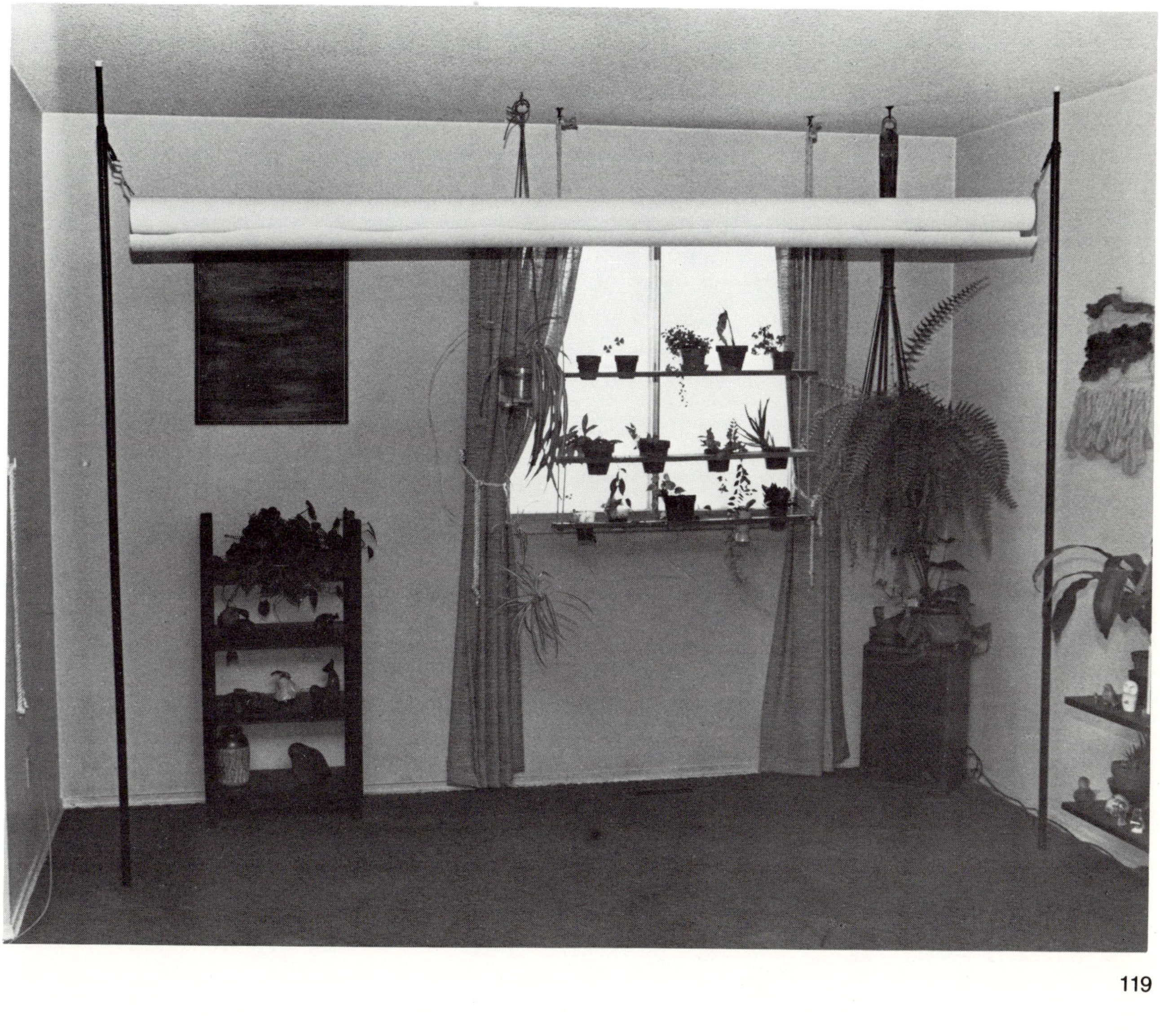

PART FOUR

CLOSE-UP AIDS

Sturdy Copy Stand

Tripods, copy stands, and other camera supports should be super rigid and extremely solid. Rigidity is almost synonymous with weight—the heavier a stand, the more stable it will be. With a tripod and most other camera supports, there are practical limits to weight because they have to be carried. With a copy stand, these limits don't exist. I have heard of professional copy stands (used for high magnification) that have a steel plate for the base and weigh hundreds of pounds. My copy stand doesn't go to this extreme, but it is a heavy and stable camera support.

A copy stand is usually thought of as something that is used to photograph flat material—drawings, documents, and photographs. But it is also useful for copying slides, for macrophotography of three-dimensional objects, and for photography with a microscope. The stable, tall professional stands are too expensive to buy, but easy and inexpensive to make.

A door or sink cutout is used for the base of the copy stand. A *door cutout* is the part of a solid-core door that is cut out when a window is installed. A *sink cutout* is counter top material removed to install the sink. These are sold in some building supply stores and lumber yards for a very low price and are just the right size and thickness for the base of the copy stand. They also make excellent bases for enlargers and tops for small tables. They come in many different sizes, so you probably can find just the size you need.

Shim brass comes in small sheets of different thickness and is sold in hobby shops and auto supply stores. You'll need a 4″ × 10″ (10.2 × 25.4 cm) sheet the thickness of drawing paper. I bought an assorted package at a hobby shop.

The rest of the materials can be purchased in a plumbing supply store or an old-fashioned hardware store. Find a place that will cut the pipe to size and will cut the threads. This is usually done for a very small fee and makes assembly of the copy stand very simple. Buy galvanized pipe and fittings—they won't rust and I think they look better than black pipe.

Begin by covering the door cutout with plastic laminate. (If you're using a sink cutout, it is already covered, so this step won't be necessary.) Plastic laminate is sold under many names and is used to cover counter tops and tables. Common brand names are Formica and Arborite. This material is usually glued with a contact-type cement, but I chose to use silicone to avoid the dangerous fumes of contact cement. If I couldn't use silicone and epoxy, I wouldn't be able to make a thing!

The silicone is slower drying than contact cement, so it should be given at least a few hours to dry. Using heat to speed the drying isn't a good idea because the plastic may buckle.

Use a special plastic-cutting razor knife to cut the laminate. This material defied cutting with my trusty regular razor knife. Two or three strokes of the knife are required to score a deep line in the top surface of the plastic. To separate the pieces, bend the plastic *toward* the scored line. This is just the reverse of the way you bend styrene and other solid plastics to break them.

After the plastic is cut, squeeze a ribbon of silicone around the edge of the base and a little more in the center. Use a putty knife or stiff cardboard to spread the silicone. The silicone is needed most at the edges. Only a little is needed in the center. After the silicone is spread, press the plastic to the wood. First attach the large piece

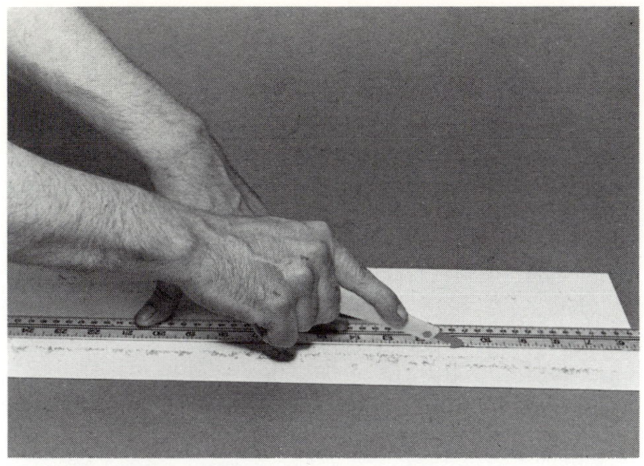

1. Use a special plastic-cutting razor knife to cut the laminate. Draw the knife across the plastic two or three times to scribe the groove deeply.

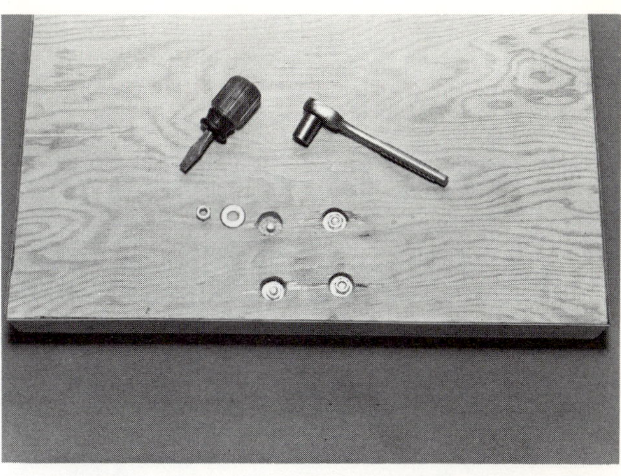

2. The holes are countersunk with a ¾″ (19.1 mm) drill bit so the bolts will be below the level of the wood. Use a screwdriver and small wrench to tighten the nuts that attach the floor plate to the base of the copy stand.

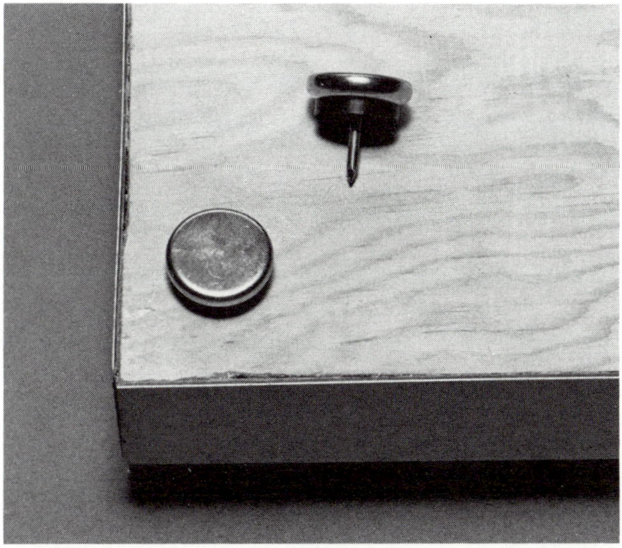

3. Glides or rubber pads can be added to the bottom corners of the stand's base. These prevent the stand from marring a tabletop.

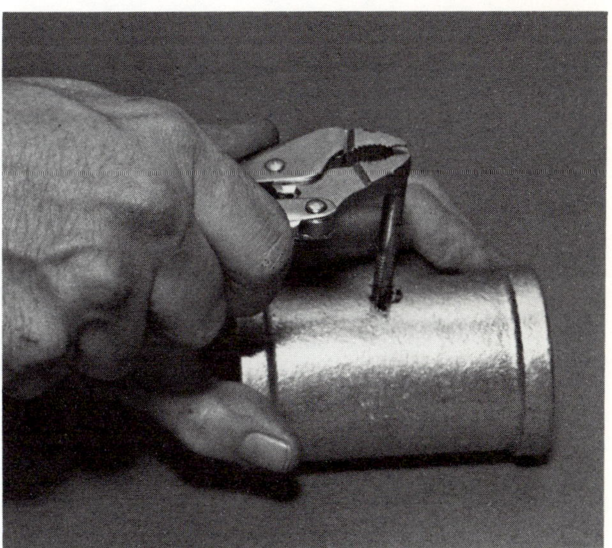

4. Use a tap to make a threaded hole in the Tee connector for the locking lever.

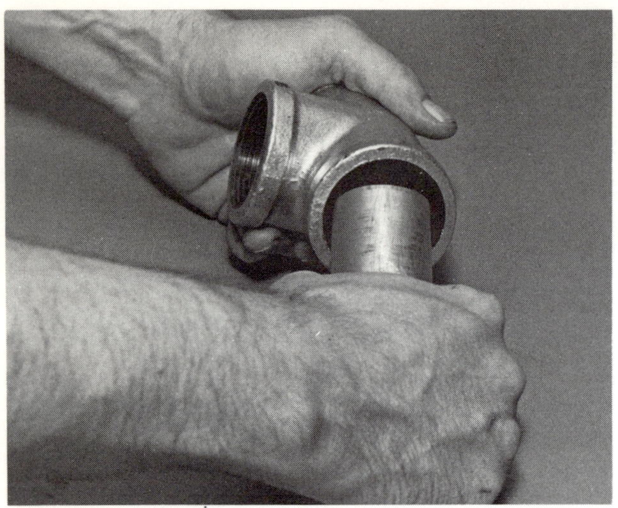

5. Make a brass bushing by rolling a sheet of thin brass and inserting it into the Tee connector. This bushing tightens the fit and makes the Tee slide smoothly on the column.

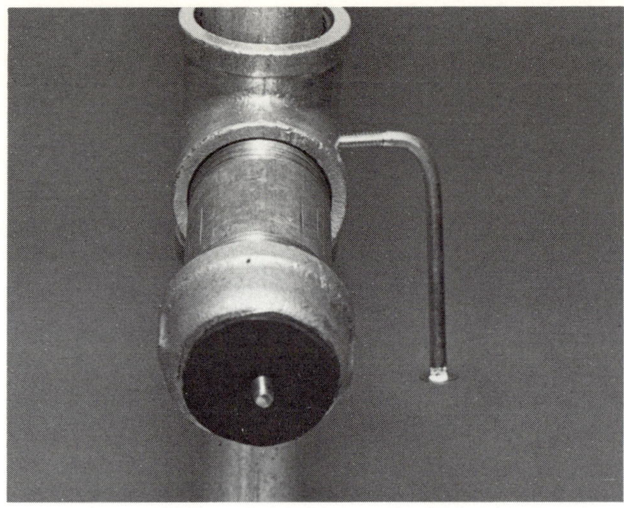

6. To make a locking lever, bend a carriage bolt and put it in the threaded hole in the Tee connector. File the end of the bolt smooth so it won't cut into the brass bushing. Glue a leather pad to the end cap to cushion the camera.

and then do the edges. If the plastic doesn't stay in place, it can be taped down with gaffer's tape until the silicone is dry. After it is dry use a wood rasp and sandpaper to smooth the edges and corners of the plastic.

Next, drill holes in the end cap and Tee. It is easier to find the center of the cap if you begin drilling from the inside. The inside has spiral scratches in the metal that indicate the center. Use a ball peen hammer and center punch to make an indentation where you wish the hole. Drill a 3/16″ (4.8 mm) hole. Use a slow speed with the drill and add a few drops of oil. A cutting oil would work best but any light oil makes drilling easier. You'll know the speed is right when the drill bit is cutting large spirals and flakes of metal. Also drill a 3/16″ hole in the Tee where you wish the locking lever to be located.

Use a ¼″ (6.4 mm) tap with 20 threads to the inch to thread these holes. Hold the tap with locking pliers. To cut the threads, just screw the tap into the metal, as if it were a bolt. Adding a few drops of oil helps the cutting. Use some soap and water to remove oil from the pipe and fitting and then wipe them dry.

Bend a 5″ (12.7 cm) carriage bolt to make the locking lever. If you have a vise, clamp it on the bolt near the threads and use a short piece of narrow pipe to bend it. The bolt bends easily with this extra leverage. If you don't have a vise, the bolt can be bent using two lengths of pipe. Be careful when doing this, and position yourself so you're prepared in case the carriage bolt breaks instead of bending.

When the silicone is dry, add the floor mount to the base. Position the mount and mark the location of the holes. Center punch the locations and drill a ¼″ hole starting from the plastic-covered side. Drill all four holes and then turn the base over. Use a ¾″ (19.1 mm) wood bit to countersink the holes for the

nuts and washers. Drill only about ½″ (12.7 mm) deep with this large bit. Attach the mount with ¼″ flat-head stove bolts, nuts, and washers. Use a screwdriver and 7/16″ (11.1 mm) socket wrench to tighten the nuts.

If desired, glides can be added to the bottom corners of the base. These are usually used on chair and table legs and can be found in hardware stores, usually near the caster section. Mine just had to be nailed to the wood.

The 1¼″ (3.2 cm) pipe for the column can slip inside the 1½″ (3.81 cm) Tee, but there is a little play. Eliminate this play with a bushing made from the shim brass. Roll a sheet of the brass, about the thickness of drawing paper, into a tube and slip it inside the Tee. The brass is springy but still easy to roll. Slide the Tee with the brass bushing in place over the column and test the fit. The Tee should slide easily with almost no play. If it is still too loose, an additional sheet of very thin brass can be added to tighten the fit.

Insert the ¾″ (19.1 mm) long ¼″ bolt in the end cap's hole and glue the bolt in place with epoxy. Cut a leather pad and punch a hole in the center. Glue the leather pad around the bolt with silicone. When the glues are dry, the parts of the stand can be assembled.

The 4″ (10.2 cm) arm is used with a ball-and-socket head to center the camera over the base. The 10″ (25.4 cm) arm is used when extra length is needed or when the stand is used without the ball-and-socket head.

Modeling lights can be added to the stand if you wish. Clamp-on desk lamps with a gooseneck or with spring-balanced, flexible arms can be used. These lamps are frequently on sale. If you decide to buy them, be sure to check the wattage. Some lamps are only rated for 60 or 75 watts, which is less than you would want. Buy lamps that are rated for at least 100 watts.

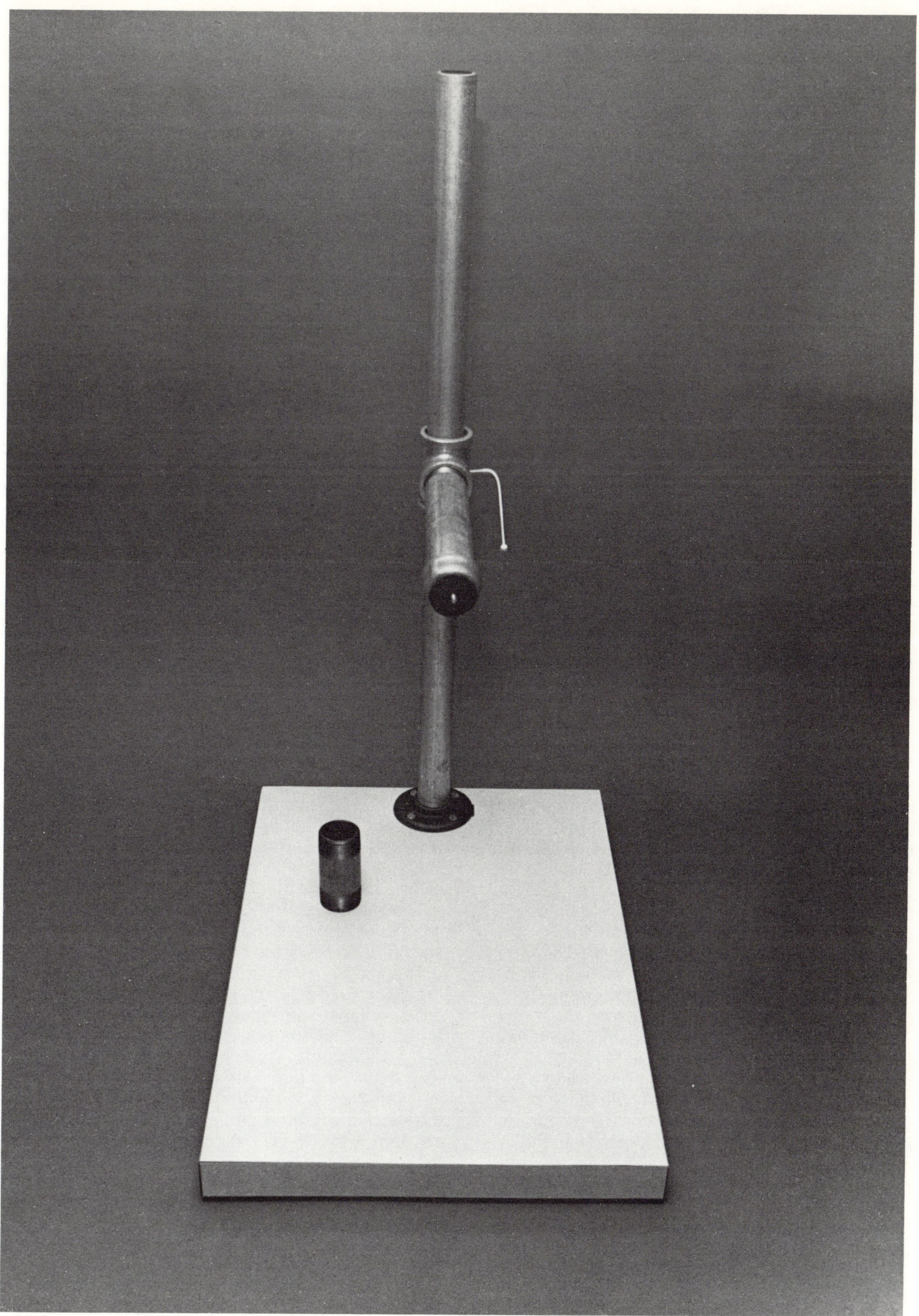

Dual Slide Copier/Light Box

MATERIALS

Square recessed ceiling light fixture
Flash opal glass or imitation
Power cord with plug
Wire connectors
Strain-relief grommet or outlet box connector
No. 211 enlarging bulb
Hose-style hair dryer or vacuum cleaner
Black felt
Silicone
White paint, heat resistant (optional)
Gaffer's tape (optional)

TOOLS

Drill and bits
Ball peen hammer
Center punch
Metal chisel
Goggles
Wire cutters
Razor knife
Coarse half-round file
Thermometer (must read to 120F or 49C)

I bought a square, recessed ceiling light fixture at an auction for $2. I didn't know what I was going to do with it, but it looked like something that I eventually would use. After a while, it dawned on me that the light fixture could be used to make a combined slide copier/light box.

Most fixtures like the one I bought have a white glass pane. Avoid those with textured glass. Flash opal glass is best for a slide copier. It has a layer of flawless white glass covered with transparent glass to protect it. Unfortunately flash opal glass is becoming expensive and you may not want to use it for that reason. An imitation of the opal glass is sold in lighting shops and hardware stores as replacement glass for this type of fixture.

I used a 75-watt (No. 211) enlarging bulb in the fixture. The enlarging bulb gives a more even light and has a more constant color temperature (2900–3000K) than regular light bulbs.

In order for it to be used for copying slides and other photography, the light fixture must be modified. Begin this modification by adding the power cord. Drill a ½" (12.7 mm) hole in the metal box where you wish to add the cord. Put a strain-relief grommet on the cord and force it into the drilled hole. This grommet prevents the power cord from being accidentally pulled out of the fixture.

Some fixtures may have knock-out plugs in the metal. These can be punched out to create a large hole. If this is the case, an outlet-box connector can be used to secure the power cord to the light fixture.

Use wire connectors to attach the wires of the power cord to the two wires inside the lighting fixture. Twist together the bare stripped wires of the power cord with the bare portion of the wire from the fixture. Screw a wire connector onto the bare portion of the connected wires. The wire connector both insulates and strengthens the joint. Pull up on the wire connector to make sure that it is strongly attached. Repeat this procedure with the other two wires. Be sure that the wire connector covers all of the bare wire.

Reassemble the fixture and install the bulb. Plug in the fixture to check if everything works. You can add a switch to the fixture if you wish, but I just use the plug to turn mine on and off.

As it is now, the fixture can be used to copy color slides with incandescent light. Use a tungsten film and an 82C light-balancing filter to match the light to the film. The next step is to modify the fixture so it can be used with an electronic flash and daylight film. The electronic flash will be placed inside the light fixture, so it must be protected from the heat of the bulb. I use a hair dryer for cooling. When the hair dryer is set on cool, it acts only as a blower and produces no heat. Some hair dryers contain asbestos-covered wires. This problem, how to identify it, and how to correct it are discussed in the Film Washer-Dryer project. As an alternative to using the hair dryer, a vacuum cleaner could be used for cooling.

With the light box unplugged, use a compass to mark a circle with the same diameter as the hose. You probably don't have a drill bit large enough to make the hole, so drill a series of small holes inside the marked circle. Knock out the metal plug with a ball peen hammer and metal chisel. Wear goggles when doing this type of hammering—it's best to be safe.

Smooth the edge of the hole with a coarse, half-round file. Drill a ½" (12.7 mm) hole in the side of the fixture opposite the bulb. This second hole is for the PC cord of the flash unit.

The inside of the fixture is already white. If you are using an old fixture like mine and the paint has yellowed, the inside can be repainted with a heat-resistant white enamel. It's best to paint and let the paint dry outside where the vapors won't affect you. If this isn't possible, paint inside in a well-ventilated area, away from an open flame. When the paint is dry, the bottom of the light box can be covered with felt. Glue it in place with silicone. The felt protects the working surface from being scratched.

Connect the blower or vacuum hose and place a thermometer inside the slide copier. Turn on the light and check the heat build-up. With the hair dryer blower, the box should stay below 120 F (49 C). With the vacuum cleaner, it will be even

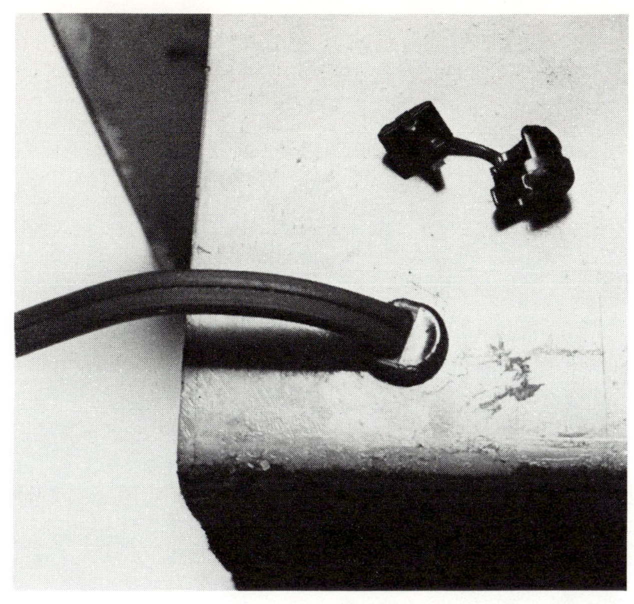

1. Left. Drill a hole for the power cord and use a strain-relief grommet to add the power cord to the light fixture.

2. Below. Use wire connectors to attach the power cord to the wire inside the fixture. Check the wire connectors to be sure they're on tightly and that they completely cover the bare parts of the wire.

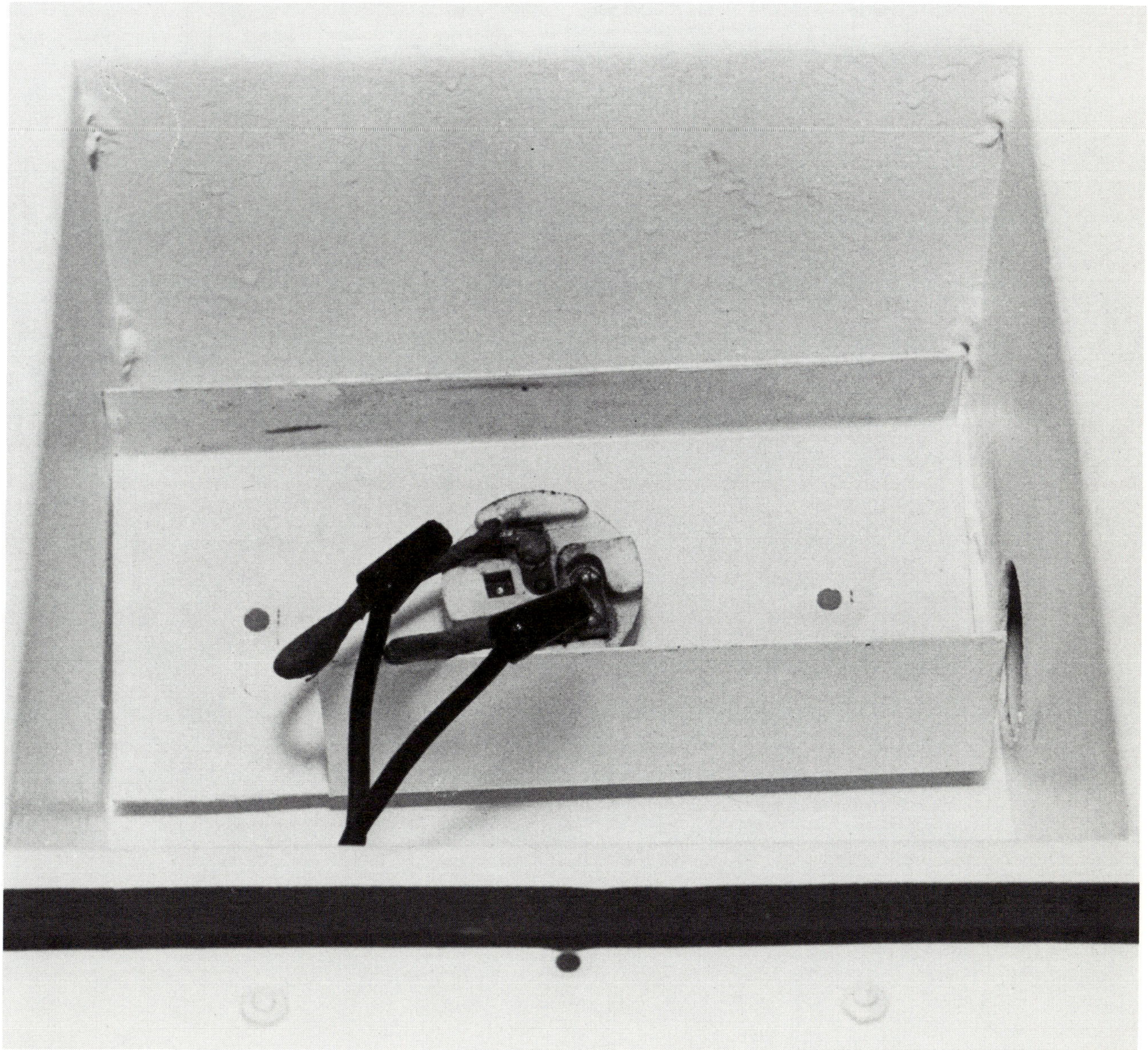

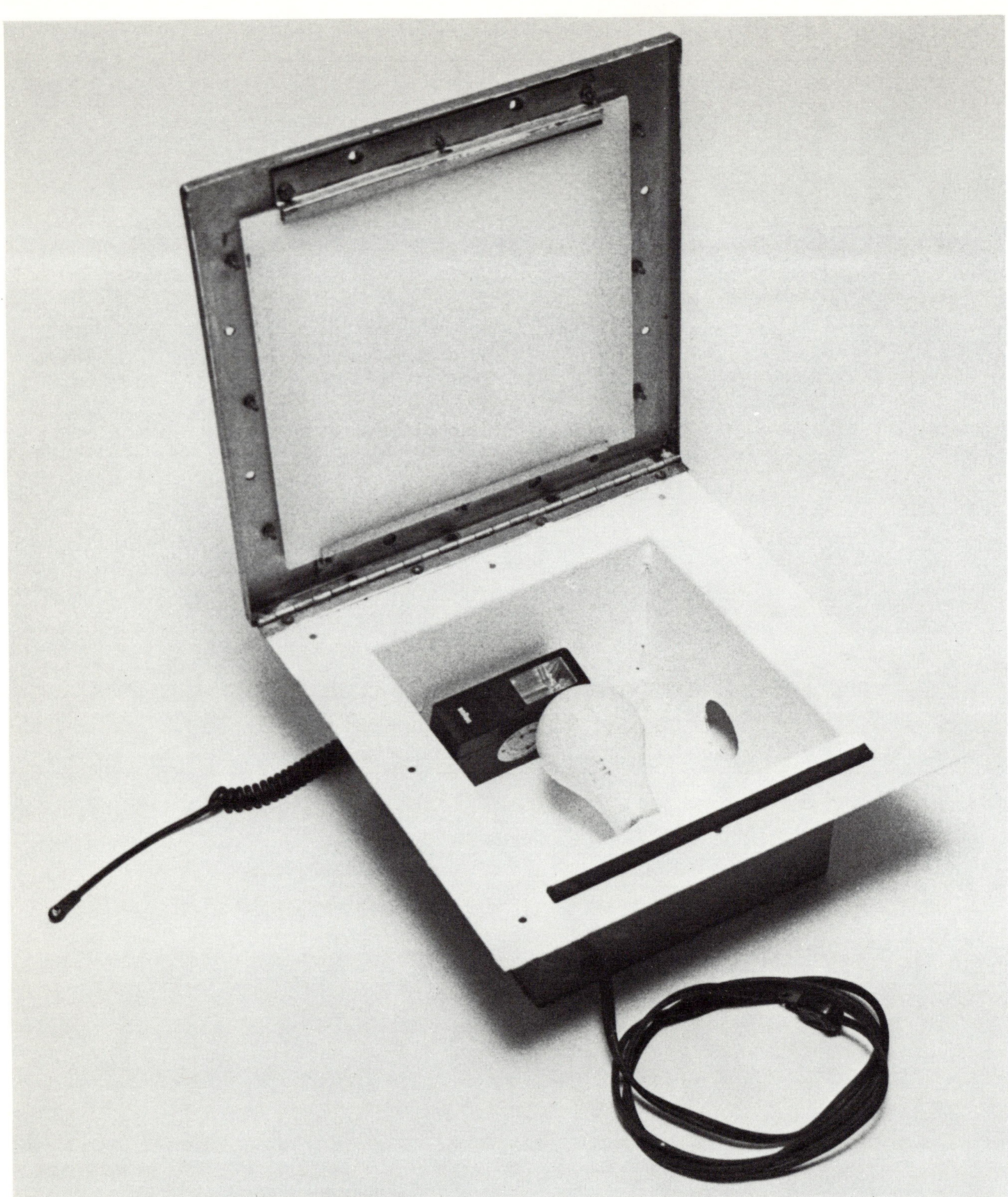

3. Place an electronic flash inside the fixture and run the PC cord through the drilled hole. The hole for the hair dryer or vacuum cleaner hose is visible on the right side of the fixture.

cooler. If it becomes too hot, a bulb with a lower wattage should be used. In normal use, mine will be about 100–110 F (38–44 C)—the temperature of a hot summer day. This temperature is safe for the flash unit. Using the light only when it's needed and turning it off the rest of the time will keep the flash unit much cooler.

Place the flash inside the slide copier as far away from the light bulb as possible. If need be, it can be taped in place with gaffer's tape. Turn on the blower and the light. The fixture has a built-in provision for air circulation around the top and down the sides. You can feel the air circulating. If it didn't, the glass might crack from the heat of the bulb.

Shoot a test roll of film to determine the correct exposure. A small- or medium-size flash unit may produce a correct exposure with an ISO 64/19 film at about *f*/5.6 or *f*/8. This is just a guesstimate, so bracket your exposures extensively. Flash matches daylight color film, so filters shouldn't be necessary unless the slide needs color correcting.

To make color corrections, place CP or CC filters beneath the slide.

For a copy stand, I use an old enlarger's base and column with a ball-and-socket head bolted to the arm. Use a small carpenter's level to make sure that everything is aligned.

Because the top is large the slide copier/light box can be used for more than copying slides. I've used it to photograph crystal, flowers, and other small objects. My wife has even used it to mark quilting lines on her quilt tops.

Using the light box, a copy stand, and a bellows to copy slides has many advantages. Small portions of a slide can be enlarged, formats changed, and new slides created by sandwiching two or more slides together. Filters can be used for more than color correcting. Slides can be given new color, and black-and-white negatives can be made from color slides.

A slide copier/light box is a creative tool that can add a new dimension to your photography.

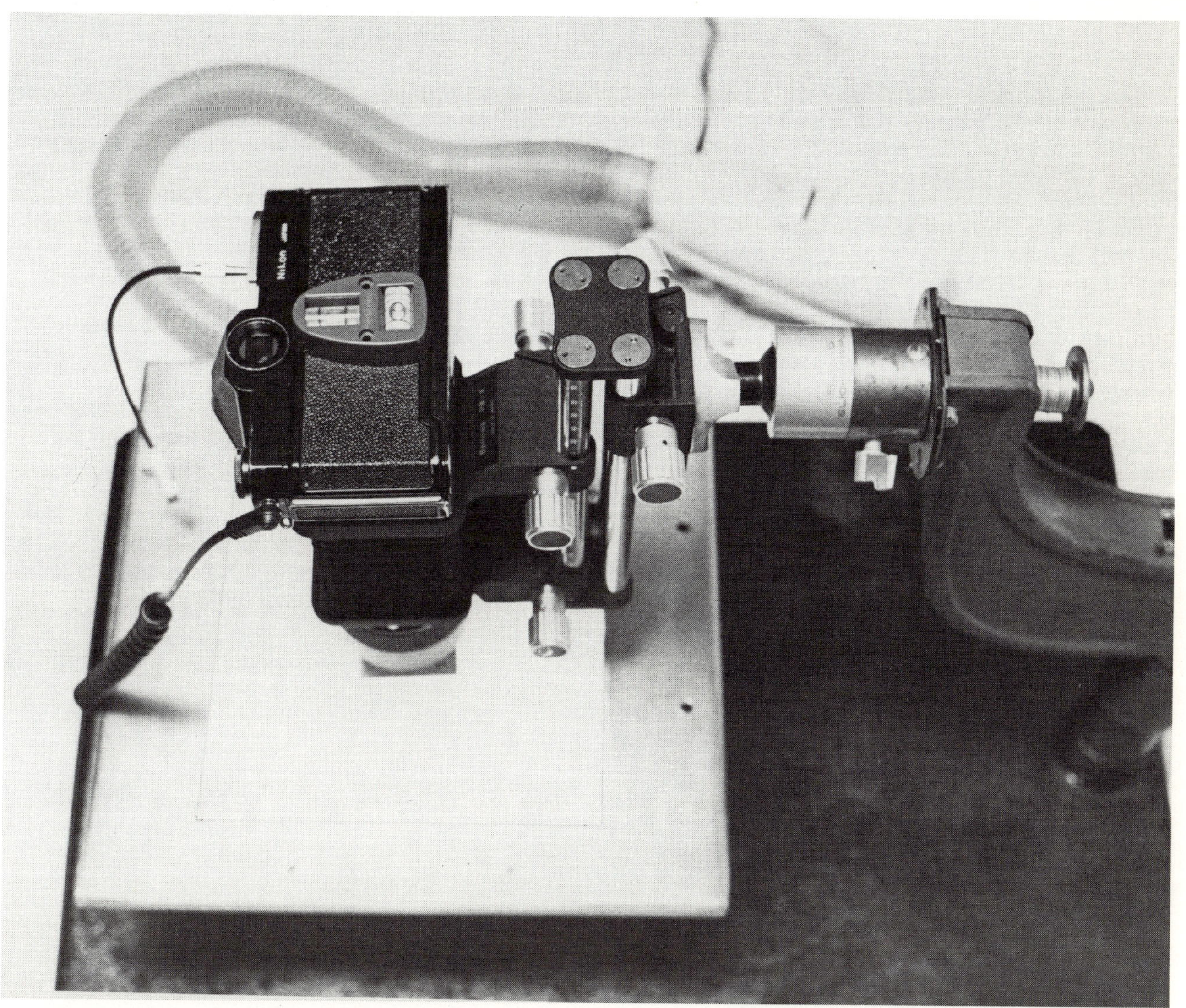

4. A level on the back of the camera is used to align the back of the camera with the top of the glass. Use a cable release to trip the shutter.

Steady, Tabletop Camera Support

MATERIALS

6″ (15.2 cm) stainless steel mixing bowl with a flat
    bottom
Scrap of leather
Felt
Plaster of paris
¼″ bolt, ½″ (12.7 cm) long (There is no metric
    equivalent of the ¼″ bolt that will work.)
Epoxy glue
Silicone cement, clear
Plastic container for mixing the plaster of paris

TOOLS

Drill and ¼″ bit
Ball peen hammer and center punch
Scissors
Razor knife
Leather punch
Stirring stick

My first experience with a table tripod was a bad one. I was using a small table tripod to take some close-ups when my camera started to topple. To save it, I yanked on the cable release in my hand. The camera's shutter release pulled out and the camera fell to the floor. After this experience, I developed an intense dislike for flimsy camera supports and easily devised an alternative.

I decided to make my own tabletop camera support—one that wouldn't fall over, no matter what. I don't know why a table camera support has to have three legs. The table already has four and this should be enough. All that should be needed is something that will hold a camera and will sit on the table.

First center punch the location for the hole in the center of the base of the mixing bowl and then drill a ¼″ (6.4 mm) hole. A sharp, regular drill bit should drill through the stainless steel. If your bit doesn't seem to be working, you can switch to a masonry drill bit. Its tungsten tip will easily drill through the bowl. Mix some epoxy and glue the ¼″ bolt in the hole and set it aside to dry.

While the epoxy is drying, cut a scrap of leather, slightly larger than the base of the bowl, and punch a hole in the center for the bolt. When the epoxy is dry, glue the leather to the bottom of the bowl with silicone.

Mix enough plaster of paris to fill the bowl. Keep adding water until the plaster is the consistency of pancake batter. It's best to mix it in a plastic container that can be thrown away. An ice cream container or large margarine container is about the right size. To fill the bowl evenly, it must sit level. With the bolt in place, you will need to support the bowl with boards on either side of the bolt. When level, fill the bowl to the edge with the plaster of paris.

The plaster sets quickly, so it should be hardened in an hour or so. Cover the hardened plaster with felt, gluing it in place with silicone. Use a slightly oversized piece of felt and trim down when the silicone is dry. The leather pad around the bolt should be trimmed to size as well.

The plaster of paris adds considerable weight to the camera support, increasing its stability. I have another support like this one that I filled with lead. It weighs about 10 lb. (4.5 kg) and is a really solid camera support. I use this extra-heavy support for high-magnification tabletop photography. The extra stability that all the weight provides is needed to hold a long, heavy bellows with extra extension. When not holding a camera, it also makes an excellent doorstop.

The large ball-and-socket head may seem oversized for a 35mm camera, but it locks securely in position and is easier to use than the smaller ones. A head from a tripod could also be used on the base.

This is a very stable and sturdy support, highly superior to a table tripod, and it's not going to tip over and accidentally drop a camera!

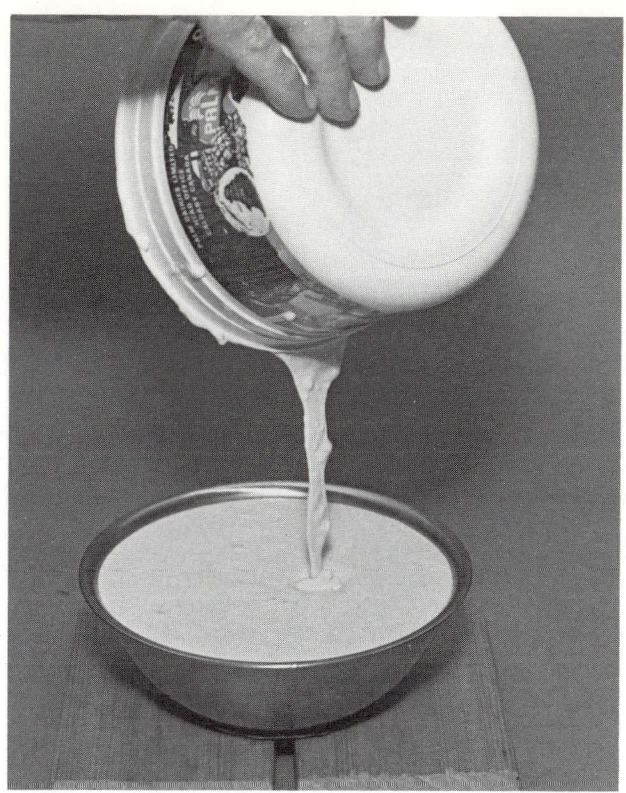

1. Above left. With the bolt epoxied in place, fill the bowl with plaster of paris.

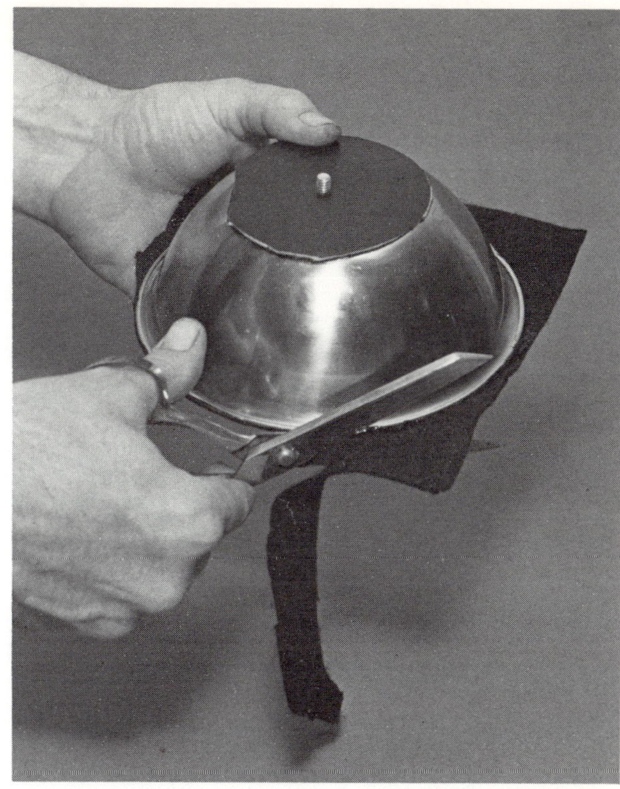

2. Above right. After the plaster is hardened, glue felt to the bottom and leather to the top of the support. Wait until the glue is dry before trimming the leather and felt.

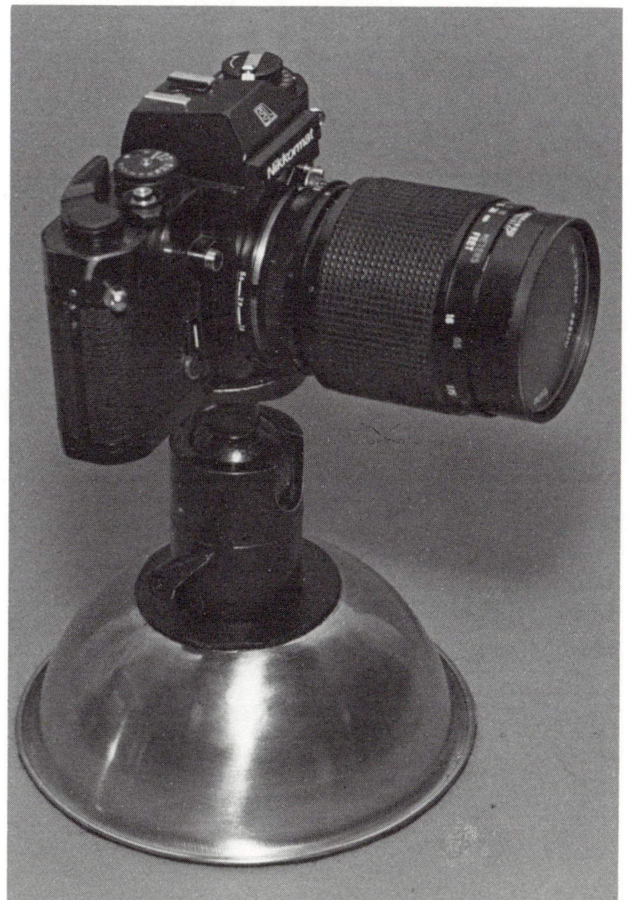

3. Left. A large ball-and-socket head works more smoothly and is easier to lock in position than a smaller one. This camera support doesn't tend to tip over like a table tripod does.

Telescoping Close-Up Clamps

MATERIALS

Miniature telescoping tripod
Three 5″ (12.7 cm) nails
Three ¼″ bolts ½″ long
Three ¼″ nuts and washers
Three paper clamps (Double Clip No. 109)
Epoxy glue
Masking tape
Small block of ¾″ (1.9 cm) wood
Aluminum foil
A toothpick or two

TOOLS

Pliers
Hacksaw
Electric drill
¼″ masonry bit

There are times I wish I had half a dozen hands. When taking a nature close-up, I have to position the subject, hold the lighting equipment (flash units, reflectors, diffusers), and still operate the camera. Clamps that can be pushed into the ground work for low subjects, but I also need something for the taller flowers and other subjects that may be a considerable distance from the ground. I finally figured out how to make clamps that can be used for subjects of different heights.

A miniature telescoping tripod has legs that can be used to make telescoping close-up clamps. The legs can expand from only 9″ (22.9 cm) to almost 4′ (1.2 m). These little tripods weren't very expensive new and might now be found at garage and rummage sales for a few dollars.

Begin by twisting the legs off the tripod using pliers. Remove the pinch spring from the top of each leg. This spring is for the top click stop and will get in the way when you begin modifying the tripod leg. The rubber tip on the bottom of each leg should also be twisted off with the pliers and discarded.

Set the legs aside while you prepare the other materials. Saw the heads off the nails so they will fit inside the small ends of the legs. Make marble-sized balls of aluminum foil and use the bolts to force one into the large opening of each tripod leg. Push the bolt in so that about half of it still extends past the top of the leg. Extend the legs and use

epoxy to glue the nails in the small tubing and the bolts and washers in the large tubing. The bolt should extend ¼″ (6.4 mm) above the washer. Masking tape can hold the bolt and washer in place while the glue is drying. The legs must be extended while gluing to prevent any sections from being accidentally fused. The aluminum foil forms a seat for the bolts as well as preventing the glue from flowing down the tubing.

While the epoxy on the legs is drying, begin working on the paper clamps. Use the drill and masonry bit to make a hole for the bolt in the center of each clamp. The masonry bit is necessary because spring steel is too hard to be drilled with a regular drill bit. A small ¾″ (1.9 cm) block of wood is used to hold the jaws of the clamp open while you are gluing. Make certain the block of wood is placed securely or the clamp will try to bite your fingers. Use a bolt to hold the nut in place inside the clamp. With a toothpick, add the glue around the outside of the nut. The epoxy can be mixed on a small piece of aluminum foil and discarded when gluing is finished.

A warm oven (150 F or 66 C) can be used to speed the drying of the epoxy on the clamps. When the glue is dry, test how well the epoxy held by springing the clamps wide open several times. If you are lucky, everything will hold. If you are not, one or more of the glue joints will fail. Reglue any nuts that come loose. Once the glue joint passes the test, it will stay glued because the clamps are rarely opened wide when in use.

These telescoping clamps can be used to hold reflectors, diffusers, the subject, or whatever else needs holding while you are taking nature close-ups. They act as extra hands for the photographer. A tripod adapter for an electronic flash lets you mount a small flash on the ¼″ bolt. Since the small head from the tripod was attached with a ¼″ bolt as well, it now can be mounted on one leg if you need greater flexibility. Other small tripod heads can also be used.

To get the maximum rigidity from the close-up clamps, use only the wider sections of the leg unless the full length is required. When pushing the clamps into the ground, grasp the section just above the spike to prevent the tubing from bending.

These small, lightweight clamps let me create a miniature studio around the subject.

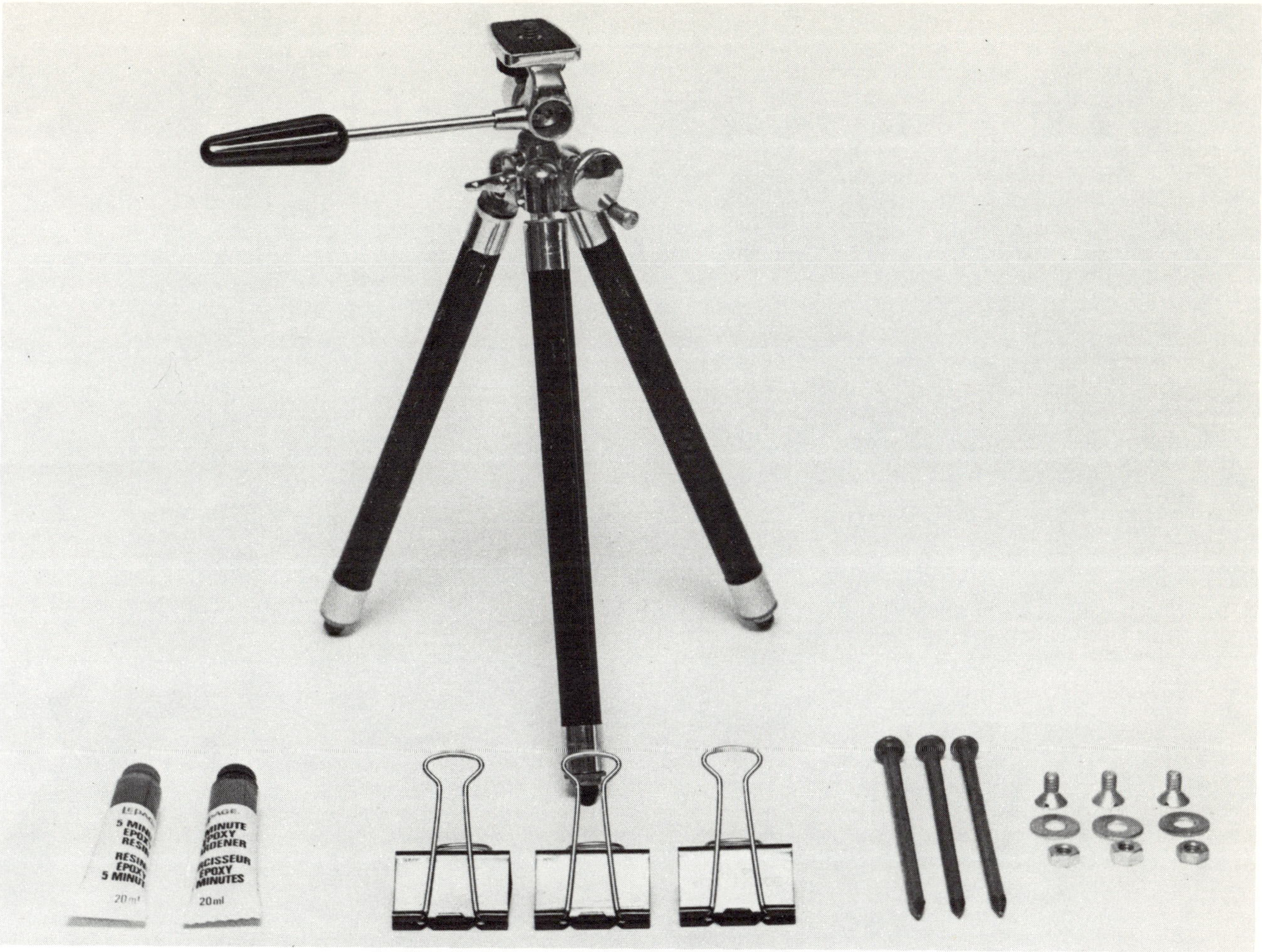

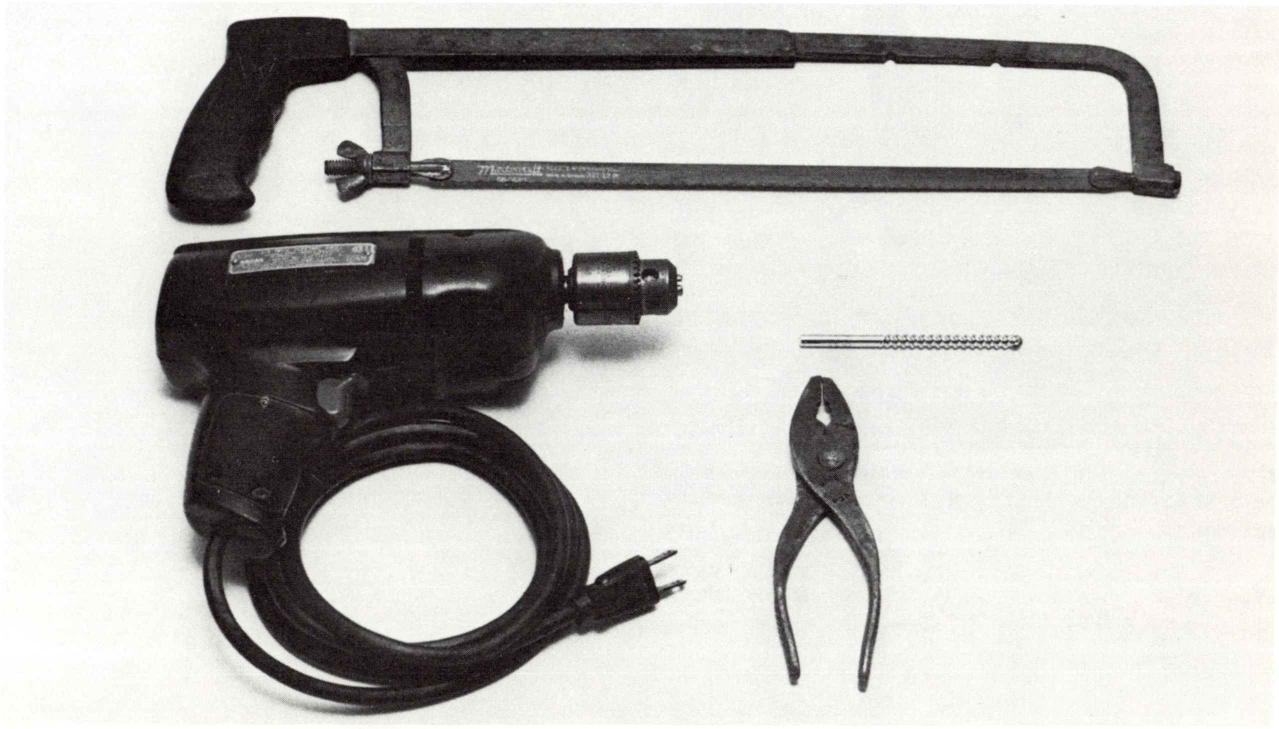

1. To turn a mini tripod into three close-up clamps, you'll need ¼″ nuts, bolts, and washers, large nails, paper clamps, and epoxy.

2. The tools needed are a hacksaw, pliers, a drill, and a ¼″ masonry drill bit.

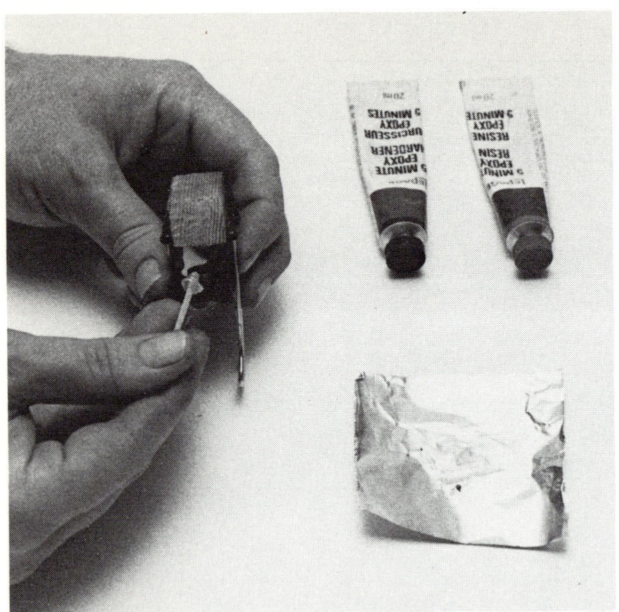

3. Hold the jaws of the clamp open with a wood block and put epoxy around the nut with a toothpick. While gluing, the nut is held in place with a bolt.

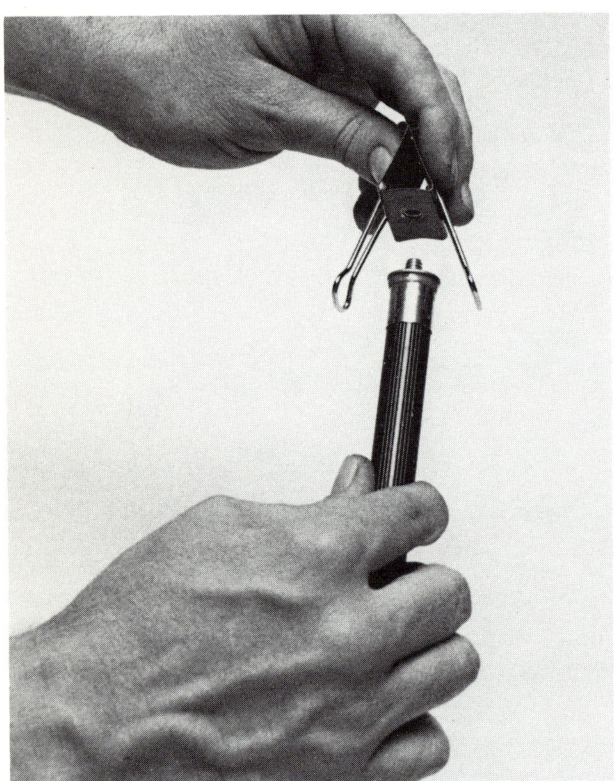

4. You can attach the clamp to the modified tripod legs. Mini-tripod heads can be added to the telescoping leg for greater flexibility.

5. Right. The finished clamps are only 12″ (30.5 cm) long with the spike and can telescope to 4′ (1.2 m). They can hold reflectors, diffusers, and electronic flash units.

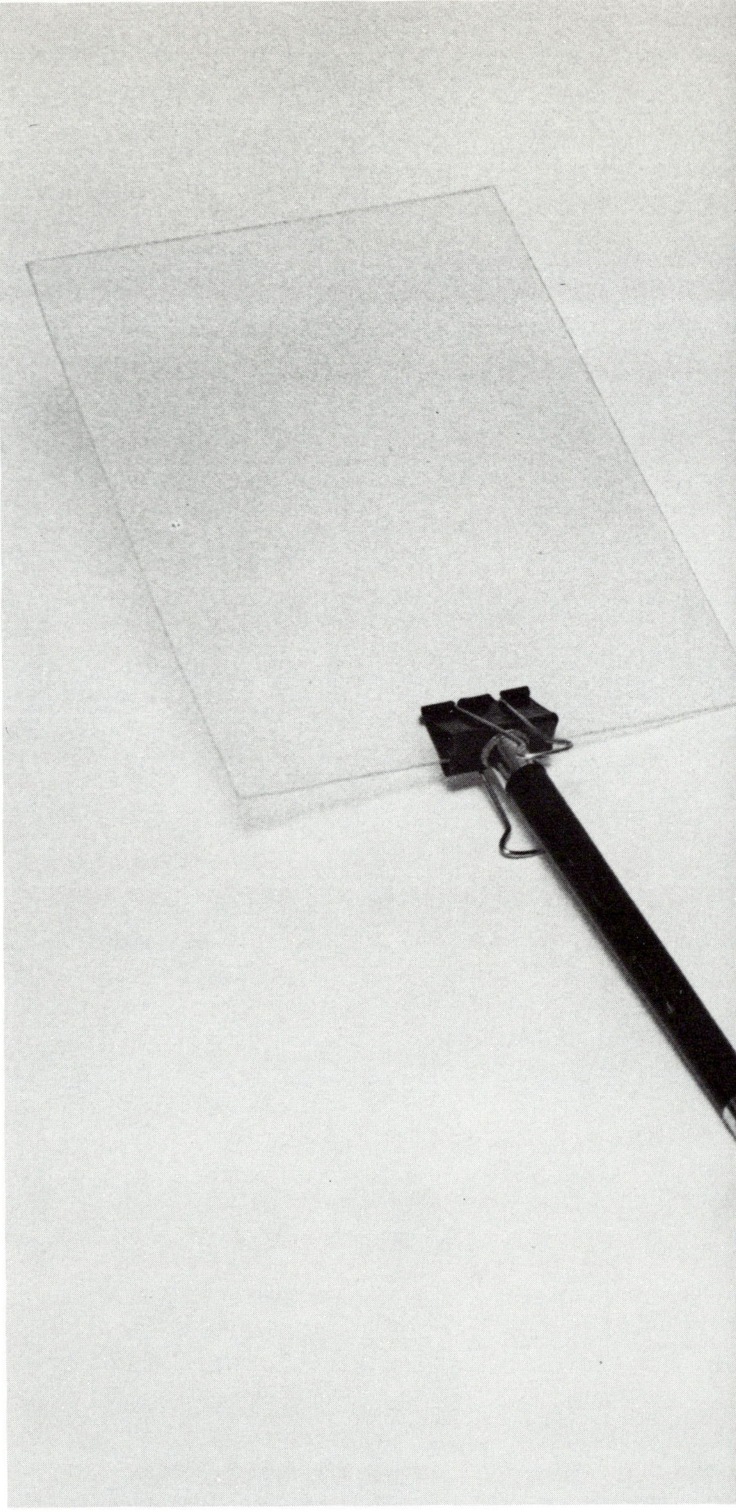

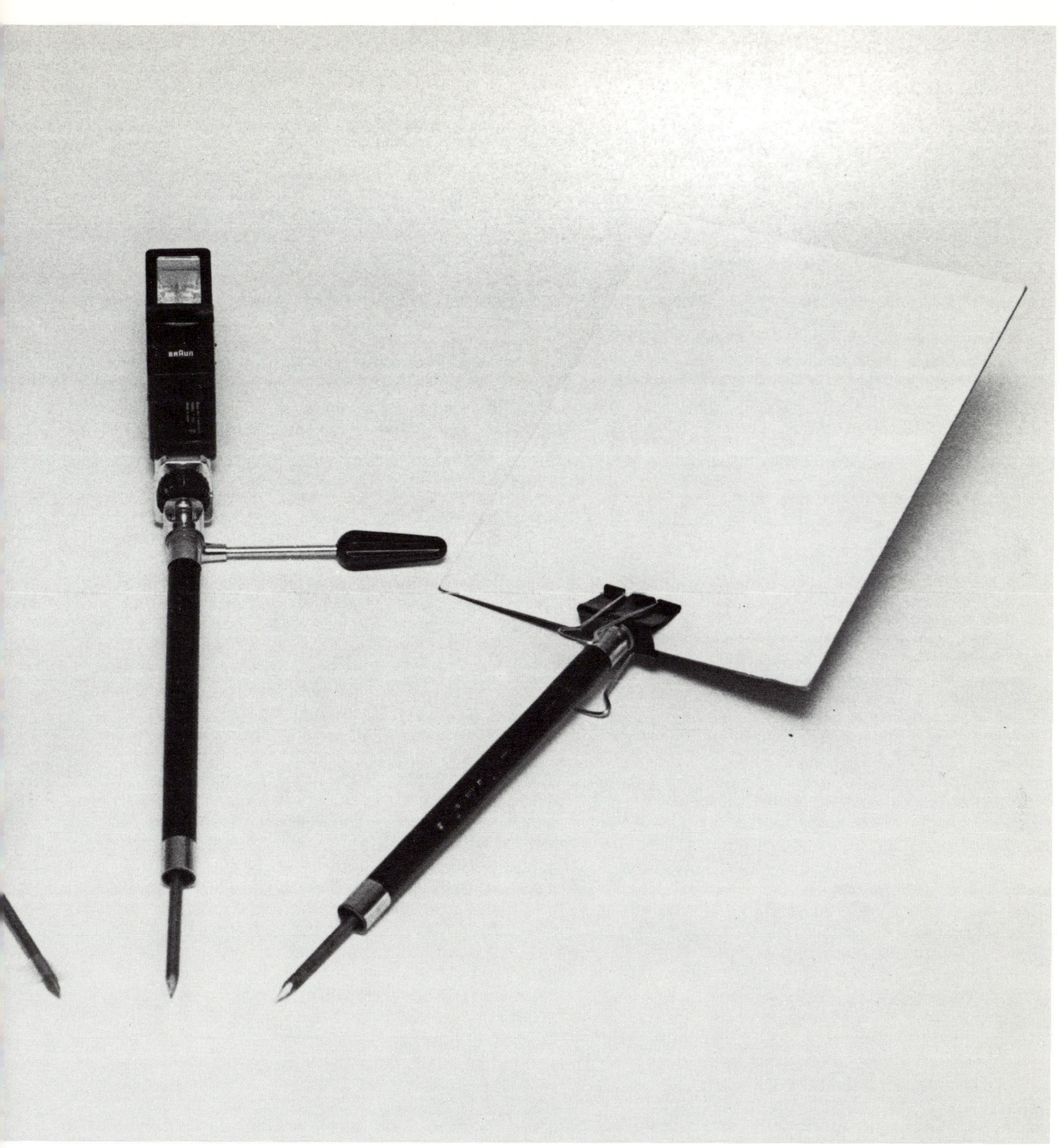

Setup for Shooting Small, Moving Objects

MATERIALS

2 small ball-and-socket heads
2 flash swivels
1/8" (3.2 mm) thick aluminum, 1½" × 9" (3.8 × 22.8 cm)
1" (2.5 cm) dowel rod, 1' (30.5 cm) long
Aluminum rod ½" (12.7 mm) diameter, 2' (61 cm) long long
Two ¼" (6.4 mm) carriage bolts, 5" (12.7 cm) long
Two ¼" nuts and small washers
Scrap of black leather
Instant glue for wood and leather
Black or clear silicone
Epoxy glue (or you can use the instant glue)
Lightweight oil
Emery paper

TOOLS

Drill and drill bits, 3/16" (4.8 mm), ¼" (6.4 mm), extra long 5/8" (15 mm) wood bit
Large flat file
Ball peen hammer and center punch
Small square file
Hacksaw
Miter box (optional)
¼" tap with 20 threads to the inch (no metric equivalent)
Razor knife
Locking pliers
Needle-nosed pliers
Vise and "C" clamp (optional)

Photographing insects and other small creatures is often done with some kind of rig. This rig consists of a bracket that can position two flash units in front of a camera with a macro lens or a bellows-lens combination.

These insect rigs aren't available commercially so each photographer must make his or her own. I make a different one every two or three years, each time trying to make it a little better than the last one. The bracket must be lightweight, but quite strong, highly adjustable, and provide for quick changes in the position of the flash units.

This is my latest attempt at making an insect rig that meets all these requirements.

First cut a 9" (22.9 cm) length of aluminum for the base of the insect rig. When buying aluminum for these projects, it is best to buy the thick aluminum already cut in convenient widths. I bought mine 1½" (3.8 cm) wide. This saves a lot of sawing. Straighten the sawed ends by drawing them across a flat file. Round the corners, and sand the edges and the corners smooth.

Next, cut the dowel into 4½" (11.4 cm) lengths. Cut one end perpendicular and cut the other end slanted about 15 to 20 degrees. The slanted face will be used to angle the handles forward so as to keep them out of the way when advancing the film. It also makes it easier to carry and to aim the combined camera and flash units.

Drill a ¼" (6.4 mm) hole through the center of the dowel. Using a 6" (15.2 cm) long drill bit helps drill the hole through, but you could use a regular drill bit and drill from both ends of the dowel. Use a 5/8" (15.9 mm) wood bit to countersink the hole in the perpendicularly cut end of the dowel rod. This large hole will hold a nut and washer and needs to be about ½" (12.7 mm) deep.

Position the dowels on the aluminum bar and find the location for the holes needed to attach the handles. Drill ¼" holes in the bar, angling the bit slightly to match the forward slant of the handles. Attach the handles with carriage bolts 5" (12.7 cm) long. These bolts have a square portion near the bolt head that requires square holes to be cut in the aluminum bar. Use a small square file to shape the round holes into square ones. File the corners first, then flatten the sides with the file to finish the hole. Test the fit with the bolt.

When the square holes are finished, insert the carriage bolts and clamp the head of the bolt and the bar in a vise. Bend the bolt forward to match the slant of the handles. Try to keep the bends close to the heads of the bolts. These bolts can be bent using pliers, but the vise really helps.

Wooden dowel rods go over the carriage bolts to make the handles. Plain wood handles will work, but I covered mine with leather to improve the appearance and then attached them to the bolts. Use a medium weight of black leather. Glue one edge of the leather to the wood with an instant glue. **Be careful with this glue**—it really does bond to skin instantly. Wrap the leather around the dowel and use more glue to attach the leather where it meets the glued edge. Slit the leather with a razor knife where the ends meet. Trim the leather at the top and bottom of the dowel. Add more glue as required to hold the leather in place. Repeat these steps with the other dowel.

Slide the leather-covered dowels over the carriage bolts and use a small washer and nut to attach the handles. Add some epoxy around the base of the handle and also around the nut and washer. The nut can be tightened with needle-nosed pliers, but the epoxy will lock it in place so that it won't loosen. This nut at the base of the handle prevents the handle from rotating.

Epoxy a ¼" fender washer to the top of each handle. Cut a leather pad with a hole punched in the center to make a neat platform on each handle for attaching the ball-and-socket heads. Use silicone to glue the leather to the washer.

Set the bracket aside while you work on the rest of the rig. Small ball-and-socket heads and flash swivels position the two flash units. I used Rowi but

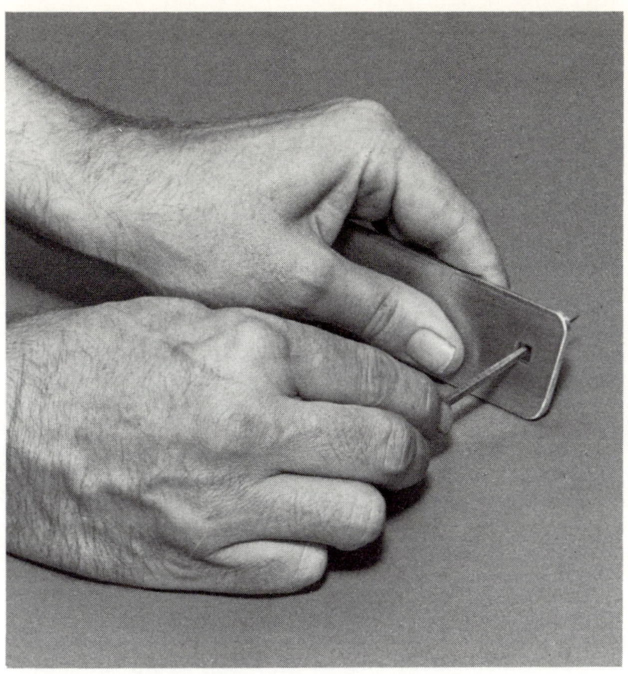

1. Use a small square file to change the shape of the round holes to square ones.

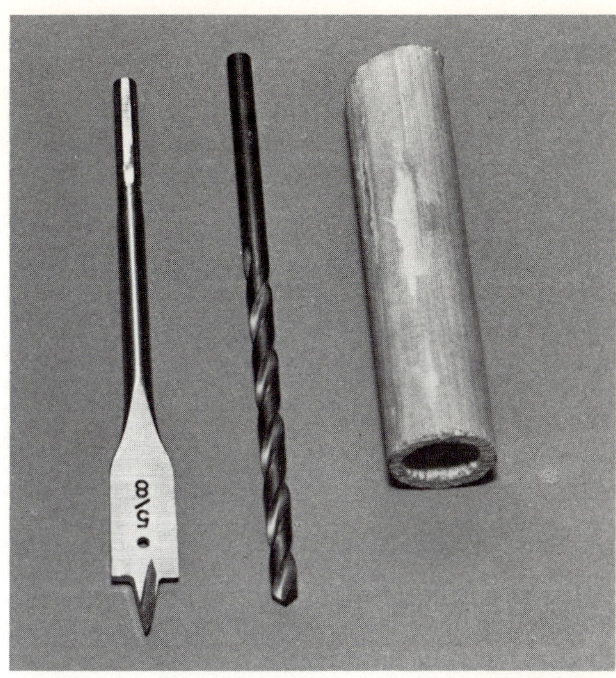

2. Use two bits to drill the handle — a bit small in diameter to drill the hole for the carriage bolt and a wood bit to enlarge the hole to hold the nut and washer.

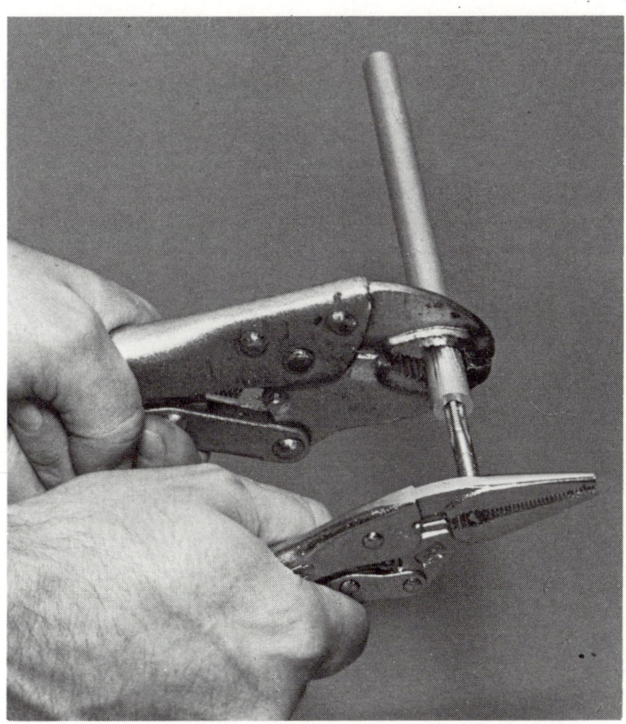

3. First drill holes in the ends of the aluminum rods and then use a tap to cut the threads. Use pliers to twist the tap into the metal.

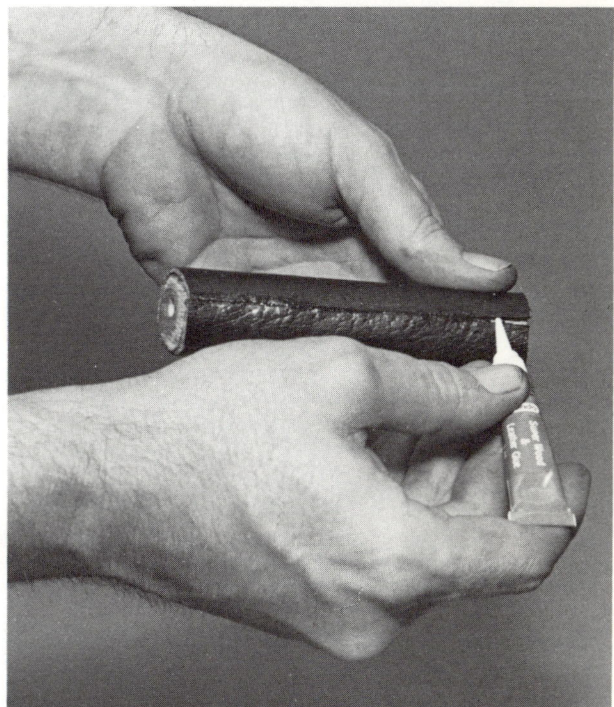

4. Use an instant glue to cover the dowel rod handles with leather.

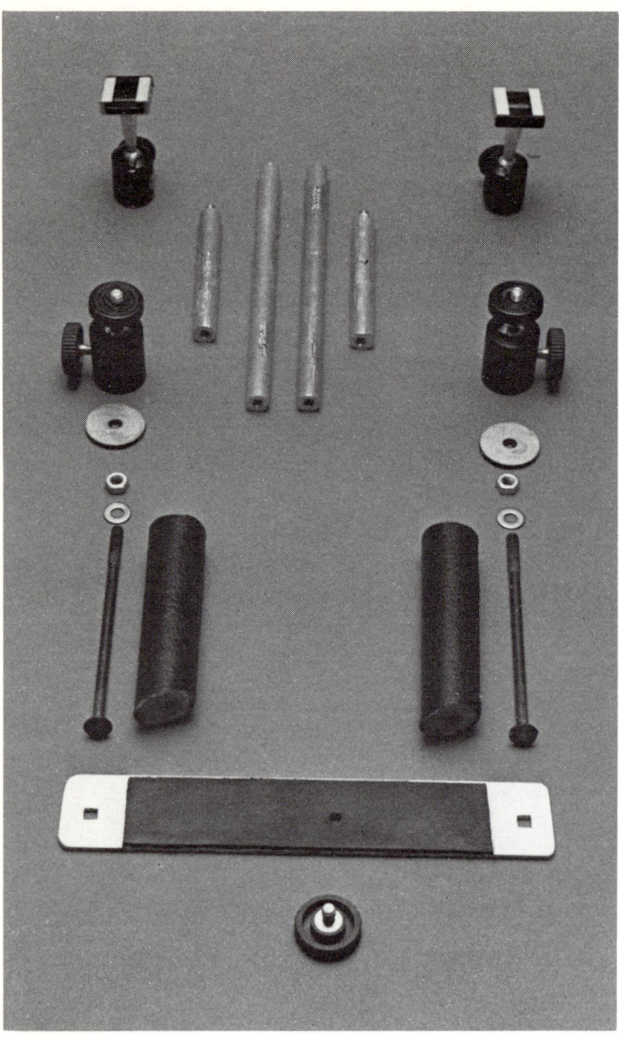

5. This is how all the parts of the insect rig go together. Assembly is simple — just bolt and glue everything together.

other brands will also work. I like the flash swivel with the extension arm. It helps to angle the flash units in toward the subject.

Use aluminum rods to attach the ball-and-socket heads to the flash swivels. Saw the rod into two 4″ (10.2 cm) and two 8″ (20.3 cm) pieces. The ends of the rods should be filed smooth and flat. Then center punch each rod end. Drill a 3/16″ (4.8 mm) hole in the end of each rod. Use a ¼″ tap with 20 threads to the inch to cut the threads. A drop or two of lightweight oil helps when cutting these. When the tap becomes difficult to turn, twist it out to remove the metal shavings and begin cutting again.

Each rod must have a male thread and a female thread. Saw four ½″ (12.7 mm) pieces of thread from a ¼″ bolt. These are the male threads. Add some epoxy to an end of each thread and screw it into one tapped end of each rod. Set these aside to dry or quick-dry them in a warm oven (150 F or 66 C).

Set your camera on the aluminum bar and find the place to drill the hole for the tripod screw that attaches the camera. Drill a ¼″ hole for the screw. Next use a razor knife to cut a strip of leather to cover the center section of the aluminum bar. The leather can be trimmed to a precise fit after it is glued in place. Punch a hole in the leather for the tripod screw and glue the leather to the bar with silicone.

Assemble the finished pieces of the insect rig and attach the camera and flash units and the insect rig is ready to use. Use the 8″ (20.3 cm) rods for lenses of longer than normal focal lengths. The short rods are for use with normal lenses and for high magnifications. Shoot a test roll of film to find the best exposure at different magnifications.

Focusing is done differently when using the rig. Don't try to focus by twisting the lens. Set the magnification you wish, and move the rig toward the subject. As the subject begins to come into focus, trip the shutter while still moving the rig forward. With practice, this method of focusing is faster and produces consistently sharper photos than focusing with the lens and trying to hold the focus.

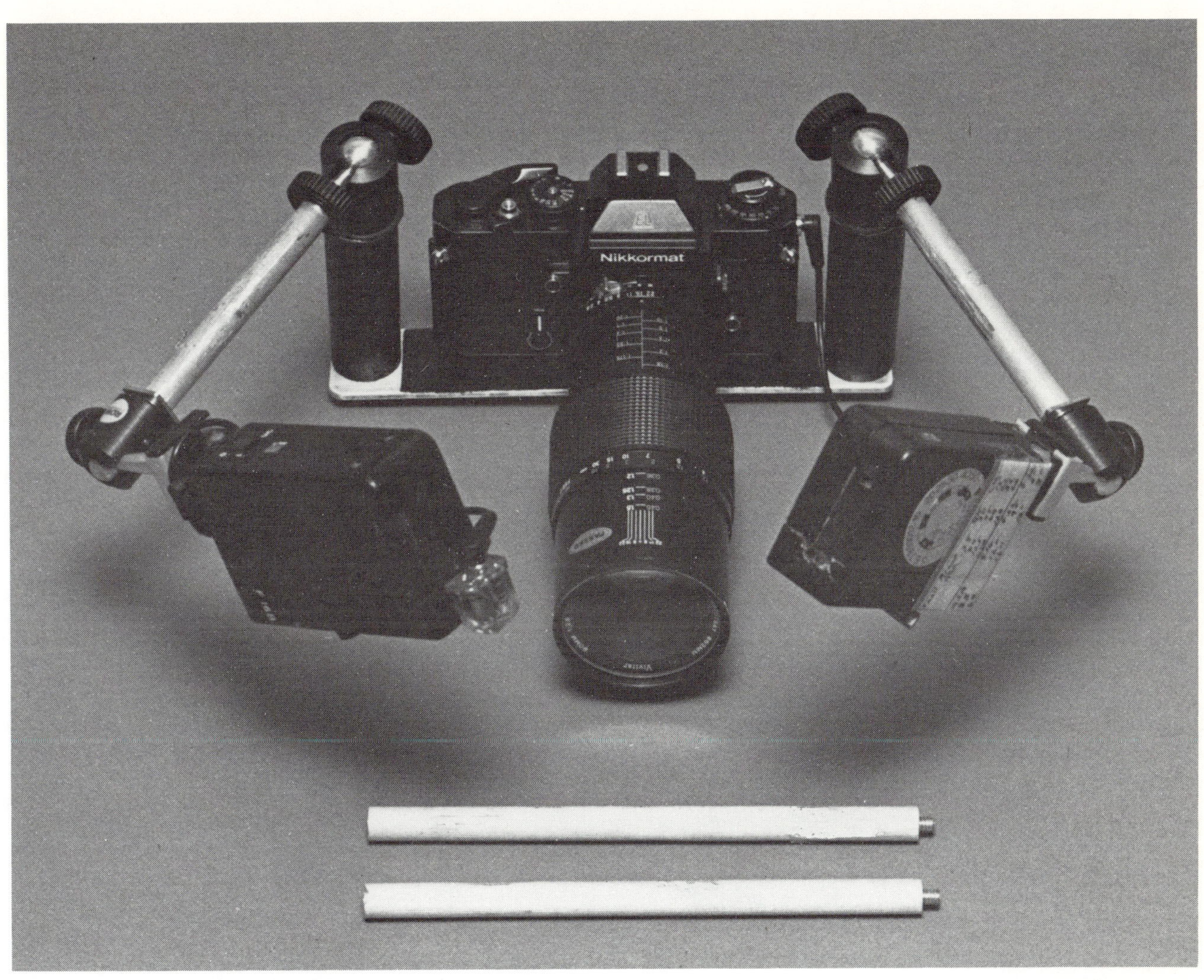

6. The ball-and-socket heads and the flash swivels let you position two flash units in front of a macro lens. The position is easily changed to vary the lighting. The extra set of rods are for changing the lengths of the arms.

Extra Long Extension Tubes

Regular extension tubes just aren't long enough for high magnification. One way to increase the magnification is to connect two or three sets of extension tubes together, but this can become rather expensive. I frequently take photos at very high magnification and need a way to increase the amount of extension. Rather than buy another set of tubes I made a long extension tube.

The set of manual extension tubes for my cameras (Nikons) screw together. Only the end pieces have the bayonet mount. The thread used for the center sections is the same as for filters (52 mm). This may be true for your brand of camera as well. You can check by just screwing a filter to the threads of the extension tubes. If the threads fit, you can make a long extension tube using threaded filter rings and the parts of the extension tubes that have the camera and lens mount. If the filters don't fit, you can use two short sections of the extension tubes to make an extra long extension for high magnification.

You'll need two filters minus the glass, so check the filters that you use. If you use UV filters to protect your lenses like I do, I suggest you check these filters. Angle them to reflect light from the front surface and look for scratches. I was appalled at how scratched and scoured some of my filters were. When they are in this bad shape, it's time to replace them.

Wrap the filters in two or three layers of cloth and use the hammer to break out the glass. Be careful of the sharp glass and use the cloth to protect your hands when removing the fragments.

If none of your filters deserve this drastic treatment, check the bargain bin at camera stores. You may be able to find used filters or adapter rings that will work.

Finding tubing the right diameter is somewhat of a scavenger hunt. Things like plastic drinking glasses, rigid plastic bottles, plastic and copper pipe may have the right diameter for your extension tube. I used the tubing from an old telescoping plastic fishing rod case.

Saw or cut 6″ (15.2 cm) of tubing. A miter box can be used to saw the tubing if you have one. Or a perpendicular cut can be made by rotating the tubing on a flat surface as it's being cut. Use epoxy or instant glue to attach the filter rings to the ends of the tubing. One end should have a male thread and the other a female thread.

When the glue is dry, the tubing should be lined with self-adhesive, black flocked paper. Remove the backing from paper that has been cut slightly too large and roll the paper to insert it into the tube. The paper's edges should overlap slightly. Use a razor knife to cut through the overlapped portion of the paper and remove the excess. This method ensures aligned edges. A flat black paint could also be used to eliminate reflections inside the tubing. Paint the outside of the tubing with black paint. When the paint is dry, the long extension tube is ready to use.

If you plan to use the tube with a heavy macro lens, test the strength of the glue joints by twisting and pulling on them to make sure of their strength before trusting them to hold your lens.

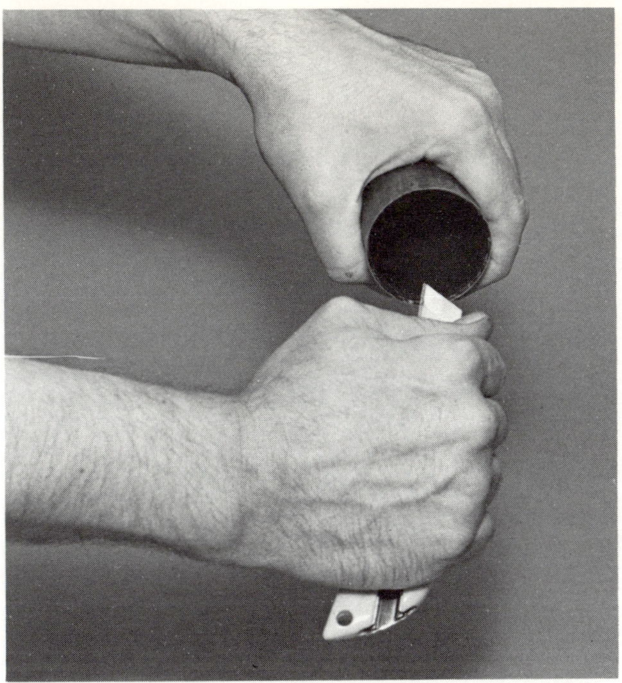 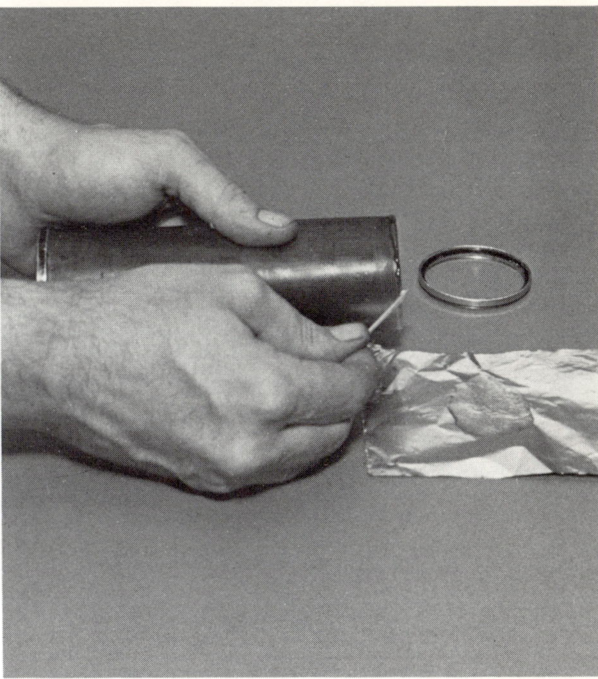

1. Use a razor knife to thin the inside edge on one end of the plastic tube so the male thread of the filter ring will fit inside. The female thread fits around the outside of the plastic tube without any modification.

2. Aluminum foil is a good palette for mixing the epoxy glue and a toothpick is a handy applicator. Only a small amount of glue is needed for a strong glue joint providing there is a large area of contact.

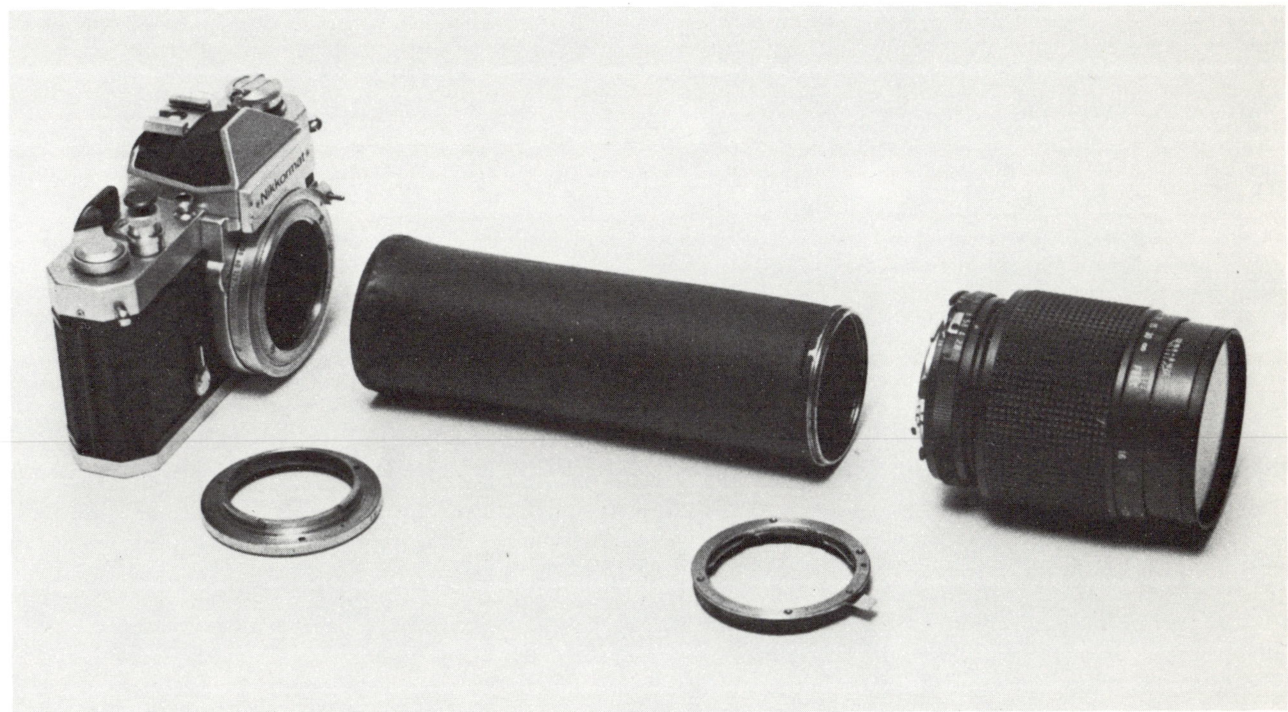

3. The long extension tube can be mounted on the camera using the short (K2) ring, on the left, from a set of manual extension tubes. The manufacturer of your brand of camera probably makes a similar ring with your camera's mount. The ring on the right has the female camera mount and can be threaded on the long extension tube to mount a Nikon lens.

PART FIVE

FINISHING AND DISPLAY AIDS

Print-Spotting Pens

MATERIALS

4 fine-line glass-tipped pens (Ultra-fine Flair, Bic
    deluxe markers, and Pilot fineliner are just a few
    that can be used)
Spotting dyes (Spotone or black india ink)
Plastic or Styrofoam cups
Acetic acid or stop bath
Photo-Flo or another wetting agent
Paper towels
Self-adhesive labels
Scratch pad
Unwanted prints

TOOLS

Pliers
Eyedropper
Tweezers

Photography is considered a twentieth century
art form. But when it comes to spotting prints, photography is absolutely medieval—relying on small
brushes and dyes to correct imperfections in
prints. Modern technology has created many new
marking instruments. First there were the ball-point
pens, then the felt tips, and now the new glass-
tipped pens. For print spotting, all that needs to be
added to these pens is the right ink or dye.

Begin by using the pliers to remove the rear
plugs from the ends of four pens. These plugs are
held in place with a small wire pin and can be
pulled out easily. At the sink, use tweezers to remove the ink-filled fiber cartridges inside the pens.
You may want to wear rubber gloves to prevent
ink-stained fingers. Some cartridges are enclosed
in a plastic sleeve that should be removed. Wash
out all the ink with running water. All the pens mentioned have water-soluble ink—other pens may
have an oil-based ink that would make them unus-
able for this project.

When the ink is gone, the cartridges will be
brown and the running water will be clear. Also
wash out the pens to remove any ink in the tips.
Dry the fiber pads in a warm oven (150 F or 66 C).
The pads must be dried because the water present would dilute the dyes when they are added.

While waiting for the pads to dry, mix four different shades of spotting dye, ranging from very light
to dark. The Spotone can be mixed to produce a
wide range of warm or cool tones, or a neutral tone
can be obtained by using the fluid straight from the
bottle. Most papers have a neutral tone and this is
the one you should use unless you frequently use
warm-toned paper. I have a problem with Spotone
dye because I can't get it dark enough to match
the black in prints. A black india ink can be used in
the spotting pens to get a darker color than is pos-

sible with the dye. When mixing the dyes, add two
drops of Photo-Flo and two drops of acetic acid to
each container. These make the dye take to the
emulsion better. Mix only about ½ oz. (15 ml) of
each tone. Test the dye on rejected prints to be
sure that it is the shade and tone you wish.

When the fiber pads are dry, put them back in
the sleeve (if they had one) and place a pad in
each cup of dye. Capillary action will suck the dye
into the pad, but to speed up the process, use the
eye dropper to add the dye to the top of the cartridge. When the cartridge is full, wipe the outside
and soak up a little of the excess with the paper
towels. Put the pads back into the pens.

Put a self-adhesive label on the bottom of each
pen. I use numbers to identify the tones—1 for the
darkest and 4 for the lightest. But you can use any
method of identification you wish.

Replace the rear caps and test the pens on
some writing paper. It will take a while for the water
to flow out of the tip, so doodle on the paper to get
the dye to flow. Each pen should have its own dis-
tinct shade, varying from very light (almost invisi-
ble) to dark. Now test the pens on an unwanted
print. Spotting is best done using small dots. Hold
the pen almost vertical and just barely touch the tip
to the paper. These pens are excellent for making
small dots.

The pens work on both RC and fiber-based papers. However, if a print has been left in the fixer
too long, it won't absorb the dye as readily as it
should. For this reason, it is important not to over
fix your prints. Some photographers use fixer
without a hardener when they expect to spot the
prints. This makes the emulsion softer so it will take
the dyes better.

The ink takes only a short time to dry. Be careful
not to smudge it. If the dots are too dark, you can
use a damp sponge to wipe the print and lighten
the color. I've used the pens for a couple of years
now and I am quite happy with them. They don't
dry out if the cap is kept on. If you forget and leave
a cap off, you can usually get the ink to flow again
by just moistening the tip.

The pens do have one unusual trait. When they
haven't been used for a while, water evaporates
from the tip and leaves ink behind. At first, the dye
will be darker than it should be. Use this to your
advantage. Have a scrap pad handy to test the
shade by doodling. The dye will quickly lighten.
This creates many intermediate shades. Doodle
with the pen until the shade you want flows out.

I use fine-line markers for writing and when one
runs out of ink, I refill it with a new shade of spotting
dye. If the tip is blunter than you wish, it can be
sharpened by using a fine whetstone under running water. These spotting pens can make print
spotting a lot easier.

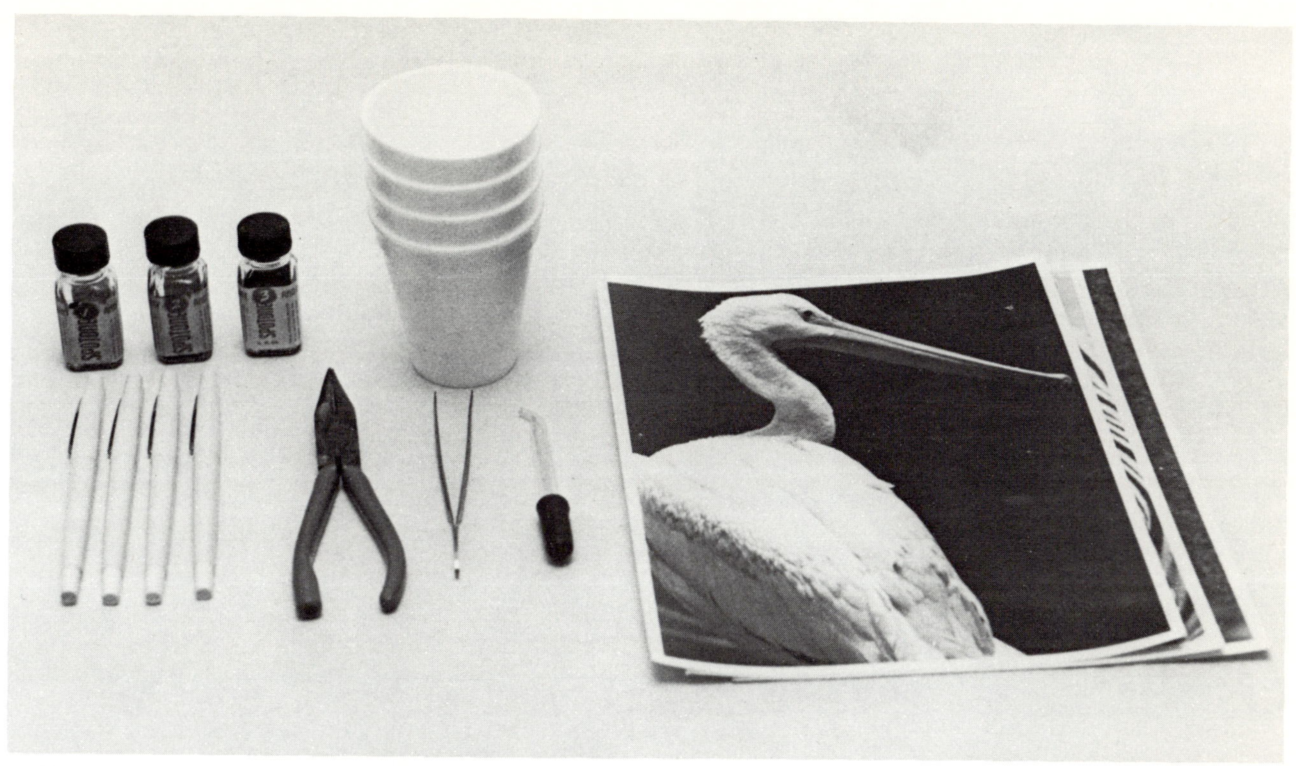

1. To make print-spotting pens, you'll need some spotting dye, fine-line markers, cups, pliers, tweezers, an eye dropper, and some unwanted prints for testing the dyes.

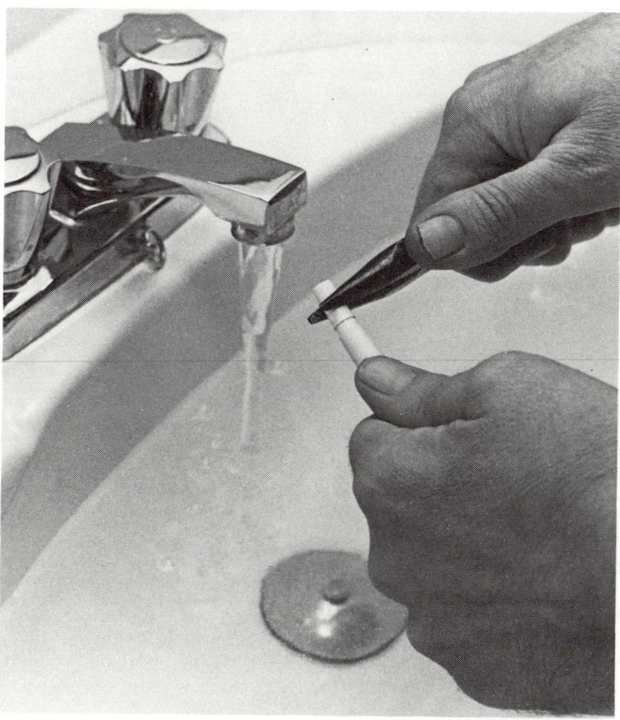

2. At the sink, use pliers to remove the end caps from the pens. On some brands, a thin wire holds the cap in place. It can be pulled out with the pliers.

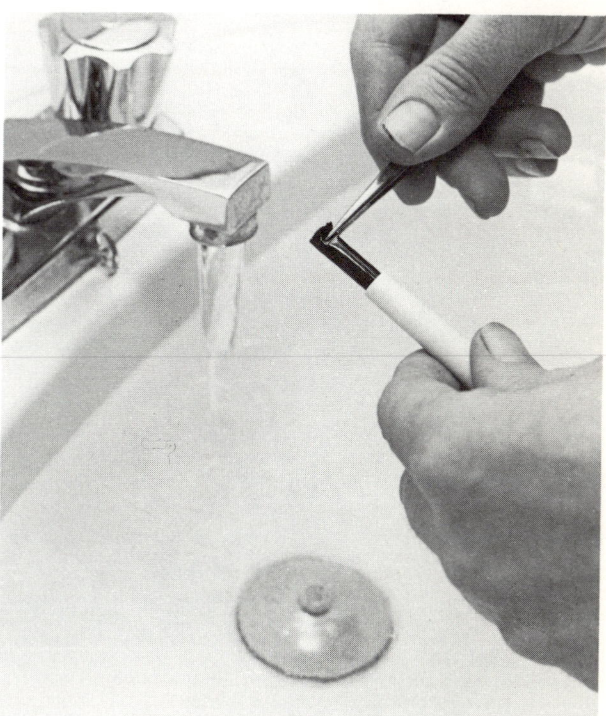

3. With the tweezers, pull the fiber cartridge out of the pen. This fiber pad is inside a plastic sleeve that you should remove before washing the pad.

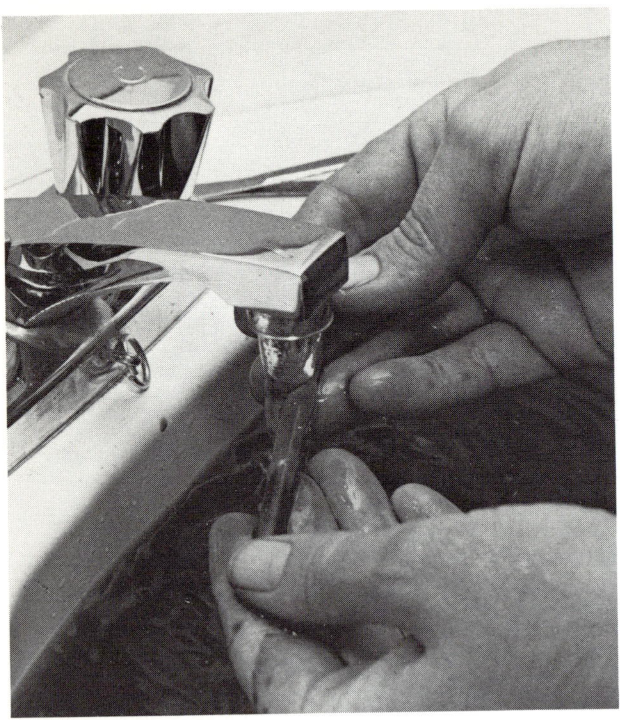

4. Hold the fiber pad under running water to wash out the ink.

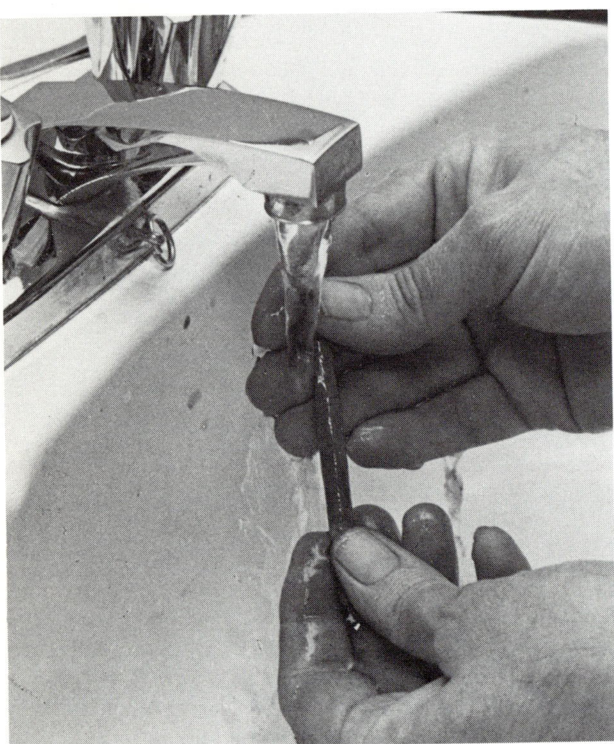

5. Keep the pad under the running water until all the ink is washed away and the water is clear. Also wash the plastic sleeve if there was one with the pen.

6. Right. Mix four different shades of the spotting dye, ranging from very light to dark. Insert a fiber pad in each cup of dye. Use an eye dropper to help saturate the pads.

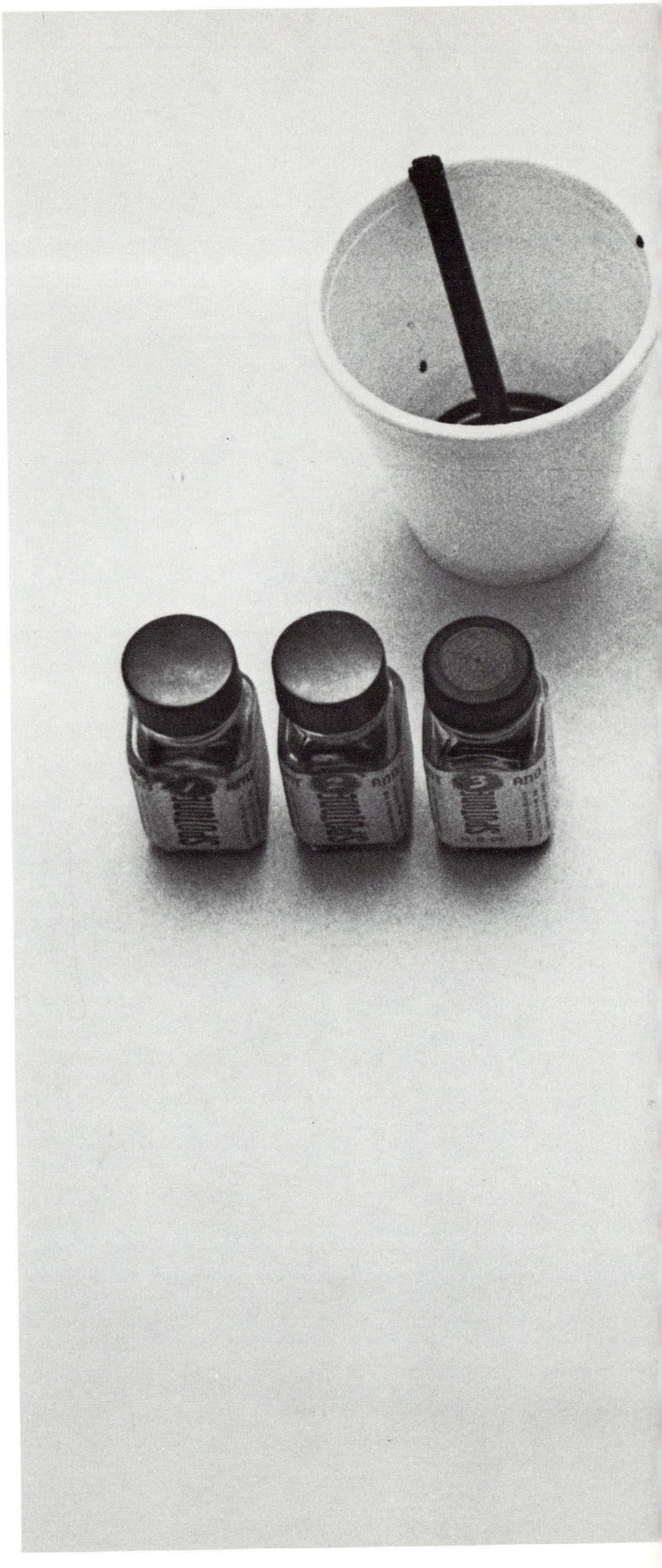

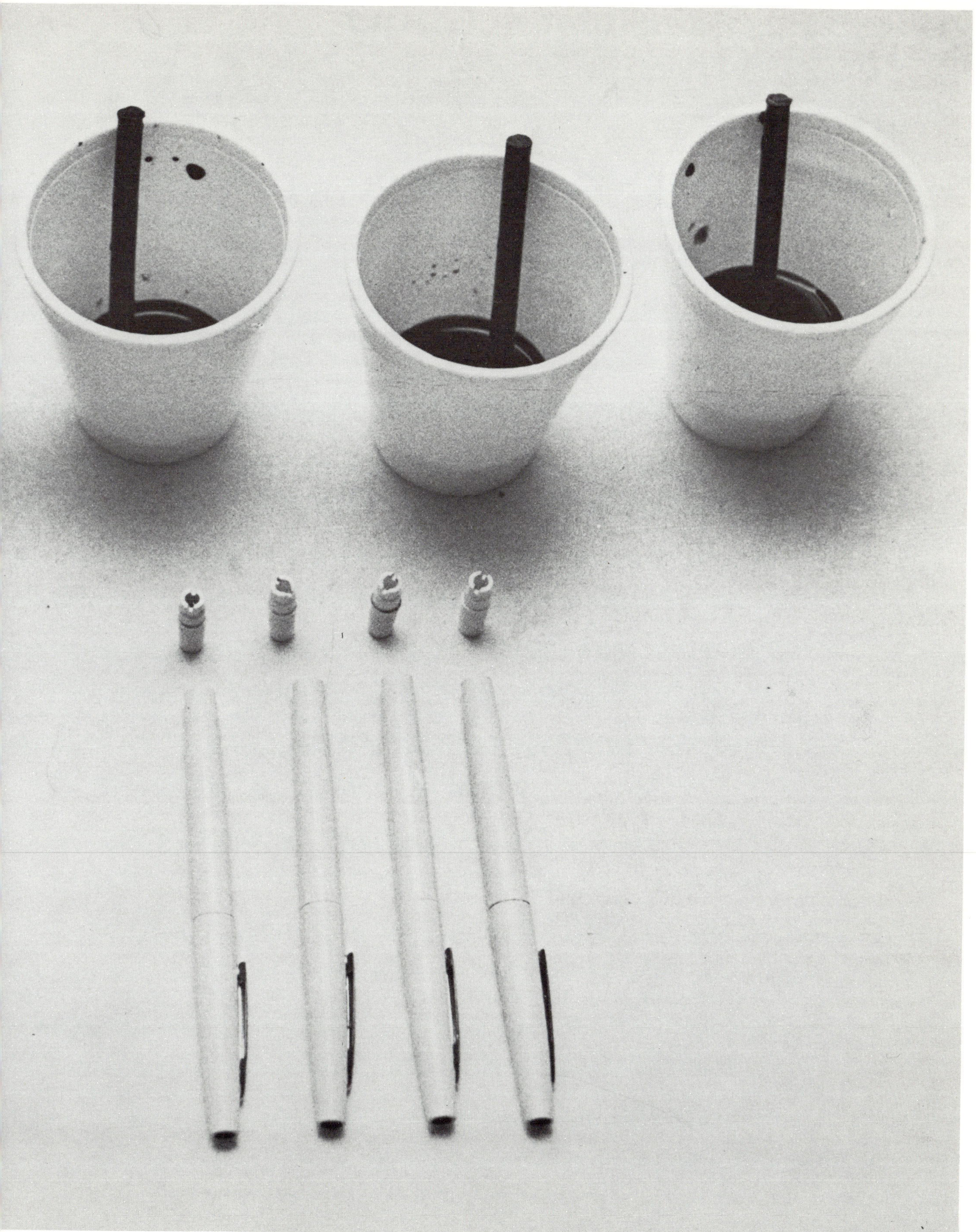

Nonslip Mat Cutter

Designing a mat cutter should be a snap. All that it has to do is hold the blade at an angle and cut a straight line. Murphy's Law prevailed and none of the prototypes I made worked. They all cut a wavy line and I couldn't figure out why. I finally found the problem—the blades were flexing under pressure and the flexing was causing the wavy cut. Another problem was that the cutter veered off the guide. I discovered that this was because the blade wasn't parallel to the guide.

I finally cleared up the defects in this design and I hope you can take advantage of the mistakes and false starts I made. Designing something for yourself can be very rewarding, but always remember that Murphy was an optimist.

The Stanley replacement blades are thicker and sturdier than the other look-alike blades that I tried. The metal ruler is an extra-wide one that I bought in a hardware store. You may have to shop around to find one like it. The extra width provides a large base for the cutter to rest on. If you can, find a ruler with indented markings. These markings are less likely to wear off than regular printed ones. A big advantage of this mat cutter is that the T square serves as the guide. I shopped around for a T square and was appalled at the prices, so I made one instead.

The first step of this project is making the T square. Align the top bar as perfectly as you can with the carpenter's square. I used a double thickness of ⅛″ (3.2 mm) aluminum for the bar, but it could also be made from wood, preferably a hardwood. The thickness allows the bar to hook onto the edge of the table or cutting board. (I use a table covered with corrugated cardboard to cut mats, but you can use a sheet of plywood on the floor instead.)

First check and double check the alignment. Then use instant glue or epoxy to attach the bar to the metal ruler. The glue holds the pieces together while you drill the rivet holes. Drilling the holes through all the metal layers at the same time solves the problem of alignment. I used regular rivets but the pop-type rivets could also be used. If you do use a riveting tool, one end of the rivets will protrude, so pound the ends flat to improve the appearance.

After you make the T square, begin work on the cutter. The cutter glides on the ruler and has rails on the base to hold it in place. These rails extend only about 1/16″ (1.6 mm) and are made from a flat piece of aluminum. To find the width for the metal, measure the width of the ruler and add an extra ¼″ (6.4 mm). The extra ¼″ allows for the bends and the lengths of the rails. Use a hacksaw or metal shears to cut the metal. Cutting the metal with shears tends to bend it, so the metal will have to be hammered flat afterwards. The width of the glide depends on the ruler you use and can be made any length, so I won't give dimensions.

A pencil can be used to mark the metal, but it is better to use a scribe. The pencil mark might rub off. A scratched line is more permanent. Scribe a line 3/32″ (2.4 mm) from the edge of the metal where you wish to make the bend. Measure this as closely as you can and mark a line for each bend.

Use a drop of instant glue or epoxy to attach the metal to a scrap of wood. This makes the metal easier to hold and the filing simpler. File a groove in the metal along the scribed line. You can use a square file if you have one, or you can use the corner of a flat file. File each groove about one-third the thickness of the metal.

When the grooves are finished, insert into the vise 1/16″ of the end of the metal that will become the rail and bend the metal over at a right angle. Repeat this procedure with the other rail. Be sure that the metal is square in the vise (the filed groove must be parallel to the jaws of the vise) to get a rail that is even across.

Test the guide by placing it on the ruler. It should be a close fit. A little hammering on the sides of the guide (rails) can tighten the fit and a little filing or unbending can enlarge the fit if necessary. The guide should slide easily on the ruler without any

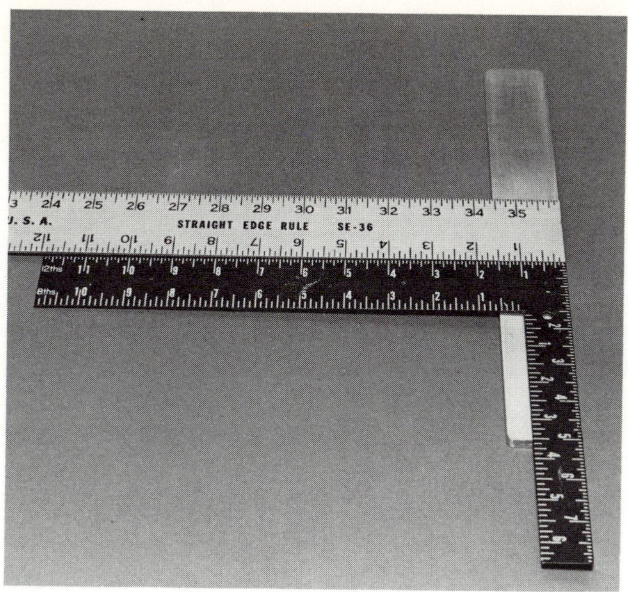

1. A carpenter's square is used to align the metal bar, which will be the top of the T square.

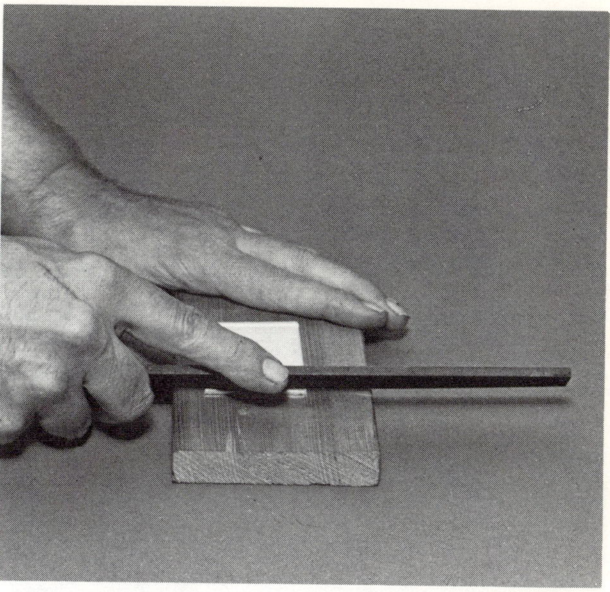

2. Gluing the sheet of aluminum to a scrap of wood makes filing the grooves for the bend easier. A tap with a hammer will break the glue bond. First carefully measure and mark where the grooves should go. Then file the grooves with a square file or the edge of a flat file. File through about one-third the thickness of the metal.

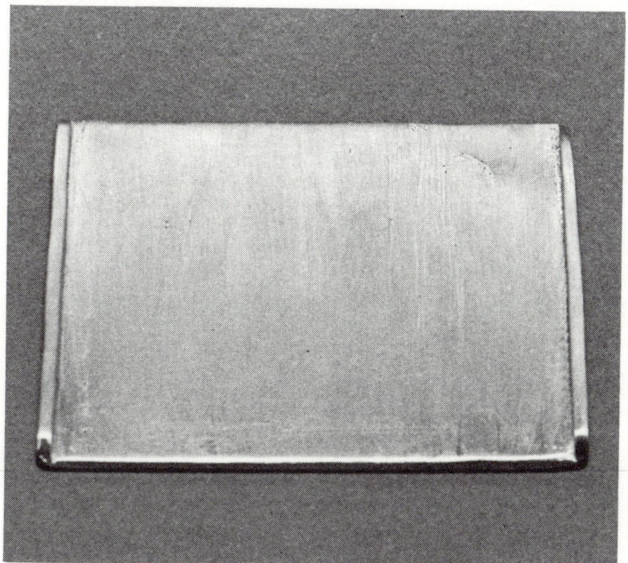

3. The finished rails only extend about 1/16" (1.6 mm) from the metal. Round the corners and sand the edges smooth. The rails should be slightly shorter than the thickness of the ruler so they won't touch the matte when sliding on the T square.

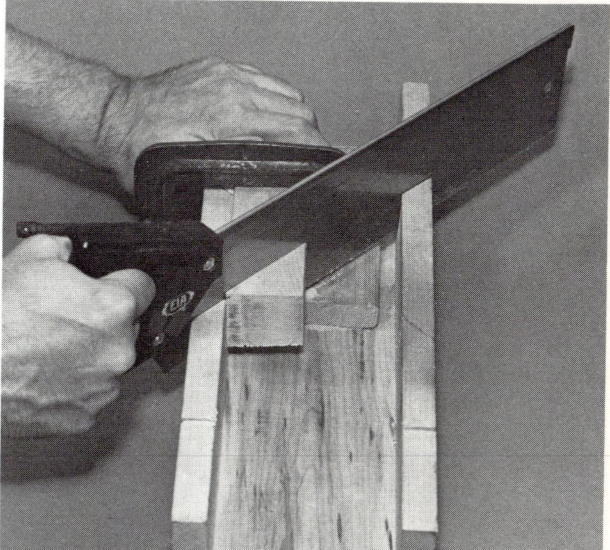

4. The hardwood is easiest to cut using a miter box. Using a C-clamp to hold the wood in place and a scrap of wood below the hardwood makes the cutting easier.

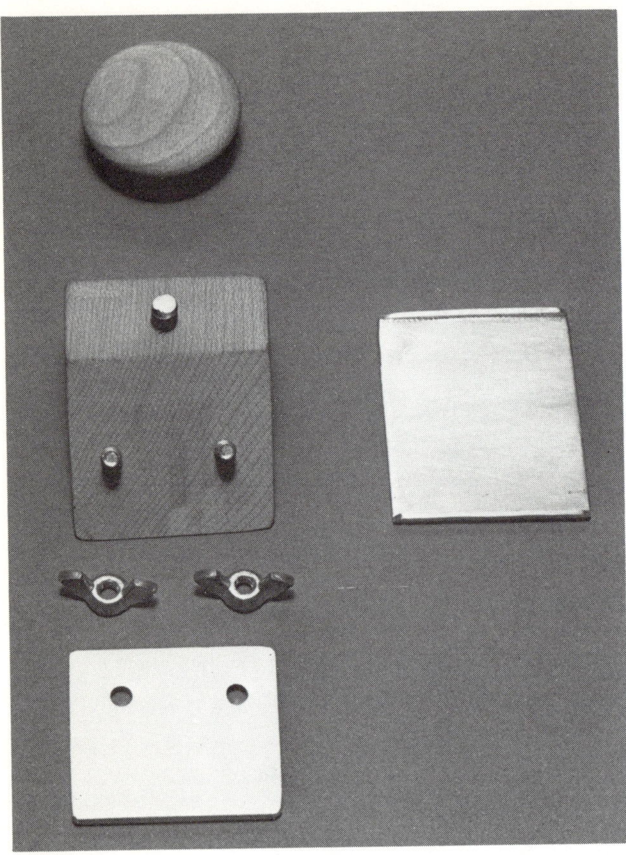

5. Here are the parts of the cutter ready to be assembled. Glue the bolts into the hardwood block to attach the blade guard and the knob. Glue the guide to the bottom of the hardwood.

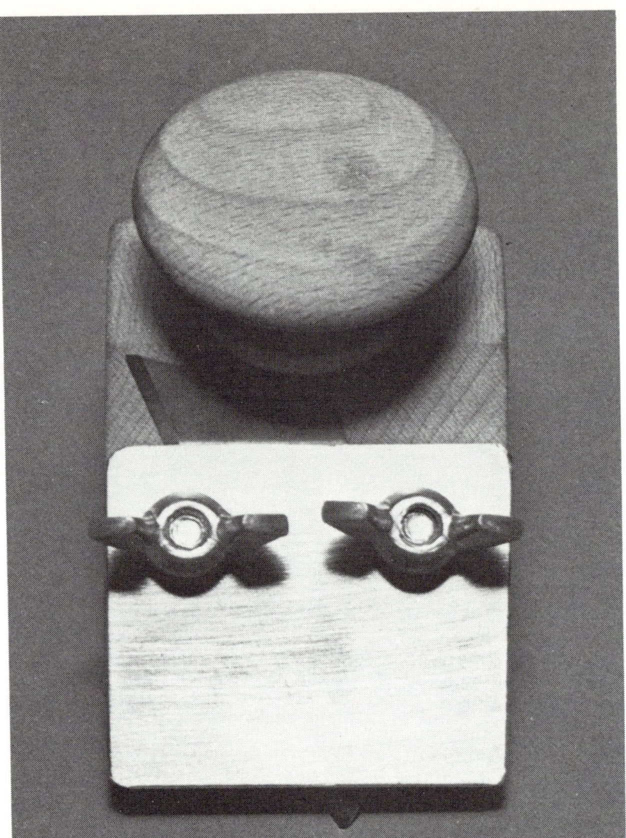

6. This is the assembled cutter with a blade. The blade guard should cover as much of the blade as possible, but the blade should still be visible when cutting mattes.

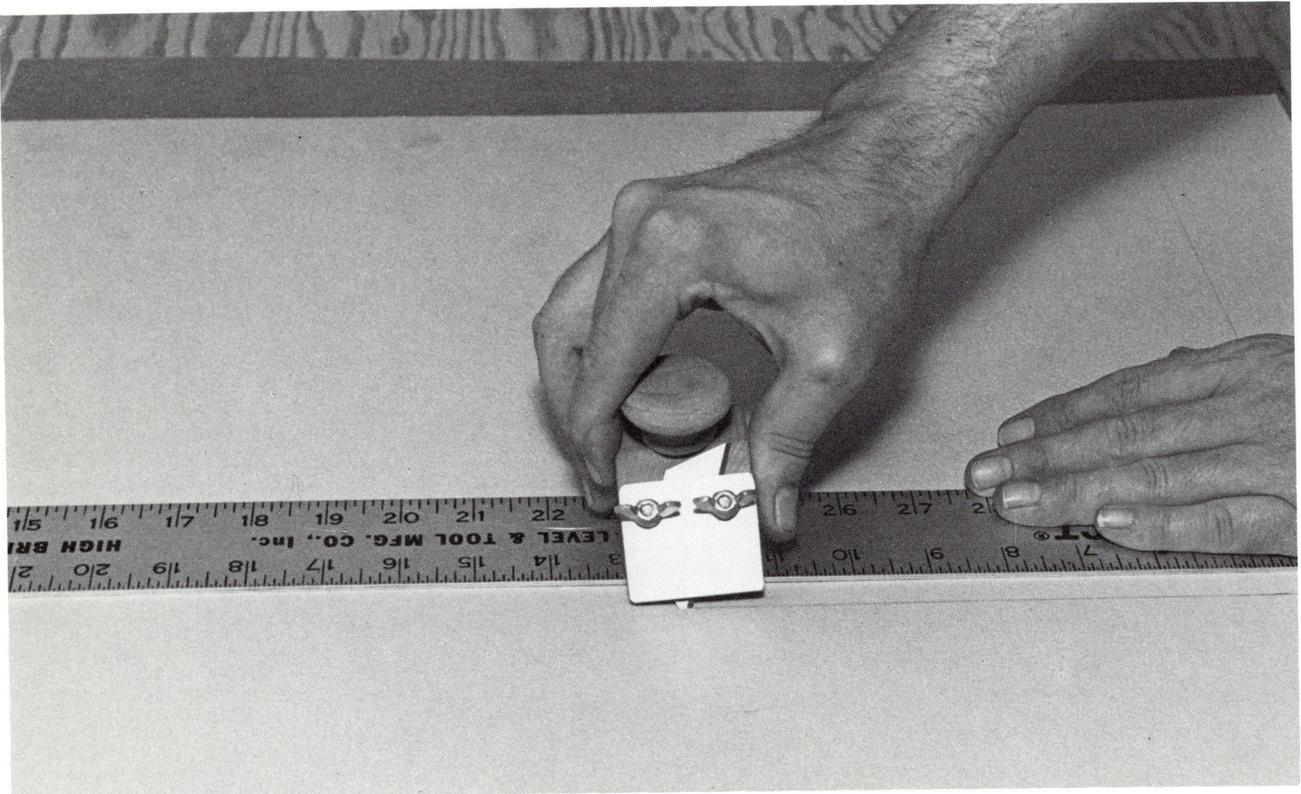

7. When beginning a cut, angle the mat cutter and push the blade into the mat. Then position it on the T square cutting guide.

150

side play. The rails should be shorter than the thickness of the ruler so that they do not touch the surface of the mat when sliding. Round and smooth the edges and corners of the guide, first with a file and then with emery paper to give it a smooth finish. This guide is the heart of the mat cutter, so take extra time to make it right.

The next part to make is the block of wood that holds the blade. I used maple to match the wood knob that goes on top, but other hardwoods could be used. Use a miter box to saw the 45-degree angle and make the other cuts in the wood. Sand the wood smooth. The wood should be cut to the width and length of the metal guide. Saw the top flat to mount the knob.

Next make the metal plate that goes over the blade. This plate prevents the blade from bending and serves as a partial shield for it. I used the ⅛″ aluminum, but a double thickness of the thinner aluminum could be used as well. Cut the face plate and attach it to the block of wood with a drop of glue. This way, holes can be drilled through both the plate and the wood at the same time.

Drill two 11/64″ (4.37 mm) holes for the 3/16″ (4.8 mm) bolts in the sloped face of the wood. These holes should be 1″ (2.5 cm) apart and perpendicular to the angled face of the wood. When drilling is finished, unglue the metal plate by giving it a sharp rap on the edge with a hammer. Enlarge the holes in the metal plate with a 3/16″ drill bit so that the bolts will slip in easily.

Add a little epoxy to the ends of the bolts and use pliers to twist them through the small holes in the wood. Twist the bolts through from the bottom until about ⅜″ (9.5 mm) exends past the top of the wood. Use a hacksaw to cut the bolts so that they will be flush with the bottom of the wood.

Drill a hole for the bolt that attaches the knob in the center of the top, flat portion of the wood block. Use a bolt that comes with the knob and screw it into the hole with pliers. Then saw off the head of the screw so the knob can be added. Glue the metal guide to the bottom of the wood with epoxy. Be sure that the guide is parallel to the sloped face of the wood—poor alignment will cause the blade to pull to the side.

When the epoxy is dry, put a blade in the cutter and set up a place to cut mats. Adjust the length of the blade so it extends enough to cut through the mat with a little extra protruding. To start a cut, angle the cutter up slightly and push the blade into the mat. Position the guide on the T square and make your first cut. The cutter will work with either a push or a pull, depending on the way you position the blade.

Mat Cutting Tips: Mark and cut the mat from the back. This way, the front of the mat is less likely to be marred.

Change blades frequently, always using a sharp blade.

When finished, remove the blade from the cutter for storage.

Dual Format Slide Sorter
(for 2¼-Square and 35mm)

MATERIALS

24″ (61 cm) fluorescent fixture, tube, and power cord
Plain white fluorescent lighting panel, 24″ × 48″ (61 × 122 cm)
⅛″ (3.2 mm) white end cap molding, 24′ (7.3m)
1/16″ (1.6 mm) white end cap molding, 16′ (4.9 m)
½″ (12.7 mm) plywood, 12″ × 24″ (30.5 × 61 cm)
1″ × 1″ (19 × 19 mm) fir, 2′ (0.6 m)
⅛″ (3.2 mm) fiberboard, 16″ × 24″ (40.6 × 61 cm)
Nails
Clear silicone cement, 3 oz. (85 g)
White paint, 1 pint
Felt, 7′ (30.5 cm), optional

TOOLS

Hammer
Saw
Screwdriver
Metal yardstick or meterstick
Razor knife
Pencil
Protractor or drafting triangle

Fluorescent lighting is the best type to use for a slide sorter—the lighting is cool and even. Fluorescent light can fool the eye, giving the slides just as natural an appearance as incandescent light.

There are even special tubes that closely match the quality of daylight. One such tube is the Vita-Lite. It has a color temperature of approximately 5500K and a color-rendering index of 91 (daylight is 100). These tubes are a bit more expensive and are available from Edmund Scientific in the United States and Efstonscience Inc. in Canada. Other fluorescent tubes of this type are also available. These special tubes are best for use in a slide sorter, but a regular fluorescent tube works very well.

If you decide to use a regular tube, take some slides with you and go to a lighting store that has working fixtures on display. Check the quality of the light by viewing your slides with different types of tubes. I like cool white light best, but you may prefer something else.

I wanted a slide sorter that had a large capacity and could handle both 35mm and 2¼-square slides. To achieve this, I made a slide sorter with two illuminated surfaces—one for each format.

All the necessary materials can be purchased in a well-stocked building supply store. Some fluorescent fixtures come already wired, complete with a tube, power cord, and switch. Others are only a fixture and other features need to be added. If you know how to wire the fixture, you can do it yourself. If not, it is best to buy a fixture that is already wired and ready to use. With the ready-to-use fixtures, you may have to change the design

slightly so that the switch is accessible. Or, better yet, buy a fixture with the switch on the power cord.

Most fluorescent lighting panels are textured, but not the plain white type. Be sure to select a panel that is free from scratches.

Begin by making the wood and fiberboard parts of the slide sorter. Make the base from the ½″ (12.7 mm) plywood and cut the triangular sides from the fiberboard, which can be cut with a saw or a razor knife. Using moderate pressure, make three or four strokes with the knife to cut about halfway through. Bend the fiberboard to open the cut and make one or two more strokes to complete the cut. This is an easy way to cut fiberboard if you don't have power tools.

The ends of the sorter are irregular triangles (not right angles) that measure 12″ × 12½″ × 16″ (30.5 × 31.8 × 40.6 cm). The 12½″-long side will go on the bottom. With these dimensions, both the front and back of the slide sorter will slope. The front (35mm) side will have a normal slope for a slide sorter—about 45 degrees. The back will only slope just enough to hold the slides on the sorter. These slopes keep the sorter as compact as possible but still provide two usable surfaces.

Brace the corners with the 1″ × 1″ (19 × 19 mm) board. First cut the board in half and position it on the fiberboard ends. Use a pencil to mark the angles that need to be cut to make the board fit the fiberboard and plywood pieces. This board only comes within ½″ (12.7 mm) of the bottom to allow for the thickness of the plywood. Cut a notch in one end for the power cord.

Nail the fiberboard and corner supports together first, and then nail both to the plywood base. Glue the lighting fixture to the back of the frame with a little silicone. This frame looks very flimsy, and it is. The strength of the slide sorter comes after the front and back plastic sheets are added.

The wood and fiberboard frame of the slide sorter should be painted white. (I didn't paint mine so it would be a little easier to photograph.) If desired, the bottom of the slide sorter could be covered with felt so it won't mar the tabletop.

The translucent plastic sheet can also be cut with the razor knife, using the metal ruler as a guide. Score a line deeply in the plastic with three or four strokes of the knife. Face the scored line away from your body and bend the plastic toward you to open the line. The plastic should break with just gentle bending. If it doesn't, score the line more deeply and try again. You have more than enough plastic for the sorter so you can practice cutting to get the hang of this method before cutting the project sheets. For the 35mm side of the sorter, the plastic should measure 17″ × 25″ (43.2 × 63.5 cm). The 2¼-square side is a plastic sheet 12″ × 24″ (30.5 × 61 cm).

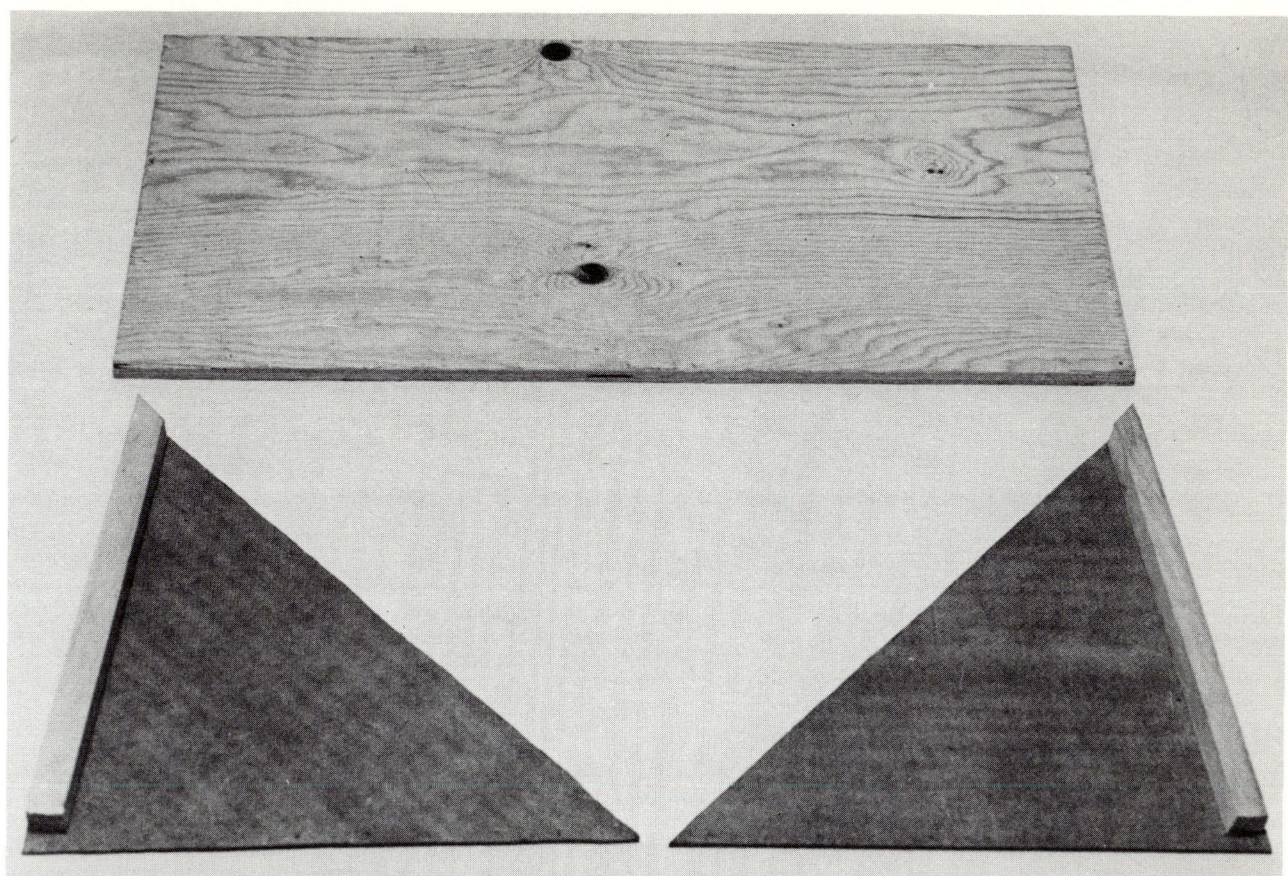

1. These are the wooden parts for the frame of the slide sorter. The corner braces are first nailed to the fiberboard ends and then the ends are nailed to the plywood base.

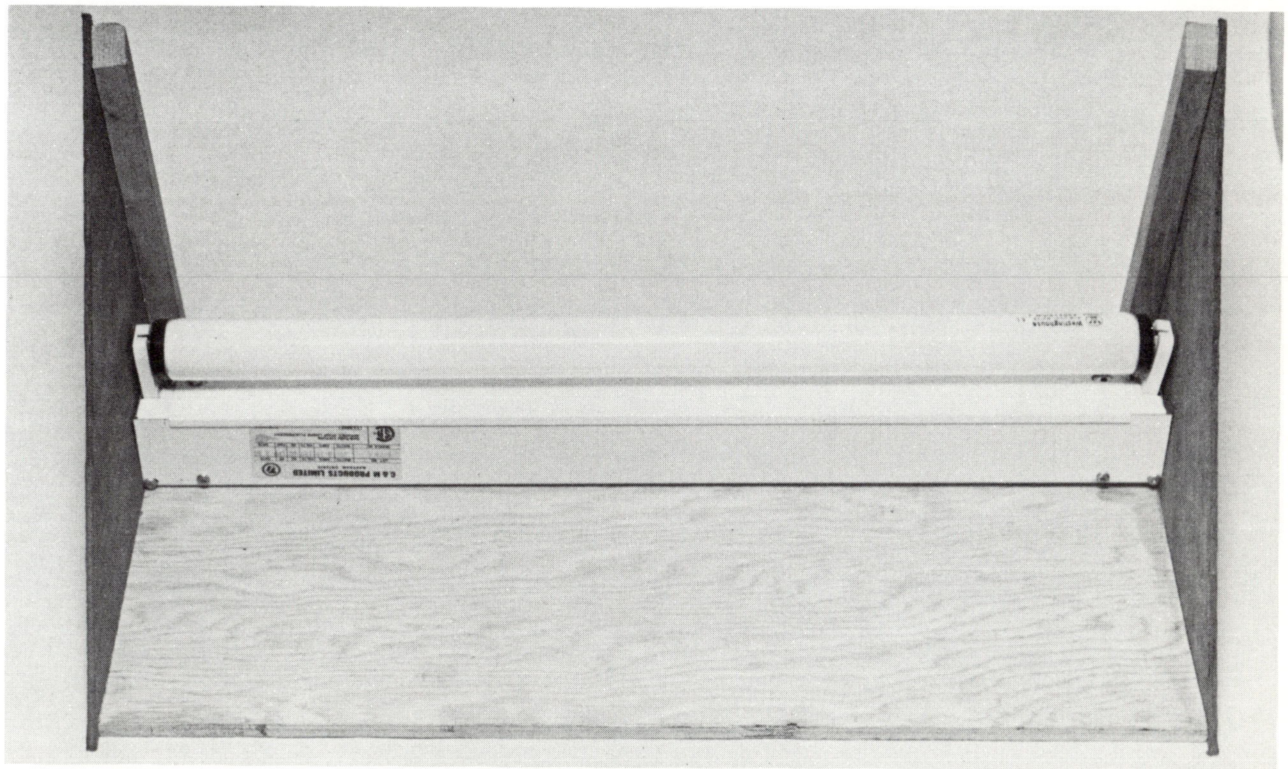

2. A fluorescent tube is used to illuminate the slide sorter. A single tube gives a sufficient amount of light. If you're going to use the sorter in a brightly lit room, you may prefer to use a fixture with two tubes.

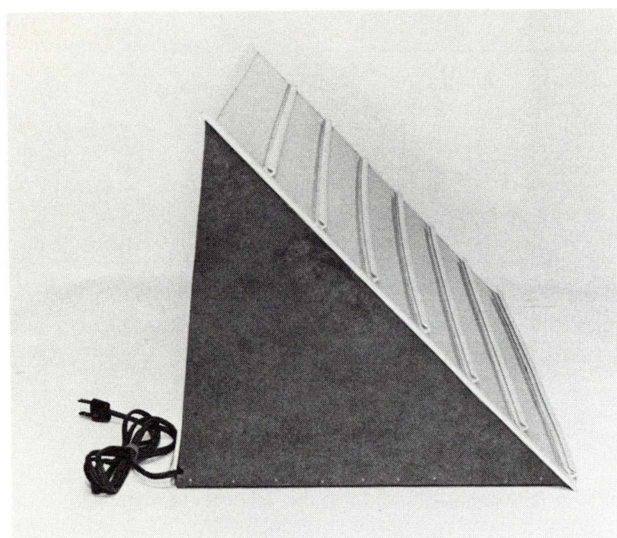

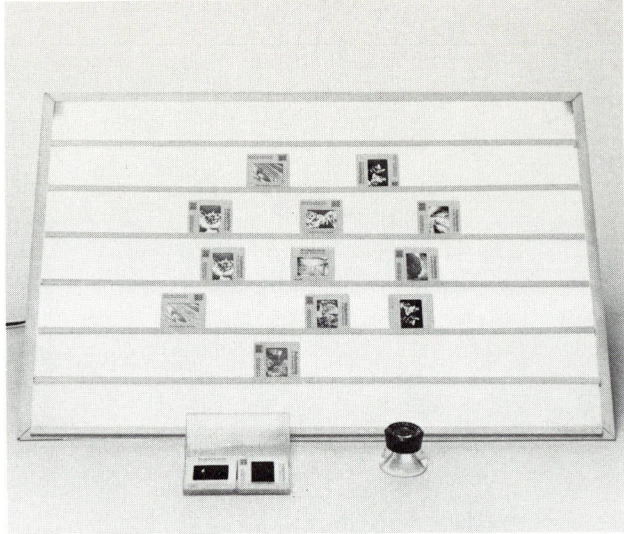

3. From this view, you can see that the back of the sorter has a very slight slope — just enough to hold the slides in place. This keeps the sorter as compact as possible.

4. The slide sorter has a large capacity. The 35mm side can hold 84 slides. The channels cut from the ⅛″ (3 mm) molding hold the slides securely in place. The slides won't fall off at the slightest jar as they do with some slide sorters.

5. Four of the channels are glued to the back of the sorter to hold 32 2¼-square slides. The distance from the top of one channel to the bottom of the next is 2¾″ (7 cm).

A U-shaped channel is needed to hold the slides. The ⅛″ (3.2 mm) end cap molding is J-shaped in cross section. To change the "J" to a "U," use the short side of the "J" as a guide and draw the razor knife along the long back part of the plastic to cut it off. In only one or two strokes with the razor knife you will produce a neat U-shaped channel. Cut all of these channels into 24″ (61 cm) lengths.

For the 35mm side of the sorter, the channels are spaced 2″ (5.1 cm) apart, measuring from the top of one channel to the bottom of the next one. For the 2¼-square side, a spacing of 2¾″ (7 cm) measured the same way works well. With these spacings, slides in plastic sheets can be placed on the sorter and the shadow from the channels will fall between the rows of slides. If you take only one size of slides, the back of the slide sorter doesn't need channels. It can be left plain to be used to view negatives or slides in plastic sheets.

Cover the edges of the translucent plastic with the 1/16″ (1.6 mm) end cap. Measure the lengths needed and cut the molding at a 45-degree angle with the razor knife. You can mark this angle with a drafting triangle or protractor. With the angled cut, the molding will make a nice frame around the outside of the plastic sheets.

Glue all of the molding to the plastic sheets with clear silicone cement. Apply only a small amount of the silicone to the backs of the slide channels so it won't spread as they're pressed in place. When the silicone is dry, glue the front and back to the wood frame. With normal use, years will go by before the fluorescent tube needs replacing. If it ever does, the back can be cut open along the glue joint to replace the tube.

This slide sorter was designed around a 24″ fluorescent fixture. A smaller slide sorter can be made using an 18″ (45.7 cm) fixture, or a really giant one from a 36″ (91.4 cm) fixture. I think a single tube fixture gives just about the right amount of light for easy slide viewing. If the slide sorter is to be used in a room with very bright lighting, you may wish to use a twin tube fixture for its greater light output.

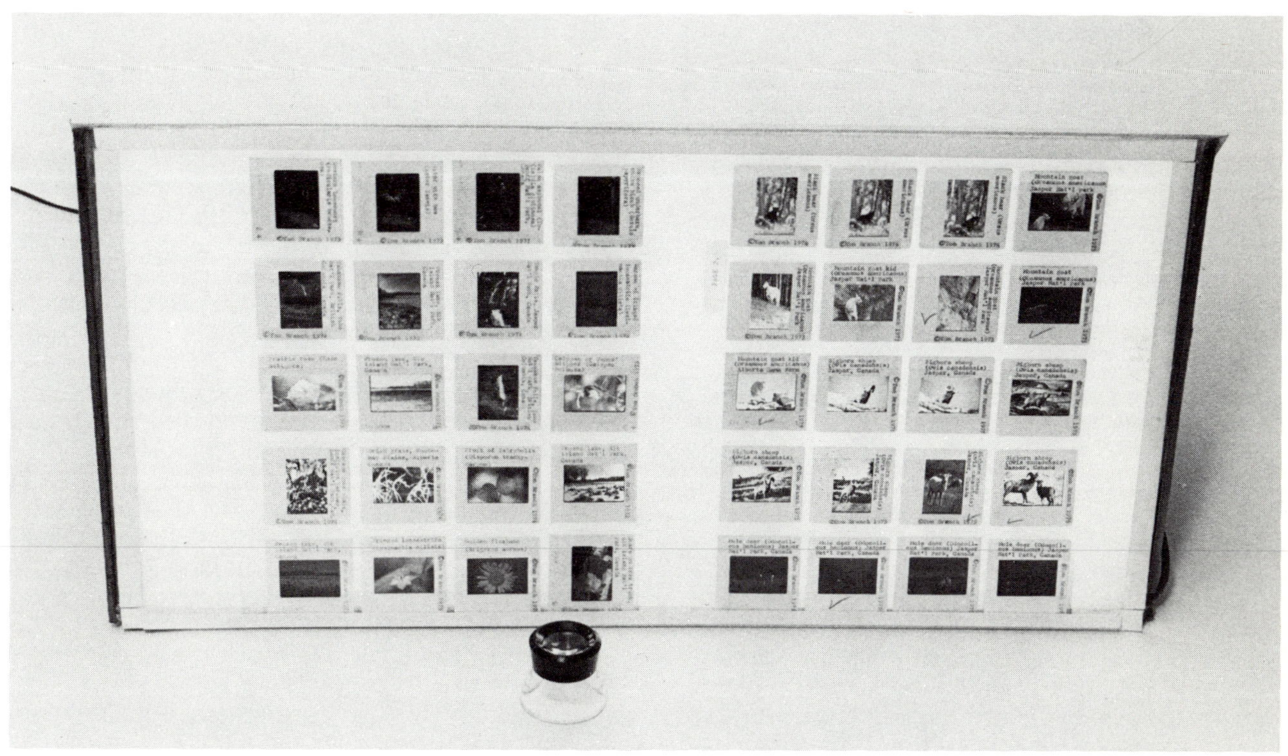

6. If you shoot only one format, a single channel can be glued along the bottom of the back side to hold sheets of slides. This back can also be used to examine negatives.

Secure Slide Projector Stand

MATERIALS

Sturdy tripod base
Sheet of corrugated cardboard
Sink cutout or ¾″ (19.1 mm) plywood
¼″ or ⅜″ "T" nuts (no metric equivalents)
Wood or epoxy glue
Sheet metal, 4″ × 4″ (10.2 × 10.2 cm), 1/32″ (0.8 mm)
    or 1/16″ (1.6 mm) thick
4 flat-head wood screws, ¾″ (19.1 mm) long
Sandpaper
Paint (optional)

TOOLS

Saw
Metal shears
Drill and bits
Razor knife or pocketknife
Ball peen hammer
Center punch
Rasp or coarse file
Screwdriver
Pencil
Ruler

Keystoning is what happens when a slide projector or other projector is tilted up at the screen. The rectangular shape of the slide is distorted, becoming wider at the top than at the bottom. This disturbing distortion can be eliminated by raising the level of the projector so it will fill the screen without being tilted upward.

Tables are always too short for use with a slide projector, so a special projection stand is needed. If you have a sturdy tripod with a detachable head, it probably can be used for the base of the stand. All that needs to be added is a platform to hold the projector.

Remove the head of the tripod—adjustments won't be needed. Removing it eliminates the possibility of the tripod unlocking and dropping the projector. Also be sure that the legs are securely locked. Use only a sturdy tripod. A lightweight one isn't strong enough to hold a heavy slide projector.

Check the size of the bolt that attaches the head of your tripod. Mine uses a ⅜″ bolt; others may use a ¼″ bolt. Both sizes should have a standard thread. This can be checked by seeing if the "T" nut screws properly onto the bolt.

Once you determine the size of the "T" nut, place the slide projector on a sheet of corrugated cardboard. First cut the cardboard to the size needed for the top of the stand. This should be about 3″ (7.6 cm) wider and longer than the slide projector. Level your projector and center it on the cardboard. Press down firmly on the top of the projector. This creates indentations in the cardboard where the rubber legs of the projector

are located. Use a pencil to poke a hole in the cardboard at these points.

Next, approximate the location of the projector's center of gravity. This is the place on the platform where most of the weight of the projector will sit, and it may not be exactly in the center. Mark this location by poking another hole in the cardboard—this is where the "T" nut will be placed.

Use the sheet of cardboard as a pattern to mark the sink cutout. A *sink cutout* is the section of counter-top material that is removed when a sink is installed. These can often be purchased at building supply stores and lumber yards. If you have trouble finding one, ¾″ (19.1 mm) plywood can be substituted. After marking the wood, cut out the top for the projector stand with a saw. Round the corners to eliminate sharp edges.

Use the cardboard to locate the position of the holes for the projector's rubber feet. First, use the ball peen hammer and center punch to indent the centers of the holes. This makes starting the drill bit easier. Use a narrow drill bit to start the hole and then switch to a wider wood bit. I used a ¾″ bit for these holes. Only drill about ¼″ (6.4 mm) into the wood—just enough to seat the legs on the projector. These holes will help keep the projector on the stand in case it is accidentally bumped.

Turn the wood over and locate the place for the "T" nut, using the cardboard pattern. Drill a ½″ (12.7 mm) wide hole about ½″ into the wood to hold the nut. Turn the nut upside down and center it over the hole. Trace around the outside of the head with a pencil. Use a razor knife or sharp pocket knife to carve out the wood to insert the nut's head. Test the depth by inserting the upside-down "T" nut. Remove plenty of wood—it's better for the nut to be below the level of the wood rather than not set deep enough. If the top of the nut protrudes, the stand will be less stable. Coat the inside of the hole and the inlay area with wood glue or epoxy and hammer the nut into the hole.

For extra strength and to provide a smooth surface for adding the tripod base, add a sheet of metal over the "T" nut. I used brass, but aluminum could also be used. When the glue is dry, sand the nut and surrounding area to make a smooth, flat surface. Use metal shears to cut the metal to a size larger than the top of the tripod base. Hammer the metal flat if it has been curved by the cutting.

Drill a hole in the center of the metal sheet for the tripod bolt, making the hole larger than the bolt— 7/16″ (11 mm) for a ⅜″ bolt, and 5/16″ (8 mm) for the ¼″ bolt. Drill holes for the flat-head wood screws in the corners of the metal and in the wood. Add some glue around the "T" nut and attach the metal sheet with wood screws. Avoid getting glue on the threads of the nut. If you do, most wood glues can be wiped off with a damp rag before they dry, and epoxy can be cleaned off with rubbing alcohol. Adding this metal plate strengthens the attachment nut considerably.

First, use a rasp or coarse file to smooth the edges of the wood and then use sandpaper to finish smoothing it. The wood can then be painted if you wish.

When the glue is dry, adjust the tripod to the desired height and add the platform by spinning it onto the bolt—don't overtighten it. Lock the legs of the tripod in place and test it by pressing down on the platform. When you're sure that everything is properly locked, the projector can be added. Place the rubber legs of the projector in the holes to keep it securely on the stand. Now you can project your slides without keystoning.

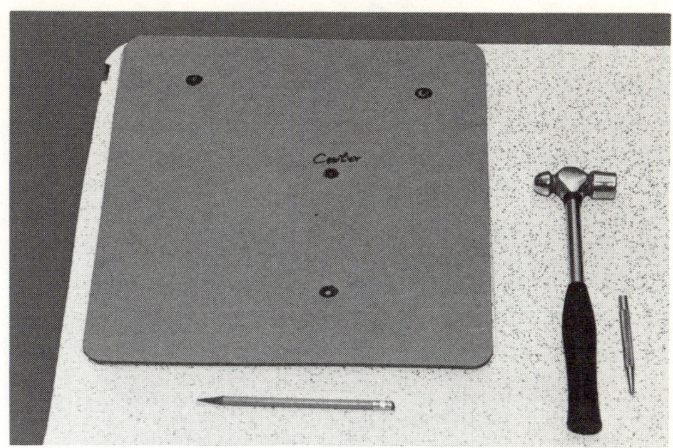

1. Make a cardboard pattern to locate the position of the projector's legs and use a hammer and center punch to punch the locations for the holes.

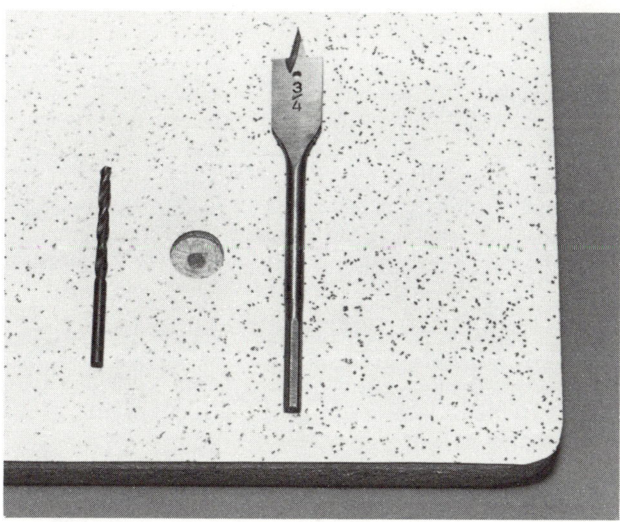

2. Make a shallow hole in the top of the platform to hold each rubber leg of the slide projector. Use a small drill bit to start the hole and then change to a large wood bit.

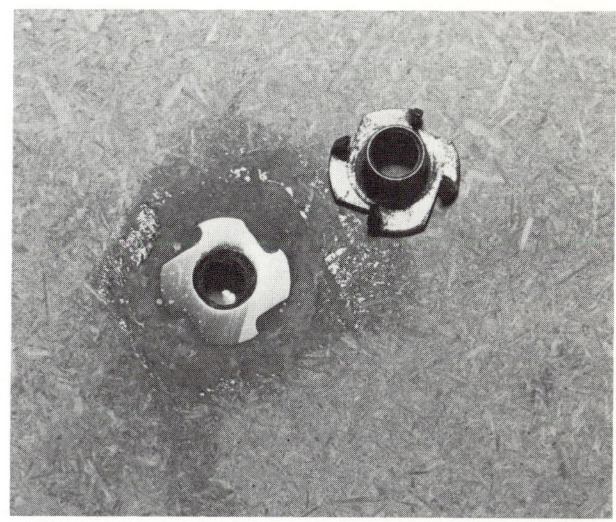

3. Position a "T" nut at the projector's center of gravity. Inlay the nut so it is flush with the wood and then glue it in place.

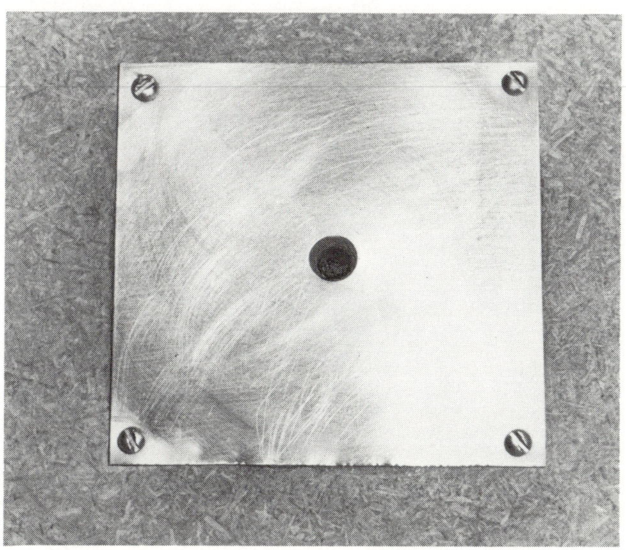

4. Attach a sheet of metal over the "T" nut with wood screws and more glue. This strengthens the connection between the platform and the tripod base.

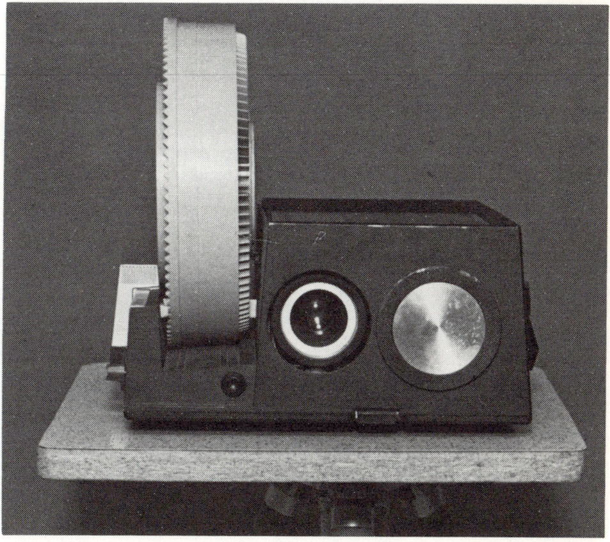

5. Use only a sturdy tripod for the base of the projector stand. Check that the legs are securely locked in position before adding the projector. Also make sure that the stand is the same level as the screen.

Magnifying Glass with Flexible Stand

MATERIALS

Gooseneck lamp
Round magnifying glass, 4″ (10.2 cm) or larger
¼″ connecting nut
Two ¼″ bolts, 1½″ (3.8 cm) long
Epoxy glue

TOOLS

Wire cutters
Drill and ¼″ bit
Hacksaw
Pliers

A magnifying glass on a flexible stand is very useful for spotting prints, examining contact sheets. repairing equipment, and for many other jobs requiring close inspection. The reason they aren't used more is that they are very expensive and the only place I know where they can be purchased is a scientific supply house.

Making your own stand is very simple—all that has to be done is to combine a few inexpensive pieces. The stand with its weighted base and flexible neck is from an old gooseneck lamp. For a few dollars this lamp can be bought at a secondhand store, a garage sale, or an auction. It doesn't matter if the lamp works since the socket and wiring will be discarded. Be sure to select a lamp with considerable weight in the base.

You may already have a magnifying glass that can be used for this project. A large (4″ or 10.2 cm) reading glass that magnifies 2 times and has a wide field of view works best. Round magnifying glasses usually screw into a handle and are the easiest type to mount on the stand. This type of reading glass is available in department and discount stores.

Begin by removing the shade, socket, and power cord from the lamp. Just unscrew the nut(s) holding on the shade and socket and cut the power cord at the socket with the wire cutters. The base can be taken apart to remove the entire power cord if you want to save it, or the cord can be cut off with the wire cutters. Only the weighted base and the flexible neck are needed. The rest of the parts can be discarded unless you have some other use for them.

Cut the head off a ¼″ bolt with the hacksaw. Epoxy the bolt into the hollow end of the gooseneck, leaving about ½″ (12.7 mm) protruding. Put this aside to let the epoxy dry.

Next work on the magnifying glass. Unscrew the handle and set it aside. Check the size of the screw on the metal frame that is around the glass. The screw should be ¼″ (6.4 mm) or smaller to fit inside the ¼″ connecting nut. If it is larger, a bigger connecting nut can be used. Mix some epoxy and glue the connecting nut to the screw on the frame. Set it aside to dry.

The handle of the magnifying glass can be modified so it can still be used to hold the glass. Drill a ¼″ hole in the handle. Saw the head off another ¼″ bolt and put it into the drilled hole. Only about ¼″ or a little more should extend beyond the handle. Glue the bolt inside the handle. The bolt in the handle can be threaded to the connecting nut if you wish to use the magnifying glass with the handle.

When the epoxy is dry, screw the magnifying glass to the gooseneck, and the magnifying glass with stand is ready to use.

If you used a ¼″ bolt and nut to hold the magnifying glass, the stand can be made even more adjustable by placing a small ball-and-socket head between the glass and the gooseneck. The stand can also be used for other things besides holding the glass. The paper clamps modified to use with the telescoping close-up clamps will also fit on the stand (see page 132). With the clamp, the stand can hold reflectors, diffusers, backgrounds, and so on for tabletop photography. With a tripod adapter for an electronic flash, the stand can even be used to hold the flash unit. I am always finding new uses for this flexible stand.

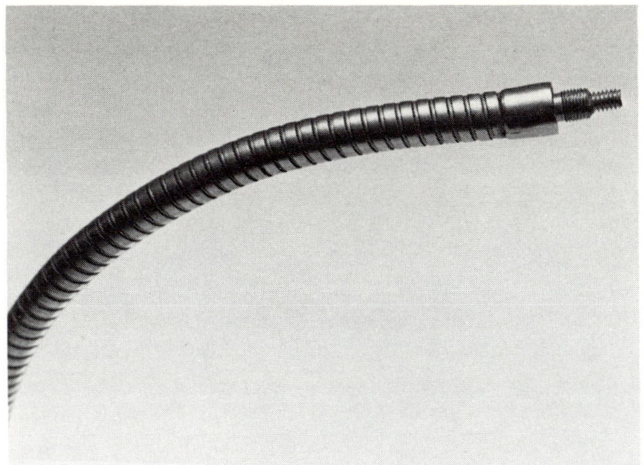 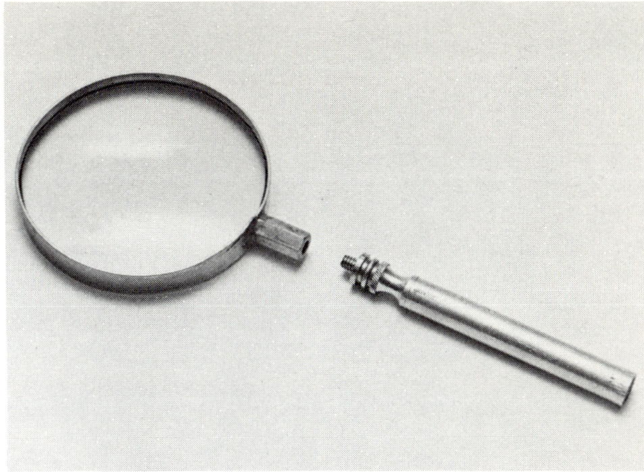

1. Remove the lamp shade and socket from a gooseneck lamp. Glue a ¼" bolt, with the head cut off, into the end of the flexible neck. Use the bolt to attach the magnifying glass.

2. Use epoxy to glue a connecting nut to the metal frame around the magnifying glass. Add a bolt that fits the connecting nut to the handle of the glass. The handle can still be used with the glass, but the glass can also be mounted on the stand.

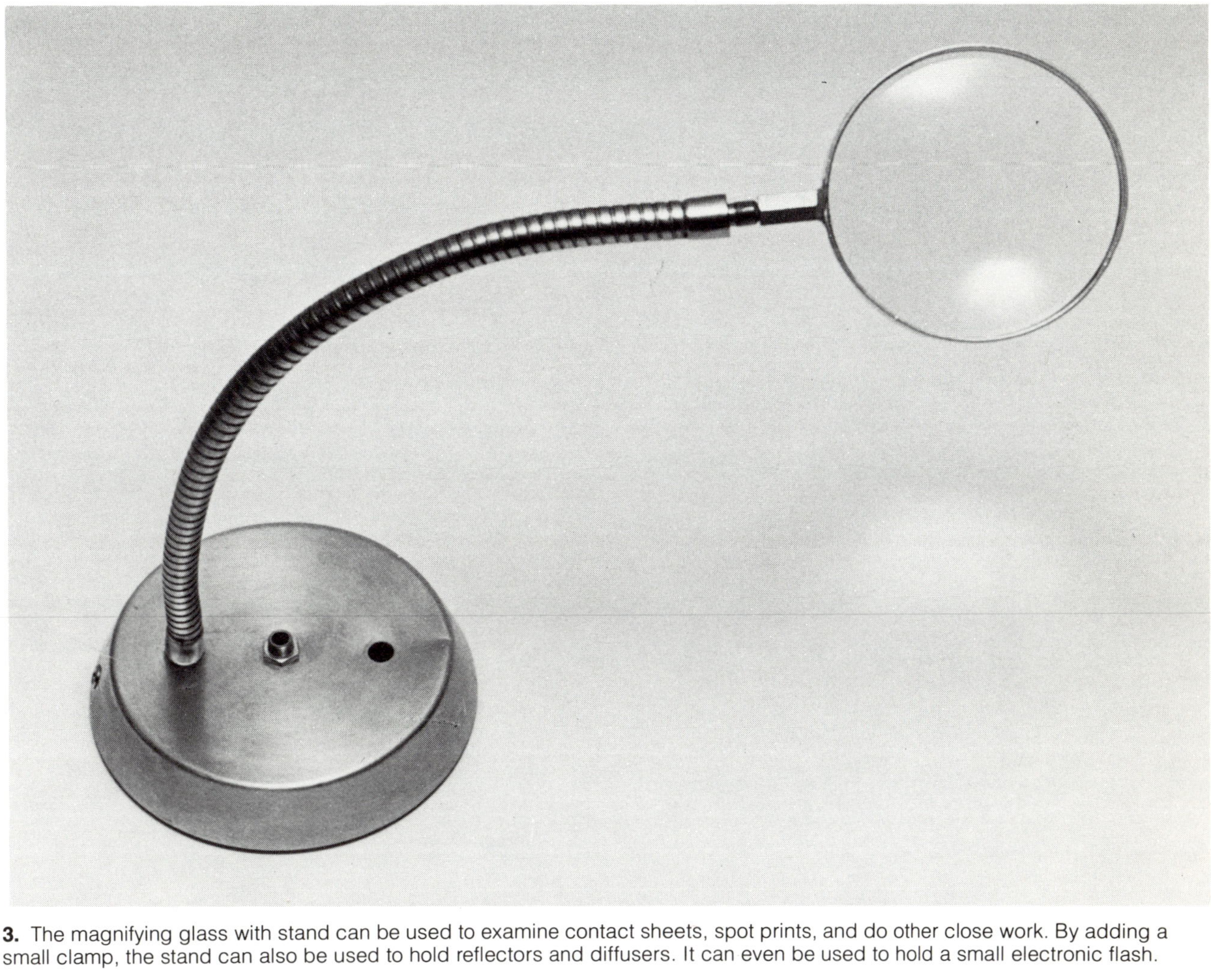

3. The magnifying glass with stand can be used to examine contact sheets, spot prints, and do other close work. By adding a small clamp, the stand can also be used to hold reflectors and diffusers. It can even be used to hold a small electronic flash.